The Logic of Fantasy

Jacques Lacan

The Logic of Fantasy

The Seminar of Jacques Lacan
Book XIV
1966–1967

Edited by Jacques-Alain Miller

Translated by A.R. Price

polity

Originally published in French as *Le Séminaire. Livre XIV. La logique du fantasme* © Éditions du Seuil et Le Champ Freudien Éditeur, 2023.

This English translation © Polity Press, 2026.

Polity Press
65 Bridge Street
Cambridge CB2 1UR, UK

Polity Press
111 River Street
Hoboken, NJ 07030, USA

All rights reserved. Except for the quotation of short passages for the purpose of criticism and review, no part of this publication may be reproduced, stored in a retrieval system or transmitted, in any form or by any means, electronic, mechanical, photocopying, recording or otherwise, without the prior permission of the publisher.

ISBN-13: 978-1-5095-6134-6

A catalogue record for this book is available from the British Library.

Library of Congress Control Number: 2025944076

Typeset in 10.5 on 12 pt Times NR MT
by Cheshire Typesetting Ltd, Cuddington, Cheshire
Printed and bound in Great Britain by CPI Group (UK) Ltd, Croydon

The publisher has used its best endeavours to ensure that the URLs for external websites referred to in this book are correct and active at the time of going to press. However, the publisher has no responsibility for the websites and can make no guarantee that a site will remain live or that the content is or will remain appropriate.

Every effort has been made to trace all copyright holders, but if any have been overlooked the publisher will be pleased to include any necessary credits in any subsequent reprint or edition.

For further information on Polity, visit our website:
politybooks.com

Contents

ELEMENTS OF LOGIC
I	The promise of a logic	3
II	Russell's paradox	18
III	Freud, logician	37
IV	From the Klein four-group to the *cogito*	52
V	Interlude	69

BUILDING THE LACAN GROUP
VI	The unconscious and the id	81
VII	From thinking to the unthinkable	96
VIII	*I* and *a*	112
IX	Alienation and repetition	133

SUBJECTIFYING SEX
X	From sublimation to sexual act	151
XI	On the structure of sexual satisfaction in its relation to the subject	164
XII	Sexual satisfaction and sublimation	178
XIII	There is no sexual act	197
XIV	On enjoyment value	212

THE ECONOMY OF THE FANTASY
XV	From truth to enjoyment	229
XVI	The Other is the body	245
XVII	From castration to the object	262
XVIII	Enjoyment obtains by the body alone	274

XIX	The question of enjoyment	288
XX	The sadist and the masochist	302
XXI	The axiom of the fantasy	317

Index 334

ELEMENTS OF LOGIC

I

THE PROMISE OF A LOGIC

Logical existence and de facto existence
Ready-to-bear the fantasy
Desire is the essence of reality
The signifier cannot signify itself
There is no universe of discourse

Today I shall be pitching some signposts that rather pertain to a promise.

La logique du fantasme is the title I have given for what I mean to present to you this year, on account of what is now becoming essential at the point we've reached along a certain path.

This path implies – I will be repeating this emphatically today – the sort of altogether special return that last year we saw being inscribed in structure and which is strictly fundamental in everything that Freud's thinking uncovers. This return is called *repetition*. To repeat is not to find the same thing anew. And, contrary to what is believed, it is not necessarily to repeat indefinitely, as we shall be spelling out shortly.

This year we shall therefore be coming back to themes that in a certain fashion I outlined a long while ago.

Indeed, it is also because we are in the time of this return, and of its function, that I believed I could no longer delay handing over to you the collection of what thus far I deemed necessary as the minimal tally of this course. To wit, this volume entitled *Écrits*, which you now find yourselves having within your reach. After all, it might be said that in a certain way I have until now been endeavouring, if not to avoid this relation to the written, then at least to put it off. I believed I ought to take this step now because this year it shall doubtless be possible to delve more deeply into its function.

I have chosen five signposts, which I shall set out before you today.

The first entails reminding you of the point we've reached with regard to the logical articulation of the fantasy, which strictly speaking is to be my script for the year ahead.

The second entails a reminder of how the structure of the fantasy relates to signifying structure as such.

The third brings you an essential and truly fundamental remark concerning what this year we need to call, if we are to place the logic in question on the foremost plane, *the universe of discourse*.

The fourth point will signpost its relation to writing as such.

Lastly, I shall end with a reminder of what Freud spells out concerning what is involved in thought's relation to language and to the unconscious.

The logic of the fantasy, then.

1

We shall start from the written formula I have already shaped, namely barred S, punch mark, lower case a ($\bar{S} \Diamond a$).

I remind you that in this formula the barred S represents, stands in for, what is at issue concerning the subject's division, which is to be found at the base of what Freud discovered. It consists in this – that the subject is struck through, in part, on account of what constitutes him strictly as a function of the unconscious.

The formula establishes a link, a connection, between the subject as thus constituted and some other thing that is called a. It is an object, and the logic of the fantasy consists in determining its status in a relation that is strictly speaking a logical relation.

Doubtless this is a strange thing, and one which you will allow me not to expand upon. I mean, what the term *fantasy* suggests in relation to *phantasia*, in relation to imagination. I'm not about to offer myself so much as a moment's entertainment marking out its contrast with the term *logic*, with which I intend to structure it. There can be no doubting that the fantasy such as we claim to establish its status is not so radically antinomic, as one might think on first approach, to this logical characterisation which properly speaking disdains it.

Thus, in spite of the imaginary aspect of what is known as the object a, the latter will appear to you as far less allied to the domain of the imaginary than it may seem at first sight. This will become more apparent as we mark out what allows this object to be characterised as a logical value. It is much rather that the imaginary hitches on to it, encases it, and amasses therein. The object a has a status that is quite other.

It is most surely desirable that those of you listening to me this year should have had the opportunity last year to get some idea or prehension of this. Of course, for everyone, and most especially for those for whom it lies at the centre of their experience, the psychoanalysts, this object is hardly something that as yet might have sufficient familiarity to be, I shall say, presentified without instilling fear and even anguish in them. *What, then, have you done*, one of them said to me, *why did you need to come up with this object a?*

In truth, taking things from a slightly broader overview, I think it was high time. Without this object *a*, the impact of which has been quite widely felt, so it seems to me, by those of our generation, a great deal of what has been done in the way of the analysis as much of subjectivity as of history and its interpretation, and notably of what we have lived through as contemporary history, has fallen short. This is especially the case with regard to analyses of what we have somewhat roughly termed using a noun that is most inapt – totalitarianism. Astonishingly, we still lack any satisfactory interpretation of this matter. Well, anyone who, having grasped this much, might be able to work at applying the function of the category of the object *a* to totalitarianism will perhaps be afforded a clearer view of what it turns around.

In the formula written up here on the board, the barred subject is joined to the object *a* by something that presents as a lozenge and which just now I called a *punch mark*. Actually, it's a sign that has been purposefully wrought to conjoin within it what may be isolated therein according to whether you section it vertically or horizontally.

When sectioned vertically it represents a twofold relation that can be read in the first instance as *greater than* or *less than*. Barred S less than or, equally, greater than, *a*.

$$\barred{S} \lozenge a \quad \barred{S} < a \quad \barred{S} > a$$

The lozenge sectioned vertically

It may equally be read as *included* or *excluded*. Barred S included in *a*, or excluded from *a*.

$$\barred{S} \wedge a \quad \barred{S} \vee a$$

The lozenge sectioned horizontally

What does this mean? What is suggested on the foremost plane of this conjunction is what in logic is called the relation of *Inclusion*, or else of *Implication*, on the condition that we make it reversible. This relation is cast in the logical articulation that is called – *if and only if*... I'm surely going over this briskly, but we shall have plenty of time to draw it out and to take up these items again. It will suffice for today to prepare the ground with a few suggestive markers.

Barred S in this sense, with the punch mark divided by a vertical stroke, is the subject barred unto this relation of *if and only if* with the *a*. This gives us pause. There exists, then, a subject. Here we have what, logically, we are compelled to write at the starting point of such a formulation. Something puts itself forward to us here, which is the dividing line between de facto existence and logical existence.

De facto existence brings us back to the existence of *being*, with the word placed between two bars.

| being |

Being, or not, speaking. Such beings are in general alive. I say *in general* because on no account is this inevitable. We have the Stone Guest, who doesn't exist solely on the stage upon which Mozart brings him to life. He also walks among us quite frequently.

Logical existence is something else and as such has its own status. Something of the subject obtains as soon as we start doing logic, that is, as soon as we have to start handling signifiers.

De facto existence, namely when something results from how there is something of the subject at the level of beings who speak, is a thing that, like all de facto existence, necessitates that a certain articulation be established already. Yet nothing proves that this articulation should be formed through a direct hold, that it should be directly due to the fact that there are beings, living or otherwise, who speak, and that they should for all that, and in an immediate way, be determined as subjects. *If and only if*... is there to remind us of this.

I am here marshalling the articulations through which we shall have to pass once more. In themselves they are so unusual, they are so seldom navigated, that I thought I ought to indicate for you the general line of my design in what I have to explicate in front of you.

2

The *a* results from an operation that has a logical structure.

This operation is effectuated not *in vivo*, not even upon the living being, not, properly speaking, in the muddled sense that the term *body* still has for us – it is not necessarily the pound of flesh, though it may be, and after all, when it is, this allows things to fall into place none too poorly – but in the end it is patent that in this entity of the body which is so little apprehended there is something that lends itself to the operation of logical structure, which we still have to ascertain. You know this much – the breast, the scybalum, the regard, the voice, those parts that are detachable yet fully linked to the body, there you have what is at issue in the object *a*.

Since we are requiring of ourselves some logical rigour, let's confine ourselves to pointing out that, to make something of the *a*, it takes some ready outfitting.

This may suffice us momentarily, but it doesn't settle anything of the very matter into which we now have to advance. In order to form something of the fantasy, something is required that is ready-to-bear-it.

You will allow me to set out a few theses here in their most provocative form, because what is likewise at issue is to peel this domain away from those fields of capture which lead it insuperably back to the most fundamental of illusions, this being what is called psychological experience. What I am going to put forward is very precisely that which will be shored up, that which will be grounded, that of which the consistency will be shown, by everything I am going to roll out for you this year.

To roll out. I've already said it. It was done a long time ago, when in the fourth year of my Seminar I dealt with the object relation. Everything has already been laid out with respect to the structure of the relation between the *a* and the Other. All of this has been gone into quite amply in the argument that the child's subjective structure will be dependent upon the mother's imaginary. What we need to argue out now is how this relation is articulated in terms which are properly logical, that is, which appertain radically to the function of the signifier.

Yet note should be taken of the consequence, for the one who back then made a summary of what I was indicating in this sense, of the merest fault, by which I mean *flaw*, with respect to the affiliation of each term for the three functions then designated as *subject*, *object* – in the sense of love object – and the *beyond zone* thereof, our current object *a*. Namely, his reference to the subject's imagination could only obscure the relationship that it was a matter of plotting out. So it was that, in failing to locate the function of the object *a* in the field of the Other as such, he was led to write that in the status of the pervert the determinants are at once the function of the phallus and the sadistic theory of coitus, when in fact this is hardly so. These two factors impact at the level of the mother.

I am therefore moving forward into what needs to be stated here. In order to form something of the fantasy, something ready-to-bear-it is required. What is it that bears the fantasy? What bears the fantasy goes by two names that concern one and the same substance, if you are willing to reduce this term to the function of *surface* such as I articulated it last year. You are already acquainted with some of the shapes of this primordial surface, which we require to make our logical articulation function. These are closed surfaces which are bubble-like, except that they are not spherical. Let's call them *bubbles* and we shall see what actuates, to what is attached, the existence of bubbles in the real.

This surface which I have called *bubble* goes, properly speaking, by two names – *desire* and *reality*. It is quite useless to tire oneself out articulating the reality of desire because, primordially, desire and reality have a relation of seamless texture. Therefore, they have no need of any stitching. They don't need to be sewn back together. There is no more *reality of desire* than it would be right to say *the underside of the topside*. There is one self-same stuff that has a topside and an underside. But still this stuff is woven in such a way that one passes, without realising, because it is seamless and uncut, from one to the other of its faces.

This is why I went on at such length about a structure known as the projective plane, illustrated on the board in the form of what is called a *mitre* or a *cross-cap*. That one should pass from one face to the other without noticing tells us very neatly that there is only one. I mean, one face.

It none the less remains that, as in the surfaces I have just mentioned – one component part of which is the Möbius band – there is a topside and an underside. It is necessary to posit this, and in an originative manner, as a reminder of how this distinction between topside and underside is grounded as already there, prior to any cut. It is clear that any entity that might be integrally implicated in this surface, like the animalcules mentioned by mathematicians, would scarcely behold a hint of the nevertheless certain distinction between topside and underside.

In the series of surfaces I have gone into with you, from the projective plane to the Klein bottle, everything that refers to what might be called their *extrinsic* properties reaches very far indeed. The greater part of what strikes you as most evident when I provide images of these surfaces for you are not surface properties. This takes on its function in a third dimension. Don't imagine that even a purely toric being could perceive the function of the hole in the middle of a torus. Nevertheless, this function is not without consequence, because it was on this basis that, my goodness, well-nigh six years ago already, I tried to articulate, for those who were listening to me back then, the subject's relations with the Other in neurosis. Indeed, it is the Other as such that is at issue in this third dimension. It is in relation

The promise of a logic 9

to the Other, and insomuch as this other term is there, that this can be a matter of distinguishing a topside from an underside.

Only, this is not yet to distinguish between reality and desire. What is topside or underside initially in the locus of the Other, in the discourse of the Other, gets played out as heads or tails. In no respect does this involve the subject, for the reason that there isn't one yet. The subject begins with a cut.

Let's select the most exemplary of these surfaces, because it is the most straightforward to handle, namely the cross-cap or projective plane. What I'm plotting out here on the board represents it for you in a shape that is merely an image, but it is nevertheless altogether necessary. This is how we represent the structure of what is at issue, in the shape of this bubble, the walls of which – let's call them front and back – cross over here, in this line which is no less imaginary.

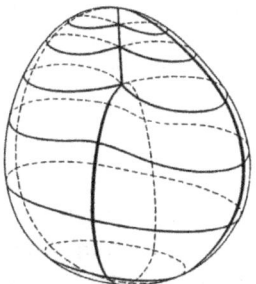

Image of the projective plane

Let's apply a cut to this, but not just any cut. Any cut that will cross this imaginary line will establish a complete change in the surface structure.

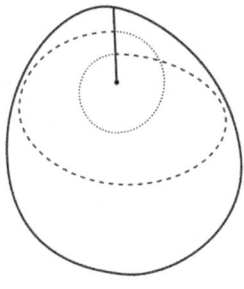

Möbius cut

The entire surface then becomes what last year we learnt how to cut out of this surface under the name of object *a*, to wit a flattenable disc with a topside and an underside, such that one cannot pass from one to the other without crossing an edge. This edge is precisely what makes such a crossing impossible, at least this is how we can articulate its function *in initio*. Through this first cut, which is enriched by an implication that doesn't leap out immediately, the bubble thus becomes an object *a*. This reminder is intended for those to whom these images are still somewhat present to mind.

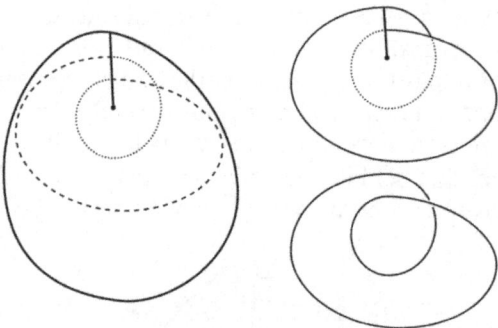

Structural transformation of the projective plane

The object at issue has a fundamental relation with the Other, or, better put, it maintains this fundamental relation, because it is there from the start, without which nothing whatsoever about it is explicable. Indeed, the subject has not yet appeared with just this one cut whereby the bubble, which is established by the signifier in the real, first allows this foreign object, which is the object *a*, to drop away.

It has to be perceived and it suffices to perceive, in the structure indicated here on the board, what is entailed by this cut in order then to perceive how it possesses the property of joining back up with itself simply by doubling up. In other words, whether one makes just a single cut or two of them, it amounts to the same thing. The gap that is here, between the two rounds which are just a single one, can be regarded as equivalent to the first cut.

However, if into the fabric which is to be cut I make a double cut, I restore what had been lost owing to the first cut, namely a surface of which the topside runs on into its underside. I restore the primary non-separation of reality and desire.

How thereafter are we to define *reality*? Well, as what I earlier called *that which is ready-to-bear the fantasy*, that is to say, that which forms its setting.

We shall then see that reality, human reality as a whole, is nothing but the *montage*, an assemblage, of the symbolic and the imaginary. Desire, which lies at the centre of this apparatus, this frame, which we call *reality*, is equally, as I have been spelling out from the beginning, what covers over what is properly speaking the real. It is important to distinguish the real from human reality. The real is only ever glimpsed when the mask of fantasy slips. This is the same thing that Spinoza apprehended when he said that desire is the very essence of man.

In truth, this word, *man*, is a transitional term that it is impossible to maintain in an atheological system, which is not the case for Spinoza's system. We can simply replace Spinoza's wording with the following, the misrecognition of which leads psychoanalysis into the greatest of aberrations, to wit – *desire is the essence of reality*.

3

Nothing of the real interplay of the relation between reality and desire can be perceived without referring to the relation with the Other, which is what I tried to sketch out for you in drawing upon the good old support of the Euler circles.

This representation is surely insufficient, but if we accompany it with its logical underpinning, it can serve our purposes.

What emerges from the subject's relation with the object *a* is defined as a first circle, that of the subject, which another circle, that of the Other, intersects. The *a* is their intersection.

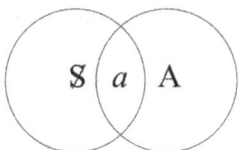

Intersection of two Euler circles

Through this relation of an originatively structured *vel*, the one with which I tried to spell out alienation for you, three years ago already, the subject will never manage to be established except as a relation of lack with respect to this *a* that partakes of the Other, unless in wanting to be situated within the Other, thus not having it but likewise amputated of this object *a*.

The subject's relation to the object *a* comprises the meaning which the Euler image takes on when it is brought to the level of the straightforward representation of the two logical operations known as *union* and *intersection*. Union depicts for us the subject's nexus with the Other while intersection defines for us the object *a*. The set of these two logical operations are those same operations that I positioned as originary, saying that the *a* is the result effectuated by logical operations of which there must be two.

What does this mean? Well, that it is essentially in the representation of a lack, insomuch as it roams around, that the fundamental structure of the bubble is established, the same that we initially termed *the stuff of desire*.

Here in the plane of the imaginary relation a relationship is established that is the exact inverse of the one that binds the ego to the other's image. The ego is doubly illusory. It is illusory in that it accedes to the avatars of the image, that is, it is equally given over to the function of disavowal or false pretence. It is illusory, too, in that it establishes a perverted order of logic, the formulation for which in psychoanalytic theory we shall be seeing later.

Indeed, psychoanalytic theory heedlessly breaches these bounds of logic whenever it presumes that at some point, at a moment that is presumed to be structurally primordial, what is rejected can be called *not-me*. This is very precisely what we contest. The order that is at issue here – and which implies, without their being aware, and in any case, without their saying so, the coming into play of language – does not allow in any way whatsoever of such complementarity [between ego and non-ego]. This is precisely what will lead us to bring to the forefront of our articulation this year a discussion of the function of Negation.

Everyone knows, and will be able to perceive in this collection which has now been put within your reach, that the first year of my Seminar at Sainte-Anne was dominated by a discussion on *Verneinung* in which Monsieur Jean Hyppolite, whose paper is reproduced in the appendix to the said volume, stressed most excellently what *Verneinung* meant for Freud. The secondarity of *Verneinung* is spelt out there so powerfully that already on no account can it be accepted that it might arise right away at the level of that first split into what we call *pleasure and displeasure*.

This is why, within this lack established by the bubble structure that forms the stuff of the subject, it is out of the question to confine ourselves to the term *negativity*, which has now become outmoded due to the confusion it entails.

The signifier is not merely what ushers in what is not there – even if, propaedeutically, the function thereof had for a while to be drummed into those ears that were hearkening to me. *Fort/Da*, insomuch as it refers to maternal presence or absence, is not the exhaustive articulation of the coming into play of the signifier. The signifier doesn't designate what is not there. It begets it. What is not there, at the point of origin, is the subject. In other words, at the point of origin, there is no *Dasein* but the object *a*, that is to say, in an alienated form that forever continues to leave its stamp upon any enunciation concerning *Dasein*.

Need I remind you of my formula, that there is no subject but by way of a signifier and for another signifier? This is the algorithm –

$$\frac{S}{\cancel{S}} \longrightarrow S'$$

Urverdrängung, or primary repression, is this – that which a signifier represents for another signifier. It doesn't bite into anything. It constitutes absolutely nothing. It makes do with an absolute absence of *Dasein*. For some sixteen centuries at the very least, the Egyptian hieroglyphs stood as solitary as they were unfathomed in the desert sands. It is clear, and it has always been clear to everyone, that this meant that each of those signifiers engraved in stone represented at the very least a subject for the other signifiers. Had it not been so, no one would ever have taken it to be writing. It is hardly necessary for a piece of writing to mean anything to anyone for it to count as writing and, as such, for it to manifest how each sign represents a subject for the next.

If we call this *Urverdrängung*, it means that we accept, it means that it appears to us to be true to experience, to think about what occurs – namely, that a subject emerges in the state of the barred subject – as something coming from one locus where it is supposedly inscribed and shifting to another locus where it will be inscribed afresh, to wit in exactly the same way that I once structured the function of metaphor, in so far as it is the model for what occurs when the repressed returns.

$$\frac{S'}{\cancel{S}} \nearrow \frac{S}{s}$$

Abolished by this first signifier – and we are about to see what this is – the barred subject comes to emerge at a site for which today we are likewise going to be able to provide a formula that has not yet been given. The barred subject, as such, is what represents, for a signifier – the signifier wherewith the subject has emerged – a meaning.

By *meaning* I understand exactly what I led you to hear, at the start of one of the previous years, in the formulation *Colourless green ideas sleep furiously*, which can be translated into French by the following, admirably depicting the ordinary order of your cogitations, *Des idées vertement fulgineuses s'assoupissent avec fureur* – and this is so, precisely, for want of knowing that they are all addressed to the signifier of the subject's lack, which a certain first signifier becomes as soon as the subject articulates his discourse.

What becomes of this first signifier? It becomes, even so, what all the psychoanalysts have perceived rather well, though they haven't managed to say anything worthwhile about it, to wit – the object *a*.

Indeed, at this level, the object *a* fulfils precisely the function that Frege distinguishes from *Sinn* under the name *Bedeutung*. The object *a* is the first *Bedeutung*, the first referent, the first reality, the *Bedeutung* that remains. It remains because it is, ultimately, what remains of thought at the end of all discourses.

To wit, what the poet writes without knowing what he says when he addresses his

> mère Intelligence,
> De qui la douceur coulait
> Quelle est cette négligence
> Qui laisse tarir son lait !

To wit, a regard *saisi*, which is the one that is transmitted at the birth of the clinic.

To wit, what one of my pupils at a recent conference at Johns Hopkins University took for a subject in calling it *The Voice and the Literary Myth*.

To wit, too, what remains after so many ponderings expended in the form of a pseudoscientific mare's nest, and which may thus be called by its name, as I did a long while ago with regard to analytic literature. It is called *shit*, as, moreover, authors readily admit. I mean that, apart from a very slight lapse in reasoning with regard to the object *a*, one of them has been quite able to articulate that there is no other support to the castration complex besides what is demurely called *the anal object*.

This is not to pin something down with a pure and unadorned appreciation. Much rather does it hinge on the necessity of an articulation, the mere statement of which ought to give further pause, since after all it has not been set down by the least qualified of wordsmiths. And so, this shall be our method for the year ahead, formulating the logic of the fantasy, to show where analytic theory stumbles over this logic. After all, I have not named this author who is known to many. Take heed – still the fault in reasoning is reasoned out, that is to say, it is arraignable. But this is not mandatory. Thus, in one particular article, the object *a* in question may show through in an altogether naked state, without for all that being appreciable on its own account. This is what we shall have occasion to show in certain texts, and after all, I don't see why I shouldn't distribute these fairly widely, as practical work. For this I will need to have a sufficient number at my disposal, but that's more or less the case already. This will come in due course, when we have to grapple with one particular register.

4

As of now I should like, even so, to mark out what prevents acceptance of certain interpretations that have been given of my function of metaphor, of the one which I have just exemplified in the least ambiguous manner. Most especially, it should not be conflated with anything whatsoever that would turn it into a sort of proportional ratio.

What I spelt out by writing that substitution – the fact of splicing a signifier to another signifier in the signifying chain – lies at the fount and origin of all signification, is correctly interpreted in the form for which today I have given you the formula, by way of the emergence of the barred subject. It still remains to supply it with a logical status, a task which the following example will allow you right away to perceive in all its urgency and exigency, or simply its necessity.

$$\frac{S'}{S} \nearrow \frac{S}{s}$$

Metaphor

Observe now how confusion has been made out of this four-fold relation – S′, the two Ss and the *s* of the signified – with the proportional relation in which metaphor was articulated by one of my interlocutors, Mr Perelman, the author of a *Treatise on Argumentation* which promotes anew an abandoned rhetoric. Reading the function of analogy into metaphor, he grounds the function of metaphor on the basis of the signifier's relation to another in so far as a third reproduces it by making an ideal signified emerge. I replied to this back at the time.

It is solely from this analogical conception of metaphor that the formula could arise which has wrongly been supplied as proceeding from mine.

$$\frac{\frac{\frac{S'}{s}}{S}}{S}$$

Flawed schema

S' over the lower case *s* of signification sits atop a first register of inscription. That which is drawn under, the *Unterdrückt*, the other register, substantifying the unconscious, would supposedly be constituted by the strange ratio of one signifier to another signifier. And we are further told that it is from here that language would derive its ballast. This formulation of so-called *langage réduit*, of reduced-state language, hinges on an error – I think you can sense this now – which is to insinuate the structure of a proportionality into the fourfold relation. And so, it is hard to see what could come out of this because the S/S relation then becomes rather difficult to interpret. In truth, this reference to a reduced-state language corresponds to the sole design, which moreover is confessed, of reducing our formulation *the unconscious is structured like a language*. Our formulation, now more than ever, is to be taken to the letter.

While it is looking like I won't get to the end today of the five points I had announced, I am none the less managing to stress what here constitutes the key to the whole structure, and renders untenable the said enterprise which happens to be spelt out at the start of the little collection which bears on this turning point in my relations with my audience that the Bonneval congress established. It is erroneous to structure any deduction of the unconscious on a presumed myth of reduced-state language, for the following reason. It is in the nature of each and every signifier not to be able in any case whatsoever to signify itself.

The hour is too late for me to force hastily upon you the writing of this inaugural point of all set theory, the axiom known as the *Axiom of Specification*, without which this theory cannot function. This axiom states, specifically, that there is no point in making a set function unless there exists another set that can be defined on the basis of a proposition that specifies certain elements x of the first set as freely satisfying a certain proposition – *freely* meaning *independent of any quantification* [, such as *for some x* or *for all x*]. What ensues when this proposition is defined simply as *x is not a member of itself*? I will begin my next lesson with these formulations.

What ensues – in positing any set by there defining the proposition which I indicated, as there specifying each x simply as *x is not a member of itself* – is that – for what interests us here, namely, for what impresses itself as soon as one wants to introduce the myth of *langage réduit*, of reduced-state language – there is a language which is not one, that is to say, which constitutes, for example, the set of signifiers. What is peculiar to the set of signifiers – I will be showing you this in detail – entails the necessity that there is something which does not belong to this set. It is not possible to reduce language, for

the simple reason that language could never constitute a closed set. 28
In other words, there is no universe of discourse.

For those who might have some trouble understanding what I have just uttered, I will remind you of what I said at the time, which is that the truths I have just uttered are merely those that became apparent in a confused manner during the *naive* period of the establishing of set theory in the form that is called, misleadingly, Russell's paradox. For it is not a paradox. It is an image. *The catalogue of all catalogues that don't list themselves*. What is meant by this? Either it lists itself, and falls wide of its definition, or else it doesn't list itself, and then falls wide of its mission. This is hardly a paradox. One has only to declare that in putting together such a catalogue, it cannot be pushed to the very end, and for good reason.

What I gave you a statement of earlier, in the formulation that in the universe of discourse *nothing contains everything*, is what exhorts us to be especially careful when handling what is called *all* and *part*, and which requires that we strictly distinguish from the outset the *One of totality* – which, precisely, I have just refuted by saying that at the level of discourse there is no universe, and which still leaves in abeyance whether we might suppose it anywhere else – from the *countable One*, insomuch as, by its very nature, it slips and slides away.

This countable One cannot be One but by repeating itself at least once. Closing in upon itself, it establishes at the origin the lack that is at issue. What is at issue is to establish the subject.

16 November 1966

II

RUSSELL'S PARADOX

> There is no metalanguage
> Writing and logic
> The surplus one
> The success of the *Écrits*

Today I am going to attempt to plot out for your usage a few relationships that it is essential and fundamental to secure here at the beginning of what is our topic this year.

I hope no one will be objecting that this has to do with abstractions. That would be an inappropriate term. As you will see, there is nothing more concrete than what I am about to put forward, even if this term does not correspond to the quality of bulk which it connotes for many.

It is a matter of making palpable for you propositions like the one that thus far I have only brought forward here in the guise of a sort of aphorism, which at one turning point in our disquisition played the role of an axiom – *there is no metalanguage*.

1

This formulation sounds like it goes against everything that is given, if not in experience, then at least in the writings of those who foray into grounding the function of language.

At the very least, in many cases they point out some differentiation in language from which they find it proper to start. For instance, they start from an *Object Language*, then to build upon this base a certain number of discriminations. The very action of an operation such as this does rather seem to imply that, in order to speak about language, one is making use of something that is not one, that would envelop it with an order distinct from the one which makes it function.

Russell's paradox

I believe that the solution to these apparent contradictions which arise in discourse, in what is said, is to be found in a function that strikes me, especially for our purposes, as essential to bring out, at least from the angle that will allow me to open this up. Indeed, the logic of the fantasy can on no account be articulated without reference to what is at issue here, namely something that, at least to announce it, I am pinpointing with the term *writing*.

This does not mean, for all that, that this is what you are acquainted with from the ordinary connotations of this word. I have chosen it, however, because it ought to bear some relation to what we have to expound.

Indeed, today we are going to have to keep teasing out the following point – that it is not the same thing, after saying something, to write it out or to write that it's been said. The second operation, so essential to the function of writing – from the angle of which the importance for our most particular references in this year's topic I want to show you today – presents with paradoxical consequences.

To put you on alert, why not start over with what I have already presented to you? Without one being able to say, I believe, that I'm repeating myself. It is fairly in the nature of the items that are being agitated here that they emerge – from some angle, from some ridge that pierces the surface upon which, from the mere fact of speaking, we are forced to keep hold – at some moment prior to taking on a function.

Here then is what I once wrote out on the blackboard. Somebody could do me the favour of writing it up there instead of me, so that I don't become submerged at the level of your dear heads. Here madam, take this stick of chalk, draw a large rectangle, almost as large as the board, and write 1 2 3 4 on the first line, inside the border. Then write beneath it the sentence – *the smallest whole number that is not written on this blackboard*.

> 1 2 3 4
> The smallest whole number that
> is not written on this blackboard

I thank the person who has kindly written out this sentence. It could have been presented differently, in the form of a little figure from whose mouth would have come what in comics is called a speech bubble, in which case you would have all concurred, and I would not have contradicted you, that it is the number 5. But it is clear that from the moment the sentence is written – *the smallest whole number that is not written on this blackboard* – the number 5, there being by this very fact written, is ruled out.

You only need, then, to look to see whether the smallest whole number that is not inscribed on the board might not by chance be the number 6. But you will fall upon the same difficulty. As soon as you pose the question of the number 6 in the capacity of *the smallest whole number that is not written on this blackboard*, this number 6 is written there. And so on and so forth.

Like many paradoxes, this holds interest only on account of what we want to do with it. It is the ensuing part that will show you how perhaps it was not unhelpful to introduce the function of writing from this angle, whereby it can present something of a riddle, a properly speaking logical riddle, and it's no worse than any other as a way of showing you the strict relation between the apparatus of writing and what is called logic.

It is also worthwhile recalling this at a moment when the new steps in logic – certainly new in the sense that they are far from being containable within the framework of a classic or traditional logic – are entirely linked to what plays out in writing.

Most of you here have, I think, an ample notion of this, and for those who have none, this might provide a handhold.

2

Let's pose a question now.

I've been speaking for some time about the function of language and I constructed the graph to articulate what is involved with respect to the subject of the unconscious. I had to do it storey by storey, with an audience who, in hearkening to me, were being dragged along by the ears. The graph is designed to give order to what, in the function of speech, is defined by the field necessitated by the structure of language and required by pathways of discourse, or what I called *the defiles of the signifier*.

On this graph, to the right on the lower line, the letter A is inscribed. This capital A can in one sense be identified with the locus of the Other. It is equally the locus where is produced everything that can be termed *statement* in the broadest sense of the term, that is to say, everything that in passing I called *the treasure trove of the signifier*.

This is not limited, in principle, to words in the dictionary. It was thus that, in correlation with the construction of the graph, I began speaking about witticisms, taking things up from the angle of the nonsensical trait they harbour. *Nonsensical* does not mean senseless. The trait of witticisms is akin to the play that English makes resonate for us with the term *nonsense*. This angle might have struck my listeners at the time as the most surprising and the most difficult, but it was quite indispensable so as to avoid any confusion. To make them hear the dimension that had to be educed, I showed the propinquity between witticisms, at least at the level of reception, at the level of tympanic vibration, with what for us was, during a trying time, the personal message. Personal messages are just as well any statement to the extent that it stands out in a nonsensical manner. I alluded to this last time by reminding you of the famous *Colourless green ideas*, etc.

The set of statements – I'm not saying *propositions* – thus forms part of this universe of discourse that is located in A.

The question that arises is strictly a question of structure, the same that gives meaning to my saying that the unconscious is structured like a language. This is a pleonasm in my enunciation, because I identify structure with this *like a language*, precisely in the structure that I am going to try to make function for you today. The question is this – how do things stand with the universe of discourse insomuch as it implies the play of the signifier, insomuch as it defines the two dimensions of metaphor, insomuch as the chain can always have another chain spliced into it by way of an operation of substitution, insomuch as, but its very essence, it signifies this sliding which is due to how no signifier belongs in its own right to any signification? Having called to mind this shifting of the universe of discourse – which allows for the sea of variations in what constitutes significations, an order that is essentially shifting and transitory, in which nothing is assured but the function of what I called back at the time, in a metaphorical way, *tufting ties* – it is this universe of discourse which it is today a matter of examining.

We have thus far defined the signifier by its function of representing a subject for another signifier. What does this signifier represent faced with itself, from its repetition as a signifying unit? Well, this is defined by the axiom, which I put forward last time, that no signifier can signify itself, even when, and very precisely when, it is reduced to its minimal form, the one we call *the letter*. What is at issue is to find out what this axiom can specify within the universe of discourse.

I know full well that mathematical usage hinges precisely on how, when we have set down a capital letter A somewhere, and not only in an algebraic exercise, we take it up thereafter as though, the second time we use it, it were still the same. So, don't quibble with me on that basis. Today is not the day for me to give you a maths lesson. Simply keep in mind that there is no correct pronouncement of any use of letters – even in what stands nearest to us today, for example in the use of a Markov chain – that would necessitate of any teacher – and this is what Markov himself did – the propaedeutic stage of giving a clear sense of what there is by way of deadlock, of arbitrariness, of what is absolutely unjustifiable in so employing the capital A, a second time, to represent the first capital A as though it were still the same. This is a difficulty that arises with the principle behind the mathematical use of this claimed identity. We are not grappling with this expressly today because what is at issue here is not mathematics. I would simply like to remind you that the fundament that *the signifier is on no account grounded from signifying itself* is accepted by the very same who do on occasion make use of it in a way that runs counter to this principle, at least in appearance. It would be an uncomplicated matter to take a look at the channel through which this is possible, but I don't have time to digress into this.

Without wearying you further, I should like simply to pursue my aim, which is the following. What is the consequence in this universe of discourse of the principle that the signifier could never signify itself? What does this axiom specify in the universe of discourse insomuch as this universe comprises everything that can be said? Does the specification that this axiom determines belong to the universe of discourse?

If it does not belong to it, then this certainly poses a problem for us. The axiomatic statement, that *the signifier could never signify itself*, would have the consequence of specifying something that, as such, would not lie within the universe of discourse, when we have indeed just said that this universe subsumes within it everything that can be said. Might we find ourselves in some diversion which would mean that what cannot in this way belong to the universe of discourse could not in any way whatsoever be said? Since we are speaking about it, clearly this does not amount to telling you that it's ineffable. I consider, and this is known, by sheer coherence and without for all that subscribing to Mr Wittgenstein's school of thought, that this thematic is tantamount to – *it is pointless to speak*.

Before coming to such a formulation, the range of which you can see I am not sparing you from, nor from the deadlock it constitutes, because this, too, we shall have to revisit, let's first be careful to test out the alternative branch – that what is specified by the axiom that the signifier could never signify itself *does* belong to the universe of discourse. I really am doing all I can to clear the way through what I'm trying to get you to follow me into.

Let's take up arbitrarily the use of a little sign that is employed in this logic grounded on writing – $\vee\vee$. In this you will recognise – this play is perhaps not accidental – the shape of my punch mark, from which in some sense the hat has been knocked off. It's as though a little box has been opened. In set theory, this sign serves to designate

Exclusion, in other words what is designated by the Latin expression for both *either* and *or* – *aut*. Either one or the other. The signifier in its repeated presentation functions only as functioning the first time *or else* the second. Between one and the other there is a radical gulf. This is what is meant by *the signifier could not signify itself.*

$$S \vee\kern-1.2ex\vee S$$

We will suppose, then, that what is determined by the axiom as a specification remains within the universe of discourse, and we are going to designate this with a signifier, B. This is an essential signifier which, you will notice, can be appropriated for the following, which the axiom sets out – that it could not, within a certain relation and from a certain relation, beget any signification. B is very precisely this signifier to which nothing objects as to its being thus specified, as to its marking out, if I may say so, this sterility. Indeed, the signifier in itself is characterised exactly thus – that it might beget a signification is neither mandatory nor spontaneous. This is what gives me the right to symbolise with the signifier B the characteristic that the signifier's relation to itself does not beget any signification.

But to begin with, let's start from the following, which does indeed seem to be crucial – it's that something which I am in the process of stating for you, namely B, belongs to the universe of discourse. Let's see what results from this.

$$B \lozenge A$$

This is why for the time being I am helping myself, because after all this doesn't strike me as unsuitable, to my little punch mark, to say that B belongs to A. Moreover, it relates to it with a richness that I shall certainly have to tease out for you over the course of the year, and the complexity of which I indicated for you last time by breaking down this little sign in all the binary fashions in which this can be done.

It's a matter of finding out whether there is any contradiction that results from B belonging to A. Can we write, not that this B doesn't signify itself, but rather that, forming part of the universe of discourse, this B can be written in the mode of what characterises what we have called a *specification*, thus – *B belongs to itself*? It is clear that this question does arise. Does B belong to itself?

I hope that enough of you here are aware that the functioning of sets is not strictly superimposable onto that of classes, but that the whole thing needs instead to be rooted from the beginning in the principle of a specification. We have learnt to distinguish the notion of specification in several logical varieties, and so we find ourselves here faced with something the kinship of which must be resonating sufficiently in your ears on account of what I brought up last time, namely Russell's paradox.

I am setting out here the function of sets in terms that are of interest to us to the extent that this function does something which I have not yet done. I'm not here to introduce this, though. It's a matter of my maintaining you in a field that, logically speaking, lies upstream of it, and to introduce something which in this connection we are afforded the opportunity to try to grasp, namely what grounds the bringing into play of the apparatus known as set theory. Not only is this theory presenting today as utterly originative with respect to any mathematical statement but, furthermore, logic, from its standpoint, amounts to no more than what mathematical symbolism is able to grasp. All in all, the function of sets would also be the principle that grounds all logic. This is what I am calling into question. If there is a logic of the fantasy, then it is indeed more principial than any logic that flows into the formalising defiles within which it is has shown itself to be so very fruitful in the modern era.

Let's try to see what Russell's paradox means when it covers something that is not far from what is up here on the board. Simply put, it holds that this type of signifier is fully enveloping, and moreover it takes it to be a class. This is an odd mistake. To say, for example, that the word *obsolete* represents a class in which it would be included, on the pretext that the word *obsolete* is obsolete, is a sleight of hand that holds interest only in that it allows for grounding as a class those signifiers that do not signify themselves. We, on the other hand, are positing here as an axiom that on no account could the signifier signify itself and that this ought to be the starting point. It should be figured out by starting from this, if only to realise that the potential to qualify the word *obsolete* as obsolete needs to be explained differently. It is absolutely indispensable to bring in here what is introduced by the division of the subject.

But let's set aside *obsolete* and pick up the argument that the likes of Russell would pitch in opposition to a formula that would be stated thus –

$$B \diamond A / S \vee S$$

Russell would draw attention to something of a contradiction. By his reckoning, it would effectively be impossible to secure the status of a subset B on the basis of its being specified in another set, A, by a characteristic such that an element of A would not contain itself.

Is there any subset defined by this proposition of the existence of elements that do not contain themselves? It is most surely an uncomplicated matter to show in this condition the contradiction that exists within it, since we have only to take an element y as an element belonging to B to notice the consequences that arise from its being an element of B and not being an element of itself.

$$(y \in B) \, (y \in A \, / \, y \notin y)$$

The contradiction is revealed by placing B in the stead of y –

$$(B \in B) \, (B \in A \, / \, B \notin B)$$

The formula plays out in the following. Whenever we make B an element of B, it results, due to the interdependence of the formula, that since B belongs to A then it must not belong to itself, while furthermore if B does not belong to itself – thus satisfying the parenthesis on the right in the formula, with B substituted for y – it does then belong to itself in being one of these y that are elements of B.

Such is the contradiction that Russell's paradox faces us with. It is a matter of finding out whether, in our register, we can stop here. At least we might perceive in passing what is meant by the contradiction highlighted in set theory, which might allow us to say in what way set theory is specified in logic, namely what stride it constitutes in relation to the more radical one that we are trying to establish here. The contradiction that is at issue at the level on which Russell's paradox is articulated hinges precisely, as the mere use of words tells us, on this – that I *say* it. If I don't say it, nothing stops this formula – very precisely the second formula – from holding up as is, *written*. And there is nothing to tell us that its use will stop here.

What I am saying here is not wordplay, for set theory has absolutely no support but the fact that I write as such. Everything that may be said regarding any difference between the elements is ruled out of the game. Handling the literal play that constitutes set theory consists in writing, as such, what I am saying here, namely that the first set can be formed at once of this nice person sitting here typing out my disquisition, the condensation on this window, and an idea that has occurred to me this very instant. This constitutes a set of three elements in that I can expressly say that no other difference exists besides the one that is constituted by the mere fact that I can apply to each of these three objects I have just named, and which you can see are fairly motley, a unary trait.

As for us, we are not at the level of such a specification because what I am bringing into play is the universe of discourse, and so my question does not encounter Russell's paradox. To wit, we can deduce no deadlock, no impossibility, as to B – which is unknown to me, but which I have begun by supposing can belong to the universe of discourse, even though wrought from the specification that the signifier could not signify itself – perhaps having with itself a sort of relation that eludes Russell's paradox. To wit, it can demonstrate something to us that would be its own peculiar dimension.

We are going to see in which status it belongs, or doesn't, to the universe of discourse.

3

If I have taken such care over this reminder of Russell's paradox, it's as like as not because I'm going to be able to make use of it to give you a sense of something else.

I'm going to give you a sense of this in the most straightforward way, and then afterwards in a slightly richer manner.

I'm about to give you a sense of this in the most straightforward of ways because I've been prepared for some time now to make every concession. They want me to put things simply? OK then, I'll put things simply. To comprehend is not to take such a direct path. You are already sufficiently trained, by my good offices, to know as much. Even when what I tell you appears straightforward, you may still have some lingering wariness.

A catalogue of catalogues. Here, on this first approach, we can see indeed how it is very much a matter of signifiers. Whyever should we be surprised that it doesn't list itself? This seems to us to have been a requirement from the beginning. Nevertheless, nothing would prevent the catalogue of all catalogues that don't list themselves from being printed within itself, on the inside. Nothing would preclude this, not even the contradiction that Lord Russell would deduce from it. But let's consider the possibility that, in order not to contradict itself, it is not inscribed in itself.

Let's posit that there are just four catalogues that do not list themselves, A, B, C and D. Let's suppose that a further catalogue appears that doesn't list itself. We add this one – E. What is inconceivable about thinking that there is a first catalogue that lists A B C D, and a second catalogue that lists B C D E? There is no cause for astonishment that each should be lacking this letter, which is the one that would designate itself. Once you have generated this series, you need only arrange it around the edge of a disc and you will perceive that, just because each catalogue will be lacking one, or even a greater number, it doesn't mean that the circle of these catalogues will not form something that corresponds precisely to the catalogue of all catalogues that do not list themselves. Simply put, what this chain constitutes will have the property of being a surplus signifier, which is constituted from the closure of the chain – an uncountable signifier, and one which, by this very fact, can be designated by a signifier. Indeed, being nowhere, there is no harm in a new signifier emerging to designate this uncountable signifier as the surplus signifier, the one that cannot be slotted into the chain.

I'll take another example. Catalogues are not made in the first place to catalogue catalogues. They catalogue objects that are in some way entitled to be there – the word *title* having every importance here. It would be easy for me to go down this path to reopen the dialectic of the catalogue of all catalogues, but, as I really must let you exercise your own imaginations, I'm going to turn to a more lively path and speak about books. With this, we are apparently entering again the universe of discourse. Yet, to the extent that a book contains a few references and may have to cover a certain area with a register of a few titles, it will include a bibliography. This is something that presents to illustrate for us what results insomuch as catalogues live or do not live within the universe of discourse. If I make the catalogue of all the books that contain a bibliography, naturally it is not from the bibliographies that I am making the catalogue. Nevertheless, in cataloguing these books, insomuch as they refer to one another in their bibliographies, I can very well cover the set of all the bibliographies.

It is exactly here that can be situated the fantasy that is properly speaking the poetic fantasy par excellence, the one that haunted Mallarmé, of the *Livre absolu*. It is at this level, where things are bound together not at the level of a *pure* signifier but at the level of the *purified* signifier – in so far as I say, and in so far as I write that I say, that the signifier is here articulated as distinct from any signified – that I behold the possibility of this Absolute Book taking shape. What is peculiar to this Absolute Book is that it would subsume the entire signifying chain, by dint of how it may no longer signify anything.

By dint of this, therefore, there is something that proves to be grounded in existence at the level of the universe of discourse, but we have to hang this existence on the specific logic that can be constituted by that of the fantasy, for this is the only one that can tell us in what way this region is appended to the universe of discourse. It is surely not ruled out that it should enter this universe, but on the other hand it is quite certain that it is not specified there by this purification of which I have just spoken, for it is hardly possible for there to be purification of what is essential to the universe of discourse, namely signification. Should I speak to you for four hours more about this Absolute Book, it would be no less the case that everything I am telling you bears a meaning.

What characterises the structure of B to the extent that we do not know where to situate it in the universe of discourse – within or without – is the trait of the *surplus one* that I stated earlier, forming for you the circle of A B C D E where, simply by closing the chain, each group of four leaves on the outside the outlying signifier that can serve to designate the group, and precisely for the sole reason that it is not represented there. And yet the total chain will come to constitute the set of all these signifiers, making this extra unit emerge, which as such is uncountable and which is essential to a whole series of structures.

It was upon precisely these structures that, back in 1960, I grounded all my operatory of identification. You will find this, for example, in the structure of the torus. You can loop a certain number of rounds on the torus, making a series of complete turns act as a cut. You can even make as many as you please. The more there are, the more satisfying it is, but the more obscure it is, too. It's enough to make two to see the third appear, which is required in order that these two should loop back, and in order that, so to speak, the line should be eating its own tail. This third round is secured by the looping of the central hole. Indeed, for the first two loops to intersect, it is impossible not to pass around there.

I'm not drawing this out on the board today because, in truth, in saying it, I've said enough for you to understand me and also far too little for me to show you that to begin with there are at least two paths by which this can be brought about. In either case, the result is not at all the same with respect to the emergence of the *surplus one* I've been telling you about.

This merely suggestive indication has nothing about it that can exhaust the richness of what is afforded us by the least topological study.

I will make do today with indicating that what is peculiar to the world of writing is that it is distinct from discourse on account of the fact that it can close upon itself. Moreover, in closing upon itself, therefrom emerges the possibility of a *one* that has a status which is quite other than that of the One which unifies and subsumes. From its mere closure, and without there being any need to go into the status of repetition, which even so is tightly linked to it, the world of writing makes emerge that which has the status of a *surplus one*, insomuch as it is sustained by writing alone. And yet it remains open in its possibilities to the universe of discourse because, as I have pointed out already, it suffices that I should write – though it is necessary that this writing should occur – what I am saying about the

Russell's paradox

exclusion of this one, for this other plane to be generated which is the one upon which unfurls, properly speaking, the whole function of logic. This matter is sufficiently signposted by the galvanisation which logic has received by submitting to the play of writing alone, with the proviso that it still wants for any recollection of how this hinges only upon the function of a lack in the very thing that is written, and which constitutes the status as such of the writing function.

Even though taking you through such simple matters might make this disquisition seem underwhelming to you, you would be wrong not to see that it joins up with a register of questions that lends the function of writing an impact that cannot help but reverberate through to what is most profound in any possible conception of structure.

If the writing I have been speaking about is indeed supported only by the return of a cut looped upon itself in the way that I have illustrated this with the function of the torus, then we find ourselves being led to speak about the function of edges, which the most fundamental of studies, linked to the furtherance in mathematical analytics, have rendered us capable of isolating. Now, when we are speaking about edges, there is nothing that can bring us to substantify this function. It would be quite unwarranted were you to deduce that this function of writing is there to limit the shifting I spoke of earlier as that of our thoughts or the universe of discourse. Far from it. If there is something that is structured as an edge, that which limits it is itself poised to enter in turn the edging function. This is precisely what we are going to be dealing with.

There is yet another facet, with which I intend to bring this to a close, and that is the function of the unary trait.

I'm going to bring up again the Book of Daniel, to remind you of what has been known since always. I've already turned to this Book to begin to get across what is involved in the function of the signifier, in connection with a tale of zouave pantaloons which are designated with a word that remains what is called a hapax, and which is impossible to translate, unless they are wooden sandals worn by the characters in question.

In Daniel Chapter 5 verse 26, you already have the theory of the subject, which is the theory I'm expounding for you. And it emerges precisely at the limit of this universe of discourse. This is the famous story of the dramatic feast, of which moreover we find not the faintest trace in the annals, but no matter. *MENE, MENE* – this is how verse 25 is expressed – *TEKEL, UPHARSIN*, which is usually transcribed into the famous *MENE, TEKEL, PERES*. It strikes me as not unhelpful to notice that *MENE, MENE*, which means *numbered*, as Daniel observes in interpreting for the unsettled prince, is expressed twice, as though to show the most straightforward repetition of what constitutes counting. It suffices to count up to two for everything that is involved in this *surplus one* to play out, which is the true root of the function of repetition for Freud – with the proviso that, contrary to what is there in set theory, it is not said.

Nor is the following said – that what repetition seeks to repeat is precisely what escapes, by way of the very function of the mark. The mark is originary in the function of repetition. Repetition plays out in the mark's repeating. But why does the mark prompt the repetition that is sought? Well, because what is being sought is that the mark should mark out the first time. Yet, at the level of what it has marked, this very mark fades away. The mark could only ever be duplicated by effacing, upon what is to be repeated, the first mark – effacing, that is to say, allowing it to slip out of reach. This is why what is sought in repetition slips away by its very nature.

MENE, MENE – in what is found, something lacks weight, *TEKEL*. The prophet Daniel interprets this by telling the prince that he has, in effect, been weighed up, but that something has been found wanting, which is *UPHARSIN*. This radical lack, this primary lack which stems from the very function of counting as such, this *surplus one* that cannot be counted, is what properly constitutes the lack for which it is our business here to supply the logical functioning, so that it may secure what is at issue in the terminal *PERES*, the one that bursts apart what is involved in the universe of discourse, the bubble, the Empire in question, the conceitedness of what closes into the image of the imaginary *all*. Here we have exactly the path by which is conveyed the effect of the entrance of what structures discourse at the most radical point.

This point is the letter. I have been saying and accentuating this from the beginning, going so far as to employ the commonest of images. But the letter at issue here is the letter insomuch as it is excluded, insomuch as it is missing.

I have, therefore, made a fresh sweep into this Jewish tradition, about which I had prepared so many items. I even went so far as to grapple with a brief exercise in Masoretic reading. All this work of mine was in a sense shelved by the fact that I was unable to present the thematic I had intended to develop around the Name-of-the-Father. Something remains of all this, though. Notably, at the level of the Creation story –

בְּרֵאשִׁית בָּרָא אֱלֹהִים

[*Bereshit bara Elohim*], begins the Book, that is to say, with a ב [*bet*].

It is said that the very letter which we have been employing today, the capital A, in other words the א [*aleph*], was not, at the point of origin, among those from which the whole of Creation emerged.

This indicates to us, but in a way that is in some sort folded back upon itself, that it is to the very extent that one of these letters is absent that the others function, but that doubtless it is in its very lack that resides the fecundity of the operation.

23 November 1966

NEXT SESSION

Restating the 'Seminar'

As I notified you last time, perhaps a little late as some of the audience had already scattered by the time I made the announcement, today you are going to be hearing a paper by Jacques-Alain Miller.

This underscores my wish that the curious name *Seminar* should maintain some basis, a name that has been attached to my teaching since Sainte-Anne [Hospital], where it was held, as you know, ten years standing.

To speak only of the last two academic years here, you know that I have been wanting this Seminar to be held in an efficacious fashion. This was a great annoyance for some of you, because my reckoning was that this efficacy ought to be bound up with a reduction of this sizeable audience, otherwise so pleasant, which you have been giving me through your assiduity and your attention. So much assiduity and attention deserve, my goodness, great respect, which made it hard for me indeed to whittle down the numbers, such that while in total there are now fewer, it is not so much so that things should have, strictly speaking, changed scale from the standpoint of quantity, which plays such an important role in communication. And so, for the year ahead, I have left the solution to this difficult problem pending. Until further notice, and without committing myself to it, I won't be closing any of these Wednesdays, regardless of whether it is the last of the month or the last but one.

Only, I should like at least the name *Seminar* to be kept, and in a more pronounced way than we saw at Sainte-Anne, though of course, until even the very last years, there were meetings at which I did entrust the floor to one or other of those who were following me back then. Nevertheless, some ambiguity has remained, which has left the appellation *Seminar* suspended between the proper use of a category, designating a place where something has to be exchanged, where the transmission and dissemination of a doctrine ought to be manifest as such, that is to say, on the path to its conveyance, and goodness knows what other use, which would not, strictly speaking, be that of the proper name – the whole discussion of proper names could be gone into in this respect – but, let's say, that of a nomination par excellence, which nomination *par excellence* would become a nomination *par ironie*.

Henceforth, to show that this is not the state in which I intend the use of this appellation to settle, you will be seeing periodically a certain number of people intervening who have shown themselves disposed to so doing.

Jacques-Alain Miller is most surely somewhat entitled to inaugurate the next part because in my book he has provided you with a *Classified Index of the Major Concepts*, which, from all I've heard, has been very welcome for a great many people who have found this Ariadne's thread most advantageous, allowing them to move around this series of articles in which some notion, or some *concept* as the term is rightly employed there, is to be found at various stages.

Just one minor detail. In answer to a question that someone asked, I will point out that the oblique numbers in the index correspond to essential passages. The upright numbers, Romanised as they say, correspond to passages where the concept is at issue more in passing – it can happen that on the designated page what is referenced is contained within a single line. This tells you how much care was put into compiling this useful little apparatus.

In this connection I've been informed that the book is – as is sometimes said in this *Franglais* to which I for my part have no objection – *out of print*. I find this expression nicer than the French *épuisé*. One starts to wonder when something is described as *épuisé*. I hope it won't stay out of print for too long.

This is what is known as a success, but a market success. Let's not jump to any conclusions about the other kind of success. We have to wait and see. It leaves the question open. It has been noted that this is a book which I was in no great hurry to bring into circulation. Given how I was so tardy about it, the question might be asked – *why now? What am I expecting from this?* It's quite clear that the reply *it ought to be helpful to you* is no less valid now than it would have been a year or two ago, and even long before that. So, the question is not so simple. It has to do with everything that is involved in my relations with something that fulfils a grassroots function, namely psychoanalysis in its *embodied* form, to put it briskly, or even its *subjected* form, in other words the psychoanalysts themselves.

Many elements lay behind how what I was trying to construct was to stay within a restricted field, so enabling the selection, which has been made, by those willing to make the decision to acknowledge the implicit consequences, in their practice, of studying Freud.

In the end, things never turn out quite as planned in these difficult matters where resistance is not narrowed down to what has to be designated under the strict sense of the term *resistance* in analytic praxis. Here it takes another form, where the social context is not without its impact. Indeed, this is what is making it rather delicate for me to explain myself on this matter before such a large audience.

I don't view with an especially favourable eye how I have been associated with all that can arise by way of fuss and bother around certain terms. I regard it merely as stemming from what I would call the outlying relationships of my teaching. Thus, for instance, the term *Structuralism*, which is currently in vogue, is not the least to inspire such wariness on my part. Unless I am pressed into it by some repercussion of what just now I referred to as the book's success, I am rather ill disposed to eating into the measured time of this Seminar to set out the reasons behind it. You can see, or sense, from your experience these last years, that I have no time to lose if I want to state things at the level of the construction I inaugurated in its style through my last Seminar, taking up those points at which I intended to lay out the groundwork of this logic which I have to develop for you over the year ahead.

It still remains, even so, that the book exists, along with the first movements that it is bringing with it, and which shall be followed by others, such that the two or three points I have just brought out as the principal ones – though there are others – run the risk of being left hanging for you. Consequently, I believe I ought to forewarn you that you will find, my word, the explanation for this – at least an explanation that will be sufficient to allow you to respond at least in part to the questions that may be left hanging for you – in two interviews that are due to be published this week, if I am correctly informed, in places that, goodness knows, are hardly free-for-alls. They are, respectively, *Le Figaro littéraire* and *Les Lettres françaises*. You might, then, come to know a little more about these points. Furthermore, as I can't help myself, whenever I am involved in one of these modes of outlying relationship, from slipping in a little of what is currently in the works, it's possible that you will find here and there something related to our disquisition of this year.

For example, I spoke to you last time about the unary trait as being established fundamentally by repetition. It may be said of this repetition that it occurs just once, which means that it is twofold. Otherwise, there would be no repetition. For anyone who wants to linger over this a little, it establishes at the outset, in its most radical fundament, the subject's division. Well, I cannot help but feel some scruple at having stated it here in front of you almost in passing, when I spent some three quarters of an hour chewing it over at the congress that was held at Johns Hopkins in the month of October, as some of you are aware. It may well be that I give greater credit to you than to my listeners back then, certain echoes since received having evinced for me that structuralist ears – to take up the term from earlier – whomever they might belong to, are quite capable of proving somewhat hard of hearing.

There are two further places, more unexpected still, where you might be able to find these little signposts which, my goodness, are never too quick in coming with respect to certain themes which I shall have to develop hereafter, on the preconscious for instance. It's curious that, for a good while now, that is to say for as long as people have been getting everything in a tangle while thinking they are keeping things distinct, they have not been dealing all that much with the functions which Freud set apart for the preconscious. If I remember rightly, this indication was insinuated in passing into one of these interviews, I don't recall which. So, to these should be added two further interviews, which I think will be unexpected for you, due to be broadcast by the ORTF [Office de radiodiffusion-télévision française].

There will be one next Friday at 10.45am, which is, so I was assured, a peak listening time. I'd like to believe it, but I think that most of you will be on shift at the hospital at that time. Well, too bad. You'll manage as best you can. I hope to be able to pass on the text, if the radio station is kind enough to give me authorisation to do so. The other of the two will take place on Monday. You can see, there's a rush on. For the first, it is Georges Charbonnier who has been kind enough, I won't say to receive this, but to give me the space. The second is Monsieur Sipriot, thanks to whom you will perhaps get something more lively than the first, because this will be a dialogue with the person best qualified to keep it up, namely François Wahl, who is here today, and who has shown himself willing to engage in this exercise with me. I won't swear to it, but it seems it's going to be on between 6.15 and 7, though they won't be speaking only about my book and I can't tell you in which slot it will appear, each having been allotted its own fifteen minutes. It's peak time, which in general is accompanied by fitness routines. There you are. We'll see what comes of all that.

Before giving the floor to Jacques-Alain Miller, I will convey some rather amusing news which was passed on to me by one of my stalwarts, drawn from a sort of specialist journal that reports on both IBM machinery and what is being done on an experimental level at the Massachusetts Institute of Technology – MIT as it is commonly termed.

It has to do with one of those machines that has been tweaked to a high level, as they are doing nowadays, and which has been given, and certainly not just for the sake of it, the name ELIZA. It's called ELIZA for the use that has been made of it, which I'm going to tell you about. Eliza is the name of a lowly flower woman on the streets of London in the well-known play *Pygmalion*. She is trained to *talk proper*, that is, she is coached to express herself in high society in such a way that no one could tell she does not belong there, but of course they do find out. Something of this register looms up with the little MIT machine.

In truth, this is not strictly speaking about a machine being capable of giving articulated responses simply when it is spoken to. I'm not saying *when it is asked*. It's a matter of what turns out to be in play, and which calls into question what, in obtaining these replies, can be produced in the one who is speaking to it. This situation is quite usable for us, even though, my word, the matter is not spelt out in a way that is altogether satisfactory for us, in other words, in a way that takes into account the framework into which we might insert it. It nevertheless provides us with a reference that is most interesting within the disquisition being pursued here, because ultimately something is suggested there that could be regarded as a therapeutic function of the machine. To spell it right out, the question that is raised is nothing less than that of the analogue of a transference that can occur in this relationship.

This matter did not displease me, and it is not unrelated to everything I am leaving open concerning how I have to handle the spread of what is called *my teaching*. It calls to mind the handling of a first symbolic chain, a notion of which, in its time, I addressed to psychoanalysts, their minds having had to adapt to it so as suitably to focus on what Freud calls *remembering*. It supplied them with a subjective model for the construction of this symbolic chain, and of what amounts to its own sort of memory. This is spelt out in what is now in this book, secondarily, in the inverted position where the Introduction to the now preceding *Séminaire sur La lettre volée* has been set just after it.

I remind those who were listening to me back then that this construction, like all the others, was made in front of them and for them, step by step. I started from a passage in Poe's text showing how the mind gets to work on the theme of whether one can win the game of *even and odd*. My second step was to devise a machine of precisely this nature, and what has effectively been produced today differs in no respect whatsoever from what I was voicing back then, to wit, simply that the machine is supposed by the subject to be equipped with a programme that takes into account the wins and losses. The subject questioned the machine by playing the game of odds and evens with it. On the basis of this one supposition – that it maintains, at least over a certain number of goes, the memory of its wins and its losses – a series of pluses and minuses can be put together. Bracketing them in patterned lengths, which each displace by one move each time, allows us to establish the trajectory which I constructed and upon which is founded this first type, the most elementary type, of model. It shows that we have no need to regard memory in the register of physiological engrams, but merely as symbolic memorial.

It was a hypothetical game. Back then, it was perhaps not yet in a state to function at this level. This was long before it was to show up squarely on the agenda of issues for those engineers who devote themselves to such apparatus – which as you know are still in progress, because they are expecting nothing less than automatic translation – but even so, this existed as such, as an electronic machine, that is to say, as something that could be written down on paper, which is the modern-day definition of the machine. It was on this basis that, fifteen years ago, I built a first model for the specific use of psychoanalysts, with the goal of producing in their *mens*, in their mind, that sort of necessary detachment from the idea that the functioning of the signifier is inevitably the flower of consciousness, which at that time amounted to introducing an utterly unprecedented step.

Over to you. *(There follows the paper by J.-A. Miller.)*

The perfect ease of this paper backs up, grounds, what I introduced last time as the utterly necessary point of departure for any logic required by the psychoanalytic terrain. But this commentary scarcely has the scope of a reduplication because it has squared up to what is in some sense the first of the groups in the logico-mathematical sense of the term, namely the Boolean group insomuch as it happens to have every appearance of being far more homogeneous with classical logic. You have thus been able to see how on the basis of this group we are enabled to construct the logical precedence, the necessity, which distinguishes radically between the status of signification and its point of origin in the signifier. You have had a most elegant demonstration of this here. At the same time as this has constituted a phase that has been necessary for assimilating what I managed to bring you last time, you have also had its complement, its check and its configuration. You will get the ensuing part next Wednesday.

30 November 1966

III

FREUD, LOGICIAN

Structure of the network
Le Paysan de la Garonne
Conjunction and Implication
Plurality of negations
On narcissistic structure

The last time we met here you were able to hear what Jacques-Alain Miller put forward. I was unable to add many observations due to shortness of time.

His paper bore the stamp of a solid familiarity with what was inaugurated in the way of modern logic as a whole by the labour and published work of Boole.

It is perhaps not unimportant to let you know that Jacques-Alain Miller had been absent from my previous lesson, nor had he been able to receive any transcript of it because I myself only got hold of the text two days ago, and so at the moment I introduced him I was not altogether sure of the subject he had chosen, as you may have been able to sense. These remarks have all their importance in view of the extraordinary convergence between what he was able to set out for you and my own design. Let's say that he undertook, wittingly of course, a reapplication of the principles and, if I may say so, the axioms around which my development has thus far been revolving.

Boolean logic marks the shift when, having wanted to formalise classical logic, it was noticed that this very formalisation not only allows for major extensions to be brought to it, but further proves to be the hidden essence upon which this logic was able to be oriented and built, while believing it was following something that was not really its fundament, namely what we are going to try to discern today, so as to distance it from the field into which we are going to proceed, insomuch as we announced this as the logic of the fantasy.

The surprising ease with which, from the fields left blank in Boolean logic – because of course the major articulation that no signifier could ever signify itself is absent in Boole – Miller was able to find again the place from which the signifier in its proper function is in some sense elided, was quite striking. It is the famous (– 1), the exclusion of which in Boole's logic he brought out most admirably, thus indicating in this very elision the place at which is situated what I have been trying to spell out here.

There is something here that carries all its importance – not that I am paying him the slightest compliment for it – because it allows you to grasp the coherence, the main course, into which is inserted the logic that we are obligated to ground in the name of the doings of the unconscious. What we ought to expect if we are what we are, that is to say, rationalists, is evidently this – not that the previous logic should be overturned, but that it should simply find here its proper foundations.

You saw being highlighted in passing the point that some time ago necessitated our bringing into play a certain symbol that corresponds to this (– 1), which Boole doesn't use and even disallows. It is by no means sure that this (– 1) is the most fitting when it comes to usage. For what is peculiar to formal logic is that it is operant, and what we have to educe are the new operators, the shadow of which is already looming in what, measured out for the ears I was addressing, I had already tried to spell out in a manageable fashion – manageable for what is to be managed, which is nothing else on this occasion but analytic praxis.

This year we are inclining to its limits, properly speaking to its edges, which is compelling us to supply more rigorous formulations in order to circumscribe what we have to deal with and which deserves, in certain of its facets, to be taken, undertaken, within the most comprehensive articulation that has thus far been afforded us in matters of logic, namely that which is centred by way of the function of sets. What Miller contributed last time, focused on Boolean logic, is worthwhile less as an articulation of what I have been developing for you than as a confirmation, an assurance and a framing, in the margins.

I will move on from this topic now, but not without pointing out that Miller also designated for you how Sartre takes up the place where this logical articulation stands – the one which constitutes our task for the year ahead – under the appellation *non-thetic self-consciousness*. This is indeed the fundamental point around which turns the special privilege of the subject which Sartre tries to maintain. It is not uninteresting to draw your attention to how what is at issue there is what is properly called a *placeholder*. It can scarcely give me further pause, unless in the register of its interpretation. There is no call to busy ourselves with this, we analysts, except in a way that is strictly equivalent to how we attend to other placeholders when we have to handle what amounts effectively to the unconscious.

It is in this respect that it cannot be said that what I am able to state about structure is in any way whatsoever situated in relation to Sartre.

1

So, logic of the fantasy.

Today we can only very briefly – like plucking a string with a fingertip to make it twang for an instant – recall here the lambency that still flickers from what pertains to the tradition here pinpointed by the term *universitarian*, if we give this term, not the meaning of designating or reviling a geographical site, but rather the meaning of *Universitas Litterarum*, the place where a curriculum is sited.

Irrespective of the further meanings, far more historical meanings of course, which can be given to the term *university*, it is not unhelpful to indicate that there is some allusion here to what I have called *the universe of discourse*. At least, comparing the two terms will not be of no avail.

Cast your minds back to the year when pretty much all of you, as many as you are, I think, went up to philosophy class, and recall the hesitation-waltz the professor would perform around logic. What is it about? Does it have to do with laws of thought or its norms? Does it have to do with how this functions, and which we will extract scientifically, or how it ought to be conducted? Even though the debate still hasn't been settled, we have the dawning suspicion that perhaps the function of the university, in the sense I have just articulated it, is to hold off this decision. All I can say is that this is a decision that is perhaps more interested – I'm speaking of logic – in what is occurring in Vietnam, for instance, than what is involved in thought, supposing it to be still suspended between its laws and its norms.

Does it have to do with laws? This is what, thenceforward, allows us to examine the question as to whether logic is applied to the world, as they say – let's say, rather, to the real – in other words, as to whether it is not dreaming. I'm not losing my psychoanalytic thread here. I'm speaking about matters which concern us, analysts, because for us, knowing whether the man who thinks is dreaming is a question that has one of the most palpable meanings. To whet your appetite, and to hold you with your breath bated, I will tell you that this year it is my intention to pose the question of awakening.

Does it have to do on the contrary with norms of thought? Here we indeed have a question that also concerns us, on the condition that it be taken in its full dimensions, not scaled down by those little efforts professors generally make to sand the rough edges off logic in their classes, such that these laws and these norms end up having the same smooth-to-the-touch presentation, allowing you to run your finger evenly across from one to the other, in other words to handle all this blindly. What has not lost its contours for us analysts is the dimension that bears the title of *the true*, and this in itself does not necessitate, does not imply, the support of thinking. This is indeed what incites the examination of what is involved in the true, in which connection the fantasy of a norm is kindled, and it is most surely apparent that, originally, this is not immanent to thought.

For us it is a matter of maintaining the contours of truth. This is what our experience hooks onto and which it is absolutely impossible to exclude from Freud's articulation. On this matter, Freud finds himself in a corner straightaway. But without anyone being obliged to intervene, because he backed into this corner himself. It was so as to draw attention to these contours and to touch those ears which had to be set aquiver, that I one day took the liberty of raising up in a written piece a figure which, for that matter, it was not so difficult for me to bring to life, that of Truth emerging from her well, as she has been depicted from the beginning, and to make her say – *I, Truth, speak*.

The way in which the field of interpretation is taken on board and the fashion in which Freud's technique offers it its opportunity, in other words free association, brings us to the heart of a formal organisation on which basis the first steps of a mathematicised logic are adumbrated that bears a name – and, anyway, it can't possibly have failed to give your ears a tickle. I'm talking about the logic of *networks*.

My job today is not to specify what is called a *lattice* in English, corresponding to the French word *treillis*, but to underscore for you how this is what is at issue as much in Freud's first *Entwurf* for a new psychology as in how he thereafter organises the handling of the analytic session as such. He builds these networks *avant la lettre*, so to speak.

At one point in the *Traumdeutung* – which I won't be able to indicate precisely because it turns out I haven't brought with me the copy in which I'd pinpointed the page for you – he responds to the following objection – *Of course, with your way of proceeding, at every crossroads you will invariably have some opportunity of finding a signified that will form a bridge between two significations. With this way of arranging the bridges, you will always get from somewhere to somewhere else.* Well, it wasn't just for the sake of it that I once put on the cover of a journal called *La Psychanalyse*, which has now vanished into thin air, a little image taken, would you believe it, from Horapollo, whose sixteenth-century treatise on the interpretation of Egyptian hieroglyphs contains illustrated renditions. The one I chose represented an ear and a bridge. It is indeed this that is at issue in Freud. That's how it functions. Each point of convergence in this network, or lattice, wherein he teaches us to ground the first questioning, is indeed a little bridge.

The objection that is put to him is that, in proceeding in this way, anything can explain everything. In other words, fundamentally what is levelled against psychoanalytic interpretation is that there is no sort of *scientific criticism*, as is imagined by those minds that go on out into the medical field with no further credentials than what they retain of their year's study in philosophy, namely that what is *scientific* is what is founded on experience. Of course, they haven't opened any of Claude Bernard's books, but they still know the titles. This is not a scientific objection. It's an objection that dates back to the mediaeval tradition, when people knew what logic was. It was far more widespread than in our times, in spite of our modern-day means of communication. Moreover, things have got to the point that, having let slip in one of the interviews I told you about that I acquired my taste for commentary from the good old practice of the scholastics, I adjured them to scrub it out. Lord knows what people might have spun out of that.

In short, in the Middle Ages, they knew that *ex falso sequitur quodlibet*. In other words, what is characteristic of falsehood is to make everything true. The characteristic of falsehood is that one deduces from it, in the same step, on the same footing, both the true and the false. It does not exclude the true. Were it to exclude the true, it would be too easy to recognise it. Yet to perceive this, one needs to have carried out a minimum of exercises in logic, which thus far, so far as I am aware, is not a component of medical studies, and this is most regrettable.

Freud's way of responding to the objection levelled at him leads us directly onto the terrain of the network structure. It would be interesting in this respect to know how he might, or might not, have benefitted from Brentano's teaching, which he was certainly not unfamiliar with since we find evidence of it in his university curriculum. Of course, Freud doesn't convey the network structure in all its details, with all the modern-day exactitude we would give it, but he is already indicating its function very well when he shows how the lines of association come to overlap, intersect and converge at select points, from which elective branches reach back out.

We know the concern, or rather, to be more precise, the veritable care with which Freud treated throughout the remainder of his life's work the dimension that is properly speaking that of truth – because, from the reality standpoint, one can rest easy, even to know that trauma is perhaps mere fantasy. In a certain way, one can be even surer of this. A fantasy, as I've been showing you, is structural. Still, this does not leave Freud – who was quite capable of coming up with that, just as capable as I am, as you can well imagine – any the less uneasy.

Where, he asks, *is the criterion of truth?* He wouldn't have written *The Wolf Man* were it not upon this trail, spurred along by this exigency that was peculiar to him – *Is it true or not?*

Freud sustains this question with what is discovered by examining the fundamental figure that is manifest in the Wolf Man's recurring dream. This *is it true?* cannot be reduced to knowing whether or not, and at what age, he lived through something that was reconstructed with the aid of this dream figure. Freud has no doubts about the reality of the primal scene, but for him the essential matter lies elsewhere and one has only to read him to perceive it. It's a matter of knowing how the subject has been able to verify this scene, and has been able to do so with his whole being. The subject has verified it through his symptom. This means that it is in this way that he has been able to articulate it in terms of the signifier. You need only recall the figure of the roman *V* that keeps cropping up everywhere, in a woman's spread legs or the beating wings of a butterfly, to comprehend that what is at issue is the signifier.

The turn whereby analytic experience joins up with the most modern logical process hinges precisely on the signifier's relation to truth insomuch as it can circumvent any thinking that supports it. Just as, on the horizon of modern logic, a sort of aim looms up which is that of reducing logic to a correct handling of what is most surely tantamount to writing alone, so too does the question of verification, concerning what we have to deal with, follow directly the line of the signifier's play in so far as from this alone is the question of truth suspended.

It's an old fact of experience that it's not so easy to foreground a term like that of the true without instantly causing all those reverberations to echo in which the most dubious intuitions, in inverted commas, insinuate themselves, and without giving immediate rise to objection. Those who venture onto this terrain know only too well that, having had their fingers burned, they can't be too careful. But who can claim that I'm opening the door to a return of the theme of Being, for example, just because I'm having you say, *I, Truth, speak*? Let's at least take a second look at this to be sure. I have drawn no one else into this, divine or human, but the very one I made speak those words. The latter is the only one concerned. Therefore, let's content ourselves with the altogether formal nexus I have just formed between truth and the signifier, this point of origin between the signifier and truth.

What relation is there between this and the point from which I started earlier? Does this mean that in carrying you onto the field of the most formal logic I have forgotten the one in which, going by what I said earlier, the fate of logic is played out? It's quite clear that Sir Bertrand Russell has taken a greater interest in what is going on in Vietnam than Monsieur Jacques Maritain has. This by itself can furnish us with an indication.

Le Paysan de la Garonne is the latest styling from Jacques Maritain. You didn't know the book was out? Well, go and get yourselves a copy. It's the latest from this author, who has dealt at length with the scholastic authors in whom the influence of Saint Thomas's philosophy was developed. There's no reason not to bring up this philosophy, to the extent that a certain way of positing the principles of Being is, all the same, not without impact on what people have made of logic. It cannot be said that it precludes the handling of logic, but it may at some moments be a hindrance to it.

I apologise for this parenthesis, but since I'm encouraging you, from the mere fact of mentioning Jacques Maritain, implicitly to find that reading him is not contemptible but indeed far from being devoid of interest, I will insist all the same on specifying the spirit in which I'm inviting you to look into this. It's the spirit of paradox that is revealed there. Indeed, having reached his advanced years, as the author himself points out, he is now evincing a sort of rigour that allows the persistence of the most unthinkable hopes to be seen being pushed so far as an exaggerated deadlock, hopes for what ought to his mind to be developing in the place of, or on the fringes of, the development of modern science, the contours of which he identifies with great exactitude. And this would be so that what he adheres to most centrally could be maintained, namely what he calls *the intuition of Being*. He speaks in this respect of *philosophical Eros*, and, given what I have put forward in front of you here about desire, there is no cause for me to renounce such a term. But using it on this occasion, in the name of the philosophy of Being, to hope for the rebirth, correlatively with the development of modern science, of a philosophy of Nature, partakes of an Eros that it seems to me can be situated only in the register of Comédie-Italienne.

Of course, this scarcely prevents, in passing – taking some distance and ultimately rejecting them – a few sharp and pertinent remarks about the structure of science from cropping up along the whole length of the book. That our science should have nothing in common with the dimension of cognisance is indeed most accurate, but it does not bear in itself any hopefulness or promise as to a rebirth of cognisance in the Antique sense, which is widely rejected, but backed up in our perspective.

After this parenthesis, I shall now resume what it is a matter for us of examining.

2

There is no need for us to shrink from using these truth tables with which logicians introduce a certain number of fundamental functions of propositional logic.

$q\diagdown^p$	T	F
T	T	F
F	F	F

Truth table for Conjunction

This is within everyone's grasp. You can find on the upper row the two values of the proposition p, which can be true or false. In the vertical column are placed the two values, true or false, of the proposition q. When p and q are combined, it's a matter of determining the value of what is called their Conjunction. The table indicates that their conjunction will be true only if p and q are both true propositions. In the three further cases, their conjunction will give a false result.

This is the type of table that is at issue. I don't need to set out its variations for you because all you need to do is open up any old textbook on modern logic to find the different tables defining Disjunction, or else Implication, or else Equivalence.

This can be a support for us, but merely a support and a prop, in the question we have to ask ourselves with regard to what we are handling, if I may say so, through speech, with regard to what we are saying in saying that truth obtains, to wit – is it permissible to write it? Writing it will in effect be the underpinning to our handling of this.

Modern logic aims to establish itself – I didn't say by means of a convention, but by means of a rule of writing. Upon what is this rule of writing grounded? Well, upon the fact that at the moment of constituting its alphabet, we posited a certain number of rules, called *axioms*, concerning how they are to be correctly handled. This is in some sense a pledge that we made to ourselves. Do we have the right to inscribe among the signifiers the T and the F of true and false as something that can be handled logically?

Regardless of the introductory, *premissial* character of the said truth tables in the little treatises of logic that might fall into your hands, it is quite sure that all the effort expended in the development of this logic was to go into constructing propositional logic without starting from these tables, even if they had to come back to them after constructing the rules of deducibility in a different way. But what is of most especial interest to us here is what it means that they should have made use of them in Stoic logic. Earlier I alluded to *ex falso sequitur quodlibet*, for example. It's something that most surely appeared a very long time ago, but it's clear that it was never better articulated – never with such force – than by the Stoics.

The Stoics questioned themselves about the true and the false along the path of logic. What would it take for the true and the false to have a relation with logic in the proper sense, in which we are positioning it here, where the underpinning of logic is to be taken nowhere else but in the articulation of language, in the signifying chain? This is how their logic was a propositional logic and not a class logic. How should the propositions link up with regard to the true and the false in such a way that this would be a propositional logic, in such a way that it might even be operant?

Either this logic has nothing to do with true and false, or it has something to accomplish – the true must beget the true. This is what is called the relationship of Implication. It brings nothing more into the balance besides two propositional clauses. The first proposition is the *protasis*. I'm not saying *hypothesis*, which would promptly rouse in you the idea that one could start believing in something, when it's a matter neither of believing nor of believing that it's true. It's a matter of *positing*, as the word *protasis* indicates, and nothing more. What is affirmed is affirmed as true. The second clause is the *apodosis*. We define Implication as nothing more than that there may be a true protasis and a true apodosis, which can only yield something that we put in parentheses and which constitutes a combination that is true.

This doesn't at all mean that this is all that can obtain. Let's suppose this same protasis false and the apodosis true. Well, the Stoics will tell you that their combination is true, precisely because *ex falso sequitur quodlibet* – from the false, the true can be implied as well as the false. Consequently, if this is true, then there is no logical objection.

Implication does not mean cause. Implication means – this combination in which protasis and apodosis are united in a certain manner, as described in the truth table that corresponds to this logical function. The only Implication that doesn't hold – at least, this is the doctrine of the one who goes by the name of Philo, who played an eminent role in this – is when the protasis is true and the apodosis false. The true could never imply the false. This is the most radical underpinning of any possibility of handling the signifying chain in a certain relation with truth.

$q\diagdown^p$	T	F
T	T	T
F	F	T

Truth table for Implication

What does all this mean? Here you have, as I said, the most radical conditions of existence for a logic. And the problem that arises for us becomes altogether obvious. It's that, for us, it's a matter of what happens when afterwards we have to speak about what's been written, in other terms, when the subject of enunciation comes into play.

To highlight this we need only observe what happens when we say *It's true that it's false that* . . . There has been no movement here, but the false has perhaps taken on a touch of lustre, of framing, that makes it pass over to refulgent falsehood, which after all is no small matter. Saying *It's false that it's true that* . . . has the same result. I mean that we have given grounding to the false. Yet is it quite the same thing as in the previous case? If we are led to employ instead the subjunctive – *It's false that it should be true* . . . – this indicates that something is happening. Saying *It's true that it's true* . . . also holds good, and leaves us with an assured truth, albeit a tautological one. But saying *It's false that it should be false* . . . doubtless doesn't ensure the same order of truth. Likewise, to say *It's not false* does not amount to saying *It's true*.

In short, the dimension of enunciation holds in abeyance something that was asking only to function quite automatically at the level of writing. The point from which the drama arises, as it were, has a slippery side to it that is noteworthy. It arises very precisely from the doubleness of the subject.

I will have no hesitation illustrating this with a little story to which I have already alluded many times because it was not without impact on, let's say, the career of my own little story. It has to do with that particular complaint, a demand even, that burst forth one day from the throat of someone who had been altogether charmed by what I had brought forward as the first articulations of my teaching – *Why doesn't he say the truth about the truth?* A touching outcry hurled up to the heavens.

This urgency, this disquiet even, would already find its response quite amply, on the sole condition of passing back to the written signifier. The truth about the truth. The T on the T. The signifier could not signify itself, except precisely when this is not what it is signifying, that is, when it is making use of metaphor. And nothing stops metaphor, which substitutes another signifier for this T of truth, from making the truth come out, with the ordinary effect of metaphor, namely the creation of a false signifier.

This happens all the time. And a discourse as rigorous as I'm trying to make this one today can still, in many recesses of what are called more or less properly your cerebra, generate confusion linked precisely to the production of the signified in metaphor. There is certainly no cause for astonishment that there should have come back to my ears, from the same source whence this wistful invocation arose, a more recent pronouncement that took as its target what I teach about Freud and which this mouth voiced so very graciously as *conceptual dilution*.

There is a certain sort of admission in this, in which is designated precisely the narrow relation that the part object maintains with the structure of the subject. The idea, or even simply the fact, of admitting that it is possible to give a commentary on one of Freud's texts by diluting its concepts evokes irresistibly what could on no account fulfil the function of the part object, insomuch as the latter must be able to be sliced through. The mustard pot, which I defined in its time as being necessarily empty – empty of mustard, naturally – could on no account be filled satisfactorily with what this dilution evokes quite well enough, to wit, watery shit.

It is utterly essential to see the coherence between these primordial objects and any correct handling of what is termed *subjective dialectic*.

3

Let's now track back to the first steps we have just taken regarding Implication.

The question that looms up from this join between truth and the handling of the written is that of knowing what can be written and what cannot.

What is meant by this *cannot*? Its definition still verges on the completely arbitrary. In modern logic, the only limit set to the functioning of an alphabet in a given system is that of the word earmarked at the outset as axiomatic. There, *cannot* most surely has a prohibitive sense, but what of this can be written? This is the problem of Negation.

The problem is to be posited here at the level of writing insomuch as Negation regulates it as a logical functioning, whereas the use of Negation necessarily arose to begin with in intuitive images that exhibited the first adumbration of what they didn't even yet know to be an edge, but rather a sort of limit. This limit is the one with which first-order logic, the one introduced by Aristotle – predicate logic – marked out the scope of a class characterised by a given predicate. What lies outside of this scope was designated as *not attached to the predicate*, the predicate thus being negated. It is not spelt out in Aristotle that this entails the unity of the universe of discourse. To give a sense of the absurdity of this approach to Negation, it so happens that I have written, with regard to the unconscious, something along the lines of – *There is black and then everything that is not* – the *unblack*. This has a meaning, and it is the underpinning of class logic and predicate logic.

Not today, but certainly in the following sessions, I will be trying to set out for you comprehensively the logical levels that writing compels us to discern with respect to Negation. By means of plain little letters, once set in place on the blackboard, I will be showing you that there are four different stages of Negation. Classical Negation, the one that invokes the law of non-contradiction and which appears to be founded on this alone, is just one of them.

This technical distinction, I mean, which can be strictly formulated in formal logic, is essential in enabling us to call into question what Freud says – and which, since he said it, has been repeated without there having been the slightest move to inspect it – namely that the unconscious knows no contradiction. It is most unfortunate that such words, sent out in the form of flaming arrows for lighting the trail to lead us to more radical developments, have been left in this suspended state, to such an extent that one lady qualified with a title which she did actually possess officially, the princess, even repeated them in believing she was saying something. This is precisely the danger with logic. Logic is supported only where it can be handled within the use of writing. But no one is able to guarantee that someone who is speaking about it should even be saying something. It is indeed this that has led it to be held in suspicion. It is also why it is so necessary for us to resort to the apparatus of writing.

Nevertheless, we also court our own danger. We must take our risks on the terrain of Negation, so as to perceive in what mode it presents, aside from in written articulation. Where does it come from? Where are we going to be able to grasp it? Are we going to be bound to write it with nothing more than the apparatus I've already come out with in front of you here?

Let's take up this Implication – proposition p implies proposition q – and let's try to see what is involved here in starting from q. What can we articulate of proposition p if we place proposition q after it? Well, we have to write the sign of Negation in front of q, or alongside it, or above it – somewhere bound to q. So, p implies q indicates – if not q, not p.

This is just one example, but one of the most manifest when it comes to the necessity of a Negation emerging in the written, a Negation that one would be quite wrong to presume to be the same as what was functioning earlier in the capacity of something complementary, namely the one that posited on its own account the universe of discourse as a unit. The two things hardly sit together, such that it suffices to state this for them to be disarticulated the one from the other, and to make one and the other function distinctly.

So, among the varieties of this Negation, there are those which put themselves forward to us as having to be examined in advance of what can be written, namely at the point from which is illuminated the doubleness of the subject of enunciation with respect to the subject of the statement, the point from which this doubleness is maintained.

First among these varieties of Negation we have the one that casts out from any order of discourse, to the extent that discourse articulates it, that of which it speaks. I point out to you that this is very precisely the one that Freud puts forward when he is spelling out the first step of the experience in so far as it is structured by the pleasure principle, which is organised, so he says, into an ego and non-ego. One is so scarcely a logician that one fails to notice that what is at issue here is nothing that might belong to the order of complementarity required by the universe of discourse. Such a reading is all the more at fault given how in Freud's text the two stages of ego and non-ego are in no way defined as complementary, but rather on the basis of the opposition *Lust/Unlust*, and given too that Freud placed on the very first line the opposition *Ich/Aussenwelt*, which does not at all belong to the same register as the other.

If the *ego/non-ego* distinction corresponded to the grasping of the world in a universe of discourse – which is strictly speaking what is being mooted whenever one considers that primary narcissism is able to intervene in the analytic session – this would mean that the child subject, at the point at which this subject is already designated by Freud in the first functioning of the pleasure principle, would be capable of doing logic. This is not what is at issue. Rather, it's about the ego's identification in what pleases it, in *die Lust*, which means that the subject's ego alienates itself here in an imaginary way and which further means that it is precisely on the outside that what pleases is isolated as ego.

This first *not* is foundational with respect to narcissistic structure. Further on, Freud will develop this into nothing less than a sort of negation of love. When this is found, as it has been, writ large in my discourse, it won't be said that I'm saying the truth about the truth, but, even so, that I'm saying the truth about what Freud says. That all love should be founded on the first narcissism puts before us one of the terms in which Freud consequently urges us to find out what is involved in this supposedly universal function, insomuch as it passes the baton to the notorious *intuition of Being* which we censured earlier.

We shall label the negation at issue here as the *mis* from *misrecognition*. It already poses a question for us.

It is distinguished from the complement, in so far as within the universe of discourse the latter designates – but can it really designate it? – the counterpart. What shall we call this? Well, if you like, let's call it *the contra*, so as not to say more by calling it *the converse*, which is perfectly distinct from it and so it is in Freud's work too.

Next comes what will make its entrance further along, and in a manner that is more wieldy than it is in the logical writing of Implication where you saw it revealing itself in the guise of those negations that flip around in a way that is utterly opaque. It may be called *not without*.

Such as it is defined in the Stoic tradition, Implication cannot be avoided, regardless of the paradoxes it entails. There is most surely some paradox in how any propositions p and q constitute an implication when combined. For example, in Stoic logic, the following implication is true – *If Mrs So-and-so has blonde hair, then the sum of an equilateral triangle is equal to 90 degrees*. There is undoubtedly some paradox to this use, but when it is flipped around so that we go back from the second clause to the first, the function of *not without* is isolated. This is *not without* . . . Mrs So-and-so may have blonde hair, this doesn't have any necessary link for us with the equilateral triangle having such and such a property, and yet it remains true that the fact that she may or may not have blonde hair is *not without* entailing the thing that, either way, is true.

Around the suspension of this *not without*, the place of what is called *cause* takes shape, together with its mode of emergence. Can we give a meaning, a substance, to this ghostly entity that no one has ever managed to exorcise from this juncture, even though everything that is developed in science plainly tends always towards its elimination and only comes to a perfect end when it no longer needs even to be spoken of? It is the function of *not without* and the place it occupies that will allow us to flush it out.

I will end with what is going to be the topic of our next meeting – what does the term *not* mean?

When it comes to be applied to the most radical terms around which I have made the question of the fact of the unconscious turn, can we make this *not* emerge as a form of complementarity? As a form of the *mis* in misrecognition? In terms of *not without*? Might it even occur to us that, when we speak of *non-being*, what is at issue is something that would in some sense lie at the outer rim of the bubble of Being? Is this *non-being* tantamount to all the space on the outside? Might it even be possible to suggest that this is what we mean when we speak – most confusedly, truth be told – about *non-being*?

I should prefer in this instance to name what is at issue here, and which the unconscious calls into question, *the locus where I am not*.

As for *not thinking*, who would go so far as to say that this is something that can in any way be grasped in what the whole of predicate logic turns around? Namely, the notorious distinction, which is no such thing, between *extension* and *comprehension*. As though comprehension were remotely antinomic to the register of extension, when it is quite clear that every stride that has been made in logic in the direction of comprehension has always occurred, and only occurred, when things have been taken up from the angle of extension. Is this a reason for Negation to remain bound to extension, and without any primary questioning whatsoever?

For us, there is not only *not being* because, equally, the sort of Being that counts for us with regard to the subject is bound to thinking. So, what is meant by *not thinking*? I mean, what does this mean at the point at which we may write it in our logic?

I will be making our next talk revolve around the question of *I am not* and *I am not thinking*.

7 December 1966

IV

FROM THE KLEIN FOUR-GROUP TO THE *COGITO*

Diagrams
I am thinking, therefore I am
No middle way in French
The *cogito* is discard
Transformations of the *cogito*

While waiting for the stick of chalk I may need, and which I trust won't be long in coming, let's talk about some little pieces of news.

The way this book of *Écrits* is being greeted in a certain sphere, the one you represent, such as you are, all of you here, is a curious thing indeed. I don't think that speaking about this lies beyond the scope of what brings us together here.

It is, for instance, curious that in farther flung universities, in which I have no reason to believe that what I have confined myself to saying in my Seminars has thus far enjoyed much of a reverberation, well, the book is being requested. As I'm making allusion to Belgium, I will point out that this evening at 10pm, channel 3 of Radio-Bruxelles will be broadcasting a short response I gave to a most pleasant person who came to interview me. I should add that the programme will be on FM, so the only people who will be able to take advantage of it in France are those who live over in the Lille area. Why yes, I know I have listeners from Lille as well. There are of course other countries yet farther away, where it is not certain whether this is enjoying such great success.

Since a segue has to be made, I'm going to begin with an idiotic question that was put to me. What I call an idiotic question is not what might be believed, I mean something that would displease me. I love questions that are *idiote*. I also love *idiotes* – and *idiots* too for that matter, idiocy not being the special privilege of either sex. To be quite open about, what I'm calling *idiotic* is something that on a given occasion is quite simply natural and proper. An idiotism is too hastily conflated with singularity, when actually it's something natural, simple and, to be frank, very often linked to the situation.

The person in question hadn't opened my book, and asked me the following question – *What link is there between your writings?*

I must say that this question wouldn't have occurred to me. I also have to say that it's a question that it wouldn't have occurred to me could occur to anyone else. But it's actually a very interesting question, which I shall make every effort to answer, and to answer, goodness me, in the way it was put to me. I mean that, as it was being put to me for the first time, it was the source of a veritable interrogation.

To go quickly, I will tell you that I responded in the following terms. Such as they may present to someone who would open them, what seems to me to constitute the link between my writings, from *Le stade du miroir* through to the last notations of what I was able to set down under the heading of the *Subversion du sujet*, is the identity of the subject, more to the point this certain something that belongs to the realm of what is called identity, to which each subject may rightfully refer so as to apply it to himself. This, ultimately, would be the link.

Although it is not quite the same thing, this is not unrelated to *the signifier could never signifier itself* – a remark with which, speaking this year about the logic of the fantasy, I believed I ought to begin, and which, moreover, for the regular attendees here has nothing new about it. But in the end, to put things in such a way that they will resonate, the point of departure of my writings, which remains a link between them right to the end of the collection and which is indeed a question that is disputed in depth throughout, is expressed in the wording that can occur to anyone and everyone, maintained with, I must say, a regrettable certitude – *I'm me, I am.*

I think there are few among you who don't have to struggle to get this conviction moving, yet even when it has been wiped off the map, it no less remains that it is still most dangerous indeed. The path down which one immediately slides, and in the most natural way, is the one that I signposted anew this year – the very same in whom this certitude is established so firmly do not hesitate in reaching such light decisions as to what isn't part of their makeup, saying *It's not me, I did nothing of the sort.*

Saying *it's not me* is not the special privilege of infants. Psychology professors teach nothing else in their theory of the origin of each and everyone's world, where the *infans*, the young infant, and then the toddler, are said to make the distinction, without further ado from the time of the first toddling steps in existence, between ego and non-ego. Once on this path, the question cannot take a single step forward because holding the opposition between ego and non-ego to be decidable based on the limit of Negation alone, entailing I suppose the excluded middle, puts quite out of play, rules out entirely, any broaching of what is nevertheless the only important question, namely that of knowing whether *for my part, I'm me*.

It is quite certain that, simply by opening my book, any reader will be squeezed into this link, and very quickly so. Yet this is not for all that a reason for the reader to stay there. Indeed, what is tied into this link affords plenty of opportunity to deal with something else, with matters that become clarified precisely on account of having being squeezed into this link – which means that they slip yet further out of the scope of this link. This is how one can come round to conceiving that it is not on the terrain of identification itself that the question can truly be resolved, but on the terrain of structure.

What is at issue here is precisely to refer not only to the question of identification but above all to everything it concerns, and in particular the question of the unconscious. It has to be said that this question presents difficulties that leap off the page with far greater immediacy when it comes to knowing with what it has to be identified.

We are employing the reference to structure because we have to start from something external to what is given immediately, in an intuitive fashion, in the field of identification. We need to start, for example, from the remark I mentioned again just now – that no signifier can signify itself.

1

Since structure is at issue, I shall begin today with the matter for which I requested these sticks of chalk.

The awkwardness I sometimes feel here stems in part from my having to take rather long detours to explain for you certain elements which, if they do not lie within your reach, cannot be through my fault. Within your reach, that is to say, within a circulation that is commonplace enough for those truths that are, if I may, primary, to be taken as read when I speak to you.

I'm going to draw up the diagram for what in mathematics is called a *group*.

I have made much allusion to what is meant by *group*, starting from set theory, for example, and I won't be going back over that today, especially given the road that lies ahead of us.

Here what is at issue is the Klein four-group. This is the same

From the Klein four-group to the *cogito*

Felix Klein whom we met with the Klein Bottle I mentioned. The group is defined by three operations, no more, which are arranged in a network. What results from carrying out each of these operations is defined, as you are going to see, by a very straightforward series of equivalences between any two of them and a result that can also be obtained differently, from the one that is the other of these two.

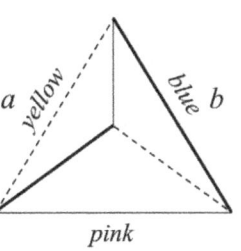

Diagram of the Klein four-group

We are going to symbolise the Klein four-group through the operations in question, which are to be arranged into a network such that each coloured line – pink, blue or yellow – corresponds to just one of these operations. You can see that each of these three operations, *a*, *b* and *c*, the nature of which for the moment I can leave completely indeterminate, is to be found at two different places in the network.

These operations are termed *involutory*. What is going on here? The most straightforward representation of this type of operation is Negation. First, you negate something. You bind the Negation sign to something, a predicate or proposition, such as *it is not true that* . . . Next, you perform another negation on what you have just obtained. Well, whatever you start from, the result will be nought. It's as though you had done nothing. This is what defines an operation as involutory.

Mark well that what is at issue here in not what you are taught, namely that two negations are equal to an affirmation, because here we don't even know what we have started from. We might not have started from an affirmation. What is at issue here is that each repeat operation – *aa*, *bb* or *cc* – is equivalent to nought. In other words, we find again what we had at the start, prior to the operation.

$$aa = 0$$
$$bb = 0$$
$$cc = 0$$

But many other operations besides Negation yield the same result – inversion of the sign, for example. I can have 1 at the start, next I will have –1, and lastly, making minus function on the minus sign, I will have the 1 from the start once again. It no less remains that, though they are different, both operations manifest as involutory.

The involutory functions do not by themselves define the Klein four-group. To these it must be added that carrying out two distinct actions successively gives the same result as carrying out the third action on its own. You just have to consider the diagram to notice that when a is succeeded by b it has the same effect as c, and that when b is succeeded by c it has the same effect as a. And so I can write –

$$ab = c$$
$$ac = b$$
$$bc = a$$

As certain intuitive exigencies that you may harbour may be seeking something more for you to get your teeth into, I will draw your attention to something that is truly within everyone's reach this week, in all the newsagents, this being the rather slim issue of a journal – you know what I think about journals so I'm not about to engage in any of my usual wordplay on *revue* – a journal in which there is not a great deal, but which includes an article, *Sur le sens du mot structure en mathématiques*. It could have been more extensive but, over the small area the author has chosen, my word, quite rightly, because what is at issue is precisely the Klein group, he chews things over with, I must say, extreme care, proceeding, it may be said, step by step, over some 24 pages, such that it constitutes nevertheless, at any rate for those who have a liking for lengthy passages, a very useful exercise and one that is fit to ease you into what is going on in the Klein group. I have chosen to present the Klein four-group here at the outset because it is going to do us a few favours. At least, I trust it will.

Let's begin again with the structure. If you care to cast your minds over some of the steps I have just taken, it may occur to you that a group so structured can, in order to function, make do with four elements, which are represented here on the network that supports it by means of the vertices at which the edges of the figure meet, as you can see plotted out here.

Observe that this is no different from the one I'm quickly chalking up for you here in white.

From the Klein four-group to the *cogito*

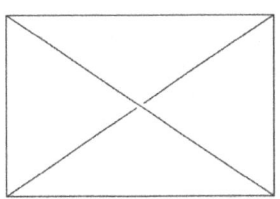 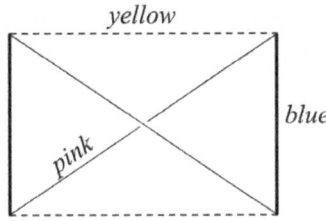

This second figure presents four vertices, each having the property of being connected to the other three. From the point of view of structure, they are both exactly the same. We need only colour the lines that connect the vertices, in pairs, for you to see that this is exactly the same structure. In other words, the crossover point in the middle of the figure has no special privilege, as the previous diagram has the advantage of showing.

That diagram has the further advantage of allowing you to get to grips with how the Klein four-group is a structure that permits of being covered by the notion of proportional relation, among others. I mean that proportion is just one of the many structures – the rest of which have nothing to do with proportion – that function in keeping with the law of the Klein four-group. This is what prompts us now to bring into play the function of metaphor, such as I represented with a four-term structure that is not proportional.

$$\frac{S\,(\text{signifier})}{S'(\text{signifier})} \times \frac{S'}{s\,(\text{signified effect})} \longrightarrow S\frac{1}{s}$$

The structure of metaphor

S, at the top left, is a signifier in the metaphorical position, the position of substitution, in relation to another signifier S'. Thus, S comes to be substituted for S', which is placed beneath it. To the extent that the link of S' to S is maintained as something that it is possible to reveal, the effect of a new signification is produced, in other words a signified effect. Two signifiers are involved, S and S'. One of them, S', occupies two positions. Then there is a fourth element, the heterogeneous element, s, the signified effect. I write the result of the metaphor as S, which has come to replace S', to become the factor of 1 over s, in brackets, which I call the metaphorical effect of signification.

As you know, I ascribe great importance to this structure. It is fundamental in explaining the structure of the unconscious to the extent that, originally, repression is an effect of signifying substitution. This is my own mode of presenting the moment regarded as originary in what is at issue in repression – it being understood that this is a logical origin and nothing else.

The leanings of the tongue, so to speak, allow us to express in an altogether vivid way the effect produced by what is substituted – the substitute has the effect of *sub-situating* what it substitutes. For, contrary to what is believed, to what is imagined, to what is even pontificated, quite wrongly in this instance, that which is substituted is not effaced, but simply *sub-situated*, placed underneath. This is how I would now translate, because it has struck me as especially practical, Freud's *Unterdrückt*.

What, then, is the repressed in this theory? Well, as paradoxical as this might seem, the repressed as such is only sustained, is only written, at the level of its return. If we refer to the formula for metaphor, it is insomuch as the extracted signifier S' comes into connection in the chain with the substitute S, that we can get a fingertip touch on the repressed, in other words the representative of the first representation in so far as it is linked to the initial logical fact of the repressed.

Are you not struck by the immediate perception that this is not unrelated to the formulation which states that *the signifier is what represents a subject for another signifier*? It is not identical, but concurrent, and this is what inclines us to recognise the functioning of the unconscious in metaphor. The S, the signifier that springs up in order to enable the return of the repressed S', finds itself representing the subject – the subject of the unconscious – at the level of something else, the effect of which we have to determine as an effect of signification and which is called the symptom. This is what we have to deal with as analysts.

It is in this respect that our four-term formula is indeed the cell, the kernel, in which it becomes apparent to us just how difficult it is to establish a primordial logic of the subject as such. This tallies with what has been borne out in other disciplines that have reached a stage of rigour far greater than our own, notably mathematic logic, namely that it is now no longer tenable to consider there to be a universe of discourse.

Nothing implies that this non-viability of the universe of discourse is included in the Klein four-group, but nor is there anything to indicate that it is not there. Indeed, while this has become evident in certain points of paradox, which are not as paradoxical as all that – as I said, Russell's paradox is no such thing – the particularity of this non-viability is that the universe does not close.

Therefore, nothing says in advance that a structure as fundamental to the order of structuring references as the Klein four-group is, should not be able to offer support to our requirement of supplying the unconscious with its structural status, and precisely in how it relates to the Cartesian *cogito* – provided, of course, we have an appropriate handle on our operations.

2

Needless to say, I have not selected the Cartesian *cogito* at random.

I have selected this because it presents as an aporia, as a radical contradiction to the status of the unconscious, and because so many debates have already turned around the supposedly fundamental status of self-awareness. But what if it were to be borne out after all that this *cogito* could present precisely as, in terms of an inner lining, the best that may be found, from a certain standpoint, for the status of the unconscious? There might then be some advantage in this.

We may already presume that this is scarcely implausible in that I once reminded you that no discovery of what is at issue in the unconscious could even be conceived of prior to the inaugural foregrounding of the subject of the *cogito*, in so far as this is coextensive with the advent of science. There could never be any psychoanalysis outside the era constituted by the advent of science, which is structuring for thought. It was on this point that we ended two years ago.

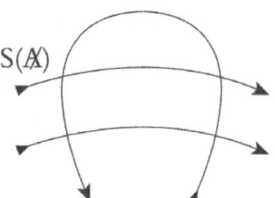

Simplified graph

Most of you are familiar with this graph, which you can now look up in my book, such as it is developed in the article entitled *Subversion du sujet et dialectique du désir*. On the level of the upper chain, to the left, we find the mark, or indication, S(A̷). What does it mean? Over the years that this has been in existence, I haven't offered that much commentary on it, in any case not enough for me not to have the occasion today to state that what is at issue here is the S of the signifier insomuch as it would be equivalent to the presence of what I called the *one extra*, which is also what is lacking in the signifying chain in so far as there is no universe of discourse.

This *one extra*, which by the same stroke is the signifier of lack at the level of the signifier, is what has to be maintained as essential and to be preserved in the function of structure – to the extent that we are following the trail along which up to now I've been leading you, since this is where you are, namely that the unconscious is structured like a language.

A little story was passed on to me recently, and I don't see any reason to doubt its veracity. It seems that in a certain place, someone, whom I would not be displeased to see showing up here one day, begins his courses on the unconscious by saying – *If there is anyone here for whom the unconscious is structured like a language, they can get out right now.*

Now that we can rest a little, I am all the same going to tell you how these things are getting commented on at the level of the pups, because since the publication of my book, even the pups are reading it. I was told about one item in particular which I can't resist sharing with you. A circle of acquaintances were speaking about one thing and another, and about those who disagree, when one of them said this, which I could never have come up with – *There as elsewhere, there are* affreuds.

Note that this is not wide of the mark. Just before the radio broadcast of one of my interviews – this caught me by surprise – the voice could be heard of a psychoanalyst, who shall remain anonymous so that I won't put anyone out of sorts when I quote her – who had been asked whether people should read Freud. *Read Freud?* replied the psychoanalyst, who had been presented as *eminent*. *Read Freud? Not on your nelly. That's not necessary at all. There's really no need. You just need technique. Technique on its own. It's not necessary at all to bother with Freud.* So, I don't have to go to much trouble to show that there are places where, *affreuds* or not, they are scarcely bothering with Freud.

Let's resume. What is our guiding thread here at the start of the year?

It's a matter of highlighting how, when we treat language – and the order which it puts forward as structure – by means of writing, the resulting demonstration on the written plane is the non-existence of this universe of discourse. The necessary *one extra* of the signifying chain, qua written, is for us the placeholder of this universe of discourse.

With modern logic, logic per se has effectively taken the path of treating logical problems by purifying them, right down to the ultimate limit of the intuitive element which for centuries used to make, for example, Aristotelian logic so satisfactory. This intuitive element incontestably used to take up a large share of that logic, making it so seductive that Kant himself, who was certainly no idiot, had nothing to add to it. But just a few more years had to pass by for it to be seen how, in merely being tempted to treat these problems by the sort of transformation that results simply from the use of writing, these problems all of a sudden swung around and the very thrust of them shifted in structure. This use of writing spread, and algebra has accustomed us to its formulas, enabling us to posit the problem of logic quite differently, to reach something within it that, far from diminishing its value, is what lends it its full worth, namely *pure structure*. Structure means *an effect of language*.

And what else can be meant by this S with, in brackets, A̶, at the level where we stand, but the designation, by a signifier, of what is involved in the *one extra*?

An objection may occur to you, as it falls quite naturally to the lips of the greenhorn whom you are starting to indoctrinate about identification – because this of course is the cutting edge upon which we are still holding ourselves – *I am not me? Then, who is me?* Likewise, around this invincible resurgence of the mirage of the subject's identity, are you going to tell me – or rather, I hope, are you going to hold back from saying – *But then, in making the one extra function, aren't we proceeding as though the obstacle were, so to speak, vincible? What if we were to allow to circulate, within the chain, that which cannot enter it? To wit, the catalogue of all catalogues that don't list themselves would be printed in the catalogue, and, as a consequence, would be discredited.* Now, this is not what is at issue.

Take, for example, a signifying chain made up of the series of all the letters that exist in the alphabet. For any one of these letters to be able to hold the place of all the others, it has at each instant to be barred from the series. One letter is each in its turn virtually struck out. And this is how we have, inserted in the chain, the function of the *one extra* among the signifiers.

But you evoke this extra signifier as such in the event that, as is indicated here, we may place it outside the parenthesis within which the bar functions. Given that the bar is always at the ready to suspend the use of any signifier whenever it might signify itself, the signifying function of the *one extra* is as such possible. Not only is it possible, it is strictly speaking that which will manifest as the possibility of a direct intervention upon the function of the subject. Insomuch as the signifier is what represents a subject for another signifier, everything we may do that resembles this S(A̶) corresponds to nothing less than the function of interpretation.

In conformity with the system of the metaphor, interpretation functions through the intervention, within the chain, of this signifier that is immanent to it as *one extra*, and as *one extra* that is apt to produce there the effect of metaphor. But what exactly will this effect of metaphor be here? Does interpretation operate by means of a signified effect, as our formula for metaphor seems to indicate? The formula does most surely indicate that it operates through an effect of signification, but this needs to be specified at the level of its logical structure, in the technical sense of the term.

This is merely a waymark. The ensuing part of the disquisition that I'm laying out for you is what will detail the reasons why this effect of signification is so specific and how it delimits interpretation – in its proper sense, in analysis – as a truth effect.

After this I shall open a parenthesis to set out for you all the grounds for my specifying the effect of interpretation in this way. I will bring these items forward as best I can, each in turn, in the same way that one nudges forward a flock of sheep.

Mark well that I said *truth effect*. The truth of the interpretation can in no way be anticipated in advance. I mean, there is nothing that would enable us to tell whether the index *true* or *false* could be assigned to the signifier of the interpretation itself.

All I am saying is that up to this point the signifier was merely an extra signifier, indeed a surplus, until it came to be the signifier of a lack, as lacking in the universe of discourse, whereupon it would bear an effect of truth.

I made a comment last time about Implication qua Material Implication, that is to say, insomuch as there exists what is called a *consequence* in the signifying chain, which means nothing else but the relation of antecedent to consequent, of protasis to apodosis. I remarked that nothing stands in the way of assigning the index *truth* when a premiss is false provided its conclusion be true.

So, put your minds on hold regarding what I have called *truth effect* until we come to know a little more about what is involved in the function of interpretation.

We are now going to be led to present something that concerns the *cogito*.

3

The Cartesian *cogito* is not at all straightforward, because even among those who have devoted their existence to the life's work of Descartes, very great divergences remain as to how it ought to be interpreted and commented on.

Am I, non-specialist that I am, going to meddle in these debates? Why, of course I am. After all, I have as much right to as anyone else. I mean that the *Discours de la méthode* or the *Meditationes* are addressed as much to me as to all the rest.

I am at leisure to ponder the function of the *ergo*, for example, in *cogito ergo sum*.

I am likewise as free as everyone else to pick up on how, in the Latin translation that Descartes made of the *Discours de la méthode* in 1644, the French *je pense, donc je suis* is rendered, if my notes are correct, by *ergo sum, sive existo*.

On the other hand, in the second *Meditation*, he formulates *ego sum, ego existo*. Moreover, in this same text, swept along by some enthusiasm or other, he compares the *cogito* to the Archimedean point, this point from which, so he tells us, so much is to be expected *si vel minimum quid invenero* . . . – *if I manage to find just one thing, however slight* – . . . *quod certum sit & inconcussum* – *that is certain and unshakeable*. This comes just after *ego sum, ego existo*.

Lastly, in the principles of the *Recherche de la Vérité par la lumière naturelle*, it's *dubito ergo sum*. For a psychoanalyst, this has a very different resonance, but I won't be venturing onto this terrain today, given how slippery it has been for contemporary tendencies, the very same that have allowed the grid of obsessional neurosis to be applied to Monsieur Robbe-Grillet. There are too many stumbling blocks, indeed there is too great a risk of absurdity, for me to stray far in this direction.

I will on the other hand underscore that what is at issue here offers a certain choice, and that on this occasion I am choosing to leave in abeyance everything that a logician might raise in the way of questions around *cogito ergo sum* and the order of Implication involved in it.

If it is merely a Material Implication, you can see where this leads us. It would mean that only in the case that the second clause, *I am*, were false could the combination of implication between the two clauses be rejected. In other words, all that counts is whether *I am* is true, because there would be no harm in *I am thinking* being false for the formulation to be admissible qua Implication. And why not? I'm the one who is saying *I'm thinking*. After all, it could well be that I believe I'm thinking, when actually I'm not. This is something that happens every day, and to a great many people. Pure and simple Implication, the one known as Material Implication, requires but one thing – that the conclusion be true.

In other words, as soon as logic is referring to truth functions and drawing up a table of them across a certain number of matrices, it cannot, if it is to remain internally coherent, define operations as *implications* except by accepting them as functions which would be better termed *consequences*. Here this word denotes the scope within which we can grant the connotation *truth* in a signifying chain. Thus, in Implication, we can place the connotation of truth upon the combination that runs from false to true, but not the other way around.

Who could fail to see that this leaves us far from the realm of what there is to be said about the Cartesian *cogito* as such, in its own realm?

It is quite certain that, taken in its own realm, the *cogito* concerns the constitution of the subject as such, which complicates what is involved in writing qua the regulating of the functioning of logical operations. Indeed, this writing doubtless does no more than represent a more primordial functioning which exceeds it. Yet, in this very capacity, this functioning does, for us, warrant being posited as a function of writing.

It is upon this functioning that the veritable status of the subject depends, and not upon his intuition of being *one who is thinking*. What has justified this intuition if not something which is at that very moment profoundly concealed from him? To wit, in seeking out this certitude on the ground of the progressive evacuation, cleansing and tidying up of everything that is put within his reach concerning the function of knowledge, *what does he want?*

And then, what ultimately is this *cogito*? *Ago, I push*, just as earlier I was pushing forward my sheep, which is part of my work when I am here – it's not necessarily the same when I'm alone or in my analyst's chair. *Cogo, I push together. Cogito.* All of this sets astir. At the end of the day, were it not for Descartes' desire, which orients this cogitation in such a decisive way, we could translate *cogito* as *I beat about*. After all, this is what is being done wherever there is cogitating going on.

Why *cogito* and not *puto*, which carries a similar meaning in Latin? It further means *to prune*, which for us analysts has a few little resonances. *Puto ergo sum* would perhaps hit a different nerve, with a different style and different consequences. We are not to know. If he had actually started by pruning, he might have finished by pruning away God. With the *cogito*, however, something else is going on.

And besides, *cogito* is first and foremost written. If we have noticed that the formulation may be written –

cogito: 'ergo sum'

it's precisely here that we can get a new hold on the intuition behind it and form some grasp of how whatever content, whatever liquid, fills it, derives strictly from structure, from the apparatus of language.

Perhaps – I say *perhaps* because I am just starting to bring this forward and I shall have to come back to it – we ought not to forget in this connection certain functions which are those within which the subject finds himself, not simply in the position of the agentive being, but indeed in the position of subject, insomuch as the subject is, more than concerned, fundamentally determined by the very action that is at issue. The ancient languages possessed a specific register for voicing this, the *middle diathesis* as it is termed by those over on this terrain, who use the suitable vocabulary. Thus, in Latin, *to speak* is, in the middle voice, *loquor*. What is at issue is language insomuch as it determines this other thing in which the subject is constituted as a speaking being.

My attempts to explain these items to those who come along to listen to me are long-standing, irrespective of whatever preoccupations might be rendering them more or less deaf to them. They might care to remember the time when I explicated the difference between *Je suis celui qui te suivrai* and *celui qui te suivra*. They don't carry the same meaning. If there are two ways of saying it, which are each to be recognised in the difference in the person of the verb after the opacity of the relative and of the *celui* that designates the subject, it's because there is no middle voice in French. Thus, *suivre* cannot be stated like *sequor* in Latin. Here, it can be seen how, from the mere fact of following, one is not the same as in not having followed.

These are not complicated matters. They are items that concern us regarding what may be said of a thought that would truly be a thought, the genuine article of true thought. How would it be said in Latin by means of the middle voice? The best way would be to find a verb that exists in the middle only, like the two I have just cited which belong to what are known as the *media tantum*. This is a riddle. Who will raise a hand to propose something?

No one. That's a pity. But it might be to press on a little too briskly to tell you already what I've found. Perhaps it will be precisely on the occasion of what a psychoanalyst does when he interprets that I will be led to tell you. But after all, we do need to move along, as we have been, step by step.

Even so, to give you a little signpost to this middle voice, and so that you won't think I'm spinning all this out on my own, I'll refer you to Benveniste's article on *Actif et moyen dans le verbe*, which fortunately we all read a very long time ago in the *Journal de psychologie*, but which has been included in the recent collection he, too, has just brought out.

In it he explains a matter which, perhaps, now that it occurs to me, might open up some ideas for you. It seems that in Sanskrit there are two ways to say *I sacrifice*. The verb is employed in the active voice when the priest makes the sacrifice to Brahma, or to whatever else, for a client. He tells him, *Come along, a sacrifice has to be made to the god*, and the fellow replies, *Very well, very well*, and he hands him his thingamabob, and swish, a sacrifice is made. Now, that is active. But the nuance is that the middle voice is used when the priest officiates in his own name. This brings into play the fault line that would have to be placed somewhere between the subject of enunciation and the subject of the statement, but it doesn't only do that. This is immediately fathomable for *loquor*, but here it's a shade more complicated because the Other is there. There is the Other that is ensnared with the sacrifice. Ensnaring the Other in one's own name is not the same thing as ensnaring him for the client who needs to have performed his duty unto the divinity and who will seek out the technician to do so.

A further riddle – I'm going from riddle to riddle – in the relation known as the analytic situation – who officiates? And on whose behalf? The question is there for the asking. Where are the analogues? I am posing the question only to give you a sense of how there is a diminishment of speech within analytic technique. I mean that it's a technical artifice that makes speech bow to laws of consequence alone. No trust is placed in anything else. One just has to get on with it. Only, this is not such a natural thing. We know from experience that people don't pick up this profession straightaway, or else they must really want to officiate. It looks a lot like a service which they are being asked to perform, as must our stout-hearted Braman when he has accumulated a bit of experience in the field and can rattle off his little prayers while thinking of something else.

Cogito ergo sum. What is *sum*-ing in this *sum*? Of course, it's not a matter of scaling down the great Cartesian stride. You know that I grant it its proper historical place. It's a matter of using it, and for this use to remain pertinent. If what I'm saying is true, then, from the moment of the *cogito*, thought started to be treated as waste. Thinking used to be quite something. It had its past and its noble pedigree. No one had ever dreamt of making the relation to the world revolve around *I'm me, I am*. The opposition between ego and non-ego was something that had never occurred to anyone. This is the price one pays, for what? Perhaps for having cast thought into the bin. After all, in Descartes, the *cogito* is discard, because he effectively puts everything he has examined in his *cogito* in the waste basket.

I think that those who have been following me can see a little of the interest that this may have, and the relation that all of this can bear to what I have been bringing forward this year.

From the Klein four-group to the *cogito*

The written formulation of the new logic allowed a certain number of items to be stated which had not hitherto unfolded in a demonstrable fashion. For example, when you want to negate both *A and B*. This is written as follows, with the convention of the bar for Negation.

$$\overline{A \cap B}$$

The advantage of these written procedures is well known – it has to run like clockwork, with no need to reflect. So, this amounts to writing *not-A or not-B*, thus –

$$\overline{A \cap B} = \overline{A} \cup \overline{B}$$

You will go and look up in Mr De Morgan, who invented it, or in Mr Boole, who reinvented it, what this corresponds to.

Well, even so, I'm going to illustrate this for you, with great regret, because I know there are people who would be put out if I didn't. But I regret it because these people will be gratified and will believe that they have understood something. It is moreover for this that I am going to show them it, but at that very moment they will be plunged into error once and for all.

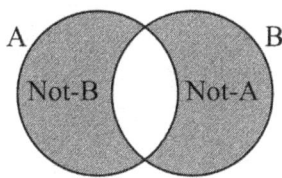

Here are two sets, A and B. Either one or the other. *Either not-A or not-B*. Here, the intersection is naturally excluded. These, the hatched areas, are what is called the *Symmetric Difference*, which is equivalent to the union of both [relative] complements. This is the function of Negation interpreted at the level of the sets.

The negation is that which is *not A and B*. And so these two other areas of either of the two sets equally fulfil this function.

I announce to you now – with the purpose of putting this off until next time because it's already 2pm – that we are going to be examining all the ways in which we can operate on *I am thinking, therefore I am*. We will be putting together an apparatus that will be the best way of conveying how we are to make use of the Cartesian *cogito*, so as to serve the subject of the unconscious as a point of crystallisation.

First, there is the falsity of the implication – *I am thinking and I am not*.

Another transformation is possible, the burning interest of which you will be able to see when I tell you that this is the Aristotelian position – *Either I'm not thinking, or I am*.

The fourth transformation overlays exactly what is here on the board, which I have chosen as a support so that you will retain something from today's stopping point – *Either I'm not thinking, or I am not* – which is the inverse of the *cogito*.

We will have to examine this inverse – which is obtained from making Negation function on the entirety of the formulation *cogito ergo sum* – in such a fashion as to uncover both the sense of the *vel* that unites it and the exact reach that Negation can assume here, so as to account for what is involved in the subject of the unconscious.

This is what I will be doing, then, on 21 December, and which will bring the year to a close. I hope so. If I hold on that long. It will provide us with the proper starting point for the rest of the distance we have to travel under the heading of the logic of the fantasy.

14 December 1966

V

INTERLUDE

Either I am not thinking, or I am not
Psychoanalysts' resistance
Wo Es war

I think that last time I gave you some proof of how I can put up with a fair amount of little tests, like this light flickering off and on. In days gone by, there were bogeyman stories in which it would be explained how in some parts people used to be led off to their sessions of self-criticism. They used lamps for that. Well, it was less disagreeable for me than for you, I must say, because I had it above my head and you full in your eyes.

You were able to note that such minor inconveniences as these are not capable of inflecting my disquisition.

This is why I hope you won't try to attribute to the doings of some vain personal prickliness the fact that today is not going to be festive, despite the time of year. I inform you right away that I won't be giving the session I had prepared with you in mind. I apologise to those who might have set back a little their holiday plans in order to benefit from it. At the very least, no one will have gone out of their way for nothing at all because I trust that you each have an offprint of my contribution to the Bonneval Colloquium which I have borne in tribute as an end-of-year gift. I haven't gone so far as to include a personal dedication in every one because too many of your names are unfamiliar to me but, well, that could still be done.

We have come to the moment when I am going to set out for you what I regard as the decisive formulations for the unconscious. These are logical formulations, one of which you saw up on the blackboard last time in the form – *Either I am not thinking, or I am not*. With the caveat that this *or* is neither a *vel* – the *or* of union, one or the other, or both – nor an *aut* – at least one, but not more, a choice has to be made. It is neither one nor the other, and this will be the occasion to introduce, I trust in a way that will be admissible in logical calculus, another function which could be named with a new term, though there is one which I made use of that might have other applications. It might create an ambiguity, but no matter, I'll bring the two together. What is at issue is nothing else but what I have indicated with the term *alienation*. But whichever, it's up to you to choose. In the meantime, let's call this operation *omega*, ω. On the truth table, it corresponds to the following – if the two propositions on which it operates are both true, the result of the operation is false. You will consult the truth tables, which you have in easy reach, and you will see that none of those that to this day have been in use – Conjunction, Disjunction, Implication, ... – meet this condition. When I say that the conjunction of true to true yields, through this operation, the false, I mean that any other conjunction is true here, that of false to false, of false to true, of true to false.

The relation that this bears to the nature of the unconscious is what I hope to be able to spell out here in front of you on 11 January, the date set for our next appointment. You may rightly think that if I'm not doing this for you today – I think you can trust me on this – it's not because my formulation isn't ready, nor the limit I could set on it today.

Nevertheless, while this is effectively due to a certain trepidation at putting this forward in its full rigour on a day when I'm in something of a bind, I have spent the last hours examining a matter which is nothing less than the opportuneness, or not, of going on with this Seminar that is bringing us together right now. I've been pondering this question because it deserves to be asked, on account of the little volume I have given you, which does need, so it seems to me, to be brought to your attention just prior to my laying out a logical formulation which in some way allows a firm and certain apprehension of what is involved in the reaction of the subject taken up in this reality of the unconscious. It is not unhelpful that this volume should be vouching for the difficulties particular to that room for those whose praxis and function consists in being there, and perhaps it is from having failed to take stock of the relation that there is between this *being there* and a certain necessary *not being there*.

This volume will attest for you to a meeting that took place around the theme of the unconscious. Among the participants, and playing an eminent role, were two of my students. They were among those dearest to me. There were others still. There were all sorts there. Even Marxists from the CNRS [Centre national de la recherche scientifique]. You will see on the first page, in very small type, a very singular manifestation. Anyone who is an analyst here will recognise what Freud alludes to at one point in one of the five major psychoanalytic case studies. I'll leave it to you to find it, which will allow you to leaf through them a little. It's a matter of what both Freud and the police force call with one same voice *the gift*, or *the calling card*. Should it ever happen that your residence is visited in your absence, you might come across the trace perchance left by the visitor in the shape of a little turd.

With this we are on the plane of the object *a*. It should come as no surprise that such things pop up in the relations of those subjects whom you track with your discourse on the pathways of the unconscious. In truth, there are strong and sizeable excuses for the shortcomings that psychoanalysts have been demonstrating when it comes to keeping up the high theoretical standards their praxis requires. One needs only to look at the place they have given to the function of resistances. On the day when I shall be trying to set out my formulations for you in their essential and their true instantiation, you will see the necessity that attaches to resistance and how it can on no account be confined to the un-psychoanalysed.

The schematic that I will be trying to set out for the relation, not of the non-thought and non-being – don't believe that I'm on the slippery slopes of mysticism – but of *I am not thinking* and *I am not*, are going to enable you for the first time, and in a palpable way, to mark out not only the difference, the non-overlap, between what is called resistance and what is called defence, but even to mark out in an utterly essential way, even though it is unprecedented, what is involved in the defence that is strictly what surrounds and exactly what preserves *I am not*. It is on account of having failed to be aware of this that everything has been wrenched out of place in that perspective wherein each person fantasises what the reality of the unconscious might be.

This something that we lack makes for the thorny issue with which we are faced – and not through some untoward eventuality – namely the new conjunction between Being and knowledge. This distinct approach to the term *truth* makes of Freud's discovery something that can in no way be critiqued by scaling it down to any ideology whatsoever.

If I have some time left, I will indicate how you won't lose anything by first having another read of Descartes. I'm not announcing this merely to dangle pointlessly before you some scrap of nothing designed to entice you, because this is also the fulcrum around which I am making this necessary return to the subject's origins revolve, in virtue of which we shall be able to take up the *cogito* in terms of the subject. How so? Well, precisely because it is in these terms that Freud voices his essential aphorism around which I not only taught myself to turn, but also those who heed me. *Wo Es war, soll Ich werden*. The *Ich* in this formulation, at the date when it was voiced in the *New Lectures*, could in no way be taken for the function *das Ich* such as it is spelt out in the second topography. I translated it as *Là où c'était, là dois-je advenir*. Where there it was, there must I come to be. And I inserted ... *comme sujet* ... as a subject, but that's a pleonasm. Here the German *Ich* is the subject.

Just as I revived the sense of the *cogito* in putting inverted commas around *I am* in such a way as to clarify it, so too will I be going into Freud's aphorism, where we find a formulation more worthy of the marble tablet upon which he had dreamt of seeing inscribed *Here the Secret of Dreams was revealed*. But if ever you were to be engraving *Wo Es war, soll Ich werden* upon it, be sure to leave out the comma. It is *Where there it was* that *Ich* must come to be. At the spot where Freud places this formulation, at the close of one of his articles, what is at issue in this indication is not the hope that all of a sudden, in all human beings, as they express themselves in a verminous language, *The ego must dislodge the id*. Rather it means that what Freud is indicating here is nothing less than the revolution in thought that his work necessitates.

Now, it's clear that there is a challenge here, and a parlous one for anybody who steps forward, as is my case, to maintain it in his stead. A certain Abelard once wrote in the following terms, which perhaps some of you still have in your ears, *Odiosum me mundo reddidit logica*. Logic has rendered me odious to the world, and it is upon this terrain that I intend to bear the decisive terms, which will put an end to the confusion over what is at issue when the unconscious is at stake. We shall see whether or not anyone might say that I am slipping out of it here, or trying to misappropriate it.

To form a grasp of what is involved in the unconscious, I want to mark out, so that you may ready your minds in some way with an exercise, that what is forbidden to us is exactly that sort of movement of thought that is peculiar to the *cogito*, which just as much as analysis necessitates the *Autre* with a capital A. On no account does this require the presence of some imbecile or other.

When Descartes publishes his *cogito*, which he articulates in the movement of the *Discours de la méthode* that he develops in writing, he addresses himself to someone. He leads this someone along the paths of an articulation that becomes ever more pressing. And then, all at once, something happens which consists in peeling away from the beaten path in order to make this other thing emerge – *I am*.

There is here that sort of movement, which I shall be trying to qualify for you in a more precise fashion, that is the one that is found only very occasionally in the course of history. It is the very same that I could designate for you in Book VII of Euclid, in the proof which still holds us in its thrall because we have found nothing else and it belongs to the same order. The latter consists in proving that, whichever formula you might come up with, if such a thing could be found, to generate prime numbers, it would necessarily be deduced – still no one has found this formula, but were it to be found – that there would be yet other primes which the formula could not name. This is the sort of knot in which is marked out the essential point of a certain relation that is the subject's relation to thought.

I touched on Pascal's wager last year with the same purpose. If you refer to what appears in modern mathematics as what is known as the diagonalisation proof, in other words what allows Cantor to inaugurate a differentiation between the infinites, you have again the same movement. And more basically, if you so wish, before the next time you might care to get hold in one form or another of the *Fides quærens intellectum* of Saint Anselm, and in chapter II – so that I won't be compelled to read it to you – you will read, though you might have to go to some lengths to get your hands on this little book – this one here is the Koyré translation published by Vrin, I don't know if there are any left but now there surely won't be – you will, by way of an exercise, thumb through what academic imbecility has caused to fall into discredit under the heading of *ontological argument*. They believed that Saint Anselm didn't know that just because one may think it most perfect, it doesn't mean that it exists. You will see in this chapter that he knew this full well, but that the argument has an altogether different reach. It has the reach of the approach I'm trying to designate for you, which consists in conducting one's opponent onto a path such that a hitherto unperceived dimension can rise up when one abruptly breaks off from it.

The horror of the relation to the dimension of the unconscious is constituted by this movement which promptly becomes impossible. Anything goes in the unconscious . . . except to articulate *therefore I am*. This is what necessitates other approaches, and specifically the logical approaches that I will be trying to plot out in front of you, which cast into its abysmal futility everything that has been voiced in the psychologist's woolly terms about self-analysis.

But while I may most certainly be experiencing all this difficulty in reviving, within a field the function of which is affirmed and crystallised precisely by difficulties – let's call them *noetic*, if that suits you – in the theoretical broaching of the unconscious, a point that is only too comprehensible and which doesn't rule out that a junction should be made with this domain on the plane of technique and precise examination, then it is exactly from having been able, for instance, to require that the terms in which training analysis is being justified should here be reopened.

For me, the question is there for the asking as to what is involved in the consequences of a disquisition on Freud, in the circumstances and also in the scheme, for me, of making use of their sinuosity, of the diversion that these circumstances imposed upon me, in opening this disquisition to a larger audience.

The gallant gentleman who has left his signature at the foot of what I have called *the gift* writes – *Is it fitting, on the pretext of liberty, to tolerate that the forum should degenerate into a circus?* Here, the gift is precious to me. The truth is coming out, even from incontinence.

It is I who, in this volume, am supposedly transforming the forum into a circus. If I really did succeed, may God bless me, for sure. In my short article on the unconscious, I did indeed have the sense, as I was drafting it, that I was practising something both rigorous and which was piercing through the limits, if not those of the circus roof then at the very least those of acrobatics, and why not those of clownery, if you wish, so as to insert something that is indeed quite unrelated to what I said at the Bonneval forum, which was, like all forums, a funfair. *(Lacan throws the booklet on the table.)*

Not everyone can pull off the precision of a circus routine, far fewer than could pull off what I'm demonstrating for you here when I speak to you about the *cogito*. It's something that does indeed take the shape of a circus ring, except that here the ring doesn't close. There is a little offset somewhere which forces the step from *I am thinking* to *I am*, which also forces at such and such a date an essential stride to be taken. Oh, how rare these revolutions of the subject are.

The last in the line which I took up is Cantor's. I will tell you that Cantor got spat on as many times as it took for him to end his life in an asylum. *(Lacan throws the booklet on the table again.)* Rest assured, this will not be my case. I am a little less sensitive than he was to comments from colleagues and others. But the question I'm asking myself is whether or not, now that I'm giving voice to this disquisition – in a dimension that is being conveyed by the fairly staggering sales of these *Écrits* – I ought to be busying myself with the funfair. For one cannot, of course, count on those whose vocation it is to push themselves forward, snatching up in passing any old item that has been latched onto in Lacan's discourse or anyone else's, to put together a paper in which they would demonstrate their originality.

Between the Bonneval congress and the time when I came over to this site, I lived in this midst of a fair. A fair where I was livestock on sale in the cattle market. That didn't bother me. First, because these operations didn't concern me. In my discourse, I mean. And then, it didn't prevent the same people who were busy with this service from coming to my Seminar and scribbling it all down. I mean, from carefully noting every last word – with all the more care given that they knew full well it wasn't going to go on for much longer, in view of their designs. So, this is not just any fair.

What is going to show up at the fair now are all these other sorts of items, which will consist – as has already been done, and already prior to the publication of my *Écrits* – in seizing hold of any one of my formulations to make it serve goodness knows what, like trying to show me that I don't know how to read Freud when for thirty years I've been doing nothing else but that. *(Lacan throws the booklet on the table for a third time.)*

So, what has to be done? Ought I to reply? Ought I to seek a reply? What a kerfuffle. Perhaps I have more useful matters to tend to. Most specifically, to busying myself with the very site where these things can bear fruit, namely with those who follow me in the praxis.

Either way, as you can see, this question doesn't leave me indifferent. It's precisely because it doesn't leave me indifferent that I have found myself asking it with the greatest intensity. I must say that there is one thing holding me back from settling it in the way that you can see it looming up here. It's not about the quality you possess, ladies and gentlemen, even though I am far from not feeling honoured to have among my listeners, today or on days past, some of the most highly trained people and such people as, in offering myself to their judgement, is never to no avail.

Nevertheless, is this alone enough to justify what can equally be transmitted by way of writing? In spite of it all, at the level of writing, it so happens that whatever is worth something tends to stay afloat, though of course in universities like those of the French university system, which have been Kantian for nigh-on a century, the heads of department, as I pointed out in one of my notes, in these hundred years over which they have been leaving their mark on the droves of students they have pushed through, have still not found the wherewithal to bring out a complete edition of Kant.

What is making me hesitate, and what is leading me perhaps – perhaps, if it takes my fancy – to continue this discourse, is not therefore your quality, but your great numbers. For after all, this is what strikes me. This is why I have given up this year on restricting the Seminar in the way I did for the previous few years. That brief trial period was the occasion to show how inefficacious that was. It is because of these great numbers, because of this extraordinary thing that is leading people to come here, when a fair share of them, whom I acknowledge because they are here as well to demonstrate to me that there is something that resonates in what I say, prove to me that it resonates sufficiently for them to come along to listen to me rather than to the speech of one or other of their professors on items that concern them on account of being part of their curriculum. They come to hear me, I who am not part of their curriculum, and this signals to me that even so, through what I say, which cannot be taken for demagogy, there must indeed be something in which they have a sense that they are concerned.

It is in this respect that I might justify myself, if it so happens, in going on with this public discourse. This is certainly, as it has been for the fifteen years it has lasted, a discourse in which most surely not everything is set out in advance, but which I have built up, and whole portions of which are still scattered about in dissertations that will make of it, my word, what they will, though there are parts that would deserve more and better.

In what I will be telling you about the formula which earlier I called the omega operation, I will be making reference to the *Witz*. For three months, in front of people who couldn't believe their ears, who kept wondering whether I was joking around, I spoke of the *Witz*. I invite you, since you are going to be on holiday, to procure, if by chance this is possible – for one never knows, Freud's works are also impossible to find – the book on the *Witz*, and to go through it. Should it happen that I, too, have to take some time off, this is the first thing from my past Seminars to which I would try to set out an equivalent in writing.

With that, you are now furnished, for the intermediary period ahead, with what I wanted to say. It's not always fun. At any rate, not always for me.

The last time I alluded to festivities was in a short written piece, which actually wasn't a piece of writing at all because I was keen that it should remain in the state of the speech that I delivered to a fairly extensive audience of doctors. The welcome it received was one of the experiences of my life. It was not, for that matter, an experience that surprised me. I won't be doing it again because I'm well aware of the results it would have. I must tell you that I couldn't resist making one modification that actually had nothing to do with the speech – the allusion to the feast, the banquet, in the *Symposium*. If allusion it was, the public will doubtless more easily recognise the allusion to the *Symposium* festivities in the bulletin of my little School than in the bulletin of the Collège de Médecine, where it is also due to be published. It has to do with two characters that crop up, the one mendicant, the other errant. You are familiar with these two allegorical characters, who are known as Πόρος and Πενία. Between the *Poros* of psychoanalysis and the *Penia* of the university, I'm wondering just how far I can let the obscenity run. Whatever might be at stake here, the matter is worth taking a second look at, I mean, even if what is at stake is what the other fellow calls, rather comically, philosophical Eros.

Merry festivities!

21 December 1966

BUILDING THE LACAN GROUP

VI

THE UNCONSCIOUS AND THE ID

Union, intersection and the negation thereof
From Being to I
Detritus, man's Being
Fantasy, support of the drive
Mutual eclipsing of not-I and I am not

I left you with the operation I had defined as *alienation*, in the form of a forced choice in which this alienation is illustrated by bearing on an alternative that ends in an essential lack.

I announced that I would at least be picking up this form in connection with the alternative through which I have been conveying the Cartesian *cogito*, and which runs as follows – *Either I am not thinking, or I am not*.

1

A logician trained in symbolic logic would recognise the transformation of the *cogito* into this alternative as corresponding to the formula brought to light for the first time by De Morgan in the mid-nineteenth century.

What was stated in this formula represented a veritable discovery, which had never before been brought to light in that form in the register of logic.

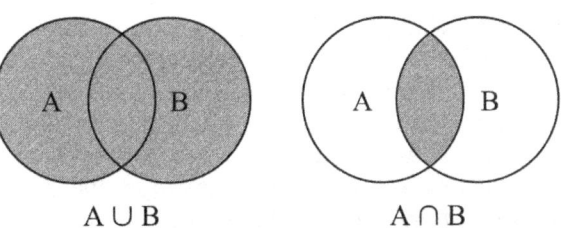

A ∪ B   A ∩ B

Here we have two propositions, A and B. The field of what is admitted in either proposition is illustrated by a circle covering an area. This one, on the left, represents the *union* of A and B. As you can see, this is not addition, because the two fields can have a portion common to both, which is the case here. If you say, for example, that it is not true that A and B are both tenable, this amounts to negating their union. *Intersection* is something else, and is represented on the right.

Well, De Morgan's statement expresses that the negation of the intersection – if you negate the tenability, say, of A and B together – is equivalent to the union of the negation of A, from the diagram on the left, and the negation of B, from the diagram on the right.

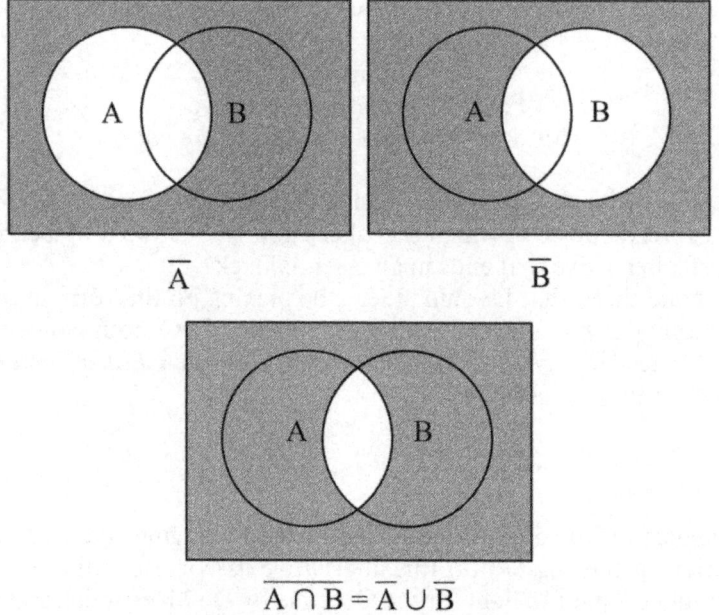

$$\overline{A \cap B} = \overline{A} \cup \overline{B}$$

The negation of the intersection

You can see in this last figure that there remains a sector that is excepted. This is the complement of the union of the two negations. It corresponds to what was negated at the outset, namely in the field of intersection of A and B.

This very straightforward formula found itself taking on such a wide scope in the developments of symbolic logic that it is regarded as fundamental, in the capacity of what is known as the *duality principle*. It is here expressed in its most comprehensive form. This is to say that we are not solely taking things up in this attempt at a literalisation of the handling of propositional logic but also bringing them onto the plane of set theory.

What was it that allowed set theory to be turned into the underpinning of the development of mathematical thinking? Well, in a masked form, so to speak, what I taught you to distinguish from the subject of the statement as the subject of enunciation is to be found somehow frozen into the primary wording of the definition of the set as such. It is wielded therein and remains implicated in it, to the extent that set theory is what allows for an expounding of the development of mathematical thought and ensures its coherence.

The progress of invention, the specific process of mathematical reasoning, is of course a different matter, which is not that of a tautology, regardless of what people say about it. Mathematical reasoning possesses its own fecundity. It wrests itself away from the purely deductive plane by this resource that is essential to it and which is known as recursive reasoning, or, to use Poincaré's term, *complete induction*. To carry this through, one has to turn to temporality, for what is constitutive of recursive reasoning is that it is founded on a process that is stepped and endlessly repeatable.

All we need to seek out at the level of set theory is an apparatus that will allow us to symbolise what has been secured within the mathematical development. This requires that, in the act of enunciation, something should be singled out as a subject – the subject of enunciation insomuch as it is different from the leading edge whereby we can recognise the subject in the statement. The existence of the subject of enunciation is secured in a veiled fashion in the notion of a set, and very precisely in so far as this notion is founded upon the possibility of the empty set as such.

At the level of set theory, De Morgan's transformation is expressed as follows. In any formula in which we have a set, the empty set, the sign of union and the sign of intersection, if we interchange them two by two – that is to say, if we replace the empty set with a set, a set with an empty set, union with intersection, and intersection with union – we preserve the truth value that was established in the initial formula.

This is what is meant fundamentally by the fact that we can replace *I am thinking, therefore I am* with a formula that unites an *I am not thinking* to an *I am not*. This is how it can be articulated to begin with, quite roughly, quite clunkily, and quite blindly, I would say. It still remains that its handling needs to be looked at closely in regard to the *or* of union and to the value of either *not*. Indeed, we are compelled to re-examine the value of the Negation function as soon as we introduce the dimension of the empty set qua representative of the subject of enunciation. Doubtless it may well be that nothing corresponds to this enunciation, but it has been established as such.

Certainly the ambiguity of negation in its grammatical use has always been evident, simply by examining the statement. Upon what does the negation bear in the expression *I don't desire*? If this *I don't desire* is transitive, it implies, by my doing, that there is something of the undesirable, something particular that I do not desire. But the negation in *I don't desire* may equally mean that I am not the one who desires, that I am relieving myself of a desire, which might equally be what is carrying me along while still not being mine. Yet it still remains that this negation can mean that *It is not true that I desire*, such that whether this desire comes from me or not has nothing to do with the question.

Trying to delineate and give order to this dialectic between the subject of the statement and the subject of the enunciation is a most useful endeavour, and especially so on the level at which we are today taking up the interrogation of Descartes' *cogito*, to the extent that this is what is going to allow us to give its veritable meaning and exact positioning to what becomes altered therein by Freud.

To say it straight out, in light of the interrogation we are conducting on the basis of this examination of the *cogito*, we are going to see a distinction between two forms that are too easily confounded and conflated, and which are called respectively *the unconscious* and *the id*.

2

It is a fact that the *cogito* is much debated in philosophical discourse.

A certain wavering that lingers in this respect is both what is enabling us to delve into this ourselves, to make it serve our own purpose, and what within it vouches for something in which it ought to have found its complement.

Why has the *cogito* gone down in the history of philosophy as a milestone? Well, to put it in its briefest terms, it's because it supplanted the relation of pathos and difficulty between thinking and Being that had lain behind the whole tradition of philosophical interrogation.

Go and peruse a copy of Aristotle's *Metaphysics*, not one of the commentaries but the unmediated text. Of course this will be easier for you if you read Greek. If you don't, there are some fine translations and very adequate commentaries in English. There is a French tradition, which is that of Tricot, which in truth cannot help draping over it the mask and veil of a constant Thomist commentary. However, to the extent that through these distortions you might try to reach the original movement of what Aristotle communicates to us, you will perceive, but after the fact, how everything that has come to accumulate around this text by way of criticism and exegesis – with some scholiast or other telling us that this or that passage is doubtful or that the order of the books has been disrupted – all these questions appear, on a first read, to be quite ancillary with respect to something fresh and direct that makes of this reading, provided you step out of the scholastic fug, a thing that will strike you for what just now I called its register of pathos, when you will see recurring and redounding from one instant to the next this interrogation of what is involved in the relation between thinking and Being, in something that does still seem to bear the trace of the very discourse in which it was formulated.

You will see such a term as the following cropping up, τὸ σεμνὸν, *that which is dignified, dignity*, which is what has to be preserved in thinking, in regard to what ought to be lifting thought to the nobility of what is involved in the grasp that is being sought, to wit, it is not merely the *entity* or *that which is* but that though which Being must manifest therein. It has been variously translated. *L'être en tant qu'être* is how it has been put [in French]. That's a terribly poor translation for the three terms I have noted up here on the blackboard, at the top left –

τὸ τί ἐστι

First, τὸ τί ἐστι means nothing else but *the what it is*. It seems to me that this is a translation that is just as valid as that of *quid*, to which people generally believe they must confine themselves.

The τὸ τί ἦν εἶναι is indeed, my word, one of the most startling features of the vivacity of the language that is Aristotle's, for *being qua being* is certainly not, and here even less so, a suitable translation for it. However unfamiliar you may be with Greek, you can read this thing that is a common, and not only literary, turn of phrase in Greek, which is patently the feature at the origin of the Greek verb and which it precisely has in common with what is connoted by the imperfect tense in French.

I have often paused over this imperfect in my lessons and have left a trace of it in my *Écrits*. It is that *c'était*, which means that *it has just disappeared* at the very same time as meaning *a little more and it was to be*. This τὸ τί ἦν εἶναι is the same thing that is said in Euripides' *Hippolytus*, when these words are spoken – Κύπρις οὐκ ἄρ'ἦν θεός, that is, *Cypris-Aphrodite, no god then was she*. This means that, in having conducted herself as she just has, surely what she was is eluding and escaping us, and thus we also have to call into question everything that has to do with a god or goddess. This τὸ τί ἦν εἶναι, *that which was to be* – that which was to be when? Well, before I speak of it, properly speaking. It is that kind of sentiment that is there, in the very language of Aristotle, of *Being* still inviolate and yet which it was already touching upon with this νοεῖν, with this *thinking*, of which all that is being agitated is to know just to what degree it may be worthy of it, that is to say, to what degree it may raise itself to the level of Being. This, then, is the original line, in which you cannot fail in some way to apprehend the root – from the order of the sacred – to which is tethered the first articulation of the philosopheme at the level of the one who is there to introduce – this much can be said – the first step of a positive science.

For τὸ ὄν ᾗ ὄν is in effect also – this last term – *the entity wherethrough*, ᾗ, *it is being*, that is to say, again this something that points towards Being. And everyone knows that the free movement of the philosophical tradition represents nothing else but a gradual distancing from this source of discovery, from this first invention, which culminates, down through the succeeding schools of thought, ever more in locking down what can be taken from this first interrogation around logical articulation alone.

Now, Descartes' *cogito* carries a meaning. It is, as I have said, that it replaces this relation between thinking and Being with the inauguration, pure and simple, of the Being of *I*. It is an effect that arises from having broken through thought, which ultimately represents something that may be called a refusal of the question of Being. This refusal begat its consequence in the form of the rise of a new broaching of the world, which is what we call *science*. Within the effects of this breakthrough there arose the Freudian discovery, or Freud's thought, indeed his thinking on thought. The essential point is that in no case whatsoever does this mean a return to the thinking of Being. Nothing in what Freud contributed, whether it be the unconscious that is at issue or the id, returns to anything that, at the level of thinking, places us back onto the plane of the examination of Being. What Freud contributed takes on its meaning only in the consequences of this break whereby the question that thinking asks of Being is supplanted, in the manner of a refusal, by the simple affirmation of the Being of *I*. I'm advancing into the domain of logic this year in order to show you how this is articulated.

What about this Being of *I*? Is there a Being of *I* outside discourse? This is the question that the Cartesian *cogito* slices through. But it still remains to be seen how it does so, and this is why it deserves to be gone though afresh. In this *cogito* we are going to find the adumbration of the very paradox that is ushered in by De Morgan's formula, the one I wrote up for you at the start.

It was in order to pose the question of the Being of *I* that we enclosed *ergo sum* in inverted commas. These inverted commas subvert what might be called its *naive* scope by turning it into an *ergo sum* that is being cogitated. All in all, its Being holds in this *ergo* alone, which, within thinking, presents for Descartes under the sign of necessity. On several occasions, as much in the *Discours de la méthode* as in the *Meditationes* or the *Principia*, he articulates it as an *ergo* of necessity.

Yet, if this *ergo* alone represents this necessity, can we not see what results from how *ergo sum* is but the refusal of the hard path that leads from thinking to Being, and a refusal of the knowledge that has to journey this way. This *ergo sum* takes the leap of being the one that thinks. Yet in thinking that there is no need to question the entity on the journey from which it takes its Being, because the question is already secured on its own account from its own existence, doesn't this amount to placing oneself, as *Ego*, out of the reach of the handhold by which Being can clasp onto thinking? Doesn't this amount to positing oneself as a pure *bethinking*, as what subsists from being the *I* of a local *am not*?

This means – *I am, only upon the elision of the question of Being. I go without Being. I am not, except where necessarily I am, for being able to say so*, or, better still, *where I am, for being able to get you to say so*, or more precisely, *to get the Other to say so*. This is how Descartes proceeds when you follow him closely.

Moreover, it is in this respect that his way of proceeding is fruitful. Strictly speaking, it has the same profile as recursive reasoning because it consists in leading the other party along a long pathway, renouncing one path of knowledge, and then another, and yet another, and soon enough all of them, then at one bend to surprise him with the avowal that, here at least, needs must that *I* be.

The dimension of the Other is so essential here that it may be said to be the sinew of the *cogito*. It is this dimension that properly establishes the limit of what can be defined and secured, at best, as the empty set constituted from *I am*, in this reference where *I* qua *I am* is constituted by not containing any element. This frame is valid only in so far as I think through the *I am thinking*, that is to say, I argue out the *cogito* with the Other. *Am not* signifies that there is no element in this set that exists under the term *I*. *Ego sum, sive ego cogito*, but without there being anything to fill it out. This meeting point makes it clear that *I am thinking* is merely apparel congruent with *I am*.

That which prepares the admission of an empty set does not play out at the level of *I am thinking* but at the level of another set, that of knowing. It was after having put to the test all the points of access to knowledge that Descartes was to ground this thinking from the emptying out of Being, avid as he was for certitude alone. From this results what we have already called a *voiding*, and this term, through this interrogation, permits of knowing whether this very operation suffices as such to give *Ego* its veritable substance.

It is from this alone that becomes thinkable, as though by means of a guiding thread, what will be at issue when Freud brings us what results from this, using the term *psychische Geschehen*. It's not *mental functioning*, as it has been misleadingly translated from the German into English, but rather *psychical events*. As we are going to see, there is nothing in Freud's examination that could reanimate or revive the thinking of Being beyond what the *cogito* has thenceforward ascribed to it as a limit. In fact, Being is so fully excluded from everything that can be at issue, that I could say, to take up one of my familiar formulations, that what we have here is a *Verwerfung*. It is very much something of this order that is at stake.

If something can be articulated in our times that might be called *the end of a humanism* – which didn't occur just yesterday, nor when Monsieur Michel Foucault voiced it, nor even myself, which is something that happened long ago – it's very precisely because a dimension is now open to us that allows us to uncover how this *Verwerfung*, this rejection, of Being plays out. In keeping with the formula I supplied for this at the start of my teaching, what is rejected from the symbolic reappears in the real. While this something that is called man's Being has indeed been rejected from a certain date forth, we can see it reappearing in the real and in a form that is altogether clear.

Man's Being, insomuch as it is fundamental in our anthropology, bears a name. The [French] word *être* is to be found in the midst of it. To find this name, and also what it designates, it's enough to leave home for a day's outing in the countryside where, on the other side of a lane, you will come across a campsite and, on the site, or more exactly around it, marking out its drossy encirclement, you will meet this *verworfen* Being of man reappearing in the real. It is called *detritus*.

We have known for some time that man's Being qua rejected reappears here in the form of these little twisted iron-bound circles which are to be found, goodness knows why, amassing around the usual sites of campers. Should we play the role of prehistorian or archaeologist, we ought to presume that this rejection of Being did not appear for the first time with Descartes, nor with the origin of science, but perhaps left its mark on each of the essential breakthroughs that enabled the stages of humanity to be constituted in forms that were marked but ephemeral and invariably precarious.

I don't need to voice for you again, in a tongue that I don't speak and which would make it unpronounceable for me, what has been pinpointed as signalling such and such a phase of technological development, in the shape of these shell-mounds that have been found in certain areas, in certain zones of what remains of prehistoric civilisations.

The point to take on board here is that detritus is not only a signal, but something essential, because it is that around which what we have now to examine in the way of alienation is going to revolve.

3

Alienation has an apparent face, which is not that we are the other, or that *the others*, as they say, misstate or mangle us when pulling us up.

The fact of alienation is not that we are pulled up, recast and represented in the Other. Rather it is essentially founded upon the rejection of the Other, insomuch as this *Autre* with a capital A is what has come in the stead of the interrogation of Being around which I am today going to be making the limit and the breakthrough of the *cogito* turn.

Would to God, then, that alienation should consist in our finding ourselves at ease in the locus of the Other.

This is surely what lends Descartes' approach its buoyancy. In his first work, his juvenilia, the first *Regulae* – the manuscript of which was discovered posthumously and a portion of which is still lost among the papers of Leibniz – the *sum, ergo Deus est* is exactly the prolongation of the *cogito ergo sum*.

The operation is of course an advantageous one. It puts everything fully in the hands of an Other secured by nothing else but from having established Being qua the Being of the *I* of an Other, which the God of the Judeo-Christian tradition facilitates by being He who presents Himself, *I AM THAT I AM*. This fideist underpinning, which remains so deeply embedded in seventeenth-century thought, is no longer all that tenable for us.

Rather, for us, it is the fact that this fundament has been subjectively struck through that alienates us for real. This is what I have already illustrated with the formula, *your freedom or your life*. It is undoubtedly a marvellous order. Who, thus ordered, could refuse this Other par excellence that death is? In view of which, as I noted for you, there remains the liberty to die. It is the same for what is voiced in the Stoic formula, *et propter vitam vivendi perdere causas*. For the sake of not losing these causes, are you to lose life itself? Already matters are here quite readable enough.

But for us what is at issue is to find out what is involved in the alienating choice between *Either I am not thinking, or I am not*. I mean – *I* as *am not*. Once the *I* has been chosen as establishing Being, we no longer have any choice. We have to move towards *I am not thinking*.

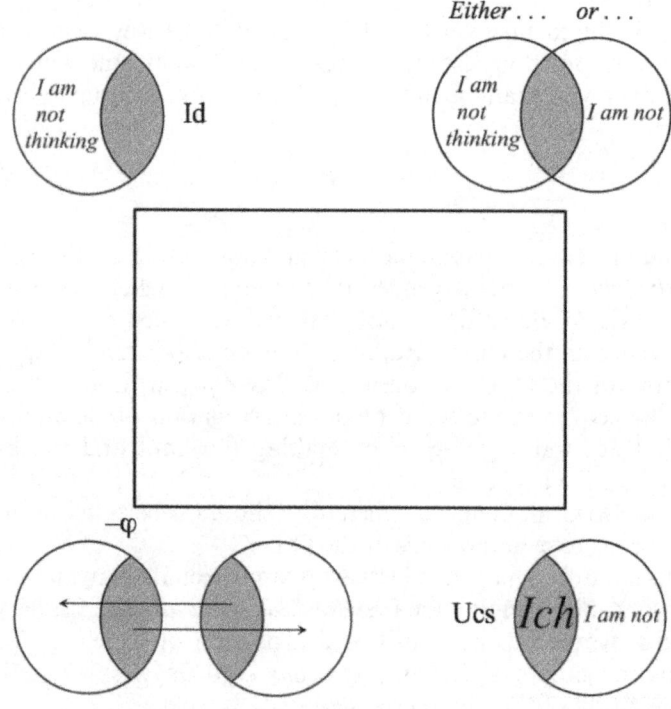

Either *I am not thinking* or *I am not*

Indeed, establishing the *I* as the one and only fundament of Being is precisely what puts a full stop to all interrogation of νοεῖν, to any way of proceeding that would turn thought into something other than what Freud, in his time and with science, made of it. *Das Denken*, so he writes in the *Formulierungen über die zwei Prinzipien des psychischen Geschehens*, amounts essentially to *a trial run of an action, displacing smaller quantities of invested energy* within the psyche, which allows us to examine, to gauge and also to plot out the path along which we have to find satisfaction for what impels and stimulates us to make our way, by means of some motor discharge, into the real.

I am not thinking is essential, but we also have to question what is going on in the loss that results from the choice – the *I am not* to which just now we gave a grounding as the essence of the *I* itself.

Does the loss brought about by this alienation boil down to *I am not*? It most certainly doesn't, and precisely because something becomes apparent in the form of Negation, but which bears not on Being but on the *I* itself, qua grounded in *am not*. Concomitant with the choice of *I am not thinking*, something looms up, the essence of which is not to be *I*. It emerges in the very place of *ergo*, insomuch as this is placed at the intersection of *I am thinking* and *I am*, in what is sustained all by itself as the Being of cogitation. In the very stead of this *ergo*, then, something unfolds that takes sustenance from being *not-I*. This *not-I*, which it is so very essential to spell out in order for it to be grasped in its essence, is what Freud brings us at the level of the second stage in his thinking, known as the second topography, under the name of the id.

There is the greatest danger of error here. In myself approaching the question of the id when I spoke of *Wo Es war* . . ., I was unable, for want of a logical articulation that would allow it to take on its veritable worth, to give a firm sense of where the essence of this *not-I* that constitutes the id lies.

Anyone who in this matter remains on the psychological trails inherited from the philosophical tradition of Antiquity seems invariably to slip into absurdity, turning the soul, or the ψυχή, into something that *is*. For them, the id will always be what some imbecile kept piping into my ears over the ten years we spent in the same vicinity – *the id is a bad ego*. Nothing of the sort could ever be upheld.

It suffices to conceive of the id in the strange anomalous positivity that it takes on in being the *not* of the *I* which, in essence, is *am not*. What strange complement is at issue in this *not-I*? Well, one needs to know how to articulate it in the way that the entire delineation of what is at issue in the id does effectively articulate it for us.

The id that is at stake is most surely not, in any way whatsoever, the first person. To have been led to come out with the comment that Freud's psychology was a psychology in the first person was a veritable error, to be consigned to the ranks of the grotesque, it has to be said, whatever respect we might show the author for history's sake. And that one of my students, in the course of the short report that is included in the opuscule I distributed to you last time, should have believed himself compelled to tread this path again, maintaining for an instant the illusion that this was the way by which I was led to formulate this for you – when after having heard me, he was quite naturally driven to formulate the contrary – is in itself a sort of bluff or confidence trick. It has no place in this question. The id is neither the first nor the second person, nor even the third, insomuch as, to follow Benveniste's definition, the third person is the one being spoken about.

We approach the id a little more closely in utterances such as *it's all ashimmer, it's raining, it's all abuzz*. But it would be to fall again into error to believe that the id would be *it* in so far as it gets uttered by itself. This does not give sufficient contour to the Freudian id. The id is properly speaking all that which, in discourse qua logical structure, is not *I*, that is to say, all the rest of the structure. And when I say *structure*, *logical* structure, understand this as *grammatical*. For it is no small matter that the very support of what is at issue in the drive, that is to say the fantasy, can be expressed thus – *Ein Kind wird geschlagen*.

A child is being beaten. No commentary, no metalanguage, could account for what is brought into the world in such a formulation. Nothing could ever repeat it or explain it away. The structure of the phrase *A child is being beaten* cannot be expounded upon. It simply shows itself. There is no φύσις that could give an account of it. There might be something in the φύσις that necessitates him getting a knock, but that he should get beaten is something else.

That the fantasy should be such an essential factor in the functioning of the drive is just what it takes to remind us of what I demonstrated for you about the drive apropos of the scoptophilic drive and the sadomasochistic drive, namely that it's an outline, a traced out montage that is grammatical, the inversions, reversions and complexifications of which are arranged by no other means but the application of various partial and select operations of *Verkehrung*, Reversal, and Negation. There is no other way of making the *I* function qua being-in-the-world, in its relationship with the world, than to pass via grammatical structure, which is nothing else but the essence of the id.

The path that lies ahead of me is sizeable enough for me not to be minded to redo this lesson on the id. I will have to make do with underscoring a pertinent remark from Freud in his analysis of *Ein Kind ist geschlagen* which is in agreement, and not by accident, with my defining the id as all that is *not-I*, as all the rest of the grammatical structure. Freud notes that the subject, the *Ich*, the *I*, is always excluded as such from the fantasy. It does have its place in the reconstruction we make of the fantasy, in the *Bedeutung* that we will give it, and in the necessary interpretation, to wit that, at some moment, the subject has to be the one who is being beaten. But Freud tells us that this phase is never avowed in the wording of the fantasy, and for good reason.

We can only account for this in marking out the dividing line between two complements, the *I* of *beat* on the one hand, this being what he is as a refusal of Being, and, on the other, what remains as an articulation of thinking and which is the grammatical structure of the sentence. This only takes on its full scope and interest, of course, when brought in line with the other element of the alternative, namely that which will be lost therein. The truth of alienation shows through only in the lost part, which is nothing else, if you follow my articulation, but *I am not*.

I am not is the crux of what is involved in the unconscious. Indeed, all that arises from the unconscious is characterised by a feature that one only among Freud's disciples managed to maintain as an essential trait, namely *surprise*. This surprise, such as it appears at the level of any veritable interpretation and which has to be preserved in its phenomenology as a tell-tale trait, has no other underpinning but the dimension of *I am not*.

This is also why the witticism is the most revealing and the most characteristic of those effects that I have called *the formations of the unconscious*. The laughter at issue there is produced at the level of this *I am not*. Take any example, and to take the first that presents on opening Freud's book on the *Witz*, that of *famillionairely*, isn't it obvious that the derisive effect of what Hirsch-Hyacinth is saying when he says that Salomon Rothschild treats him *quite famillionairely* resonates with the twofold inexistence, of the wealthy man's position insomuch as it is mere make-believe, and of the position of the one who is speaking, who is reduced to a sort of being for whom there is no place anywhere? This is where the effect of derision lies.

But quite to the contrary of what was going on when we were defining the id, and in which you were able to recognise, in this reference to grammatical structure, that what is at issue is an effect of *Sinn*, of meaning, here we are dealing with *Bedeutung*. Which is to say, there where *I am not*, what is going on needs to be pinned down with the same sort of inversion that guided us earlier. The *I* of *I am not thinking* inverts, and also becomes alienated, in something that is a *think-thing*.

This is what gives its true meaning to what Freud says about the unconscious, which is that it is made up of thing-representations, *Sachvorstellungen*. This is no obstacle at all to its being structured like a language, for it's not about *das Ding*, the ineffable Thing, but rather the part that is perfectly articulated, but insomuch as it prevails, as *Bedeutung*, over anything that can assume an order.

So, how can what is involved in the unconscious be designated with respect to the register of existence and its relation to the *I*? Just as we have seen that the id is a thinking that is bitten into, not by a return of Being, but by a *Being-laid-waste*, so too the inexistence at the level of the unconscious is bitten into by an *I am thinking* which is *not-I*.

I once indicated the fleeting unison of the id with this *I am thinking* that is *not-I* as an *It speaks*. Yet this is a short-circuit and a mistake. The model of the unconscious is undoubtedly an *It speaks*, but on the condition that we take careful note of how here there is no Being. The unconscious has nothing to do with what Plato still, and others further along after him, maintained as being the level of ἐνθουσιασμός. There may be something godly in *It speaks*, but what characterises the function of the unconscious is very precisely that there is no god. If for us the unconscious must be discerned, located and defined, then it is to the extent that the poetry of our century no longer has anything to do with what was the poetry of, for example, the likes of Pindar. If the unconscious has played such a referential role in everything that has been traced out by way of a new poetry then it is very precisely by dint of this relation of a thinking that is nothing but not being the *I* of *I am not thinking*, to the extent that it bites into the field defined by the *I* qua *I am not*.

While just now, in speaking about *It speaks*, I might have given the impression that the id has something that overlaps with the unconscious, what I want now to end on is how precisely they do not overlap.

At the start, on the top right, you will find the two circles, the two fields that we have set in opposition as representing the two terms of *I am not thinking* and *I am not*, thus constituting the contrasting relations of *I* in thinking and in existence.

Only one of these two comes to the access point in the real of alienation – here, on the top left. In a subsequent phase, the operation will come to a close in a fourth term, the quadric term, which will be situated here on the bottom left.

With this quadric term, the circle of *I am not thinking* qua correlate of the id is summoned to conjoin with *I am not* qua correlate of the unconscious, but in such manner that they eclipse one another, they hide one another, by each overlying the other. The id will come to the place of *I am not*, positivising it into an *I am id*. Likewise, in the opposite direction, the unconscious comes to the place of *I am not thinking*.

This *I am id* is nothing but sheer imperative, an imperative which is very properly the one that Freud formulated in *Wo Es war, soll Ich werden*. If this *Wo Es war* is something, then it is what we said earlier. If *Ich soll*, if I must thither, *werden*, come to be, then this means it is not there.

It was not for the mere sake of it that earlier I pointed out the exemplary character of sadomasochism, and you can be sure that the year will not pass without our having to examine more closely what is involved in this position of *I* as essential to the structure of masochism. It will suffice for now that I remind you of the comparison I drew between Sade's ideology and Kant's imperative. The *soll Ich werden* may be just as impracticable as Kantian duty. It is precisely because the *I* is not there that it is summoned there, not, as it has been ridiculously written, in order to dislodge the id, but to lodge there, and, if you will allow me this equivoque, to lodge itself in its logic.

So, conversely, it can also happen that the eclipsing of one circle by the other can happen in the opposite direction. And thus the unconscious in its poetic essence and its essence as *Bedeutung* comes in the stead of this *I am not thinking*. What it then reveals to us is that which in the *Bedeutung* of the unconscious is struck with some kind of obsolescence in thinking.

In the first occultation, in the stead of *I am not* was the revelation of something that is the truth of structure. We shall be seeing what this factor is, and to say it now – it is the object *a*. So too, in the other form of occultation, is a fault-line produced, a rift in thinking, a hole in the *Bedeutung*, to which we have gained access only after taking the pathway of the process of alienation which was plotted out in full by Freud. The meaning of this process of alienation, what it reveals, is the incapacity of any *Bedeutung* to cover what is involved in sex. What is manifested here is nothing else but the essence of castration, to wit that sexual difference is sustained only by the *Bedeutung* of something that lacks, in the guise of the phallus.

I shall therefore have set out for you today the outline, the apparatus, around which we are going to be able to pose anew a certain number of questions. Might you have managed to catch a glimpse of the privileged role that the object *a* plays in this as an operator? It is the sole element that has remained hidden in today's explication.

11 January 1967

VII

FROM THINKING TO THE UNTHINKABLE

The Other and the grounding of mathematical truth
I am not thinking and the id
The unconscious and I am not
Phallic signification makes its appearance
The truth operation

Today I will be coming back to the operation that last time I introduced under the name *alienation*, to spell it out once again and more emphatically still, because the use I am making of it transforms the way it has hitherto been used.

In what I have been expounding for you, alienation is the pivotal point in virtue of which can and must be preserved the value of what, from the angle of the Freudian instauration of the subject, may be called the decisive step in Freud's thought. Further still, the praxis that is maintained with his patronage under the name *psychoanalysis* has carried this through in a way that, once brought to our consideration, is equally decisive.

We will be speaking about a thinking that is *not-I*, which is how on a first vague approach the unconscious presents. Though this wording is certainly insufficient, it does have the merit of placing the term *I* at the fulcrum of what Freud produces for us as decisive.

This does not, of course, allow us to content ourselves with so vague a wording, even if it is poetic – and which, moreover, is never extracted from its poetical context without a little misuse – as is advanced in *Je est un autre*. To say *I is an other* is not to say everything, and does not exempt us from the necessity of supplying a more precise logical articulation.

1

The function of the Other, which as you know I write with a capital A [for *Autre*], is the determining function without which it is impossible to articulate the logic of thinking such as is established in the Freudian experience.

Without bringing into play this function of the Other, it is likewise impossible to comprehend anything of the step that, in the philosophical tradition such as it came down to us prior to Freud, the fact of placing the function of the subject at the heart of the reflection represents.

The Other, bearing the mark of this capital A, is defined as what takes on the function of being the locus of speech. What does this mean? We never return to this often enough, even though I do believe I've been banging on about it a fair bit.

When Freud tells us about this thinking that is *not-I*, for instance at the level of what he calls dream thoughts, *Traumgedanken*, he seems to be telling us that this thinking remains singularly independent of any logic. He first emphasises how the system of these thoughts is not bothered by any contradiction, but more than one feature is spelt out. Those who say, from a first approach, that negation as such can never be represented therein, nor causal articulation, subordination and conditionality, seem to be avoiding what in these thoughts appears to link up in a chain, only to be found again in its main thread along the paths of the freest association. I remind you of this because for many it is still the commonplace preconception about what is involved in the realm of the unconscious.

In fact, to say with regard to the untied link presented by the thoughts that we identify at the level of the unconscious, which are indeed those of a subject or ought to be so, that these thoughts do not follow the laws of logic is merely an initial broaching which presupposes something of an antinomy with a preconceived real. Or rather, it is a preconception about what the relations between any thought and the real ought to be. As for us, we believe that the real, as the right and proper order of any efficacy of thinking, ought to impose itself upon thought. In truth, this is too bound up in a pedagogical logic based on an adaptive scheme for it to be justified by anything other than the fact that Freud, in making this reference, was speaking to minds that had received no other training but what the common run of his audience could receive. Any reflection that reports on how different a subject's relation with the real can be, due to the fact that the subject is established only on the basis of how the powers of language are present in the real and as such exert a hold over it, compels us to carry our examination further.

The step that Freud leads us to take certainly remains no less astonishing and, truth be told, takes on the value of astonishment that it is up to us to hear in it only when we articulate it more precisely with what it recasts in thinking's relations with Being. And this is most surely a theme that has been put on the agenda by the discourse of contemporary philosophers, foremost among whom stands Heidegger.

In all the noise that has arisen around what Heidegger has voiced, it would be most naive, concerning goodness knows what reminder that Being ought itself to be issuing to thinking at the turning point we've reached so that it should break off from what has led it, by following the same thread for some 3,000 years, to goodness knows what deadlock in which it can no longer form any grasp of its own essence – and where it may still be asked, as Heidegger does, *Was heißt Denken?*, *What is called thinking?* – to hope for the overhaul of the word *thinking* only from some kind of trans-metaphysical accident that would amount to a complete upheaval in everything that thought has traced out. This is most certainly not where the sense of Heidegger's text lies.

For those inclined to linger here, we could bring up the funny and derisory metaphor of the girl who knows no better way to offer herself than to spread out on a bed with limbs flailing akimbo, waiting for the initiative to come from him to whom she thinks she is giving herself. This is not so rare a lark in a mediocre period of civilisation, and it is no secret that the one who finds himself faced with this is not for all that especially fired up to perform.

Thinking ought not to be translated into an image of this kind. However, it would be fitting that it should acquiesce to the reminder that true conjugations do not always happen without going to a little trouble.

If what we are brought by the path that Freud plotted has something to contribute to the issue of Being, then it does so not otherwise than by gauging the consequences for thinking that result from what we have called, in keeping with a sort of well-founded historical convention, the Cartesian step. This decisive step, this decisive slicing, confines the instauration of Being per se to the instauration of the *I am* of the *cogito*, in other words, to the *I am* that is implied in the pure functioning of the subject of *I am thinking* as such, in so far as it has the appearance of being transparent to itself, of being what we might call an *am-thought*.

Allow me to use this neologism to translate, or caricaturally to sustain, what is usually called *self-awareness*, a term that resonates poorly and inadequately when put up against the Germanic make-up of the *Selbstbewusstsein*. But likewise, at the level of Descartes and the *cogito*, it is strictly an *am-thought* that is at issue, an *I am thinking* that cannot be situated but at the very moment when it is no longer supported unless by articulating *I am thinking*. It is in the ramifications of what results from this first decisive stride, namely a determined thinking, that Freud's discovery takes up its place.

I spoke of the Other. It is quite clear that, at the level of the Cartesian *cogito*, the consequences of this step are put in the Other's charge. *Cogito ergo sum* is not tenable if it is not complemented by a *sum, ergo Deus est*, which most surely makes matters easier. You can find this writ large in Descartes' *Regulae*, in which the conditions that determined the same in full as thought can so very clearly be read. And yet, even if the articulation of the *cogito* is not tenable as a philosophical articulation, it no less remains that benefit has been obtained from this approach which reduces Being to the slim margin of the thinking being that thinks it can ground itself, from this thought alone, as *I am*.

Something is obtained, then, from this approach, the consequences of which can be read, and furthermore very promptly so, in a series of contradictions. This is the place to emphasise, for instance, that the claimed fundament of simple intuition, which would see the radical distinction between *res extensa* and *res cogitans*, was soon demolished by the Newtonian discovery. It is never underscored often enough that the characteristic that this discovery ascribes to *res extensa* – which Descartes had founded upon an exteriority of one of its parts with respect to the other, upon the fundament of *partes extra partes* – is that in each of its points, so to speak, no mass is unaware of what is going on at that very same instant in all the other points. Scholars at the time, and most especially the Cartesians, found it very hard to accept this evident paradox.

This is a resistance that has not run dry, and in which is demonstrated something that for us is complemented by how the *res cogitans*, such as it impresses itself upon us on the basis of the Freudian experience, is no longer this thing that is always being signalled as an indissoluble unification, but is much rather characterised as being fragmentary and even fragmenting. The *res cogitans* bears within it that same mark which is expanded and in some sense demonstrated across the whole development of modern logic. To wit, what we call *machine* is, in its essential functioning, the closest thing there is to a combinatory of notations. And this notational combinatorics is for us the most precious fruit, and the most indicative, of the development of thought.

Freud brings forward his contribution here by demonstrating what results from the effective functioning of this facet of thinking in its relations, not with the subject of mathematical demonstration, whose essence we will be reminding ourselves of presently, but with the one that Kant called the *pathological subject*, that is to say, the subject who can feel pathos from this sort of thinking. The subject suffers from thinking insomuch as, says Freud, he represses it. The fragmentary and fragmenting character of repressed thought is what we are taught on a daily basis from our experience in psychoanalysis.

It follows that it is a coarse and dishonest mythology to presentify, as the core of our experience, goodness knows what yearning for a primitive unity, for a pure and simple pulsation of gratification in a relation with the Other which here is the only one who counts, and who is illustrated, who is represented, as the Other of a nursing relation. The next move, which if I may say so is yet more outrageous than the first and which is inevitably what has been voiced long-windedly in the new-fangled psychoanalytic theory, is the conflation of this nursing Other with the sexual Other.

There is truly no salvation for Freud's thought, no possible preservation of the truth it ushers in, nor even any technical integrity, unless one steps away from this shoddy lure and the disgraceful misuse it represents. It is a sort of backwards pedagogy, a deliberate employment of capture by a sort of illusion, which is especially untenable for anyone who casts a steady gaze over what goes on in the psychoanalytic experience. Restoring the Other in its only valid status, which is that of the locus of speech, is the necessary point of departure for each item in our analytic experience to take up its rightful place once more.

To define the Other as the locus of speech is to say that it is nothing else but the locus in which an assertion is posited as truthful. By like token, it means that the Other has no other kind of existence. But since saying so is to call upon the Other to situate this truth, it makes it rear its head again each time I speak. And this is why, ultimately, I cannot *say* that it doesn't have any kind of existence, but I can *write* it. Furthermore, this is why I write S, signifier of the barred Other, S ($\bar{A}$), as constituting one of the nodal points of the network around which is articulated the whole dialectic of desire insomuch as it is hollowed out from the interval between statement and enunciation.

There is no shortfall, no reduction to goodness knows what gratuitous gesture, in affirming that this written notation, S ($\bar{A}$), plays a pivotal role for our thought. Indeed, what is called mathematical truth has no other fundament but the recourse to the Other, to the extent that those to whom I'm here speaking are being asked to refer to it in order to see there the inscription of the signs of our initial conventions, so far as what I've been handling in mathematics is concerned.

Mathematics is very precisely what Sir Bertrand Russell, an expert on the subject, made so bold as to designate in the following terms – that *we never know what we are talking about, nor whether what we are saying is true.* And indeed, why not? Yet, in a certain field that corresponds to a limited use of certain signs, it is incontestable that, having spoken, I can write and maintain what I have written. Recourse to the Other is nothing else but this.

If I am unable at each phase of mathematical reasoning to perform this back-and-forth movement between what I am articulating through my discourse and what I am inscribing as having been established, then there is no possible progression of what is called mathematical truth. In this lies the entire essence of what is known as *proof* in mathematics, and what is at issue here belongs to precisely the same order.

In any effect of thought, recourse to the Other is absolutely decisive. Not only does the *I am* of the Cartesian *I am thinking* not avoid it, but it is grounded therein even prior to being compelled to place this Other at a level of divine essence. Already, just to obtain the *therefore* of the *I am* from the interlocutor, this Other is called upon directly. Descartes defers to this Other, to the reference to this locus as a locus of speech, for a discourse that appeals for consent to do what I'm doing right now in front of you. *In exhorting me to doubt, you will not deny that I am.* From this stage forth, the argument is an ontological one.

While Descartes' reasoning doesn't have the cutting edge of Saint Anselm's argument, and while it is more sober, it is not without consequence, the very same consequence that results from having to write, with a signifier, that this Other is nothing else but this.

It is to this consequence that we are coming now.

2

I asked you to refer over the holidays to a particular chapter in Saint Anselm. So as not to leave this matter up in the air, I will remind you how this famous argument runs, an argument that has been unjustly disparaged and which is firmly cut out to provide the function of this Other with its proper contours.

Contrary to what the textbooks say, on no account does the argument bear on the idea that the most perfect essence would imply existence.

Take a look at Chapter II of the *Fides quærens intellectum*. It spells out the argument in addressing *the fool*, the one who, according to the Scriptures, *hath said in his heart, There is no God*. The argument consists in telling him – *Fool, it all depends on what you call God, and as it is quite clear that you have called God the most perfect being, you don't know what you are saying. I, Saint Anselm, know full well that it is not enough that the idea of the most perfect being should exist as an idea for this being to exist. Yet, if you consider that you may rightly hold this idea, and you say that this being does not exist, what would you look like if, perchance, it were to exist? The idea you have formed of the most perfect being is an inadequate idea, because it is sundered from the following – that this being can exist and, qua existent, it is more perfect than an idea which does not imply existence.*

In short, this is, from a certain critical bias, a demonstration of the feebleness of thought, of the inoperancy of thinking, in the one who is voicing something about thought. It is a matter of demonstrating to him that in voicing something about thought, he doesn't know what he's saying. This is why what has to be looked at again lies elsewhere, at the level of the standing of this Other where I not only *can* but *cannot do otherwise* than establish myself each time something is articulated that belongs to the field of speech.

As one of my friends recently wrote, no one believes in this Other. In our times, from the most devout to the most libertine – supposing this term still to carry some currency – everyone's an atheist. Philosophically speaking, anything that would be founded on any form of the existence of this Other is untenable. This is why the scope of *I am* consecutive to *I am thinking* boils down to the following – that this *I am thinking* makes sense, but in exactly the same way that any old nonsense makes sense.

I have already taught you that anything you may voice, so long as it is maintained in a certain grammatical form – need I go back over *Colourless greens ideas...?* – makes sense. This means nothing more than that, on this basis, I cannot go further. In other words, the strict consideration of the logical scope entailed in any language operation is affirmed in what amounts to the fundamental and certain effect of alienation. Alienation doesn't at all mean that we defer to the Other. On the contrary, it means that we perceive the obsolescence of everything that is grounded on this recourse to the Other alone.

All that can endure of this is what grounds the path of mathematical proof from recursive reasoning. It is a reasoning of the kind – if we can prove that something holds true for the integer n, then it also holds for $n - 1$. It suffices to know what is involved for $n = 1$ to be able to affirm that the same holds true for the whole series of

From thinking to the unthinkable 103

integers. And then? This does not entail in and of itself any other consequence than the nature of a truth such as the one that just now I pinpointed with Bertrand Russell's assessment.

For us, insomuch as something reveals to us the truth that lies hidden behind this consequence, we have no cause to recoil from the following crucial point. The status of thought, to the extent that alienation becomes a reality therein as the Other's downfall, is composed of what, in this white field at the top left of the rectangle, corresponds to the status of the *I* that is articulated from an *I am not thinking* which is not only proud but even glories in this affirmation. In view of which, what completes it is what I have designated as the id, the Freudian *Es*. I spelt this out last time as a complement, but one which comes from the part that has fallen away in this alienation, namely what comes to it from the locus of the Other that has disappeared. What remains is *not-I*, which I designated as grammatical structure.

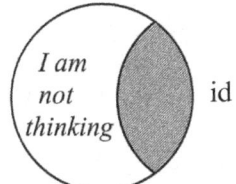

I am not thinking / The *Es*

Conceiving of this in this way is certainly not the prerogative of a Freudian. Read the *Tractatus Logico-Philosophicus*. Don't believe that the step that Mr Wittgenstein took amounts to nothing, just because a whole school of thought that calls itself Logical Positivism keeps harping on about a whole heap of the most insipid and mediocre anti-philosophical considerations. Wittgenstein's attempt to articulate what results from a consideration of logic such that it can bypass any existence of the subject deserves to be followed in detail, and I recommend reading his book.

For us Freudians on the other hand, what the grammatical structure of language represents is exactly the same thing that leads Freud, when he wants to spell out the drive, not to be able to proceed otherwise than by way of grammatical structure, which alone provides the complete and ordered field to what, in point of fact, when he speaks about the drive, comes to dominate – I mean, when he puts together the only two examples that function as drives as such, namely the scoptophilic drive and the sadomasochistic drive.

Only in a world of language can *I want to see* take on its dominant function, leaving open whence and wherefore I am regarded. Only in a world of language, as I pointed out in passing last time, does *A child is being beaten* carry its pivotal value. Only in a world of language does the subject of action elicit the question that sustains him, namely *for whom does he act?*

Doubtless nothing can be said about what is involved in such structures. Our experience affirms that, in giving their law to the function of desire, it is they that are dominant, and not what lurks around goodness knows where, backstage of the analytic assembly, namely a drive that is said to be genital, which anyone would be quite incapable of defining as such. So, nothing can be said of these structures, unless to repeat the grammatical articulations in which they are constituted, that is to say, to expose in the sentences which underpin them what will be able to be deduced from the diverse ways in which the subject will lodge within them. Nothing, I repeat, can be said thereof, except what we do in fact hear, namely the subject in his complaint.

To the extent that the subject cannot get his bearings in this, the desire that is founded therein holds for him the ambiguous value of being a desire that he cannot take upon himself, that he can want only in spite of himself. It is in order to revisit this point that we have been spelling out everything that we have to work through together here. It is indeed because this is how it is, and because we have dared to say so, that needs must examine the point of departure of this discourse.

Well, this point of departure is the following. There is a point of experience from which we can behold the truth of what I shall call the obscurities, the constrictions, the deadlocks of the subjective situation, in this strange instance, the ultimate mainspring of which is to be grounded in the status of language. It is to be found at the level where thinking exists as – *it is* not-I *that is doing the thinking*.

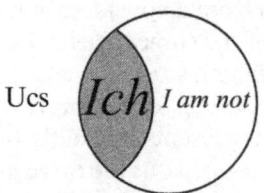

The unconscious / I am not

This thinking, which has the status of unconscious thoughts, is supported here by this little shuttling in the lower right corner of the diagram. The status peculiar to this thinking is that it implies that it can neither say *therefore I am* nor even utter the *therefore I am not* which, even so, does complete it and is its virtual status at the level of the Other. For it is here and here alone that the Other maintains its agency, and this is where the *I* as such comes effectively to be inscribed only with an *I am not*.

This *I am not* is supported by as many others as there are to constitute a dream. Freud tells us that dreams are essentially egoistic and that in everything which a dream presents to us we have to recognise the instance of the *Ich* beneath a mask. But this also means that, in so far as it is not articulated there as *Ich*, it is only present there if it masks itself. This is why the place of all the dream thoughts is marked by this grey area on the left of *I am not*, where it is designated that the *Ich* as such, the *I*, is to be found, as Freud indicates, in each of these thoughts.

How is the *Ich* spread right across what Freud calls the *Trauminhalt*, namely the set of signifiers from which a dream is constituted by means of the various mechanisms of the unconscious, such as condensation and displacement, *Verdichtung* and *Verschiebung*? To say that it is in all of them is to say that it is completely dispersed. What does this mean? And what status is left to the thoughts that constitute the unconscious? Well, Freud tells us that they are the signs whereby each thing – in the sense I said last time, of items, the things one meets, *Sache* – plays one upon the other, sending each to the next, playing out this function which, in the psychoanalytic operation, makes us lose a certain amount of time in their abundance, as though in an orderless world.

Whatever those who have lately been reading me for the first time might say, and who are stunned that I have been saying for so many years that the unconscious is structured like a language, at the beginning of the chapter on *Die Traumarbeit* in the *Traumdeutung*, Freud spells out plainly that *Der Trauminhalt*, the dream content, is set out, *ist gleichsam*, as it were in a pictographic script – this designates hieroglyphic script – the characters of which have to be *zu übertragen*, translated one by one, *in die Sprache der Traumgedanken*, into the language of the dream thoughts. The ensuing sentence on the *Zeichenbeziehung*, their symbolic relation, and then on the comparison with a rebus, on the fact that a picture-puzzle can be understood only when it is read and spelt out, because otherwise it is absurd to see an image composed of a house with a boat on its roof, or of a running figure with an apostrophe for a head – all this carries meaning only in a language.

This is what Freud spells out, after we have been told that the world of dream thoughts is illogical in nature. I ask you to refer to Freud's text, and not merely to attest for you to what is altogether patent and illustrated in broad terms on every single page, namely that what is being spoken of is never anything else but language. Rather it is so that you can see that what Freud spells out here are all the ways in which the grammatical functions are preserved in the dream world. This world is undoubtedly a world of things, but things that mean something. They are *Bedeutungen*. A rebus does indeed carry meaning. What does Freud do with the images comprised by the picture-puzzle? He shows us how the distortions of these images designate the index that allows us to recover in their sequence all the grammatical functions that were eliminated at the start.

Read the vast chapter VI on *Die Traumarbeit*. He shows us how the relation between a subordinate clause and a main clause is expressed. He shows us how a causal relation is expressed, and also how the form of negation makes its re-entrance. And most especially, you will find things that have an obvious kinship with the scheme I have been setting out for you here, like the function of *either . . . or . . .*, which serves, says Freud, to express a conjunction, because one cannot do so otherwise. When you look closely, you will find exactly what I said to you – *either . . . or . . .*, suspended between two negations, has the same value as the negation of the conjunction.

The material I've been laying out here will surely strike you as standing a little more at the forefront in its results than what Freud gives you, but he tells you quite enough to prompt you to take the same route. Just take the Secerno dream, the one where you are requested to close *the* eyes or *an* eye, and you will see what it signifies. One cannot have at the same time *one* eye open and *both* eyes open. It's not the same thing.

In sum, Freud is here plotting out the path to a logic of dream thoughts.

As such, this requires the support of the locus of the Other, and this locus can be articulated only by way of a *therefore I am not*.

It is in this respect that the whole chapter, to speak of this chapter alone, prepares for us, and grounds the legitimacy of, the logic of the fantasy.

3

A brief aside now, inspired by this *therefore I am not*.

At the level of this function, we find ourselves suspended from a *Thou art not, therefore I am not*. Doesn't this tickle your ears in a certain way? Don't we have here the language, I would say the most inopportune language, of love itself? Does the meaning of this need

to be pressed further, so far as the following, which gives it its truth?
– *Thou art but what I am.*

Everyone knows and is able to recognise that if this wording, *Thou art not, therefore I am not*, is indeed what gives the sense of love, then in its turmoil and in its naive rush, as in many of its discourses, love does not commend itself as a function of thinking.

If it is from such a formulation that emerges the monster whose effects in everyday life we are well acquainted with, then this is very precisely to the extent that the truth of *Thou art not, therefore I am not* is rejected in love. As I state with respect to any *Verwerfung*, and this is indeed yet another illustration of it, love manifests itself in the real by the most incommodious and the most depressive of effects. The ways of love are nowhere else to be designated as so easily plottable.

In Descartes' time, these ways were, of course, unknown to no one. We were in the era of Angelus Silesius, who dared to say to God – *Were I not here, well, Thee God, qua existent, Thou wouldst neither be here*. We can project ourselves back into such an era in order to gauge what is creating a deadlock in our own time.

Let's come back to what Freud tells us in carrying further the examination of his logic.

If you still harbour the faintest doubt about the nature of this subversion, which makes the *Bedeutung* – in so far as we grasp it at the moments of its distortion, its twisting as such, its amputation and even its excision – the mainspring that can allow us to recognise in dreams the re-established function of logic, you will doubtless see this doubt evaporating when you see how Freud reintegrates into dreams everything that becomes apparent in them in the way of judgements, both when these judgements are internal to the dream experience and, even more so, when they present as apparent judgements on waking.

When an obscure patch, an interruption, a *Lücke*, a lacuna – as I used to say at the time when I was reporting on these lacunae – an *Unterbrechung*, a break, is revealed in the dreamer's telling of the dream, it is to be restored as part of the dream text. To allow you to grasp what this designates it will be enough for me to take up the example that Freud gives us.

I was going into the Volksgarten Restaurant with Fräulein K... then came, says the dreamer, a *dunkle Stelle*, the passage about which he has nothing to say. He no longer remembers. And so to resume – *then I found myself in the salon of a brothel, in dem ich zwei oder drei Frauen sehe, where I saw two or three women, one of them in her chemise and drawers.*

The analysis is as follows. Fräulein K. was the daughter of his former boss. The circumstance in which he had got to speak with her is altogether distinctive and he describes it in these terms – *we did as it were acknowledge our sexuality, man sich gleichsam in seiner Geschlechtlichkeit erkannte, as much as to say, Ich bin ein Mann und du ein Weib, I am a man and you are a woman.*

Here we have precisely why Fräulien K. was chosen to constitute the dream's opening, but also, no doubt, to determine the syncope. For what is about to follow in the dream is exactly what will disturb this fine relation so full of certainty between man and woman. To wit, the three people who for him are tied to the memory of the restaurant, and who also represent the three whom he meets in the brothel's reception room, are his sister, his brother-in-law's sister, and his sister-in-law, three women with whom it cannot be said that his relations were marked by any frank and direct sexual approach.

In other words, Freud demonstrates for us the following strict correlation – a syncope in the *Trauminhalt*, a lack of signifiers, always occurs whenever is broached in language, and not merely in the mirage of looking each other in the eye, anything whatsoever that would bring into question what has to do with relations of sex per se. The original logical sense of castration, to the extent that analysis uncovered its dimension, lies in how at the level of *Bedeutungen*, significations, language, insomuch as this is what structures the subject as such, very certainly falls short with respect to the relation between the sexes, reducing it to what we can designate as best we can by this thing to which language reduces sexual polarity, namely *having or not having* the phallic connotation.

This is very precisely what is represented, and represented alone, by the effect of analysis.

No approach to castration as such is possible for a human subject unless within a renewal, at another level, separated by the full height of the rectangle which I have drawn out here, of the function that earlier I called alienation. I remind you that this alienation is where the function of the Other intervenes as such insomuch as we must mark it as barred.

This is precisely where analysis, through its work, comes to invert this relation. Having turned everything that belonged to the order of the subject in its *I am not* into an empty field, a non-identifiable subject, this field will come to be filled in, here, in the bottom left-hand corner.

From thinking to the unthinkable

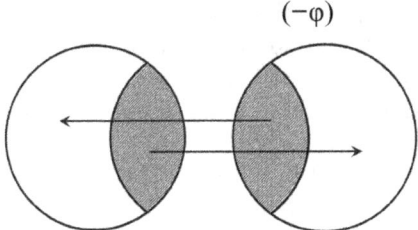

This is where, conversely, the $(-\varphi)$ of the failing in the articulation of sexual *Bedeutung* makes its appearance. I titled the lecture that I gave in German on the signification of the phallus, *Die Bedeutung des phallus*. It is on this basis that the question must be posed as to what distances the two equally alienating operations – that of pure and simple logical alienation and that of the re-reading of the same alienating necessity in the *Bedeutung* of unconscious thoughts. You can see that, though they do seem the same, they have a different result, and the whole distance that lies between one and the other consists in their fields of departure.

They are reconstructed from the fields of departure on the top right, on the basis of which I have designated the underpinning of the whole logical operation, namely the choice that is offered of *Either I am not thinking or I am not*, this being the true sense of the Cartesian *cogito*.

The operation leads, on the top left, to an *I am not thinking* and to the underpinning of everything that makes the human subject submit, most especially, to the two drives that I have designated as scoptophilic and sadomasochistic.

Something else is manifested on the basis of sexuality, down here on the bottom right, on the basis of unconscious thoughts. This is very precisely the meaning of Freud's discovery, but it is also what designates the radical incompatibility between thought and the reality of sex.

The question is not to get past what in this is unthinkable – unthinkable and yet salubrious. Herein lies the whole spirit of why Freud clung so essentially to the sexual theory of libido. One has to read, from Jung's shamanic pen, his stupor, his indignation, upon receiving from Freud's lips something that seemed to the latter to constitute goodness knows what utterly anti-scientific stance. Freud tells him – *Above all else, my dear Jung, promise me never to abandon this theory. But why?* Jung asks him. *As a bulwark*, says Freud, *against the* Schlammflut, *the black tide of mud of occultism*. Freud knew full well what was entailed by the fact of not having touched the limit which is here so precisely designated. It's a limit that doubtless constitutes the essence of language, in the fact that, to the extent that the fundament of sex is perhaps most deeply tied to the essence of death, language does not dominate what is involved in sexual reality. Such is the sober lesson that Freud teaches us.

But then, why are there two paths, two points of access? Undoubtedly there is something that deserves a name in the operation we have been speaking about, the operation that makes us pass from the level of unconscious thought to this logical and theoretical status. And, conversely, in the operation that makes us pass from the status of the subject qua subject of the scoptophilic and sadomasochistic drives to the status of the analysed subject, in so far as for him this carries the meaning of the castration function. We call this operation the *truth operation*, because, like truth itself, which gives whispered prompts, it becomes a reality wherever it wants to, whenever it speaks.

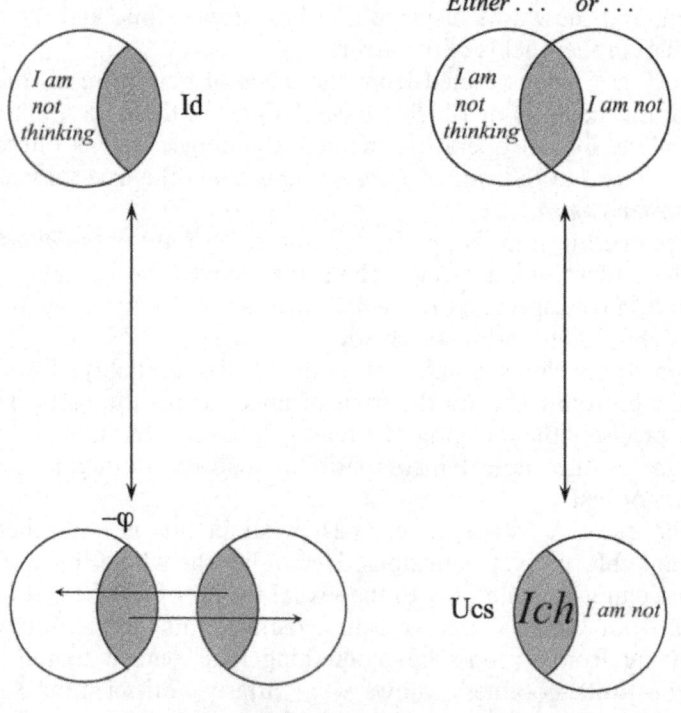

Truth operation

This, which has been linked to the discovery, to the irruption, of the unconscious, to the return of the repressed, allows us to conceive of how we are able to find again the instance of castration in the kernel-object, the core-object, around which the status of the grammatical subject turns.

This can be designated and translated on the basis of this nook, which has been obtained from the fact that language is, in its very status, antipathetic, so to speak, to sexual reality.

This is none other than the locus of the operation that is going to enable us to define the function of the object a in its logical status.

18 January 1967

VIII

I AND *a*

The Other is marked
Critique of representation
The vigilant agency in dreams
The *I* as stain and picture
Cogito ergo Es

Last time I left you having made a first round of the rectangle to which we will be referring again as a suggestive support with respect to the grounding of what we're trying to build this year in the way of a logic of the fantasy.

The choice set out at the start of the development of these logical operations is the sort of altogether special alternative that I have been trying to spell out under the name, which is proper to it, of *alienation*.

The choice is between *I am not thinking* and *I am not*, with what this entails by a way of a forced choice, because it heads on its own account to *I am not thinking*.

We have surely covered enough ground to know now how the analytic reference to the discovery of the unconscious is situated, to the extent that this discovery imparts the truth of this alienation. And it has already been amply indicated that what supports this truth goes by the name, which has been many times repeated for you, of the object *a*.

Certainly, all of this is possible only because I've been speaking about this object long enough for it to be able already to represent some support for you. Yet the special articulation that it has with this logic has still not been pushed to its end. Far from it.

At the end of our last appointment, I simply wanted to point out that castration is surely not unrelated to this object.

1

Castration represents the following. The object *a* as cause of desire dominates everything that it is possible for the subject to discern as a field, as a prehension, as a grasp, of what is called, strictly speaking, in man's essence, *desire*. Needless to say, *man's essence* is a Spinozian reference and I am not granting any further accentuation to the term *man* than I would normally give it. Castration represents how this desire, insomuch as it is limited to this causation by the object *a*, is exactly the same point that necessitates that, at the level of sexuality, desire is represented by the mark of a lack. Everything in sexual relations such as they are produced in speaking beings originates in castration and is arranged around its sign, namely the phallus, in so far as it represents the possibility of an object that is wanting.

Castration is therefore something like an awakening to how sexuality – I mean, everything thereof which becomes a reality in a psychical event – bears the mark of a lack.

For example, such a sign can arise from how the Other, the Other of the inaugural experience in the child's life, must at some moment appear as castrated.

This Other, which we designate in analytic vocabulary as *the Mother* and which supports the first apprehension of castration, is not to be taken purely and simply as the personage who is tasked with sundry functions in a certain typified relation at the origin of the little human's life, because it also bears the most profound relation to the Other that is brought into question at the origin of the entire logical operation I have been expounding. The regular correlative horror that arises upon discovering that the Other is castrated leads us to the heart of what is at issue with regard to the subject's relation to the Other, in so far as it is grounded therein.

Such as it is lived through, such as it is operative, in everything that we can plot out in our analytic experience, sexuality is something that on this point represents fundamentally a self-defence against following up on the truth that there is no Other.

This is what I have to comment on for you today. While I have taken the inroad of the philosophical tradition to announce that this Other doesn't exist, and to bring up in this connection the atheist correlation that professing this entails, this does not of course mean that we can stop here. We need to go further into the thrust of the question of what is meant by the fall of A, designated by the S of barred A, $S(\bar{A})$, which we posit as the term that is logically equivalent to the inaugural choice of alienation. Such a fall can only afflict what stands here in A.

If A is not, we posit that there is no locus where the truth constituted by speech can be secured. It's not that words are empty, but rather, should it be said instead that words have no place that justifies their being called into question, again in accordance with the common consciousness of how, so people say, *they are only words*, then what does the formulation S(A̶) bring in addition? What is brought by this formulation which I have given you as the key that allows us to set off with a sure step, and which we can keep up at some length in elaborating the logic of the fantasy? Well, if I am using a mathematical-type algorithm to support this S(A̶), it is most surely in order to assert that there is another sense, a deeper meaning, to be uncovered. Is it the case that, if truly, as I say, modern consciousness, be it the consciousness of the religious or of those who are not, is on the whole atheistic, the mere assertion that this A doesn't exist would only amount to something like blowing out a shadow? Isn't there something else at issue behind this?

There are many ways of perceiving that, indeed, something else is at stake. What is meant by A being marked by a bar? Well, I have just said it. There's no need to go hunting any further. It is marked. The Other to whom it was so essential for Descartes to refer, and which enabled us to take our first sure step, the Other that Pascal called the *God of philosophers*, the Other that is indeed so necessary for the construction of any philosophy and which is even to be found among the mystics who were contemporary with that same stage of a reflecting upon this theme of the Other – isn't this Other characterised essentially as not bearing this mark? Negative theology. And what is meant by the perfection of the Other invoked in the ontological argument, if not precisely that no mark makes a dent in it?

In this sense, the symbol S(A̶) means that we can reason our experience only on the basis of this – that the Other is marked. Indeed this is what is at issue right back at the first approach to the primeval castration that strikes the maternal being. The Other is marked. We perceive this very quickly, from tiny little signs. Before I proclaim here in the way of a lecturer – which is always to abuse a little the credibility of the role of the one teaching – what is involved in this marked Other, we might try to see it in these little signs, which can be seen in what one does when one translates.

If I were speaking in German, you might enquire as to how I would translate *l'Autre* – a question I've been harping on about for many a year. *Das Anderes* or *der Andere*? You can see the difficulty that arises. It's not due, as people say, to the fact that German is one of those languages in which the neuter would constitute unmarked gender. That's quite absurd. The notion of gender is not to be conflated with the masculine/feminine bipolarity. The neuter is also a gender and it is marked. What is peculiar to those languages in which it is not marked is that whatever is unmarked can regularly be accommodated under the masculine. This is what allows me to speak about *l'Autre*, in French, without you having to wonder whether it would be translated as *das Anderes* or *der Andere*.

I would have to talk to an English-speaker – and there is no shortage of them in my audience, but I haven't had the time – about the wherefore of drawing the translation over to one side or another. I was able to perceive this while preparing my recent talk for Baltimore. It seems that it is not self-evident to translate it as *the Other* in English. I imagine that this is due to the altogether different value of the definite article *the*. In order to speak about this Other, my Other, I had to use [the English term] *Otherness*. It was again a matter of going in the direction of the unmarked. We took the path that we could, in English. We leant towards an uncertain quality. Otherness is something that essentially shrinks away. Wherever we meet it, it will always be otherwise. I cannot say that I am altogether comfortable with finding in *Otherness* a representative of the sense I wish to give to *l'Autre*, and nor were those who suggested this translation to me. Yet in itself this is quite significant enough with regard to what is at issue, and very precisely with regard to the aversion that there is to introducing the function of the mark into the category of the Other.

When you are dealing with *the God of Abraham, of Isaac and of Jacob*, well, there you don't have to go without this mark. This is precisely why it is not self-evident, and why those who deal with this sort of Other, directly, personally, collectively or bodily, have a destiny that is, for them too, thoroughly marked.

For the few youngsters in this tribe that has gathered around me, I had envisaged doing them the favour of clarifying a little the question concerning their relation with the Name, the God of the unutterable Name, the one that is expressed in the register of the *I*, it has to be said. Not *I am the one who is*, which is the feeble transposition of a Plotinian thinking, but, quite simply, *I AM THAT I AM*. As I said, and I will be coming back to this again, I thought of doing them this favour, but we won't be going any further so long as I haven't taken up once more the question of the Name-of-the-Father. I have spoken of the youngsters, but there are also most certainly the elders, the Jewish elders who have no need of me when it comes to facing up to their God.

We here, however, are dealing with the Other qua field of truth. And whether we like it or not, as philosophers, this Other is marked from the very first approach by castration.

This is what we are dealing with today, and against which, once analysis exists, nothing can prevail.

2

This is why I consider that, on a certain terrain, there is every reason to break off.

With respect to certain speculations, one ought not to allow oneself to give in to the penchant, not of judging, as has been imputed to me, but simply of going in search of what these speculations attest to unwittingly, namely the truth that is wanting in them.

What's the point in flagging this in the thought of one contemporary philosopher or another? That at some such point something should come to take the place of a lack, and which is expressed more or less awkwardly, like *non-thetic self-consciousness*, there is really nothing to say about it, unless to note that it is not an *Unsinn*, because an *Unsinn* is not *nothing with respect to Sinn*. Rather, as we know, *non-thetic self-consciousness* is, properly speaking, *sinnlos*.

This is still to say too much, because it amounts to conceding that this point could be the mark of the locus itself, which would be this something that is being indicated as lacking. Yet it is nowhere. It lies in nothing of the like. It is not in the unthinkable anteriority of what is established as the point of the *Selbstbewusstsein* that we should seek out the nodal point which for us, from the position at which we have placed ourselves, would be the turning point where the locus of the *cogito* could be found again. It is necessary to define this point, because it is findable, as you are about to see.

It is no small matter, however, that the Other should reappear in such a speculation, to the extent that I'm bringing it up. I am speaking about it in order to show how, even in the details that are pursued, only a breaking off can correspond to the search that was plotted out beforehand. If I don't want to pin its label on the thinking that I'm bringing up here, this is precisely so as to mark out firmly how what we have to settle decisively along the path of thought could not in any way be authorised by a label, and less so by mine than any other.

Take a look at where this thinking leads us when it's a matter, for example, of the voyeur's befuddlement, the stress that is put on the regard, and this thinking, too, which in order to justify his befuddlement heads in the direction of his surprise when he is caught unawares by the regard of another, the regard of one who just rolls up, who comes out of nowhere, while the voyeur has his eye at the keyhole, such that this regard is already amply evoked by the portentous little noise of the other party arriving.

What is at issue with respect to the status of the voyeur's act is very much something that we have to name thus as a *regard*, but which is to be sought out altogether elsewhere, namely in what the voyeur wants to see. The voyeur misrecognises that what he wants to see is what regards him most intimately, what freezes him in his voyeur's fascination, to the point of making him, too, as inert as a picture.

Without picking up the outline of what I have already developed quite fully enough, I shall say that this radical straying is the same that is expressed in *Huis clos* in the slogan, *Hell is our image infixed forever in the Other*. This is false. If there is a hell somewhere, it's in *I*.

Moreover, there is no bad faith to be invoked in all this straying. *Mala fide* is just as much of an excuse as the apologetic Christian ruse of *bona fide*, designed to tame the sinner's narcissism. There is the right path or there is the wrong path. There is no transition. Any stumbling along the wrong path has no value so long as it has not been analysed, and it cannot be analysed in this instance except from a radically different point of departure, namely the acceptance, at the base and as a first principle, of the unconscious and of the search for what constitutes its status as such.

What makes up for the failing of the *Selbstbewusstsein* could not in any way whatsoever be situated as its own specific impossibility. We have to look elsewhere for its function, if I may say so, since it would not even be the same function.

I have had to tarry a while on this trail – which I am now going to leave behind – because of some confusion in which it seems that it is almost necessary to implicate oneself, because I heard from the lips of analysts that, even so, there was something to be held onto in the reconciliation that some were trying to establish, on the outside, from the appearance of a certain thinking, on the supposed basis of a philosophy that it claimed was being attacked and even subverted. It is most surprising that the possibility of such a reference could even be accepted, and by someone who is an analyst, as one of the possible effects of what on this occasion is called *alienation*. I heard this from the lips of someone who certainly doesn't always go wrong, at a date when I had perhaps not yet made reverberate sufficiently in his ears what is truly involved in what ought to be thought of the term *alienation*.

Alienation has absolutely nothing to do with what results from distortions and losses in communication. I would even say, in the most traditional way, and now that it's been established quite well enough by a thinking which is called Marxist, that it is clear that alienation in the Marxist sense has nothing to do with what is properly speaking mere confusion. Moreover, Marxist alienation in itself doesn't presuppose at all the existence of the Other. It consists simply in my not recognising my labour in this item that I have produced. That this labour of mine should come back to me and that I should have to pay for it at a particular price, has absolutely nothing to do with opinion. No sociological persuasion could modify this in any case whatsoever. It is something that cannot be resolved by any direct dialectic. It presupposes the interplay of all sorts of very real links, should one wish to modify, not the chain, nor the mechanism, which it is impossible to break, but rather its most noxious effects.

The same goes for what is involved in alienation, and this is why what is important in what I'm stating here about alienation derives its contour not from someone or other remaining more or less deaf to what I have been spelling out, but from its effects upon those who comprehend it perfectly, on the sole condition that they be concerned in it in a primary way.

This is why it is at the level of analysts that, over the more advanced items which I have been setting out, I sometimes receive from them the signs of an anxiousness that can extend, let's say, so far as restlessness.

Last time, for example, I formulated in a lateral fashion, designed to offer its veritable clarification to what I was defining as the position of *I am not* qua correlative to the function of the unconscious, the wording which I gave for the truth of what love here allows itself to put into words. *If thou art not, I die*, says love. We are familiar with this cry. And I translate it as, *Thou art nought but what I am*. Freud articulates purely and simply that the fundament of *Verliebtheit*, of love, is the *Lust-Ich*, and that this love is nothing else – for this is asserted by Freud – but the effect of narcissism. To go no further than this remark, which is implied in a certain commandment which I think is not unknown to you, it is in what is most secret to your own self that the mainspring of the love for your neighbour is to be sought. The wording that I have given certainly goes far beyond what it traces out by way of an opening to love, simply in that it indicates that the *Verwerfung* it constitutes arises precisely from this alone – that love does not think. Isn't it strange that such a wording, which immediately appears as infinitely more open, should be able to conjure up in an analytic ear goodness knows what alarm, as though what I was uttering there were derogatory? It was taken as though I were committing some imprudence in allowing myself to come out with a comment, to twenty-five year-olds, that would reduce love to nothing. Oddly enough, from the twenty-five year-olds I received only reactions that were particularly wholesome – to the best of my knowledge, of course, though there are some who come over to confide in me during the week that follows my Seminar. However austere the wording might be, it struck many as salubrious.

What is it, then, that could possibly set the condition for an analyst's disquiet, if not very precisely what I have marked out here in this formulation? –

Thou art ⌒ *but this* ⏋ *which I am*
 ⸝nought⸍_____⌋

The little hook displaces the *nought* by nothing at all. The formulation is no less true than the previous formulation, in so far as it refers us to the key function that, in the status of *I* in *I am*, falls to this little *a* which is, in effect, the whole question. I should like to dwell on this a little further.

Indeed it is conceivable that the function of the *a* concerns the analyst because in the operation of analysis – where the *a* has to be finished off with a signifying tail – it alone allows us to go far enough into thought's relation to Being at the level of the *I* for it to be this that introduces the function of castration. On the path that the analysis plots, the *a* is the analyst. It is because the analyst has to occupy the position of the *a* that, for him, this wording does indeed give rise quite legitimately to the right kind of anxiety – if we remember what I formulated about anxiety, namely that it is *not without object*. It is especially well founded on the side of the analyst in that he is called upon, through the signifying operation that analysis is, to find himself in the stead of this object and thus roused at the very least to take an interest in how he is taking it upon himself.

These are items that are still rather distant from the consideration we might bring to it here. But how could we fail to recognise that there is nothing here that should throw us any further off course than what was worded long ago along the aphoristic short-circuits of a wisdom that, while it has certainly been lost, still retains some echo, in the form of *Tat Tvam Asi, Recognise yourself, Thou art that*.

Of course, from a certain angle of the philosophical tradition, this formulation could only remain opaque. If the *Tat* can in no way be identified with the correlate of representation – wherein, in this tradition, the subject is ever more established – then nothing could be more empty than this formulation. That I should be my representation is something to which one can only too easily point as what has been corrupting the whole modern-day development of a certain thinking under the name of idealism. The status of representation as such needs to be revisited by us. If these words carry a meaning that is called *Structuralism* – I don't want to name any others – even *New Criticism*, they must of course begin by articulating something to do with representation.

Just in opening *Du miel aux cendres*, the latest volume of Claude Lévi-Strauss's *Mythologies*, isn't it clear that the analysis of myths, in the way that it is presented to us, knocks the function of representation completely off its axis? Here we are most surely dealing with dead matter, where there is no longer any relation of *I*. This myth analysis is a game, and a fascinating one. On the very first pages we can see being articulated the relations of honey – which is conceived of as a nourishing substance prepared by non-human others and which dates in some sense from before the distinction between nature and culture – and what operates beyond the raw and the cooked of cuisine, namely what goes up in smoke – tobacco.

From the author's pen we find the remark that, before tobacco came to us, its place had already been prepared by the contrast between ashes and honey. This is a peculiar notation, which he hitches onto certain texts, mediaeval ones, for example. In some sense, the *res meli* had for a long time been lying in wait for the *res tobacco*. Whether or not you follow Claude Lévi-Strauss in his analysis, isn't it cut out to suggest what we are familiar with in the practice of the unconscious, and which impels us to press a little further the critique of what Freud voices with the term *Sachvorstellungen*?

In the idealist perspective, they think that *thing representations* means *things that are represented*. And after all, why wouldn't Freud have written in this sense? But why should we be averse to thinking about the relations of things as supporting representations that belong to the things themselves? Things *signal*, with all the ambiguity that you can read into this term. They signal among themselves. They motion one to the next and await one another, and can be arranged as an order of things. It is most surely upon this that we play each time that, interpreting as analysts, we make something function as *Bedeutung*.

It no less remains that, however amusing the game may be, this is where the trap lies. Nor does analytic work consist in uncovering in the unconscious the latticed weft of ancient myths. On that score, we would always be well served. Whenever it's a matter of *Bedeutung*, we will find whatever might take our fancy by way of structures from the mythical era.

This is why, after a certain while, the game went stale for analysts. They realised that it was too easy. The game isn't easy when it's a matter of attested texts, which have been gathered up, of existent myths that are not just any old myth. But at the level of the unconscious of the subject in analysis, the play of the *I* is far more flexible. Why so? Precisely because it is untethered, because it comes to conjoin with *I am not*. As I said last time, this is sufficiently manifest in those forms in dreams which make the function of *I* omnipresent yet never completely identifiable.

But what ought to be detaining us is something else, namely the holes in this play of the *Bedeutung*. How can it be that no one has noticed, despite its blinding presence, the aspect of bunged *Bedeutung*, as it were, by which is manifested everything that touches on the object *a*?

Of course, analysts do everything to tie it to some primordial function which they imagine to themselves they have grounded in the organism. For example, when it's a matter of the object of the oral drive, this is why they will go on, quite incorrectly, about good milk or bad milk when what is actually at issue is nothing of the sort, since it's a matter of the breast. It is impossible to link milk to an erotic object, the latter being essential to the status of the object *a* such. When it comes to the breast, the objection is not the same, but who cannot see that a breast is something that – have you ever pondered this, my friends – is not representable?

I don't think those for whom a breast can represent an erotic object are much in the minority here, but are you able to define in terms of representation by reason of what this should be so? What, for instance, is a *beautiful breast*? Despite the term being a commonly uttered one, I defy anyone to give any support whatsoever to the term. If there is something that the breast constitutes, then it would require what one apprentice poet from not so far away articulated, towards the end of the little quatrains that he set down, with the words *nuage éblouissant* of breasts. It seems to me that there is no other way but to play on this cloudy register, while adding to it something of the realm of reflections, namely something less graspable still, by which it is possible to support in the *Vorstellung* what is involved in this object that, much rather, has no other status but the one we can name with every opacity in the following terms – *a point of enjoyment*.

But what does this mean? While striving to focus what on this occasion I will call the syncope of the *Bedeutung*, to give you a sense of how this is the point that the *Sinn* comes to fill, it occurred to me all of a sudden that what is most apt to support the role of the breast-object in the fantasy, insomuch as it is truly the specific support of the play of the oral drive, is the formulation I have served up to you umpteen times already to illustrate the purely structural character of *Sinn* – *Colourless green ideas sleep furiously*. These are what breasts are. It seems to me that nothing can better express the special privilege of this object. Nothing could express it in a more adequate way, that is to say, in this instance, a poetic way. On occasion, they sleep furiously, and it is no small matter to wake them. This is what is at issue when it's a matter of breasts.

This is just what it takes to put us on the trail that brings us closer to the question left in suspense as to what might make up for the *Selbstbewusstsein*.

This is none other, of course, than the object *a*. Only, we need to know how to find it where it is.

Knowing its name in advance doesn't mean that we will meet it and, for that matter, meeting it doesn't signify anything, if not some occasion for amusement.

3

If we are taking things up at the level of dreams, what does Freud come to voice on this matter?

We will surely be struck by what he lets slip, so to speak, about a certain vigilance of the subject during sleep.

If the want of the Other is, as I have designated, fundamental to alienation, and if the *I* is nothing more than the opacity of logical structure, and if the intransparency of truth is what sets the style of the Freudian discovery, then isn't it strange to see Freud saying that such and such a dream which contradicts his theory of desire means nothing else here but the desire to prove him wrong?

Isn't this enough to show both the accuracy of the formulation I have spelt out, that *desire is the desire of the Other*, and the abeyance in which the standing of desire is left if this Other can be said not to exist?

Isn't it yet more remarkable to see Freud, at the end of one of the sections in the same Chapter VI to which I paid particular attention last time, specifying that the dreamer arms himself and defends himself most surely with the idea that, *after all, it's only a dream*. In this respect, Freud ventures so far as to insist that there is an agency that always knows – he does indeed say that it *knows* – that the subject is asleep, and that, though this might surprise us, this agency is not the unconscious but rather the preconscious, which in this instance represents, he tells us, the desire to sleep.

This gives us pause to reflect on what happens upon waking, because if, through the intermediary of the sleeping state, the desire to sleep happens to be so complicit with the function of desire as such, insomuch as it stands in opposition to reality, what is it that guarantees that, in emerging from sleep, the subject should be further protected against desire insomuch as it frames what he calls reality? The moment of waking is perhaps only ever a brief instant. A moment when one changes curtain. But let's set aside this first unresolved question. I will be coming back to it, but I just wanted to touch on it, which is why as you can see I've written the word *awakening* on the blackboard.

Let's follow Freud. Dreaming that one is dreaming must be the object of a function, of course, so that we can say that in every instance it designates the imminent approach to reality. Can we not see that, if something can perceive that it is shielding itself with a function of error so as not to identify reality, then we have here, albeit by a path that is exactly the opposite, the assertion that an idea is transparent to itself. Don't we have here the trace of something that deserves to be pursued?

To give you a sense of how to hear this, it seems to me that I can do no better than take the path that is offered by a well-known fable, drawn from an ancient Chinese text, the *Zhuangzi*. Goodness knows what people have read into the poor fellow [whose name is the title of the text], and into this well-known dream in particular. It concerns what he is supposed to have said after dreaming that he was a butterfly. He is said to have questioned his disciples about how to distinguish Zhuangzi dreaming that he is a butterfly from a butterfly which, as fully awake as he believes himself to be, would merely be dreaming that it is Zhuangzi.

Needless to say, this is absolutely not the meaning that is usually given to this text from the *Zhuangzi*. The ensuing sentences show us what is at issue here and where this leads us. They have to do with nothing less than the training of beings, namely those things and those paths that have long eluded us to a very large extent. I mean, with respect to what exactly was thought by those who have left written traces of it.

I am going to allow myself to suppose that this dream was reported inexactly, and that, when he was dreaming that he was a butterfly, Zhuangzi told himself – *This is only a dream*.

This would be in full conformity with his mindset. He doesn't waver for a second in overcoming the trifling problem of his identity as Zhuangzi. He tells himself, *This is only a dream*, and it is precisely here that he misses reality. He misses reality to the extent that something that is the *I* of Zhuangzi resides in this, which is so essential to any condition of the subject, namely that the object is in view.

Nothing better enables us to overcome what is so treacherous about this world of vision, which is presumed to support this kind of resembling, whether you call it *the world* or *res extensa*, of which the subject is supposedly the only support and sole mode of existence. What is it that forms the consistency of the subject qua seeing subject? That is to say, in so far as he possesses only the geometry of vision, in so far as he can say to the Other, *This is on the right, This is on the left, This is inside, This is outside.* What is it that enables him to situate himself as *I*, if not that, as I have already underscored, he is himself a picture in the visible world?

Here, *butterfly* is nothing else but what designates him as a stain in the world. And I already underscored in its time what is originative about the stain in its appearance at the level of the organism for something that will form vision. It is indeed insomuch as the *I* itself is a stain on a ground that what he will question of what he beholds is equally what he cannot find again and which shrinks away, namely this point of origin of the regard – which is so much more tangible and manifest, in being articulated for us, than the light of the sun when it comes to inaugurating what belongs to the realm of *I* in the scoptophilic relationship. *I am only dreaming* is precisely what masks over the reality of the regard, in so far as it is there for the uncovering.

This is the point to which I wanted to bring you today with this reminder of the function of the object *a* and its strict correlation with the *I*.

However, whatever the link might be that is supported, that is indicated, as a frame, by the *I* of all the fantasies, we are unable as yet to grasp in a multiplicity of these objects what gives the object *a* this special privilege in the status of *I* insomuch as it posits itself as desire.

There is only what we are enabled to designate, to inscribe, in a more precise fashion, by calling upon repetition.

The trait by which the subject is secured is drawn in the field of repetition. If, in relation to this field, the subject can inscribe himself into it in a certain relation of loss, then it's because this field possesses a structure, which is, let's say, the one we have put forward with the term *topology*. We have already made a rigorous approach to what is meant by the object *a* in the image of something that can be cut up into certain privileged surfaces in such a manner as to allow something to fall away. This falling object detained us, and we gave an image of it in a small surface fragment, but this was still a crude and inadequate representation.

Neither the notion of surface, nor the notion of the effect of the trait and the cut, are to be brushed aside, but we cannot content ourselves with the shape of some shred or other, however suitable it might appear as an image when likened to what is utilised in analytic discourse under the term *part object*.

I and *a* 125

The surface we have defined is not to be considered from the spatial angle, but rather as something whose every point attests to a structure that cannot be excluded from it. I mean that, in each point, it is in so far as we manage to articulate certain transecting effects that we come to be acquainted with something, in these fading points, which we can describe as objects *a*.

25 January 1967

NEXT SESSION

Questions for Jakobson

I thank you for having shown up in such large numbers today when this is, as no one can ignore, a day of industrial action. I thank you all the more in that I also have to apologise to some of you because it is certainly on account of my recent announcement that I would be holding what is called my Seminar that a portion of those who are here are here.

I did indeed intend to hold it, and to hold it on the humorous theme I've written up here, *cogito ergo Es*, at the top of these white sheets of paper I'm using to compensate for the poor lighting on the blackboard. As you may have gathered from the different coloured pen, this *Es* is a play on words. It plays on the approximate homophony between the Latin *es* and the German *Es*, the latter designating what you know in Freud, namely what has been translated into French by the function of the *Ça* [the id].

Cogito ergo 'Es'

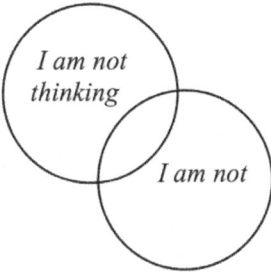

A logic – which is not a logic, which is a wholly unprecedented logic, a logical layout which I didn't want to name until it was established because, even though I have a layout right in front of me that seems to me to be valid, it still struck me as more suitable to wait until I had developed it sufficiently before designating it – a logic, then – with a curious point of departure wrought from this alienating choice that is put to you, between *I am not thinking* and *I am not* – one can all the same wonder what the place might be, on account of the fact that we are here, for something that could fairly be called, *We are thinking*.

This would already lead us quite far because, on the paths along which I've been moving, which are those of the barred Other, this *we* does most surely pose a question, as you can sense. Be that as it may, my producing something that really does look like it is drawing you onto the pathways of thought is certainly not without constituting the motivation for such a large audience. The status of thought would at the very least deserve to be indicated as forming a question, on the basis of such premises. Today, however, I shall be confining myself to the following. Like any man who applies himself, who imagines in any case that he is applying himself, to this operation of thinking, I am a firm friend of order, and one of the most essential fundaments of our order, of the existing order – this is always the only one to which one can refer – is industrial action. As the whole of the public service is on strike today, which unfortunately I found out a little late, I have no intention of being an exception to it. This is why I won't be giving today the lesson you might have been expecting, and not in particular on this *cogito ergo Es*, save from having announced it as such.

However, I am not sorry to be here, and for a good reason, perhaps the very reason that blinded me, a little longer than should have been the case, to the fact that it would be better for me not to be giving my lesson, namely the presence in our midst today of Professor Roman Jakobson, to whom as you know we are indebted with respect to what is being pursued here in the way of teaching.

He arrived in Paris yesterday evening and he is doing me the honour of being my guest. Certainly I was delighted at the prospect of giving my usual lesson in his presence, but he concurs fully with me that it would be better if I didn't do so. At the very least, he has come here, and if someone has a question to ask him, he is quite prepared to reply – an act of courtesy which has nothing to do with our appointment today being maintained.

I am still going to say a few more words to give you time to get your bearings. If anyone has the presence of mind to get a question ready to put to Professor Jakobson, who is here in the front row, they have time while I amuse the gallery and get everyone warmed up. If the question is a veritable question, the reply might on this occasion hold great interest for everyone.

To keep you on tenterhooks, I'm going to indicate down which path we are led by this *cogito ergo Es*. I think you already have a sense of this. What would be the point of your rolling up here so assiduously if you couldn't foresee to what more or less burning moment the next part of our disquisition is leading us?

I had already planned that next Wednesday I would not be holding my Seminar, for personal reasons to do with the Mardi Gras break which this year has been transformed into a fairly long holiday. Please be aware that the next appointment will be on 15 February. I trust that the thread of what is uniting us this year along a single line of attentiveness will not have slackened off too much.

To point up what is at issue in this *cogito ergo Es*, I will say that it's a way of reposing the question of what this famous *Es* is all about, which is not especially self-evident. I even allowed myself to qualify as imbeciles those who happen too easily to get their bearings from seeing in this a sort of other subject and, to say it in full, an ego that would be constituted otherwise, an ego of a suspect quality, an outlaw ego or, as some have put it most crudely, a *bad ego*.

Of course, giving its status to this entity is no straightforward matter. To think that it would be suitable to substantify this *Es* only through what comes to us by an obscure inner thrust does not in any way remove the problem of its status. In truth, if it were this, it would be nothing else but what has always constituted this sort of subject that is called *the ego*, and quite legitimately so. You have a firm sense of how it is on the basis of the barred Other that we are going to have, not to rethink this *Es*, but quite simply to think it through. Now, to the extent that it is our point of departure as the locus in which speech is affirmed, this barred Other very much calls into question the status of the second person.

Since the beginning, a sort of ambiguity has been established by the very necessity of the step that made me introduce, via the path of *Fonction et champ de la parole et du langage*, what is involved with respect to the unconscious. The term *intersubjectivity* surely still lingers, and will long do so, because it is written in black and white in what constitutes the journey of my teaching. Yet, while I did employ the term, it was never without accompanying it with a few reservations, even if they were reservations that were not intelligible for the audience I had at the time. As everyone knows, this term is only too readily accepted, and of course it is going to remain the fortress of everything I am fighting against in the most precise fashion.

The term *intersubjectivity* harbours a number equivocations in the psychological realm, and foremost among them is one which I have always designated as the most hazardous to underscore, namely the status of reciprocity. This is the bulwark for everything in psychology that has been most forcibly wrought to ensconce every stripe of misrecognition concerning psychical development.

People have set out the status of reciprocity as what marks out the statutory limit at which the subject's maturity is supposed to be developmentally established. Well, to symbolise this for you in a sort of image that is at once resounding and coarse, I shall refer to *The Confusions of Young Törless*. I think there are enough of you here who have seen the film adaptation at the cinema for me to get across what I'm going to say. The rest will have to ask around. I will say that the status of reciprocity is what constitutes the firm seat of the college of professors who do their supervising but don't want to know anything about, or touch on anything to do with, this atrocious story. This is what makes it only more evident that, regarding the shaping of an individual, and most especially a child, the educators, before striving to perceive at what level, at what stage, it would be possible to consider *I* and *you* as reciprocal, they would do better to enquire as to what the best pathways are that might be allowing him to situate himself as being, through his very existence, prey to the fantasies of his young classmates.

Here we have what is clearly at issue in what we are putting forward this year under the heading of the logic of the fantasy, and which brings with it concerns of importance. Of course, this hardly goes in the direction of a solipsism, but precisely in the direction of knowing what is at issue with respect to this big Other whose place has been sustained in the philosophical tradition by the image of this divine Other, the empty Other, whom Pascal designates with the name, *God of philosophers*. We absolutely cannot content ourselves with this any longer, and not for reasons of thought, or freethinking. Freethinking is like free association – let's not breathe another word about it.

I will take advantage of this opportunity to say, and to chase away goodness knows what gadfly whose chosen victim I might happen to be, that Freud's thinking, the thread and trace of which we are here to follow, is not Freud's thinking in the sense that an historian of philosophy might, even with the assistance of the most attentive textual criticism, define it, in the ultimate sense of minimising it, that is to say, in the ultimate sense of pointing out that, on one issue or another, Freud didn't go any further, or imputing to him, at some bend or other in what he set out, goodness knows what fault or loophole or poorly executed reworking. On the contrary, if Freud still exercises a hold over us it's not on account of what he thought as an individual at such and such a bend in the life he effectively led. What interests us is the object he discovered.

The importance that Freud's thinking carries for us hinges on how we can observe that there is no better path for finding again the ridges of this object than to follow its trace in his thinking.

What legitimises the place that we ascribe to it is precisely how, at every instant, these traces do nothing else but mark out for us which object is at issue, and in a way that is all the more rending in that these traces are rent. They lead us back to what is at stake, and what it at stake is not to misrecognise it. In the current state of things, to misrecognise it is surely the irresistible and natural tendency of any constituted subjectivity.

This is indeed what intensifies the drama with what is known as research. You also know that for me the status of research is not entirely free from suspicion. We are about to come back to this, and I think that next time we will be able to pose the question of the status that we can give to the word *research*, behind which the greatest bad faith commonly takes shelter. What is research? Well, surely nothing more than what we can ground as the radical origin of Freud's step with respect to his object. Nothing will furnish us with the status of research if not what appears as the irreducible point of departure of the Freudian innovation, namely *repetition*. This research is in some way itself repeated by the question that is raised by what I will call our relations, the relations between you and me, namely what is involved in this teaching.

This teaching does indeed suppose that there are subjects for whom the new status of the subject that is implied in the Freudian object has been realised, in other words, that there are analysts, that is to say, subjects who could sustain in themselves something that approaches as close as it can this new status of the subject that is required by the existence and the discovery of the Freudian object. These are subjects who would be equal to the fact that the Other, the traditional big Other, does not exist and that, even so, there is indeed a *Bedeutung*. This *Bedeutung* has no other name but the one I'm pinning on it here, and which shall suffice for all those who have followed me closely enough for the words that I use to have a meaning, namely *structure*, insomuch as it is real.

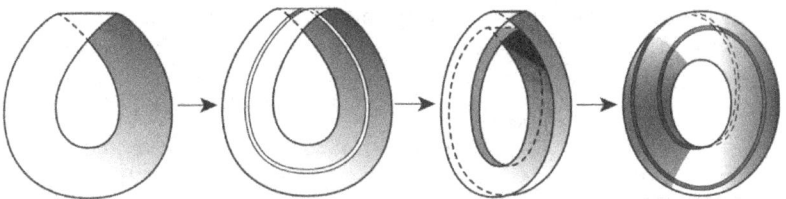

From the Möbius band to the torus

My lesson today was supposed to be running through these little images I've spread out here. You will recognise once again the

Möbius band. Once the band is cut in two, in so far as it doesn't separate but rather slips over itself in some manner, doubling itself in the smoothest of fashions, as you can observe if you manage to copy down correctly what I've taken the trouble to sketch out, there obtains in the end something that is perfectly closed, which has a within and a without, and which is this fourth figure up here, that of a torus. Structure is about how something like this is real.

I'm not saying that this, all by itself, is structure. I'm saying that what is real under the name of structure is exactly of the nature of what is drawn out here, and that there is in some way a structural substance. This is not a metaphor. To the extent that something is possible through this, which we can bring together as a set of cuts, what we are dealing with exists.

What about a teaching which also supposes the existence of what most surely does not exist? For, as yet, there is to all appearances no analyst who could support in himself this position of the subject. And this leads to nothing less than the posing of the question – *what is it that authorises me to take the floor as though to address these as yet non-existent subjects?* You can see that things are not without being supported, as has been noted with a snigger, by a few suppositions, about which the least one may say is that they are dramatic. This is not, however, to turn all this into a psychodrama, because we have to close it with a logical closure. This is our object for the year.

It still remains that, whatever it might be that does authorise me – and perhaps we will be able to say a little more on this matter – it is quite clear that I am not alone.

If I myself had to put a question to Professor Roman Jakobson – I give my word that I gave him no inkling of this on our way here in the car, and it's not that this is occurring to me just now but rather that it's just now that it has occurred to me to put it to him – I would ask him whether he too, whose teaching on language has been of such consequence for us, thinks that this teaching is of such a nature as to require a radical change of position at the level of what constitutes, let's say, *the subject*, among those who follow him.

I would also ask him another, but this is a most *ad hominem* question. I don't want to use any big words, and I'm steering clear of words that can suggest the ambiguity that attaches to the word *askesis*, or even to the word that lingers around in science-fiction novels – *mutation*. We are certainly not at the level of this poppycock. It's a matter of the logical subject and what it entails by way of discipline in the thinking of those who are introduced into this position by their thinking. My question for Professor Jakobson would pertain to whether for him, in the consequences of what he teaches, things reach this far. Does the word *disciple* have a meaning for him?

I would say that for me it doesn't have any. Quite rightfully, any such meaning is literally dissolved, evaporated, by the mode of relation that such thinking establishes. *Disciple* can be distinguished from the word *discipline*. If we are inaugurating a discipline which is also a new era in thinking, something distinguishes us from those who came before us in that our speech does not require any disciples.

If Roman might care to begin by responding to me, should he so wish, then please go ahead.

R. JAKOBSON – *Do you think, perhaps, that it might be better if several questions were to be posed and I respond to them all together?*

Quite so. Who has a question for Roman Jakobson?
(The professor fields questions from, in turn, Luce Irigaray, Jean Oury, Lucien Mélèze and Stoïan Stoïanoff-Nenoff.)

R. JAKOBSON – *There remains the question from my friend, whom I admire so very much and whose work is always a source of instruction for me, such that I feel myself to be – to use Dr Lacan's word – his disciple. Even so, I must say that I find it very hard to reply to his question. I should like him to rephrase it in a more succinct manner, otherwise it would necessitate a response as voluminous as his recent book. Or else I will promise him that I shall answer this question on my next visit to Paris.*

Do you think that, to take any linguist among your pupils, a deep training in the linguistic discipline generates in them a mark such that their way of broaching all manner of issues, including moral issues, bears an absolutely original stamp? Second, given that you are the one who transmits this sort of discipline, precisely because it is not just any discipline but the one that stands closest to our own, that of the psychoanalysts, is it the case that the mode of relating that the fact of being the one who transmits this discipline gives rise to on your side is such that there is a dimension of what it means to be a disciple? And is this something that is essential, something requisite, something which matters to you?

R. JAKOBSON – *I must say that I could reply to this question in the same way that I replied to the question about the issue of the difference between the grammatical structures of diverse languages. That is to say, it's possible for a linguist to try, at certain moments, to stop being merely a linguist and to see the issues from another side, from another angle, that of a psychologist, that of an anthropologist, that of a biologist, and so forth. All of this is possible, but the pressure of the discipline is enormous.*

What is the mental type of linguists? Curiously enough, becoming a linguist is something that almost never happens. Psychologists have shown that mathematics, music, linguistics, and so on, are passions, prepossessions, capacities, which appear at a very early age, in childhood. If you read the biographies of linguists, you can see that they are already predisposed to become linguists at six, seven, eight years of age. This was Saussure's life, and the life of a number of linguists.

What does this mean? Well, I will allow myself to say that the vast majority of children know very well how to draw and paint, but at a certain age the majority of them lose this capacity, while those who become painters maintain a particular childhood acquisition, a particular childhood trait. Linguists are people who have maintained a particular attitude towards language since childhood. A tongue interests a linguist just as it interests a child. It becomes for him, so to speak, the most essential phenomenon in a complexity of threads and it enables a linguist to see very sharply the inner relations, the structural laws, of a tongue. But there is a danger, too, that the relation between what amounts to language and other phenomena can be easily twisted, due to the somewhat overly unilateral emphasis on the tongue. This is where we meet the great necessity of the work that goes by a name that is most ambiguous and altogether vague, but which is also important, that of interdisciplinarity.

I saw from my experiences in New York, from my contact with psychoanalysts and with an anthropologist like Lévi-Strauss, that when I and some other linguists discussed our issues together, it was important to become for a moment the disciple of other disciplines, so that a language can be beheld from the outside, like the earth can be beheld from without by sending up a Sputnik.

I won't take the floor again after Roman Jakobson except to thank him on behalf of everyone, and to repeat these thanks that you have just given him with your applause.

And so, I will say – until 15 February.

1 February 1967

IX

ALIENATION AND REPETITION

> Repetition, memory, recurrence
> Loss, regression, demand
> Alienation, *passage à l'acte*, acting out
> Topology of the act

I need to press on, and to demonstrate in the same move what the nature of analytic knowledge is – very exactly, how it comes about that this knowledge passes into the real.

We are positing that analytic knowledge passes all the more into the real commensurate with the ever growing claim from the *I* in asserting itself as the *fons et origo* of Being.

This is what we have posited. But, of course, this elucidates nothing about what I have just called the passing of this knowledge into the real. I'm alluding here to nothing else but the formulation I gave for *Verwerfung*, or rejection, which is that anything that is rejected from the symbolic reappears in the real.

There is a prevalence of the *I* at the height of something that it is quite hard to grasp without giving rise to misunderstanding. To say *the age*, or even, as we have said, *the era* of science is always to open up some leeway for a hint of something that could be pinpointed fairly well with the term *Spenglerism*, for instance. The idea of human phases is certainly not something we can settle for, and it gives rise to a great many misunderstandings. Let's take as our sole point of departure the following – that it is true that discourse has its empire, and I think I have demonstrated that psychoanalysis is thinkable only in counting the discourse of science among its precedents. It's a matter of finding out where it positions itself in the effects of this discourse. Is it inside? Is it outside?

As you know, we have been trying to grasp it here as a sort of quivering fringe, something analogous to those most tangible forms in which the organism reveals itself. Even so, there is a step to be taken before recognising in this the lineament of the animate because thinking, as we understand it, is not animate. It is the effect of the signifier, which is to say, ultimately, the effect of the trace. What we call structure is this. We track thought in its traces and in nothing else, because the trace is invariably what has caused the thought.

One can get an immediate sense of how this way of proceeding relates to psychoanalysis, so long as one is able to imagine it, or indeed to have some experience of it. What I defended was that Freud, when inventing psychoanalysis, did so by introducing a method for detecting a thought-trace right where thought itself masks over it by recognising itself therein in a different way – a way that is different from how the trace designates it. No deployment of Freudism as an ideology – naturalist ideology, for instance – will ever prevail over this.

That such a stance – which is a stance of the history of philosophy – should have of late been pushed to the fore by people who authorise themselves in the occupation of psychoanalyst is indicative of what lends greater precision to the response necessitated by the question I posed at the start, about how it comes about that analytic knowledge should come to pass into the real.

So, oddly enough, the path by which what I have been teaching passes into the real is none other than *Verwerfung*, the effective rejection of the psychoanalyst's position, which we can see occurring at a certain generational level insomuch as this generation doesn't want to know anything about what nevertheless constitutes its only knowledge. What is rejected from the symbolic must be focused somewhere in a subjective field, to reappear at a correlative level in the real. Where? Doubtless, right here. What does that mean? This *here* touches you. And what vouches for this point is what the journalists have already identified under the label of *Structuralism*. It's a matter of nothing less than your interest, the interest you take in what's being said here, an interest that is real.

Naturally, there are psychoanalysts among you, and there is this generation – it is already here – of psychoanalysts in whom will be embodied the correct position of the subject, insomuch as this is necessitated by the analytic act. When this generation has reached its maturity, it will be possible to measure the distance travelled – on reading those unthinkable items, fortunately in print so that they will bear witness, for whoever knows how to read, to the prejudices from which the outline necessitated by this actualisation of analysis will have had to be extricated.

Among these prejudices and these unthinkable items, there will stand Structuralism, too. I mean, what now goes by this name with a certain value set by the markets of cogitation.

If those of you who lived through what was characteristic of the first part of this century – the ordeals we went through of outlandish manifestations in civilisation – had not been sent to sleep thereafter by a philosophy that quite simply went on with its noise-making, I would now have less of an avocation to try to mark out those lineaments that are necessary for you not to be completely out of your depth for the phase of the century that is now to ensue.

1

It is in his own *Jenseits*, in *Beyond the Pleasure Principle*, that Freud introduces for the first time the two concepts of repetition, *Wiederholung*, and compulsion, *Zwang*, which combine in compulsive repetition, *Wiederholungszwang*.

When he introduces this in order to give the subject of the unconscious its definitive status, does one measure the full scope of this conceptual intrusion?

It is called *Beyond the Pleasure Principle* precisely because it breaks away from what had hitherto supplied the model of psychical functioning, namely the homeostasis that echoes the one necessitated by the substance of the organism, which duplicates and repeats, and which is the one that, in the nervous apparatus isolated as such, Freud defines as the law of the lowest tension.

What is introduced by *Wiederholungszwang* stands in stark contrast to the original law set out in the pleasure principle and this is how Freud presents it to us. We who have read the text, I assume, can go straight to its furthest extreme, which Freud formulates as the *Todestrieb*, the death drive. This means that he cannot stop there and must extend the *Zwang*, the pressure to repeat, to a field that doesn't merely envelope that of living manifestation but exceeds it, thus to include it in the parenthesis of a return to the inanimate. He appeals to us, therefore, to allow to subsist as *living* – and we really must put this term in inverted commas here – a tendency that extends its law beyond the duration of the living.

Let's take a closer look at this because, so long as the matter has not been understood, this is what becomes the obstacle that draws a prompt objection from a line of thinking accustomed to providing the term *tendency* with the very support I have just mentioned, when putting inverted commas around the word *living*. In Freud's thinking, life is therefore no longer, to cite Bichat, *the full set of forces that resist death*, but rather the full set of forces wherein is signified that, for life, death is its rail.

In truth, this would not lead very far were it not a matter of something else besides the entity of life. Indeed, what is at issue is what we might on a first approach call its *sense*, that is to say, something that we can read in signs that possess an apparent vital spontaneity, because the subject doesn't recognise himself in this, yet there does indeed have to be a subject, for what is at stake can on no account be a mere effect of fallout from the bursting of the vital bubble, leaving the place in the state it was in before. It must instead be something that, wherever we follow it, is formulated not as a mere return but as a return thought, as a repetition-thought.

Where in everything that Freud tracked so closely in his clinical experience was this problem to rear its head? Well, in what he calls the *negative therapeutic reaction*, or again in what he broaches at this level as a fact – with a question mark – of *primary masochism*, as that which insists in a subject's life in such a way as to remain in a certain medium ... let's say, to get things straight, of illness or failure. This is what we have to grasp in a repetition-thought.

A repetition-thought has to do with a domain that is different from that of memory. Memory does most surely evoke the trace as well, but what is it that allows us to recognise a memory trace if not precisely its effect of non-repetition? If we seek to determine experimentally how a microorganism is endowed with memory, we will see it in how it doesn't react to a stimulant the same way the second time as the first. This is also what leads us sometimes to speak of memory – with care, with attention, and with suspicion – in respect of certain inanimate organisations. But repetition is something quite different.

If we make repetition the guiding principle of a field, insomuch as repetition is strictly subjective, we cannot fail to formulate what unites the identical and the different in the manner of a copula. To this end, we are again compelled to employ the unary trait, the elective function of which we acknowledged in connection with identification.

I'll go over the crux of the matter in straightforward terms, having been made aware that such a simple function can appear astonishing in a setting that comprises philosophers, or self-professed philosophers. This was an experience I had recently. They found obscure, and even opaque, the very simple remark that the unary trait plays the role of a symbolic marker precisely on account of how the principle of differentiation is based neither on similitude nor even on difference.

I have already underlined quite amply here that the use of the countable *one*, as distinct from the unifying *one*, is that it may function by designating as so many *ones* such heteroclite objects as a thought, a veil, and any other object that might be lying about here in easy reach. And since I have listed three of them, the count is 3. It entails that even their most extreme difference should be taken as null and that their differentiation should be established by something else. Here we have what yields us the function of number and everything that is established through the recurrence operation. As you know, the proof of recurrence is drawn from this model alone – that what is true of $n + 1$ is true of n. It suffices for us to know what is involved for $n = 1$ for the truth of the theorem to be secured. This founds a being of truth that is through and through one of slippage. This sort of truth is, if I may say so, the shadow of number. It remains without any purchase on any real whatsoever.

But if we now go back in time, into what is being asked of you here today, so as to take up again the identificatory schema of alienation and to see how it functions, we will notice that the basal 1 of the operation of recurrence is not *already there*, because it is established only by the repetition itself.

2

Let's start over.

Repetition cannot be deduced dynamically from the pleasure principle.

We are taking note of this only to give you a sense of the contours of what is at issue, namely that maintaining the lowest degree of tension does not on any account imply repetition. On the contrary, finding again a situation of pleasure in its sameness can only be the source of operations that are invariably more costly than simply following the way of the least tension.

Following this like an isothermal line, if I can express it thus, will lead, from one situation of pleasure to the next, to the desired maintaining of the least tension. Should this imply some looping back, some return, this can only be along the path, so to speak, of an external structure. This is scarcely unthinkable, because I mentioned just now the existence of an isothermal line.

However, it is not at all in this way, on the outside, that the existence of the *Zwang* is implicated in the *Wiederholung*, in Freud's repetition.

A situation that repeats, like a situation of failure for example, implies coordinates not of a waxing and waning of tension but of signifying identity, of plus or minus as signs of what must be repeated. Yet this sign was not borne as such by the initial situation. You can understand very well that this situation is not marked by the sign of repetition, otherwise it would not be the first. Further still, it has to be said that it becomes the repeated situation, and that by this very fact it is lost as an originary situation. Something is lost through the very fact of repetition.

Not only is this spelt out perfectly by Freud, but he voiced it long before having been led to state the beyond of the pleasure principle. Back in the *Three Essays on Sexuality*, we can see the principle of re-finding looming up as impossible. That the metabolism of the drives should comprise as such the function of the lost object is something that the mere approach of clinical experience had already prompted Freud to uncover. It furnishes the very sense of what emerges under the heading of the *Urverdrängung*. This is why it has to be acknowledged that, far from there being a jump and a break here in Freud's thinking, there is rather a preparative, by means of a glimpsed signification, to a notion that finds at last its final logical status in the shape of a law that is constituent, even though not reflexive, of the subject himself, and this is repetition.

I think that you have all seen the graph, if it can be put thus, doing the rounds in the shape I gave it.

I furnished this topology of return with the said shape as an intuitive, imaginative support, so that it should unite the part, which is just as important as its directive effect, to this effect that is itself imaged, namely its retroactive effect. As I have just said, what is at issue here is what happens when, through the effect of a repeat, what was there for the repeating becomes the repeated. The line by which what is repeated sustains itself, qua repeating, must loop back to find again at the point of origin the line that, by this very fact, thenceforth marks the repeated as such.

This outline is none other than that of the double loop, or else what I called, when I first introduced it here, the inverted 8.

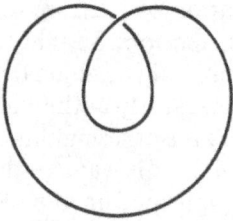

The inverted 8

Here you have it, coming back on what it repeats. The first, fundamental, operation, the initiator as such of the repetition, yields this retroactive effect which cannot be detached from it.

This effect compels us to entertain a third relation, which from 1 to the 2 that constitutes the return comes looping back to the 1 so as to produce this non-numerable element which I have been calling the *one extra*. On account of not being reducible to the series of natural numbers, being neither addible to nor subtractable from the 1 and the 2 that follow on one from the next, it even warrants the title *one-to-spare*. I designated this as essential to any signifying determination and, moreover, as being always ready, not only to appear, but to make itself fleetingly apprehended, detectable in lived experience, as soon as the counting subject has to count himself among others.

We can observe that this is the most radical topological shape and that it is necessary when it comes to introducing what asserts itself in Freud's work in the polymorphic forms with which we are acquainted under the term *regression*. It may take a topographical, temporal or formal shape, for this is not homogeneous regression. The root common to each of these forms is to be found in this return effect of repetition.

It is certainly not without reason that I have put off for so long the examination of these functions of regression. It would suffice to refer to a recent article, *À propos de la régression*, published on neutral ground, in a medical journal, to see the veritable gulf that is left open when a mind that has grown accustomed to too little light tries to coalesce theory with what is intimated to him by psychoanalytic practice. The curious sort of valorisation that regression has been receiving in some of these most recent theoretical studies does doubtless correspond to something in the experience of analysis, whereby the progressive effect that regression comprises does indeed deserve to be examined, it being essential, as everyone knows, to the very process of treatment as such.

But consult this article, which is in the latest issue of *L'Évolution psychiatrique*, and it is enough to see the distance that lies between everything that of Freud's formulations is newly evoked and what is deduced from it when it comes to usage in practice, for one to get a sense of the extent to which the regression involved there is liable to prompt the question as to whether this might amount to anything else but a theoretical regression. In truth, here lies precisely that major mode of rejection which I am designating as essential to a certain present position of psychoanalysts. In taking up such questions again, at their point of origin, as though they had not already been decisively settled elsewhere, they are drawing out the pleasure. And this is certainly not, in this matter, the pleasure of those for whom we have responsibility. I will be coming back to this in due course, because if there is in all these effects something that belongs to the order of clumsiness, this does not for all that remove all reference to something that belongs to the order of dishonesty, should such formulations happen to coalesce with and justify a treatment aim that finds itself covering the ego's coarsest illusions, that is to say, what is most opposed to analytic reform.

What is meant by what we have contributed under the heading of alienation when we start to clarify it with this apparatus of the signifying involution, if I may put it thus, of repetition?

We first asserted that alienation is S(A̸), the signifier of the Other insomuch as it turns the Other into a field marked by the same finitude as the subject. What finitude is at issue here? Well, the same that is defined in the subject by the fact of depending on the effects of the signifier. The Other as such, I mean, this locus of the Other to the extent that it is evoked by the need to secure a truth, is, if you will permit me this word of my own improvising, *fractured*. In the same way that we can grasp this in the subject himself, very precisely in the way that the subject is marked by the topological double loop of repetition, the Other, too, finds itself under the impact of this same finitude.

Division thus finds itself poised at the very heart of the conditions of truth, whence results a complication that carries onto any requirement of a Leibnizian type, of the safeguarding of truth. The *salva veritate* that is so essential to any order of philosophical thought is a little more complicated for us, and not only by the doing of psychoanalysis since it is manifest across all the points of the elaboration that is being carried out at the level of mathematical logic. At any rate, it utterly excludes any form of intuitive absoluteness, for example attributing to the field of the Other the dimension of the Eternal, however Spinozianly qualified you may wish this to be.

This permanent diminishment of the Other is inextirpable from the givens of subjective experience, which is what places at the heart of this experience the phenomenon of belief in its ambiguity, which is constituted by how it is not at all by mishap, nor out of ignorance, that truth should present itself in the dimension of the contestable. This phenomenon should not therefore be regarded as the fact of some failing but as a fact of structure.

It is at this point that we are called upon to proceed with a step that is more careful and more discreet. I mean, a step that is more discerning, in order to designate the substantial point of this structure. Indeed, it's a matter of not giving rise to the confusion people rush into, doubtless not uninnocently, by suggesting here a revamped positivism. We ought much rather to be finding our models in what remains so uncomprehended and yet so vivid about what tradition has passed down to us fragmentarily in the exercises of Scepticism, in so far as they were not simply those sparkling acts of juggling between opposed doctrines but, on the contrary, veritable spiritual exercises which most surely correspond to an ethical praxis that lends its veritable density to what remains under this heading and under this category in the way of theory.

Let's say that what is at issue for us now is to give an account, in the terms of our logic, of the necessary emergence of this locus of the Other insomuch as it is thus divided.

Here we are required to situate not simply this locus of the Other, the one that answers perfectly for truth not being false, but much more precisely how it is possible, across the different levels of subjective experience that clinical practice impresses upon us, that exhortations are inserted into this experience which cannot be articulated otherwise than as the Other's *demand*. This is what neurosis is.

We must not fail at this juncture to speak out against the excessive misuse of certain terms that we have introduced and highlighted, like that of *demand* for example, when we see it being taken up by the pen of some novice or other, and holding some sway over the plane of analytic theory, who insists on marking out how essential it is – here the upstart shows his perspicacity – to place at the centre and at the start of the venture *a demand*, as he puts it, *of current exigency*. In fact, this is what people have always been putting forward, making analysis revolve around the duo of *frustration* and *gratification*. Here, the term *demand*, which has been borrowed from me, is there only to put people off the scent of what makes for the essential part of this, namely that the subject doesn't come into analysis to request anything whatsoever that might arise from a current exigency, but to know what his demand is, which leads him very precisely to the demand that the Other should demand something of him.

The problem of demand is situated at the level of the Other, and the neurotic's desire turns around the Other's demand. The logical problem is to know how we can situate this function of the Other's demand upon the support that the pure and simple Other is, as such, the barred A, $\bar{A}$. A good many further terms are also to be mentioned as having to find their place in the Other, like the Other's anxiety for example, the true root of the position of the subject as a masochistic position. Let's also say how we ought to conceive of a point of enjoyment as being essentially identifiable as the Other's enjoyment.

This is a point without which it is impossible to comprehend what is at issue in perversion, while also being the sole structural referent that can account for what is traditionally apprehended as *Selbstbewusstsein*. Nothing else in the subject really penetrates the self, pierces it as such, but this point of enjoyment that makes for the Other's enjoyment. I will try one day to sketch out for you some childhood model of this.

We mustn't move into these issues with a hurried step. We need today to trace out the lesson to be drawn from the relation that this graph of repetition maintains with what we have punctuated as the fundamental choice of alienation.

3

It is easy to see that the more the double loop clings to itself, the more it will tend to divide. If we suppose that the distance between one edge and another is reduced, it is easy to see that what will come to be isolated are two rings.

What relation is there between this *passage à l'acte* of alienation and repetition itself? Well, very precisely, what one can and must call *act*. What I am going to be putting forward today is what presages a logical situating of the act as such.

This double loop, outlined by repetition, imposes a topology, because it cannot have an edge function on just any surface. Try tracing this out on the surface of a sphere and tell me how you get on. Try making it so that it comes back to here, looping back in such a way that it should form an edge, that is to say, so that it doesn't cross over itself. As I showed you a while ago, it's impossible. One can only loop it back on a certain type of surface, such as the torus, or what I called in its time the cross-cap or the projective plane, or else, thirdly, the Klein bottle. The important thing is to know what in each of these surfaces results from the cut constituted by the double loop and what the structure of the surfaces thus established is. On the torus, this cut will produce a surface with two edges. On the cross-cap, the double loop will produce a cut with just one edge. The most characteristic surface to illustrate for us the function we are giving to the double loop is the Möbius band. As you know, it's a surface with a single edge, and the double loop is the edge in question.

We can take this surface to be symbolic of the subject, on the condition of course that you regard it as being constituted by its edge alone. Indeed, if you make a cut down the middle of the strip, the cut itself will concentrate within itself the essence of the double loop. It is easy to demonstrate that, being a cut that turns back on itself, as it were, it constitutes in and of itself the whole Möbius surface. And the proof of this is that when you have made this median cut, there is no more Möbius surface at all. The median cut has removed it from what you believe you are seeing here in the shape of a surface.

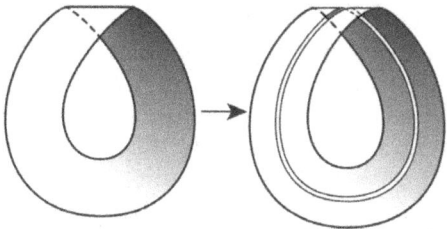

Median cut along the Möbius band

This figure shows you how, once cut down the middle, the surface which previously had no topside or underside, which had but one face just as it had only one edge, now does have a topside and an underside. You just have to imagine that the two colours indicated in the diagram each pass onto the underside of the other, right where, due to the fact of the cut, they are continuous. In other words, after cutting there is no more Möbius surface. There is, however, a surface that can be applied onto a torus.

If you take the surface you have ended up with after cutting, and slide it back on itself, if I can express it thus, you can, by nestling the edge at issue in a different way, constitute a new surface which is that of a torus, upon which the same cut is still marked out, constituted by the fundamental double loop of repetition.

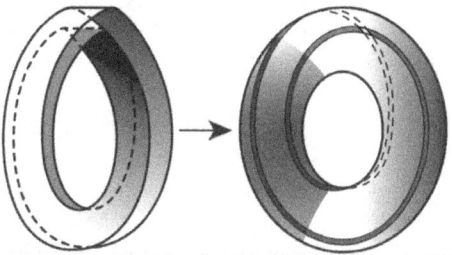

Surface of the cut Möbius band nestled on the surface of a torus

These topological facts are extremely propitious for us when it comes to illustrating the relations of alienation and repetition.

Alienation has been illustrated in the two distinct directions in which two different operations are carried out. One of them represents the necessary choice of *I am not thinking*, with the *Es* of logical structure lopped off. The alternative element, which one cannot choose, faces it and conjoins the kernel of the unconscious – this being something that has nothing to do with a thinking attributable to the *I* instituted as a subjective unit – to an *I am not*. The latter is marked out very well in what I defined in the structure of the dream as an immixing of the subject, namely the unpinnable, indeterminable character of the subject taking upon himself the thinking of the unconscious.

As for repetition, it allows us to bring into correlation two modes in which the subject can appear to be different, in which the subject can be manifest in his temporal conditioning. These correspond to two defined statuses, that of the *I* of alienation and as that which reveals the position of the unconscious in specific conditions which are none other than those of analysis. At the level of the temporal diagram, we find that *passage à l'acte* corresponds to what is allowed in the operation of alienation. Corresponding to the other term, which in principle it is impossible to choose in the alienating alternative, is *acting out*.

What does this tell us? I mean the act, and not some manifestation of movement. *Motor discharge*, as they put it at the theoretical level, in no way suffices to constitute an act. If you will allow me a rough-and-ready image, a reflex is not an act. But actually this zone of *non-act* has to be extended much further. What is solicited in studies on the intelligence of higher animals, *la conduite du détour*, for example the fact that a monkey will realise that he has to take an about path to get hold of a banana on the other side of a pane of glass, has absolutely nothing to do with an act. In truth, as you can well imagine, very many of the movements that you will perform from now until the day is out are a far cry from acts.

How is an act to be defined? It is impossible to do so otherwise than on the basis of the double loop, in other words, on the basis of repetition.

It is in precisely this respect that the act founds the subject. The act is, in and of itself, the equivalent of repetition. It is the very repetition in a single stroke which I designated earlier in the cut that can be made down the middle of the Möbius band. It inheres in itself – the double loop of the signifier. It might even be said – though this would be a mistake – that in its case, the signifier does signify itself. We know that this is impossible. It is none the less true that it's as close as can be to this operation. Let's say that, in the act, the subject is equivalent to his signifier. He remains none the less divided.

Let's try to clarify this a little and position ourselves at the level of this alienation where the *I* is founded by an *I am not thinking* that is all the more propitious in leaving the entire field of the *Es* of logical structure. If *I am* all the more in that *I am not thinking*, I mean, if I am but the *I* established by logical structure, then the medium, the stroke, by which these two terms can be joined is *I act*.

As I have said, this *I act* is not a motor performance. For *I'm walking* to be an act requires the fact that I am walking to signify that I am indeed walking and that I am saying so. There is an intrinsic repetition in any act. It is allowed only by the effect of retroaction that, due to the fact of the signifying impact which lies at its heart, is exerted upon what is called *the case* at issue, whatever it may be.

Of course, it's not enough for me to proclaim that I'm walking. It's the beginning of an action. It's a farcical action – *Marchons, marchons* [in the words of *La Marseillaise* – March on, March on]. It's also what is called, in a particular ideology, *commitment*, which is what lends it its well-known comical character.

The important thing to detect regarding what is involved in the act is to be sought out right where logical structure as such offers up the possibility of transforming into an act what on first approach might be nothing but passion, pure and simple. *I'm falling down*, for example, or *I'm stumbling*.

Reflect on this fact of a signifying doubling. There are two things in my *I'm falling down*. There is the affirmation that I'm falling to the ground, while *I'm falling down* transforms my fall into something signifying. I fall down and thereby perform the act in which I demonstrate that I am, as they say, *down*. Likewise, the fact that I might stumble, which in itself bears so manifestly the passivity of tripping up, can, if it is taken up and doubled with the affirmation *I'm stumbling*, be the indication of an act in so far as I myself take upon myself the meaning, as such, of this stumbling.

There is nothing here that goes against Freud's inspiration, if you would care to recall the page in the *Traumdeutung* on which he designates for us the first lineaments of his research on identification. He underscores, thus legitimating in advance the intrusions I've been making of the Cartesian formulation in the theory of the unconscious, how *Ich* has two different meanings in the single sentence *Wenn* ich *daran denke, was für gesundes Kind* ich *war*. As he puts it very exactly, *I think, I meditate, I reflect upon, I delight in* . . . the thought of *what a healthy child* I *was*.

The essentially signifying character, as such, lies in the doubling of the act. Here, in the repetitive and intrinsic impact of repetition in the act, we have what allows us to coalesce in an original way, and in such a way as to be able thereafter to satisfy the analysis of each of its varieties, the definition of the act.

I can only indicate in passing, because we will have to come back to it, that what is important lies not so much in the defining of the act as in its repercussions. I showed you earlier what results from the impact of the cut along the centreline of the Möbius band, namely a change in the structure of the initial surface. Whether, after the act, the surface has another structure in one case, whether it has yet another structure in another, or whether even, in some cases, it cannot change, each offers us a model for distinguishing what is involved in the impact of the act, not so much in the determination of the subject as in the mutations thereof.

Now, I left to the attempts and gustations of those around me, without responding plainly, the objection that has been raised, and which has been put to me for some time, that *Verleugnung* is the term to which ought rather to be referred those effects that I have been setting aside for *Verwerfung*. I have spoken enough of the latter today not to have to go back over it. As for what belongs to the realm of *Verleugnung*, I will simply point out here that it is invariably what has to do with the ambiguity that results from the effects of the act as such.

I'm crossing the Rubicon. One can do that all on one's own. One just has to get on the right train at Cesena. Once you're on the train, you can't do anything else about it. You're crossing the Rubicon. But it's not an act. Nor is it an act when you cross the Rubicon thinking about Caesar. That is an imitation of Caesar's act. But you can already see how, in the dimension of the act, imitation takes on a quite different structure from the one that is ordinarily supposed of it. It's not an act, but even so it can be one. There is not even any other possible definition for such exorbitant suggestions as those that go by the title *The Imitation of Christ*, for example.

In regard to the act, whether imitation or original – Caesar's historians tell us that the meaning indicated by the dream that preceded the crossing of the Rubicon was none other than that of incest – it's a matter of finding out, at each of these levels, what the effect of the act is. This is the labyrinth proper to the recognition of these effects by a subject who cannot recognise them, because he has been wholly transformed, as a subject, by the act. It is these effects that are being designated whenever the term *Verleugnung* is being rightfully employed.

The act, then, is the only locus at which the signifier has the appearance – the function, in any case – of signifying itself, that is to say, of functioning beyond its possibilities.

In the act, the subject is represented as pure division. Division, we shall say, is his *Repräsentanz*. The true sense of the term *Repräsentanz* is to be taken at this level, because it is on the basis of this representation of the subject as essentially divided that one can have a sense of how the function of *Repräsentanz* can affect what is called *representation*, which makes the *Vorstellung* depend upon an effect of *Repräsentanz*.

The hour is bringing us to a halt. Next time, it will be a question of finding out how it is possible for the element that it is impossible to choose in alienation to be presentified, namely the vertex that corresponds to the conjunction *Unconscious/I am not*. The thing really is well worth the trouble of displacing into a disquisition set aside for this alone, because it's a matter of nothing else but the status of the Other, right where it is evoked for us in the most urgent fashion, which ought not to lead to precipitancy or error, namely the analytic setting.

Let's say, before we take leave of one another and as a parenthesis, that the model that the act provides us with as the division and the last support of the subject is the point of truth that explains the rise of the function of existence to philosophy's summit. This is surely nothing but the veiled form in which the originary character of the act in the function of the subject presents for thought.

But why does this act remain veiled, and in the work of those who best knew how to mark out its autonomy – I'm thinking of Saint Thomas – contra Aristotle, who hadn't the faintest idea of it, and for good reason? It is doubtless because the other possibility of cut is afforded us in the part of alienation that it is impossible to choose, which even so is brought within our reach by means of analysis.

When this cut intervenes, this is what is called *acting out*. We shall be trying to define its status next time.

15 February 1967

SUBJECTIFYING SEX

X

FROM SUBLIMATION TO SEXUAL ACT

Bodily enjoyment is my only good
Repetition, *passage à l'acte*, acting out, sublimation
Verleugnung of the act
Harmonic division
The couple and castration

We will be picking up with a reminder of where we left off – alienation.

Let's summarise the point we've reached, for those who have already heard and above all for the rest.

Alienation, in so far as we have taken it as the point of departure for the logical path that we have been trying to plot this year, is the elimination – to be taken in the proper sense of *expelling over the threshold* – the ordinary elimination of the Other. Over which threshold? The threshold at issue is the one that determines the cut in which the essence of language consists. Linguistics is useful to us, and essentially so, in that it furnishes us with a model of this cut.

This is why we find ourselves placed on the side of linguistics that is approximately qualified as *structuralist*. The developments in linguistics, and most notably and curiously what has been recently designated as *semiology*, are not all of equal interest to us, which might at first blush seem surprising.

So, elimination of the Other. What is meant by the Other qua eliminated as a closed and unified field? It means that we assert, with the best reasons for so doing, that there is no universe of discourse, that there is nothing assumable under this term.

And yet language in its radical practice, which is psychoanalysis ... Note that I could also say *in its medical practice*. Someone, whom I am surprised not to see here today in his usual place, asked me what I might have given in Latin, which is stricter, for *I think*. I'd left it as a riddle. If no one has found it, I shall come out with it today. I had indicated that it could only be conceived in a verb in the middle voice. It's *medeor*, from which comes both the *medicine* I have just mentioned and *meditation*.

Language in its radical practice is integral with something that we will now have to reintegrate, to conceive of in some way, in the mode of an emanation from this field of the Other, once we start having to regard it as disjoined. It is not hard to name this something. It is that from which the field of the Other derives, precariously, its authorisation. It is called – a dimension specific to language – *truth*. In order to situate psychoanalysis, one might say that it comes to be constituted wherever truth gets acknowledged solely in that it surprises us and impresses itself upon us.

Here is an example to illustrate what I have just said.

No enjoyment is given to me, nor givable, but that of my body. This doesn't impose itself right away, but one suspects as much. Thenceforward this enjoyment is indeed my only good, and one sets up around it the protective grating of the law that is said to be universal and which is called *human rights*. No one can stop me from deciding at my own discretion what happens to my body. The result, at the furthest limit, is something on which we other psychoanalysts put a finger or foot – that enjoyment has dried up for everyone. This is the nether side of the little article I came out with under the title *Kant avec Sade*. Obviously it's not spelt out upfront, but on the nether side. It was not for all that less dangerous to say it the way Sade said it, and Sade is all the proof of this one needs. Yet as I was merely explicating Sade, it was less dangerous for me.

Truth manifests itself in an enigmatic way in the symptom. Which is what? A subjective opacity. Let's leave to one side what is clear – namely that the enigma has already something about it that has been resolved, which is that it is just a rebus – and let's base ourselves for a moment on the following, which could be passed over in going too quickly. The subject can be non-transparent. Moreover, *évidence*, what seems evident, can be hollow, and so it would doubtless be better henceforth to revoice the word in the past participle, *évidé*, hollowed out.

The subject is perfectly thing-like. And the worst kind of thing. The Freudian Thing, precisely. As for *évidence*, we know that it's a bubble and that it can be burst. We have already experienced this on several occasions. It is the plane on which modern thought has trodden its path. Marx was the first to set the tone, then Freud. If

From sublimation to sexual act

the status of what Freud contributed is less evidently triumphant it is perhaps precisely because he went further. And one pays for that.

One pays for it, for example, in the thematic that you will find being developed in the two articles I'm bringing to your attention, for your study if you have enough spare time at your disposal for it, because they are going to shape the backdrop against which what I have to put forward here is going to find its place.

1

I'm going to be picking things up where I left them last time.

I'm going to be completing the quadrangle by connecting up to it what I started to plot out around repetition.

Repetition is a temporal locus, in which is agitated what I first hung upon the purely logical terms of alienation across the four poles I punctuated. First, the alienating choice. Next, the establishment of these two poles – the *Es*, the id, and then on the other side, the unconscious. At the fourth of these poles, I put castration. These four terms, which might have left you in a state of suspense, have their correspondents in what I began to articulate for you last time to show the fundamental structure of repetition.

I situate repetition at the top right of the quadrangle. Across from it I put this privileged and exemplary mode of establishing the subject, the *passage à l'acte*. At the third pole I place acting out, which is situated at the elided place where something of the field of the eliminated Other manifests itself, as I have just reminded you, in the form of veridical manifestation. This is, fundamentally, the sense of acting out.

Building the quadrangle of repetition

I ask you simply to be patient in following me because I can only bring in these terms and the structure to which they refer in a headfirst manner, as it were. In wanting to make our way by a progression from, even proceeding by way of a critique of, what has already been sketched out in the theories that have to date been expressed in analysis, we cannot help but get lost, quite literally, in the same labyrinth that these theories constitute. This is not to say, of course, that we would reject their data or their experience, but rather that we would submit what we are bringing in the way of new formulations to the test of seeing whether it might not be precisely our formulations that would allow not only the soundness but also the meaning of what has already been initiated to be narrowed down.

You can already sense the pertinence of foregrounding acting out in this situating of the field of the Other which for us it's a matter of restructuring, so to speak, be it only in that the history of analysis, like the experience such as it is being pursued, indicate to us at the very least a certain overall correspondence between this term and what the analytic experience establishes.

I am not saying that acting out occurs only during the course of analysis. I'm saying that it's from analyses, and from what is produced in them, that the fundamental distinction arises, isolating the act, the *passage à l'acte* – such as it can pose us problems as psychiatrists and be established as an autonomous category – as distinct from acting out. I was therefore simply putting forward a correlate, which links acting out to the symptom as a manifestation of truth. It is certainly not the only one and it requires further conditions. I hope, then, that at least some of you will, in parallel with the remarks that I will be led to put at your disposal, be able to browse through the article by Otto Fenichel from the 1946 *Yearbook of Psychoanalysis*, one of those volumes they started bringing out after the last war. The wording of the title is *Neurotic Acting Out*.

To move on, which term are you going to see being inscribed at the fourth point of support of these operating functions which determine what we have been articulating on the base of repetition? It may well surprise you, though I think I am able to uphold this as fully as possible for your appreciation. It's something that, peculiarly enough, has been left in a certain state of abeyance in analytic theory, which has most surely turned it into the conceptual point around which the most pother and pretence has accrued. To name it, and it is already written up here on the blackboard, it is *sublimation*.

From sublimation to sexual act

Quandrangle of repetition, complete

In this regard, I ask you to consult the 1955 *Notes on the theory of sublimation* by Heinz Hartmann in *The Psychoanalytic Study of the Child*, to seize hold of a typical fruit of the analytic setting as such.

Sublimation is a term that is, I won't say *mediating* because it's not that at all ... but one which allows us to inscribe the basis and conjunction of what is involved in the subjective base insomuch as repetition is its fundamental structure. It entails the essential dimension over which the greatest obscurity still lingers in everything that has thus far been formulated with respect to analysis, namely *satisfaction. Befriedigung*, says Freud. In this you can hear the presence of the term *Friede*, the common sense of which is *peace*. Given the era we live in, this word might not strike you as being all that evident.

What is the satisfaction that Freud conjugates for us as essential to repetition in its most radical form? It is in this mode that he produces for us the function of *Wiederholungszwang*.

Wiederholungszwang not only encompasses the altogether localisable functioning of life under the term of the pleasure principle, but indeed supports this life. We can nowadays allow of everything with regard to this life, up to and including what has become a tangible truth, which is that there is nothing in the material it acts upon that, in the end, is not death. I mean, which is not, in its nature, inanimate. It is nevertheless clear that life will render the material it gathers together unto the domain of the inanimate *only in its own fashion*. This is what Freud tells us. That is to say, life inheres all the while in this satisfaction which entails its passing again and again down the same paths it has already laid out – but how? – vouching most surely for how its essence is to tread them over and again unto death.

Let's be modest. There's a world of difference between this theoretical moment and its verification. Freud is not a biologist. It could lead to disappointment were we to reckon that ascribing the chief place in his thinking to the powers of life would suffice to give rise to anything whatsoever that might resemble the construction of a science that could be called biology. We analysts have contributed nothing at all to anything that even looks like biology.

So, why do we insist so firmly on designating the satisfaction that we are dealing with when repetition is at issue – with all the infelicity and imprudence that the term can entail at the point we've reached in biological research – as *sexual*? Well, designating it as sexual is Freud's bulwark, which I would go so far as to label fideist, to keep back *the black tide of mud* of the thinking he designates as a recourse to occultism. According to Freud, if one doesn't stand firm on this matter, occultism will inevitably ensue, and this was the reason he put to the stupefied Jung.

Does this mean that everything should go so straightforwardly? I mean, do so many assertions suffice to shape an actionable articulation? This is the question I'm trying to put forward today and which is leading me to foreground sublimation as the locus that, having been thus far left abandoned and covered with coarse scribblings, is, even so, the one that is going to allow us to understand what is at issue in the fundamental satisfaction that Freud articulates as a subjective opacity, namely the satisfaction of repetition, this conjunction that is so basal for logic as a whole.

If we are dragging the requirements of logic with us into this marginal locus of thought in which analytic action develops – this shady, twilight zone – what we are being led to do ultimately warrants the label, which I think is the best we can pin on it, of *sublogic*.

2

I'm uttering this term just when it's going to be a matter of fathoming what is involved in sublimation. Even though he didn't develop it at all, and for the same reasons that are necessitating the developments I'm adding, Freud proceeded in accordance with the ordinary mode of his thinking, which consists – as was said by a certain Bossuet, by the first name of Jacques-Bénigne – in keeping a firm grip on both ends of the chain.

First, he asserts that sublimation is *zielgehemmt*, and naturally he doesn't explain to us what that means.

I tried to mark out the distinction that is already inherent in this term by turning to English as a more accessible reference with its differentiation between *aim* and *goal*. Say it in French and it's not so clear, because we are forced to employ words that are already in use in philosophy. There is the word *la fin*, which is the weakest word because the whole pathway has to be integrated back into it, which is what is at issue in *aim, la cible*. It's the same distance that exists in German between *Zweck* and *Ziel*. On no account are we told that the *Zweckmäßigkeit*, the sexual finality, is *gehemmt*, inhibited, in sublimation. What is claimed to be the object of the hallowed genital drive that delights us so, is precisely what can be extracted quite harmlessly from the sexual drive. It can be completely inhibited, absent, in the sexual drive without the drive losing anything of its capacity of *Befriedigung*, of satisfaction.

This is, back at the time of the first appearance of the word *Sublimierung*, how Freud defines it without any equivocation whatsoever. There is *Zielgehemmt* on the one hand, but on the other there is satisfaction that is met without any transformation, displacement, distraction, reaction or defence. This is how Freud introduces the function of sublimation and places it before us.

Heinz Hartmann's article on sublimation, which I referenced earlier, is exemplary of what to our eyes is on no account outmoded in the psychoanalyst's position. His approach to what he is dealing with as a responsibility of thought invariably corners him from one angle or another with one of those two terms that I will designate in the mildest fashion as *banality*. Everyone knows that for a long time now I have designated Fenichel as the most eminent representative of such banality. May he rest in peace. For us his writings have the very high value of being the most scrupulous gathering together of everything that can arise as holes in experience. It simply lacks, in the stead of these holes, the necessary question marks.

As for Hartmann and his way of upholding the problem of sublimation over some fourteen or fifteen pages, I think it cannot escape the notice of anyone who comes to it with an open mind that such a discourse, which I ask you to judge by consulting it where I've sourced it for you, is strictly speaking a mendacious discourse.

The whole apparatus of an ostensible energeticism is proposed, which consists precisely in upending the broaching of the problem, by presenting sublimation first of all as identical and undisplaced in relation to something that, with the inverted commas that this use of the term *drive* calls for, is all the same properly the sexual drive. Through a series of little touches, the article examines what is involved in sublimation as linked to functions of the ego which are posited in the most unwarranted fashion as autonomous, as arising from what in this confusional language is called *non-instinctual sources*. Was it ever a question of that for Freud? All analytic thought rejects any notion that the bare functions of the ego could be bound to a taking measure of reality, producing reality in an essential way and thus re-establishing, at the heart of analytic thought, that there is a relationship of pure thought, a relationship that is isolated, direct, autonomous and identifiable, with a world that it would be capable of broaching without being itself crisscrossed with the function of desire. And so, one wonders how it is that there can arise from elsewhere, from the instinctual source, goodness knows what shine, what tonality, what colouration, which in his text is called *sexualization of ego functions*. Once introduced in this way the question becomes literally insoluble, or at any rate excluded forever from everything that offers itself to the praxis of analysis.

To broach what is involved in sublimation we need to introduce the primary term by virtue of which it is possible for us to orient ourselves in the problem, the same I started from last time when defining the *act*. The act is *signifying*.

3

The act is a signifier that repeats, though this occurs in a single move, for topological reasons that make the existence of the double loop created by a single cut possible.

Second, it sets the subject up as such. That is to say, with a veritable act, the subject emerges as different. Third, owing to the cut, the subject's structure is modified.

Fourth, its correlate of misrecognition, or, more exactly, the limit imposed upon its recognition in the subject, or further, if you wish, its *Repräsentanz* in the *Vorstellung*, is *Verleugnung*, namely that the subject never recognises it in its veritable inaugural scope, even when the subject is, if I may, capable of having committed this act.

Well, it is here that we need to remember the following, which is essential to any understanding of the role that Freud ascribes to sexuality in the unconscious, namely that we speak of a sexual *act*. This might at least suggest to us what is obvious elsewhere, because as soon as one thinks on it, it can be touched right away, namely that the sexual act is not pure and simple copulation. The sexual act possesses every characteristic of the act that I have just called to mind. In the way we handle it, in the way it presents to us with its symptomatic sediment and everything that causes it to get stuck and to stumble, the sexual act does indeed present first and foremost as a signifier. And it presents as a signifier that repeats something, because this is the first thing that was introduced here in psychoanalysis. What does it repeat? Why, the Oedipal scene, of course. It is a curious thing to have to call these things to mind, which constitute the very soul of what I have propounded that ought to be perceived in the analytic experience.

That something should be set up that is without return for the subject is what certain privileged sexual acts, precisely those that are termed *incest*, allow us quite literally to put a finger on. I have enough analytic experience to affirm that a boy who has slept with his mother is not at all a subject like others in analysis. And even if he knows nothing about it himself, this changes nothing in the fact that analytically it's just as palpable as this table in front of me here. His personal *Verleugnung*, the disavowal that he might bring to bear on what possesses the decisive value of a breach, doesn't change anything.

Of course, all this deserves to be substantiated. My assurance is that I have listeners here who have analytic experience and who, were I to say something over-the-top, would start yelling. Believe me, they won't say the contrary because they know it as well as I do. This doesn't mean that people know how to draw lessons from it, for want of knowing how to articulate them. Be that as it may, this might lead us to try to introduce a little logical rigour into it.

The act is founded upon repetition. What, on first approach, could be more welcoming for what is involved in the sexual act? Let's recall the teachings of our holy mother the Church. In principle, one doesn't do such things together, one doesn't get one's leg over, except to bring forth into the world a new little soul. There must be people who think of this when they're at it. This is a supposition. It's not established. It may well be that, however much this thought conforms to Catholic dogma, wherever it occurs it is merely a symptom. This has all it takes to suggest that there might perhaps be some cause to try to tighten up a little the function of reproduction that is lying there, behind the sexual act, and to see from what angle it is admitted, because when we deal with the subject of repetition, we are dealing with signifiers insomuch as they are the precondition of a thought.

The way this biology is going, which we leave so well to its own devices, it is curious to see that the signifier has been rearing its head, right at the root, at the level of chromosomes. For the moment at least, it's teeming with signifiers, the vehicles of highly specified characters. We are told that genes, whether DNA or RNA, are constituted like short, carefully serialised messages which, after being brewed in a certain way in the big urn, spill out goodness knows what, the new breed of zany that the whole family has been expecting to gather around with a cheer.

Is this the level at which the issue comes forward?

It is here that I should like to introduce something which I didn't invent just yesterday.

In a volume that is called my *Écrits*, there is an article that is called *La signification du phallus*, and on page 693, on the tenth line, I write – *le phallus comme signifiant donne la raison du désir (dans l'acceptation où le terme est employé comme moyenne et extrême raison de la division harmonique)* [*the phallus as signifier affords the ratio of desire (in the acceptation where the term is employed as the mean and extreme ratio of harmonic division)*].

I was simply laying down a little white stone designed to tell you that this is what the signification of the phallus is. It's been pinpointed. So, let's try today to put a little order, some measure, into what is at issue in the sexual act insomuch as it relates to the function of repetition.

4

Well, it's blindingly obvious, not that people misrecognise the Oedipus complex, because we've been cognisant of it from the beginning, but that they don't know how to recognise what it means, namely that the product of repetition in the sexual act qua act, that is to say, insomuch as we participate in it as submitted to what it possesses by way of signifier, has its points of impact in the fact that the subject that we are is opaque, in the fact that the subject has an unconscious.

It ought to be noted that the fruit of biological repetition, of reproduction, is already there in this space that is well defined for carrying out the act and which is called a *bed*. The agent of the sexual act knows full well that he is a son, and this is why, in so far as this concerns us psychoanalysts, it was brought back to the Oedipus complex.

Let's try to see what results from this in the signifying terms that are defined by what I have just called *mean and extreme ratio*. Let's suppose that we are going to give this signifying relation the most straightforward support, the same that we have given to the double loop of repetition, a simple line. For yet further ease, let's make the following template. We can form two lengths on this line. We can cut this double loop wherever we like and, once we have cut it, we can try to make use of it. Let's place along it the four points that define the mean and extreme ratio.

From sublimation to sexual act   161

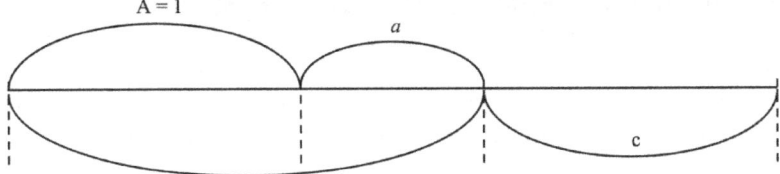

The couple in the sexual act

The lower-case *a* is the lovable product of a previous copulation which, since it happened to be a sexual act, created the subject, which is there representing the sexual act.

What about the capital A? What is it? If the sexual act is what we are taught it is, then the A is, as a signifier, the Mother. We can find right across analytic thinking the trace of everything that the significant term of the Mother brings with it in the way of a fusional thinking, a thinking that falsifies the unit that alone is of interest to us – namely the countable unit – by passing from this countable unit to a unifying unit. We will assign to this the value 1. What does this value 1, as a unifying unit, mean? We are in the signifier and its consequences for thinking. The mother as subject is the thinking of the 1 of the couple. *And they twain shall be one flesh*. It is a thinking of the realm of the maternal A.

Such is the mean and extreme ratio of what links the agent to what is patient and recipient in the sexual act. I mean, insomuch as it is an act, in other words, insomuch as it has a relation with the subject's existence.

The 1 of the unity of the couple is a thought determined at the level of one of the terms of the real couple. What does this mean? It means that something has to surge up subjectively from this repetition which re-establishes the ratio, the mean ratio such as I have just defined it, at the level of the real couple. In other words, it means that something should appear that, as in this fundamental handling of the signifier that the harmonic ratio is, would manifest as follows – the measure c has the same value in relation to the two others, A and *a*, as the lesser, *a*, in relation to the greater, A.

$$\frac{c}{a+A} = \frac{a}{A}$$

But this is not all. It possesses this scope insomuch as the value of c, the lesser in relation to the greater, is the same value as the greater possesses in relation to the sum of the first two.

$$\frac{a}{A} = \frac{A}{a+A} = \frac{-\varphi}{a+A-\varphi}$$

I have drawn something out here on the right which possesses a value that is none other than the minus phi by which castration is designated. Minus phi over *a* plus big A minus phi is in effect the signifying relation of the phallic function as an essential lack of any juncture between sexual relation and its subjective realisation.

Designating with the very signifiers that are fundamental to the sexual act, even though called upon, yet still stealing away, the shadow of unity lingers over the couple. Even so, the mark of something that has to represent a fundamental lack here necessarily appears, and this is due to its very introduction into the subjective function. This is called *the function of castration qua signifying*.

There is castration only in so far as man does not introduce himself into the function of the couple save along the path of a relation that cannot be immediately inscribed into sexual conjunction and which does not find itself being represented there, unless in the same exterior in which you can see being sketched out what is called, for that very reason, *extreme ratio*. The relation that is assumed by the predominance of the phallic symbol in relation to conjunction qua sexual act is the one that provides both the measure of the ratio of agent to patient and the measure, which is the same, of the thought of the couple, such as it is in the patient, to the real couple.

Everything that belongs to the realm of sublimation is able to reproduce exactly the same type of repetition. I would prefer not to be forced here to evoke it specifically in the form of what is called the creation of art, but, since I have to, this is what I shall bring in. It is very precisely to the degree that something, some object, can come to the place taken by the $(-\varphi)$ in the sexual act as such, that sublimation can subsist by affording exactly the same order of *Befriedigung* as is afforded in the sexual act. This hinges, as you can see, on the fact that what lies purely and simply within the couple is not satisfying.

This is so true that the rather boorish homily that is introduced into the theory under the heading of *genital maturation* is put forward, when whoever it may be is trying to set it out, as nothing more than a catch-all dumping ground. Nothing about it can truly suffice to conjoin the fact of a copulation – a *successful* copulation, they add, but what does that mean? – to those elements that are qualified as tenderness or acknowledgement of the object. But which object, I ask you? Is it really so clear that the object is there, when already we have been told that behind any object whatsoever the Other is looming, the object that provided shelter over that nine-month interval between the conjunction of chromosomes and the coming forth into the world?

I am well aware that this is where all the obscurantism takes refuge, which clings so hopelessly to analytic demonstration. But nor is this a reason not to speak out against it, if this enables us to advance more strictly into a logic. You are going to see next time how this logic becomes concentrated at the level of the analytic act itself.

The quadrangle enables us to establish certain proportions. The *passage à l'acte* here fulfils a certain function in relation to repetition and, as is suggested by the way the terms are arranged, this must be the same that separates sublimation from acting out. In the other direction, sublimation's relation to the *passage à l'acte* must have something in common with what separates repetition from acting out.

There is assuredly a far greater gap here. There is the one that most surely makes the analytic act something that also deserves to be defined as an act.

We will be trying to grasp this through what we will be saying next time.

22 February 1967

XI

ON THE STRUCTURE OF SEXUAL SATISFACTION IN ITS RELATION TO THE SUBJECT

On the different orders of satisfaction
The anharmonic relation
The object a, incommensurable with 1
Sublimation and identification with woman
Detumescence and cognisance

$$2 + a = \frac{1}{a} + 1 = \frac{1}{a^2} = \frac{1}{1-a}$$

$$1 + a = \frac{1}{a}$$

$$a + a^2 = 1$$
$$a^2 + a^3 = a$$
$$a^3 + a^4 = a^2 = 1 - a$$

In red on the blackboard

Yesterday evening I read somewhere, where some of you may have come across it too, the peculiar title, *Connaître Freud avant de le traduire* ['Know Freud before translating him'].

Hénaurme, as was once said by a certain someone whom I do not claim to resemble, because I don't stroll around with a cane as he did, though I do sometimes don a hat. *Hénaurme*.

Be that as it may, it is quite clear to my mind that trying to translate Freud is a path that certainly imposes itself as a prerequisite to any pretension to knowing him.

That psychoanalysts should say they know psychoanalysis is just about admissible. But knowing Freud before translating him insuperably suggests the foolishness that one could know him before having read him. This presupposes, of course, all the necessary broadening of the notion of translation.

I don't know whether we could ever advance something that resembles this pretension to knowing Freud.

1

Within the perspective of Freud's thought, once he has got to the end of its development, he puts before us the model of subjective gratification in sexual coalescing.

Can you take full measure of what this means? Isn't the experience that was Freud's starting point very precisely the locus of subjective dissatisfaction? And has the situation improved for us?

Quite frankly, in a social context dominated by the function of the individual's employment, whether one sets this employment by the measure of his pure and simple subsistence or by the measure of productivity, what margin is left in this context to what might amount to proper time for a culture of love? And doesn't everything vouch for how this is the reality that for us is most excluded from our subjective community?

I won't say that this is what persuaded Freud to articulate this function of satisfaction as a truth, but it is doubtless what appeared to him to shield this truth from the risk he admitted to Jung, that of seeing a shallow theory of the psyche slipping back into the rut of what he called *occultism's black tide of mud*. While sexuality had over the course of the centuries presided over what today strikes us as follies, like those delusions of the gnosis about the copulation of the sage, and of σοφία, and by what a path, Freud could indeed think that in our century, under the reign of the subject, there was no risk that sexuality might presume to be any sort of model for cognisance.

This is no doubt why he started whistling the game leader's tune, finely illustrated by the Grimm fairytale of the Pied Piper of which he was so fond, trailing behind him the audience who can fairly be said to have represented the dregs of the earth so far as any wisdom was concerned.

On the line he plotted out for us, one really needs to start from its end-term, namely the formulation of repetition.

And here, one needs to take full measure of what separates it from the Πάντα ῥεῖ of the thinker from Antiquity who tells us that nothing ever passes anew into its own trace, that never do we bathe in the same stream. One needs to take full measure of what this signifies by way of a deep wrenching of a thought, which cannot grasp time but is something that moves towards the indeterminable only at the price of a constant rupture from absence.

What is added by introducing the function of repetition here? Well, certainly nothing much more satisfactory, were it not for renewing always and incessantly a certain number of circuits. The pleasure principle certainly doesn't guide us towards anything, and least of all towards a fresh grasp on any object whatsoever. What can the pure and simple notion of discharge account for? It is modelled on the established circuit that goes from the *sensorium* to something that is rather vaguely defined as *motor*. The stimulus–response circuit, as they say. Who could fail to see that, in sticking to this level, the sensorium can only be the guide for what, at the simplest level, makes the frog's leg recoil when irritated. It's not going to grasp anything else in the world. It's going to flee what hurts it.

What is it that ensures the constant defined in the nervous apparatus by the pleasure principle? Well, an even stimulation, an *isostim*, I would say, to imitate the isobar or the isotherm I was speaking about the other day. Or even *isoresp*, the *isoresponse*. It is hard to found anything on the *isostim*, because it is no longer a *stim* at all. The *isoresp*, the feeling around for an even resistance, is that which in the world can define this isobar, which is that the pleasure principle will lead the organism to slink away.

In any case, nothing in all this nudges towards the search for, the grasping out for, the constituting of, an object. The problem of the object as such is left intact by this entire organic conception of a homeostatic apparatus. It is altogether astonishing that until now this fault line has not been marked out. Freud, to his credit, underscored how the search for the object is conceivable only when the dimension of satisfaction is introduced.

And yet here once again we run up against the following oddity.

There are a fair number of organic models of satisfaction. Digestive repletion, for a start, and Freud mentions the satisfaction of a few other needs as well. It is quite remarkable that these are layouts in which satisfaction is never transformed by the subjective agency. Oral gratification can admittedly send the subject to sleep and so, at a push, it is conceivable that sleep should be the subjective sign of satisfaction. But it is infinitely more problematic to assert that the true order of subjective satisfaction is to be sought out in the sexual act when it is here that it proves to be the most ruptured. It is infinitely more problematic to assert that all the other realms of gratification, those that we have just listed as being mentioned by Freud, only take on their meaning when placed in a certain dependence – which I defy anyone to define and to render conceivable otherwise than by formulating it in terms of structure – in relation to sexual satisfaction. This dependence is – let's put it in broad terms – symbolic.

These are the terms in which I propose to formulate the problem which I'm taking up again today.

What is at issue consists in trying to give you the signifying articulation for what is involved in the repetition implied in the sexual act, if the latter truly is what I've been saying it is, which the words themselves advertise and which our experience certainly doesn't disconfirm, namely an act.

Having emphasised what the act entails in itself as being conditioned first and foremost by the repetition that is internal to it, I am going to go further in regard to the sexual act. At least I believe that we ought to go further in order to grasp its full scope.

The repetition that it implies entails, if we follow Freud's indication, an element of measure and harmony, and this is most surely evoked by the directive function that Freud ascribes to it. But we certainly do still have to specify this, because if there is something that is produced and promoted in any one of the analytic formulations, then it's that in no case whatsoever could this harmony be conceived of as belonging to the realm of the complementary, namely the conjunction of male and female, however straightforwardly people imagine it to themselves in the mode of a conjunction between lock and key, or whatever else might present in the usual modes of the gamic symbols. Everything indicates that the mode of measure and harmony implied in the sexual act belongs to a structure that is altogether different and, to say the word, more complex. Here I need only highlight the fundamental function of the third-party element that turns upon the phallus and castration.

This is what I had started to formulate just before taking leave of you last time, bringing in, because it's a matter of harmony, the relation that is said to be anharmonic.

On a simple line that has been drawn out, a segment can be divided in two ways. Either by a point that is internal to it, a point C between A and B, this division yielding whichever relation, for example 1:2. Or else one locates a point D outside the initial AB segment and the same 1:2 proportion can be produced between the segments DA and DB. This had already appeared to be most suitable for ensuring what is at issue according to all our experience, namely the relation of one term to another term which presents for us as a locus of unity. By this I mean the *couple*. It is in relation to the idea of the couple, there where it is to be found, effectively, in the subjective register, that the subject has to situate himself within a proportion that he may find has to be established by introducing a mediation that is external to the confrontation that he constitutes, as subject, to the idea of the couple.

This is just a first approximation and in some way the simple layout that allows us to designate what needs to be secured, namely the function of the third-party element that we can see appearing at every turn in what might be called the subjective field in the sexual relation. What is this third-party element? Two things are at issue. It is what, subjectively speaking, appears here in the most distant fashion, namely its organic product, which is always possible, whether or not it is deemed desirable. It is also this element that can seem to be so different from the first fact, even contrary to it, yet which is immediately conjoined with it by the analytic experience, namely this requirement of the phallus which in our experience seems to be so internal to the sexual relation such as it is lived subjectively. Isn't the pertinence of the *child* = *phallus* equivalence something that we are tempted to designate in a certain synchrony that we ought surely to have uncovered here, which of course does not mean simultaneity?

Furthermore, doesn't this third-party element bear some relation to what we have designated as the division of the Other itself, the $S(\bar{A})$?

It is so as to lead you onto this path that today I am bringing in the relationship that belongs to an order that is structured quite differently from the simple harmonic approach which came at the end of my last disquisition.

2

The true mean and extreme ratio is not simply the relation of one segment to another insomuch as this relation can be defined twice over, in a fashion that is internal to their conjunction or external to it. Rather, it is the relation that posits at its starting point an equivalence of relation between the lesser to the greater and the greater to the sum of them both.

The indeterminacy, the perfect liberty, of the anharmonic relation is no small matter when it comes to establishing a structure. I remind you that last year we already had to bring up this relation as fundamental to any structure that may be said to be projective, but however directive the mean and extreme ratio may be in the manifestation of projective constants, let's leave this aside so as to engage the following.

Numerically speaking, the relation of mean and extreme ratio is not just any relation. It is perfectly determined and unique. I have

On the structure of sexual satisfaction

set out on the blackboard a figure that allows us to give a support to what I have been stating.

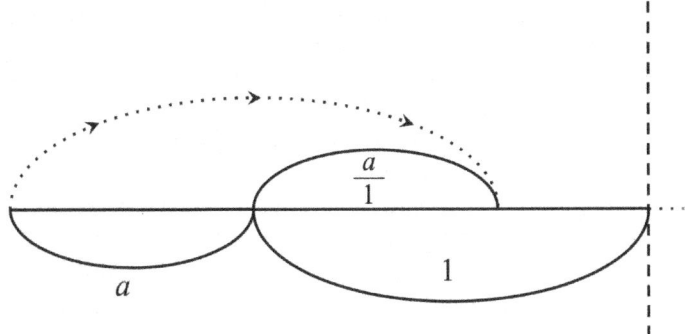

The relation of mean and extreme ratio

I have marked the first segment on the line with the lower-case letter a. For us this stands as the sole element with which we may content ourselves in order to build everything that will be involved in this relation of measure or proportion, on the sole condition that we give it its correspondent, the value 1, as you can see. I don't want to give names of letters to the points that determine the indicated segments since that could give rise to confusion and set your ears awhirl.

When we ascribe the value 1 to this segment, we can content ourselves, within the relation known as mean and extreme ratio, with ascribing to the other segment the value $a/1$, which on this occasion means that we have furthermore posited that the $a/1$ relation is the same as the relation $1/(1 + a)$.

$$\frac{a}{1} = a = \frac{1}{1+a}$$

This relation is perfectly regular and has extremely important mathematical properties, which I have neither the time nor the inclination to develop for you today. Please be aware simply that its appearance in Greek mathematics coincides with the decisive step of bringing some order to what is in involved in the commensurable and the incommensurable.

What is specific to two commensurable values is that there is always a point at which the two measures will fall together on an equal footing. Two commensurable values will always end up with a certain multiple, different for one and for the other, constituting the same magnitude. Two incommensurable values never will.

The relation 1/*a* here is incommensurable. In seeking out the mode by which one might define how the succession of points afforded by either series staggered out by two units of measure are each covering the other, the hardest thing to imagine, when they are incommensurable, is how they might slot together.

But how do the two measures commingle? It was in this line of research that a procedure was defined that consisted in folding the lesser into the field of the greater, then to ask what becomes of the remainder from the standpoint of measure. For the remainder that we have here, which obviously is $1 - a$, we proceed in the same way. We fold the lesser into the greater, and on and on to infinity. I mean, without ever being able to get to a point where the process would end. The incommensurability of a relation that, even so, is so very simple, consists in this.

Of all the incommensurables, this is the one that, as it were, within the intervals defined by the rational of the commensurable, always leaves the greatest gap. This is a mere indication on which I cannot comment further here. Be that as it may, you can see that what is at issue here is something that, within this order of the incommensurable, is specified by an accentuation at the same time as a purity of the relationship, both of which are quite special.

Much to my regret, because I think that all the entrails of occultism are going to be quaking on this occasion, I am very much forced, for honesty's sake, to tell you that this relation of the *a* is what is known as *the golden section*. Following which, of course, you will feel quivering in the depths of your cultural acquirements, most notably as far as aesthetics are concerned, some evocation of whatever you will, cathedrals, Albrecht Dürer, alchemical crucibles, and any number of tinkerings of the same ilk. I do hope, however, through the seriousness with which I introduced the strictly mathematical character of this matter and very precisely what is problematic about it, which can hardly give rise to any idea of a measure that would be easy to appreciate, to give you a sense of how what is at issue is something else.

Let's see now what some of the remarkable qualities of this *a* are.

The fact that $1 + a$ should be equal to the inverse of *a*, that is to say 1/*a*, was already secured sufficiently in the premises afforded by the definition of this relation, because the notion that it consists in the relation of the lesser to the greater qua equal to that of the greater to their sum, gives us the following formula, which is the same as the fundamental formula, $a = 1/(1 + a)$. On this basis, it is very easy to perceive other equivalences, the non-essential character of which is marked here by the fact that I have written them out in red. In truth, they don't hold any great importance for us at the present moment.

On the structure of sexual satisfaction

$$2 + a = \frac{1}{a} + 1 = \frac{1}{a^2} = \frac{1}{1-a}$$

The only important thing to note is that $1 - a$ can be equal to a^2, which can be demonstrated very easily. On the other hand, $2 + a$, which as you can see can easily be deduced from $1/a + 1$, represents what happens when, instead of involuting the folding over of segments upon themselves, they are on the contrary developed outwards.

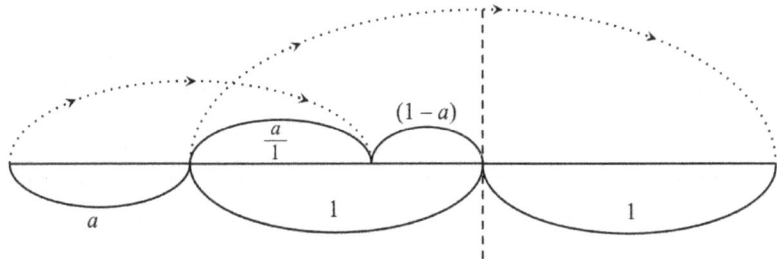

Thus, $1/(2 + a)$, which earlier corresponded to our external segment in the anharmonic relation, equal to 1 in being obtained by the external development of the 1 represented by the greater length, has the same value as the initial value from which we started, that is to say $1/(1 + a)$.

$$\frac{1}{2+a} = a = \frac{1}{1+a}$$

These are the properties of mean and extreme ratio insomuch as they can allow us to understand something of what is at issue in genital satisfaction.

3

I told you that a is one of the terms – whichever – of the genital relation. I mean, whichever its sex might be.

In the sexual relation, in the experience of the subjective relationship it entails, defined by analysis as Oedipal, both girl and boy enter it first of all as child, in other words, as already representing the product.

I am not picking this term at random. We are going to have to take it up later, in so far as it allows us to situate, as different from what is called *creation*, everything that in our day and age has been circulating everywhere, and even indiscriminately, under the name *production*. The most current, the most imminent question that is being put to thought is indeed that of how to define the subject's relation to what is involved in production. To put forward a dialectic of the subject in which it cannot be seen how the subject himself can be taken as production would be worthless for us, which doesn't mean that it would be so easy to secure what is involved in production by starting from such a root.

It is so far from easy to secure that, if there is one thing that an unprepared mind might surely wonder at, then this is the remarkable silence, the silence of a Valentin Conrart, which psychoanalysis is maintaining with respect to the delicate question, which I must say is none the less doing the rounds in our journalistic, political, domestic and everyday lives, and at any other level you might wish, even the commercial, and which is called *birth control*. We have yet to see an analyst saying what he thinks about it. It's all the same rather curious in a theory that claims to have something to say about sexual satisfaction.

There must be something in this regard that is bound up, and I must say in a way that is not particularly convenient, with the religion of the Word, because after the very surprising hopes about being freed from the Law fostered by the Pauline generation in the Church, it seems that thereafter a good many dogmatic pronouncements have taken a harder line. Whatever for? Why, for the sake of production, the production of souls. That which, for the sake of the production of souls, was announced as the very imminent passing from humanity to beatitude, has undergone, so it would seem, a certain postponement.

But it ought not to be believed that the problem is confined to the religious sphere. A further announcement has been provided, about man's liberation. It seems that the production of proletarians has played some role in the precise forms that Socialist societies have found themselves taking, on the basis of a certain idea of the abolition of man's exploitation of his fellow man.

On the side of this production, they don't seem to have come to a much clearer measure of what they are producing. Just as the Christian field has, for the sake of the production of souls, continued to allow beings to appear in the world of whom the least that can be said is that their quality of soulessness is fairly mixed, so too, for the sake of the production of proletarians, it seems that what has come to light is nothing else but something that, while certainly respectable, does have its limits, and which could be called the production of executives.

The question of production, and of the status of the subject qua product, is therefore being presentified for us at the level of what is indeed the first presentification of the Other – the Mother. We know about the unifying function of her presence. We know it so well that the whole of analytic theory, and practice with it, has literally toppled over into it and succumbed completely to its fascinating merit. This is the principle that lies behind a conception that goes so far as to maintain – and this you were able to hear in a debate that brought our last year to a close – that the analytic setting is founded on the ideal of unitive fusion, or founding unification, as you like, which is supposed to have united child and mother over nine months.

However we might qualify this union of child and mother, whether or not we make it the function of primary narcissism or simply the choice locus of frustration and gratification, it's not a matter of repudiating this register but rather of moving it back to its proper place. This is what our theoretical efforts are going into.

How derisive it is to assert that the unit of the couple at the level of sexual encounter is constituted by what the religious pronouncement worded as *one flesh*. Who can assert in any way whatsoever that in the clasp that is said to be genital, man and woman form one flesh, unless the religious pronouncement has recourse here to what has been brought in by analytic investigation, to that which in sexual conjunction is represented by the maternal pole?

I repeat, this maternal pole which, in the Oedipal myth, seems to be conflated purely and simply with the partner of the little male, in reality is a far cry from the male–female contradistinction. Any girl, like any boy, is dealing with this maternal locus of unity as representing for her that with which she is confronted at the moment of broaching what is involved in sexual conjunction.

For both boy and girl, what they are as a product, as *a*, has to confront the unity established by the idea of the child's union with the mother. It is within this confrontation that the $(-\varphi)$ looms up, which will bring us this third element insomuch as it also functions as the sign of a lack, or, if you will, to employ the humorous term, the sign of *the small difference*, which comes to play the chief role in what is involved in sexual conjunction to the extent that it concerns the subject.

Of course, commonplace humour, or common sense, turns this small difference into the fact that, as they say, there are haves and have nots. In fact, this is not at all what is at issue because, as you know, the fact of not having plays such an essential role for woman, a role that is just as mediating and constitutive in love as it is for the man. Moreover, as Freud underlined, it seems that her effective lack confers upon her a few advantages, and this is what I'm going to try to articulate for you now.

225 In effect, what can we see if not that, as we said earlier, the extreme ratio of the relation, in other words the one that reproduces it on the outside, will serve us here in the form of the 1 that reproduces the correct proportion, the one defined by *a*, on the outside of the relation thus defined as a sexual relation. For one of the partners to pose himself in relation to the other as a 1, in other words, for the dyad of the couple to be established, we have here, in the relation thus inscribed into the measure of the mean and extreme ratio, the support of a second 1. It is inscribed here on the right and it restores the proportion to the whole, on the condition that the third-party term of *a* be maintained here.

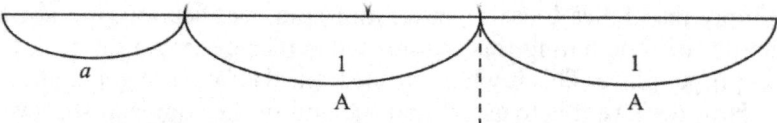

Here stands what supports our saying that, in the sexual relationship, it is in so far as the subject manages to make himself the Other's equal, or to introduce into the Other the repetition of 1, that he finds himself reproducing the initial relation, the one that maintains the constancy of the third element, here formulated by the *a*.

In other words, we find again here, in a new form, the process that I once set out around a dividing bar as forming part of the subject's relation to the big A. In the mode wherein a division is produced, the barred A is given, in relation to which a barred S comes to be inscribed, while the remainder is given by an *a* that is the irreducible element of the division.

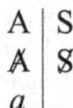

Division of the Other

It is here that we can start to conceive of how it can come about that an organ as local, if I may say so, as the penis, and which in appearance is so purely functional, is able to play a role that allows us to glimpse what the true nature of the satisfaction in the sexual relationship is.

Indeed, somewhere in the sexual relationship, something can symbolise, as it were, the elimination of this remainder. It is to the extent that the organ is the seat of detumescence that the subject can
226 have the illusion, somewhere, which is certainly deceptive but none

the less gratifying, that there is no remainder, or, at the very least, that there is merely a remainder that will vanish away. In truth, this would be simply comical, and it does certainly belong to the comic register, because at the same time this is what sets its limit on what can be called enjoyment insomuch as enjoyment would lie at the centre of sexual satisfaction. The fantasised idea of the discharge of drive tension is in reality supported by this framework, where it can be seen to impose this limit upon enjoyment on the basis of the function of detumescence.

There is no more disappointing aspect that can be supposed of a satisfaction, if indeed what were at issue were purely and simply enjoyment. But everyone knows that if there is something that is present in the sexual relationship then it is the ideal of the Other's enjoyment, and this is also what constitutes its subjective originality.

The fact is that, in limiting ourselves to organic functions, nothing is more precarious than this intertwining of enjoyments. If there is indeed something that experience reveals to us then it is the radical heterogeneity between male enjoyment and female enjoyment. It is precisely for this reason that there are so many well-meaning souls busy keeping an eye, more or less scrupulously, on the strict simultaneity of their own enjoyment with their partner's. Well, today is certainly not the day for me to run the gamut of failures, illusions and trickery to which this lends itself. But also, this is about something quite different from these little exercises in erotic acrobatics.

We know the place that this has held in a certain psychoanalytic verbiage. If something does come to be founded around the Other's enjoyment, then it is in so far as the structure that we have set out today gives rise to the phantom of the gift. It is because she doesn't have the phallus that woman's gift takes on a privileged role with regard to Being. This gift is called love, which I defined as the gift of what one doesn't have.

In love relationships, woman finds an enjoyment that belongs, as it were, to the order of the *causa sui*, to the extent that what she gives in the shape of what she doesn't have is also the cause of her desire. She becomes what she creates, in a purely imaginary fashion, and she creates precisely what makes her an object, insomuch as, in the erotic mirage, she can be the phallus. Being it and at the same time not being it. What she gives, in not having it, becomes, as I have just told you, the cause of her desire.

Because of this, it may be said that she alone wraps up in a satisfying way the genital conjunction. But, of course, this is so to the extent that, having furnished the object that she doesn't have, she doesn't disappear into it. I mean that, this object cannot disappear – leaving her to the satisfaction of her essential enjoyment – but through the intermediary of masculine castration. In sum, she loses nothing in all this because she has put in only what she doesn't have, and because, quite literally, she creates it.

This is why it is always through identification with woman that sublimation produces the appearance of a creation. If in certain human activities, which it will remain for us to examine to see whether they are mirages or not, there may be what is called creation or ποίησις, for example, it is invariably in the mode of a genesis that is obscure – and is certainly so prior to my having exposed its lineaments here – but very strictly bound to the gift of womanly love insomuch as it creates this vanishing object. Furthermore, this is so inasmuch as this is an object that she lacks, and which is the almighty phallus.

The phallus is therefore indeed, from one angle, the penis, but in so far as it is its shortcoming in relation to enjoyment that defines the subjective satisfaction to which the reproduction of life happens to be referred.

In fact, in coupling, the subject cannot really possess the body onto which he clasps. He doesn't know the limits of possible enjoyment, I mean, of the enjoyment that he might have of the body of the Other as such, because these limits are uncertain, and this is everything that constitutes the beyond zone defined by scoptophilia and sadism.

That phallic flagging should take on the ever renewed value of the fading of the subject's Being is what is essential to men's experience, and it is what causes this enjoyment to be compared to what is called the return of the little death. This fading function of the phallus is far more directly felt in men's enjoyment, which ascribes to the male the privilege from which the illusion of pure subjectivity arises. If there is an instant, a somewhere, where the man can lose sight of the presence of the third-party object, then it is the vanishing moment when he loses, because the object is flagging, what is not only his instrument but also, for him as for the woman, the third-party element of the relationship of the couple. It was on this basis that, even prior to the advent of what we are here calling the status of pure subjectivity, all the illusions of cognisance were built.

The imagination of the subject of cognisance, whether from before the scientific era or after, is a male figment, a figment of the male in so far as he partakes of powerlessness, in so far as he denies the *minus something* around which the causation effect of desire is formed, taking this minus for a zero. We have already said that taking the minus for a zero is what is proper to the subject, and the proper name is here designed to mark out its trace.

The rejection of castration marks the delusion of thought. I mean, the entering of the thinking of the *I* as such into the real. This is what, in our first quadrangle, constitutes the status of *I am not thinking* insomuch as syntax alone sustains it.

Here you have what is involved, structurally speaking, in what enables a raising up of what Freud designates for us concerning sexual satisfaction in its relation with the status of the subject.

We will leave it there for today, leaving for next time what we have now to put forward about the function of acting out.

1 March 1967

XII

SEXUAL SATISFACTION AND SUBLIMATION

Critique of the genital stage
A remark about acting out
The field of the sexual Other, desexualised in analysis
The structure of sublimation

All in all, what I am establishing amounts to a whole method.

Within a certain field, what defines this field, namely the presence as such of the subject, remains implicit. The method I am establishing allows for a parrying, so to speak, of everything that the subject's implication in this field introduces into it from the beginning by way of fallacy and fallaciousness.

That this method possesses such overall comprehensiveness is something one realises only upon taking a step back. I would even say, furthermore, that I myself am only realising this after the event because I didn't, of course, start with such a comprehensive aim. It may come about one day that this method will be made use of to rethink matters where they are the most interesting, on the political plane for instance.

Whyever not? It is quite certain that, with sufficient concessions, some of the schemas I have provided would find their application there. It might even be there that they will have the most success because on the ground upon which I devised them this is not a foregone conclusion, given how it is perhaps here, on this ground of the psychoanalyst, that a certain deadlock, which is precisely the one manifested by what I am calling the fallacies of the subject and which are not univocal, finds it can best resist.

Well, it no less remains that this is where these concepts will have been devised, and one might even say further that the whole possibility of the venture, namely the very mode of what these concepts will have to confront, for example analytic theory such as it has already been devised and such as revisions are being introduced into it, the very dialectic of what the introduction of these revisions into analytic theory will have entailed by way of difficulty and even resistance – which in appearance is altogether accidental and exterior – all of this comes in some way to contribute to the modes in which I will have secured them. I mean that what may be called *the resistance of psychoanalysts themselves to their own field* is perhaps what vouches most glaringly for the difficulties that need to be resolved and for their very structure.

With this, we are landing on ground that is a little keener still, at a moment when I am going to have to speak about what I located for you at the first of the vertices on the quadrangle and which I qualified as the one that connotes the moment of repetition. Responding to this, as foundational to the subject, is the *passage à l'acte*.

Regarding the status of the act, I showed you the importance that the sexual act has here. I paid particular attention to it and I will be coming back to it again today, because we have to.

1

Without defining the sexual act as an act in the fullest sense, it is absolutely impossible to conceive of the function that Freud ascribed to sexuality with respect to the structure that has to be called, as he called it, satisfaction, *Befriedigung*. It is a subjective satisfaction that cannot be conceived in any other locus but the one in which the subject as such is established.

This is the only notion that functions in a way that can give meaning to *Befriedigung*.

In order to furnish this sexual act with the structural bearings beyond which it is impossible for us to conceive of its place in what it at issue, namely Freudian theory, we have been led to give a functional role to one of the most exemplary mainsprings of mathematical thought. When I make use of such means, it is to be understood that, for anyone who is familiar only with what I have helped myself to as an instrument, it is always verging on something partial. But the situation may of course be different for anyone who knows from what place I, doubtless with my own share of inexperience, am extracting the mainspring. Still, please believe that this is not without being wise to what the ramifications of what I'm helping myself to are in mathematical theory as a whole, and not without having made sure that anyone who should like to make more in-depth use of it would find all the extensions that could allow accurate expansion to be given to the precise points I have chosen for the grounding of such a structure as this.

An echo came back to me that, in hearing me speak about the sexual act, making use, in order to structure its tension, of what was furnished by the proportion of the golden section in the way of a ternary, someone let slip through gritted teeth the following remark – *Next time I'm going to get my rocks off, I'd better not forget my slide rule.*

While this remark has all the amusing character that is attributed to witticisms, for me it remains half-heartedly between earnest and jest when the one responsible for this funny outburst is a psychoanalyst. In truth, I think very precisely that any assurance of enjoyment in bed comes essentially from forgetting whatever might be found on the slide rule. Why so? I'll be focusing on this once more in a short while. It is even here that lies the mainspring of what there is that is satisfying in what, moreover, subjectively speaking, is translated by castration.

It is quite plain, however, that psychoanalysts cannot forget, in so far as another act concerns them, which we shall call, to introduce its term today, *the psychoanalytic act*, that some recourse to the slide rule can clearly be requisite.

To avoid any misapprehension I will specify that on this occasion it's not about using the slide rule to read what is there to be read when two little lines meet – we haven't got to that point yet – but rather for what it bears in itself by way of a measure that has no other name but that of *logarithm*. The logarithm furnishes us with something that is not altogether unrelated to the structure I've been talking about.

What is striking about the psychoanalytic act, to name it thus in reference to the theory as a whole, is that it allows us to make a remark that might have already occurred to some, on the fringes of what I have thus far set out here.

I have been concentrating on the character of act that the sexual act entails. It could be noted in this connection that everything that is being uttered in psychoanalytic theory seems designed to efface, for the use of those beings in our charge who are in various ways suffering or dissatisfied, the character of act in what is involved in the sexual act. Analytic theory on the whole has been accentuating the more or less gratifying mode of what is called the sexual relationship. One form or another of sexual relationship is declared gratifying, or less so, rightly or wrongly, in any case in various capacities, and capacities over which I have allowed myself on several occasions to voice a few objections. It could be asked whether this is not a way of eluding, or even of drowning out, what is keen about the sexual act and, strictly speaking, what is sharp about it, because what is at issue here is something that has the same cut-structure as belongs to any act.

This is a cut that is not self-evident, as all our experience demonstrates most abundantly, and which does not yield a result of simple equity, as all sorts of structural anomaly attest. Moreover, these anomalies have been perfectly articulated and pinpointed, indeed conceived of in their true scope, by analytic theory. It is quite clear that the fact of eluding what is involved in the contours of the act as such is most surely something that is bound up with what I will call the temperament, the tempered fashion, in which theory edges forward with the manifest aim of not bringing with it too much scandal.

The worst of such scandals, and which doesn't seem for all that to have been scaled down by this cautiousness, is the one I shall tell you about now.

In libertine circles from the start of the century, a few examples of which were still surviving, keeping afloat in certain milieus or on other ground that was serious in its own way, I mean revolutionary ground – which had been loosely inherited from experiences that were complex in a different way, those that date from what is known as the heyday of the man of pleasure – among certain of their exaggerated slogans one could still come across the one that maintains that, when all is said and done, the sexual act should not be taken as holding any more importance than drinking a glass of water.

That used to be said, for example, in certain zones, certain groups, certain sectors, in Lenin's circle. I remember reading a nice little volume in German entitled, if I rightly recall, *Wege der Liebe*. This was even the beginning, before the war, of something that was to bear a strong resemblance to the paperback, and the cover sported the ravishing mug of Mrs Kollontai, who belonged to the first team and was, if memory serves, an ambassador in Stockholm. The book consists of charming tales on themes to do with love life. With the passing of time, and Socialist societies having assumed the structure you are familiar with, it appears that, regardless of our aspirations towards freethinking, and contrary to what some have asserted in one zone or another and to the objective examination that falls within the remit of ethics, the sexual act has not yet passed over to the ranks of what can be gratified in a snack bar.

Whether the theory acknowledges it or not, accentuates it or not, matters little to us. Experience proves most abundantly that the sexual act still brings with it, and will for long to come, the strange sort of effect of goodness knows what, of discordance, or deficit, of something that never falls into place, and which is called *guilt*.

I don't believe that all these writings by the lofty minds around us, bearing titles like *L'univers morbide de la faute*, as though it had already been conjured away – it was written by a friend of mine and

I always prefer to quote people of whom I'm fond – have settled the question. Nor do they mean that we don't have to deal, and most likely for a long time ahead, with what still cleaves to this universe around, let's say, the misfirings of the structure of the sexual act. These misfirings, or non-misfirings, may be essential to it and it is a matter precisely of giving due consideration to their status.

In view of which, I believe I need to come back, certainly very briefly, but to come back all the same, to what is insufficient about the definition given to us in a certain register of blessing homilies, in connection with what is called the genital stage, about what supposedly forms the ideal structure of its object. There is nothing pointless about consulting this literature. In truth, that the dimension of tenderness evoked in it should be a respectable thing is not to be contested, but that one should consider it to be a dimension that could in any sort be structural is an assertion I don't think it vain to contest. *(Smoke and a burning smell start emanating from the audio recording device on the rostrum; unrest in the audience.)*

Let's resume.

This incident affords me the opportunity to cut short what I had to say on the slightly stale topic of this famous tenderness. One could pinpoint one facet of tenderness, and perhaps tenderness as a whole, with a slogan along the lines of – *tenderness is what it befits us to have by way of pity for powerlessness to love*. Structuring this at the level of the drive is not easy.

Furthermore, to illustrate what ought to be articulated with regard to what the act and sexual satisfaction entail, it might be helpful to recall what experience dictates to psychoanalysts in respect of love's ambiguity. They call it *ambivalence*, a word that has been used so much it no longer means anything at all. Is a sexual act less a sexual act, is it an immature act, ought we to relegate it to the field of an inchoate subject, a subject still stuck in the backwardness of some archaic stage, if the sexual act is committed quite simply in hatred? This case doesn't seem to have caught the interest of analytic theory. It's odd, but I haven't seen it being raised anywhere. To introduce some consideration of hatred in love, I had to turn – in a Seminar that is already some time behind us, back when the seminar was a seminar – to Claudel's well-known play, or more exactly his trilogy which opens with *L'Otage*. Do the love relations between Turelure and Sygne de Coûfontaine amount to an immature conjunction?

What is admirable in it is what I think I brought out amply enough in the merits and the points of impact in this tragic trilogy without any one of my listeners, so far as I am aware, having perceived its scope. This is not surprising, because I wasn't minded to lay the accent on this precise question and, in general, going by all the feedback that reached me, this point can easily be passed over by listeners. There are two kinds. There are those who follow Monsieur Claudel into the religious resonance on the plane upon which he sites a tragedy that is most surely one of the most radically anti-Christian tragedies ever to have been devised, at the very least with regard to a Christianity of good form and tender emotion. Those who follow him into this mood reckon, of course, that Sygne de Coûfontaine remains intact throughout all of this. This is not what she seems to express in the drama, but no matter. It's there to be surmised through certain screens. What is curious is that those listeners who seem not to have to be bothered by this screening, namely those listeners who have not been religioned in advance, do seem, in the same way, not to want to hear anything of what is very precisely at issue.

Be that as it may, since we don't have, from the heights of a bully pulpit, any other reference in arm's reach, I will, even so, let the question stand as to whether a sexual act consummated in hatred would be any less of a sexual act, I shall say, of full scope. Raising the question to this level would lead on to a good many inroads that would not be unfruitful, but I cannot go into this today.

Let it suffice me to mark out another feature, which it seems to me doesn't connect especially well with those of which use is being made in the prevailing theory concerning the genital stage, namely the as-it-were limited, moderate and tempered character that mournful sorrowing is purported to take on.

It would supposedly be normal, and a sign of maturity, if the object that has been made a reality in the partner – because, after all, this is a package deal that tends to adapt to mores that are as conformist as might possibly be wished – could be mourned within a time limit that we may call *decent*. There is something here that gives one to think that it would fall within the norm of what is called *affective maturity* if the other were to go first. It makes us think of the fine tale which Freud relates somewhere, from someone who was in analysis, a gentleman, Viennese of course, who in this Viennese story says to his wife, *If one of us dies, I shall move to Paris.*

Here I am simply noting, by way of this rough-and-ready contrast, that nothing has ever been mentioned in the theory concerning the mourning that the mature subject will leave behind him. This, too, could be a characteristic that one might contemplate very seriously concerning the status of the subject. In all likelihood this would be of less interest to the customer base, and so it draws the same blank.

There are further remarks which this little incident [of the smouldering device] is forcing me to abridge due to the time we have lost.

2

I should simply like to pose the following question. Aren't the insistence and the proliferation of developments that have to do with the analytic *setting*, or else the analytic *relationship*, just what it takes to allow us to elude what is involved in the analytic *act*?

Of course, people will say, *the analytic act is interpretation*. But, as interpretation is, in a way that continues to grow – in the direction of decline – the very matter on which it seems to be most difficult to articulate something in analytic theory, we shall for the time being merely *prendre acte* of this deficiency.

Even so, we note that this theory is not without some promise of conjugating the function of the analyst – I'm not saying *the analytic relationship*, an expression at which I have just wagged my finger in order to say that on this occasion it bears a screening function – with something of the register of the act.

This promise hinges on the following reason. If the analytic act is indeed to be situated at the point which for us is the keenest and the most interesting to determine, and which lies on the bottom left of the quadrangle where the unconscious and the symptom are at issue, this act possesses, I would say, in a way that is rather in line with the structure of repression, a sort of off-beam position. A representative, if I can put it thus, of its deficient representation is given to us under the name *acting out*, and this what I have to introduce to you today.

All those of you here who are analysts have at least a vague notion of this term. Its axis, its centre, is set by certain acts with a structure that not everyone will necessarily agree on, but which all the same one can acknowledge as being likely to occur in the course of analysis and in a certain relation of dependence that is more or less sizeable with regard, not to the analytic situation or relationship, but to the precise moment of the analyst's intervention and thus of something that must bear some relation to what I consider has not been defined at all, namely the psychoanalytic act.

In a field as difficult as this, we can ill afford to go charging in like a bull in a china shop. We have to tread gingerly, to maintain with acting out something onto which it seems possible to draw the attention of those who have experience of analysis in a way that promises concord. We know that there are things that are called acting out and that this bears a relation to the analyst's intervention.

I designated the page in my *Écrits* on which, in my dialogue with Jean Hyppolite on *Verneinung*, I highlighted a very fine example of acting out. It's an excellent account, which is admissible for us because it's one that is truly innocent, make no mistake. It is in the article that Ernst Kris came out with under the title *Ego Psychology and Interpretation in Psychoanalytic Therapy* in *The Psychoanalytic Quarterly*, Volume XX, issue 1, January 1951. The text of mine is easy to find. It's the one that follows *Fonction et champ de la parole et du langage*, in other words, the *Discours de Rome*.

In this text I highlighted at some length what it entailed for Kris to have intervened, in keeping with the methodological principle that is promoted by Ego Psychology, in the field of what he calls *surface* and which we for our part shall call the field of *an appreciation of reality*.

In the analytic interventions, or in any case in the analyst's terms of reference, this appreciation of reality plays a considerable role. It is not one of the least distortions of the theory to go so far, for example, as to say that it is possible to interpret what are called *manifestations of transference* by giving the subject the sense that repetitions, which would constitute its essence, have something about them that is inappropriate, misplaced, unsuitable, with respect, not to the analytic setting, but to the confines of the analyst's consulting room, which is regarded as constituting such a straightforward reality. This has been written, and printed, in black and white. The fact of saying, *Can't you see how inappropriate it is for something to be repeating in this field in which we find ourselves three times a week?* – as though the fact of being together three times a week were such a straightforward reality – most surely gives firm pause to ponder the definition that we have to provide for the reality that is involved in analysis.

Be that as it may, Kris doubtless positions himself in a like perspective when, dealing with a patient who to his mind is pinning on himself the auto-accusation of plagiarism, and having got his hands on a document that plainly proves that the subject is not really a plagiarist, he believes he must, as an *exploration of the surface*, spell out to him that he, Kris, can assure him that he is not a plagiarist, because he has gone and found the volume in which the subject believed he had discovered proof of his plagiarism and he can see nothing of any particular originality which the subject, his patient, could have turned to his profit.

I ask you to consult my text and also the text by Kris, and, if you manage to get your hands on it, Melitta Schmideberg's too. She had the subject in analysis for a first period or stint. You will be able to see how utterly exorbitant it is to take such an inroad in order to broach a case in which quite clearly the essential thing is not that the subject might or might not really be a plagiarist, but rather that his whole desire is to plagiarise. This is so for the simple reason that he feels that it is not possible for him to formulate something that could have worth unless he has tapped it from somebody else. This is the essential mainspring. I can break it down so narrowly because this is its mainspring.

Be that as it may, after Kris's intervention, the subject falls into a short silence, which Kris processes. Next, Kris reports that the patient then comes straight out with this little doing – for some time now, when he leaves Kris, he has been going off to consume a nice little dish of fresh brains.

What is this? I don't need to say it, because already, right at the start of my teaching, I accentuated how this is an instance of acting out.

In what way is this acting out? It wasn't so fully articulable then as I can make it now. The oral object *a* is presentified here, brought in on a platter – quite literally – by the patient, in connection with the analyst's intervention.

And so? What then? This holds interest for us now – though indeed it has always held long-standing interest for any analyst – only if it allows us to move forward a little in the structure.

So, this is called acting out. What are we going to make of this term?

I think we won't dawdle over the notion that making use of what is called *Franglais* would amount to lapsing into some idiosyncrasy. I must say for my part that, whatever taste I might have for the French language, using Franglais doesn't bother me in the slightest. I really don't see why we shouldn't turn the use of our tongue to the employment of words that are not part of it. It's no skin off my nose. Especially so, given how I haven't managed to find any translation for the term *acting out*. It's a term of extraordinary pertinence in English. I'm pointing this out in passing because to my mind it is a sort of confirmation of something. I'm not about to rehearse the history of the authors who introduced the term because time is of the essence, but they made use of it because they knew full well what they wanted to say, and I'm going to bring you proof of this.

I won't be referring to what I thought I might find in an excellent philological dictionary which I have in thirteen volumes, the new *Oxford English Dictionary*, because it bears no trace of *act out*. Rather it was enough to open up the *Webster's*, which is also an admirable instrument, albeit in a single volume, which is published in the US, to find under *act out* the following definition – *To represent (as a play, story, etc.) in action, as opposed to reading; as, to* act out *a scene one has read.*

So, there are two phases. You have read something, some Racine, out loud. But you've read it poorly. I'm betting on your reading it out in a loathsome manner. Someone who is there wants to show you how it's done, and plays it out. That's what it means to act out.

I'm supposing that those who chose this term in the English literature to designate acting out knew what they wanted to say. In any case, it matches perfectly. I act something out because it has been read to me, translated and articulated for me, signified to me, in a way that is insufficient or off beam.

I would add that, were the experience I have just illustrated to befall you, namely should someone wish to give you a better presence of Racine, this would not be a very good starting point. It would probably be just as poor as your way of reading it. At any rate, it would already amount to starting from a certain stance that is out of kilter. There is something off beam, even deadened, in the acting out that is introduced by such a sequence.

This is the remark around which I mean to approach what I am only now, today, putting into question.

3

In order to speak of the logic of the fantasy, it is indispensable to have at least some idea of where the psychoanalytic act is situated. Here we have what is going to compel us to back up a little.

It goes without saying, though it goes better still when we do say it, that the psychoanalytic act is not a sexual act. It is not even possible to have the two of them commingle. They are quite contrary the one to the other. But, since we're doing logic, let's note that the contrary is not the contradictory.

To give a sense of this I need only bring up the analytic couch. After all, it does count for something. In the topological realm, something I noticed that really is a problem is that the myths don't make much of it. And yet the bed is something that has to do with the sexual act. The bed is not merely what Aristotle speaks to us about to designate the difference between φύσις and τέχνη, and to presentify for us a wooden bedstead as though it might be able to start sending up a shoot from one instant to the next. I had a good look, and in Aristotle there is no trace of the bed regarded as what I in my language – which is not that far removed from Aristotle's because he, too, had a certain sense of the τόπος when the realm of Nature was at stake – would call *the locus of the Other*. It's very curious, but having spoken about the bed in Book H of the *Metaphysics*, if memory serves, he never considers this fine and wonderful bed as a τόπος of the sexual act.

One says [in French] *enfant du premier lit*. This is, all the same, to be taken to the letter. Words don't get joined together randomly.

Under certain conditions, the fact of entering the zone of the bed might perhaps qualify an act as having a certain relation with the sexual act. Take, for instance, the *ruelles* of the Précieuses. The analytic bed also signifies a zone that is not without a certain relation to the sexual act. It's a relation of contrariety, namely it could never in any fashion whatsoever pass over to it. But it no less remains that it's a bed and that it introduces the sexual in the form of an empty field, or an *empty set* as they say in certain quarters.

If you refer to my little structural layout, because that's where we have already placed the sexual Other, this is also where the analytic act has no business whatsoever. It stops here, at the capital A. There remains this, the big A, and this, the little *a*, and their relations.

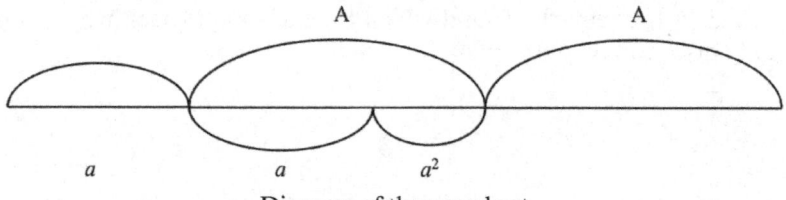

Diagram of the sexual act

I should like now and again to be able to omit the heavy stuff, but well, for those who are deaf, who have never heard me, I will specify that this does indeed concern the field of the Other, not insomuch as it is duplicated but insomuch as it splits into two in such a way that it's a question, within it, of an Other qua field of the sexual act. And then there is this Other, here, which seems not to be able not to come along with it, and which is the field of the Other of alienation. This field of the Other is the one that introduces the Other of the barred A, which is also the field of the Other in which truth presents for us, but in a way that is broken up, parcelled out and fragmentary, which constitutes it properly speaking as an intrusion into knowledge.

Before so much as daring to pose the question *Where is the psychoanalyst?*, we need to remind ourselves about the status of what is designated here by the *a* segment. I think you have already been able to sense that there is clearly a relation between this *a* and the big A, and that they even have the same function in relation to two different things.

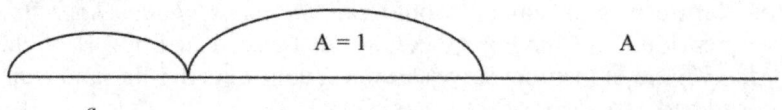

Sexual satisfaction and sublimation

The little *a* has a closed form. It is the form that is given at the start of the analytic experience, the form in which the subject presents. It is a production of his history and even, we will further say, the discard of this history.

This form, which is the one I designate under the name of the object *a*, has the same relation with the A of the sexual Other as this A of truth – the A of the field of an intrusion of something that hobbles along, that errs in the subject, under the name of the symptom – has with the first two [1 + *a*] . . .

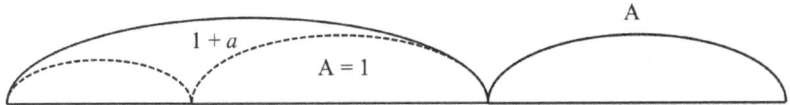

. . . and as the field of the *a* [*a*, *a*, a^2] has with the whole.

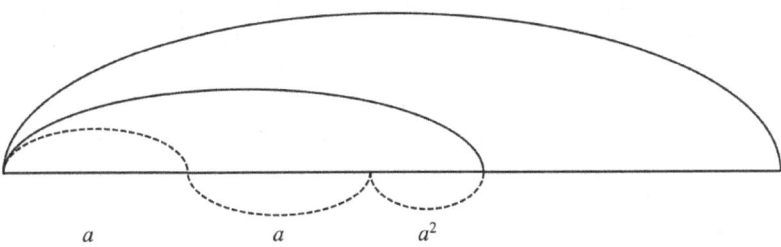

Where is the analyst? Given that he proceeds into this field of truth, one might clearly be somewhat tempted to identify him with the field of the Other, like in those coarse analogies between the analyst and the father, for example. It might also be here that the measure designed to determine all the relations of the whole, and notably those of the little *a* with the field of the sexual A, functions. Let's not rush, I beg you, into such hasty formulations, and especially given how false they are.

This doesn't stop there being the narrowest possible relation between the field of the A of the truthful intervention and the way in which the subject comes to presentify the *a*, if only, as you have just seen to all appearances in the exemplification borrowed from Ernst Kris, in the manner of a protest against a cut that comes ahead of time. There is just one infelicity, which is that Kris's intervention wasn't brought to bear in the field of truth, but in the field of the sexual Other, in so far as, in analysis – I'm saying, *in analysis* – this is a desexualised field.

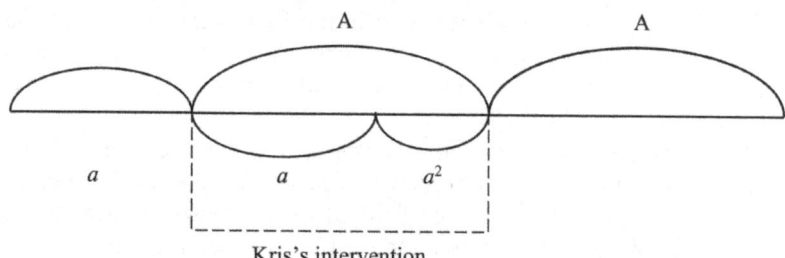

Kris's intervention

I mean that, in the subjective economy, it is upon the desexualisation of the field that is specific to the sexual act that this economy depends, together with the repercussions that the other sectors of the field shall therefore have on one another.

I won't be going any further into this until after the Easter holidays, for the reason that the next of our sessions, which will be the last before the break, will be reserved for someone who has asked me whether he might chime in on what I have been putting forward, since January at least, concerning this topology, which includes as much the four terms of alienation as those of repetition. Under these conditions it would be right to pause over what is involved in this field within which, in analysis, the place of the sexual act finds itself set aside.

So, I will be coming back now to the fundament of the satisfaction of the sexual act insomuch as it is also what sets the status of sublimation. I am coming back to it so that I won't have to push any further this year what I'm introducing on this point.

4

What is involved in the satisfaction of the sexual act?

It results from the following, with which we are acquainted from analytic experience, namely that there is, not from one partner to the other, but from whichever one of the partners to the idea of the couple as 1, the lack which we can define variously – want-of-Being, want of the Other's enjoyment – this lack, this non-coincidence of the subject as product in so far as he advances into the field of the sexual act. At that moment, he is nothing else but a product. He needs neither to be nor to think. He doesn't need to have his slide rule either. He enters this field and he believes he is equal to the role he has to hold there, be it that of man or that of woman. In either case, the phallic lack, which is called *castration* in one case or *Penisneid* in the other, is what symbolises the essential lack.

Sexual satisfaction and sublimation 191

And why does the penis find itself symbolising this? Well, precisely because, being that which, in the form of detumescence, materialises the want of enjoyment, it materialises the lack that derives, or more exactly which appears to derive, from the law of pleasure. It is effectively to the extent that pleasure has a limit, at which too much pleasure amounts to displeasure, that it comes to a stop here and seems not to lack anything. Well, this is a miscalculation.

It is exactly the same miscalculation that I can assure you I would be making if I were to pull off the sleight of hand, in giving myself over to a certain number of little equations concerning this a, this $1 + a$, this $1 - a$ which is equal to a^2 and everything that follows on from it, of suddenly passing off, as though it were nothing, this $2 + a$ which you can see here in the form of this a that is here and these two segments which are each worth 1, transformed, by error of course, into a $2a + 1$, without you noticing a thing.

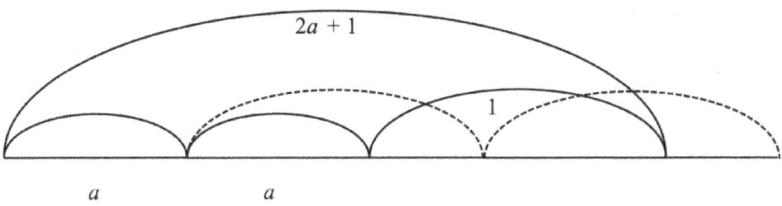

Erroneous transformation of $2 + a$ into $2a + 1$

I don't have time today, but if you like, once we've had our little debate together next time, it would be easy to do. It's even most amusing. There's nothing so amusing as this very lovely function that is called *the golden section*.

The $1 - a$ that is here, and which can easily be demonstrated to be equal to a^2, is what is satisfying about the sexual act, namely that, in the sexual act, one doesn't notice what is lacking. And here lies all the difference that separates it from sublimation. Not that in sublimation one is aware of it all the time, but one gets to it as such in the end, if there is an end to sublimation.

This is what I am going to try to materialise for you by making use of the relationship known as mean and extreme ratio.

What happens in sublimation? The interest of this relationship lies, as I told you last time, in being able to proceed by way of a successive reduction, which is produced thus. You fold back the a^2 here and you get, concerning what remains, namely the a that is here – here with a^2 to form 1 – another subtraction of a, that is to say $a - a^2$. It is easy to demonstrate that its value is equal to a^3, just as a^2 was equal to $1 - a$.

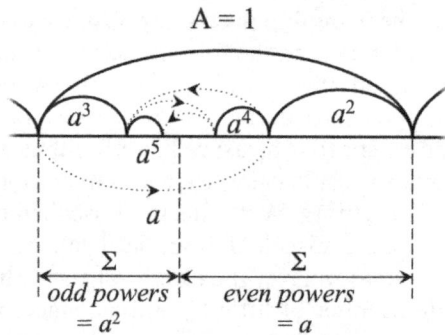

Structure of sublimation

This is what you get when you take each time the remainder and not, of course, what you have reproduced by way of a^2. If you fold back a^3, you get a sector that has the value of a^4. Then you fold this back and you have a^5, here. All the even powers are on one side and the odd powers on the other. It is easy to see that they will keep reaching out, one towards the other, to total up to 1. The point at which the cut between the odd powers and the even powers occurs is easily calculated. It is precisely determinable by the fact that it is equal to a^2, which was produced here at the start.

What does this yield as a structure of the sublimatory function? First of all, unlike the sexual act pure and simple, its point of departure is lack and it is with the aid of this lack that it constructs what amounts to its work and which always amounts to the reproduction of this lack. Whatever it is, and however it is taken, the work of sublimation is not at all necessarily a work of art. It can be many other things besides, including what I am doing here with you, which is a far cry from a work of art. This reproduction of lack, which goes so far as to narrow down on the point at which its final cut is strictly equivalent to the starting lack of a^2, is what is at issue in any completed work of sublimation.

Of course, this implies a repetition within the act. It is only through reworking the lack in an infinitely repeated fashion that the limit is reached that gives its measure to the work as a whole. For this to function, the measure still has to be right, from the beginning. Indeed, observe how, with the measure a that we have given as an especially harmonic measure, you have the following formula, $1 + a + a^2 \ldots$ etc., up to infinity with respect to the said powers, is equal to $1/(1-a)$.

This is not only true for the a of the right measure, the measure of the golden section, in so far as it serves us as an image commensurate with the subject in relation to sex, in an ideal case. This functions for any value x, on the sole condition that this x should be included between 0 and 1, that is to say, that it should thus entail some shortcoming, some lack, in relation to 1.

Of course, it will not be so readily handled in respect of the repetitive function of sublimation. The question is indeed as to what is involved in this a at the beginning. This a doesn't have to do only with the sexual function in the subject. It even stands anterior to it. It is tied purely and simply to repetition per se.

The relation of a to the barred subject, in so far as the barred subject strives to be situated in keeping with sexual satisfaction, is here what is called, strictly speaking, the fantasy. This fantasy is what we wish to broach this year, but before we could see how we might gain access to it, it was necessary for me to spell out these articulations for you, in a way that admittedly might seem far removed from the facts, but which, as you are going to see, is not so far removed as you might believe in joking about the presence, or not, of a slide rule in your pocket.

You are going to see, on the contrary, that by introducing these novel articulations into the structural realm, a great deal of the confusion, telescoping and obfuscation of theory can be cleared away in a fashion that has its inevitable consequence in the order of efficacy.

8 March 1967

NEXT SESSION

A visit to Sainte-Anne

I wish to give over all the time that is usually reserved for our talk to Dr Green, whom you can see on my right. I am therefore beginning just a little earlier, quickly to give you the few words of introduction I had been thinking of for this occasion, without, moreover, even knowing in advance that he had, as he has just told me, a great many things to tell us, such that he will in all likelihood fill up the hour and a half.

In accordance with the secret fabric of my superego, which is as steadfast as ever, as I had implicitly given myself a day off today, I found the means to have to speak yesterday evening, at five o'clock, to the young generation of psychiatrists at Sainte-Anne. That is to say, my goodness, to the generation of analyst candidates.

Honestly, what business did I have to be there? In truth, precious little, given that those who preceded me, and notably some of my students, and those best cut out to inform them what might have been marked out to enlighten them about my teaching, Mme Aulagnier for example, Piera – what will we not found upon this *piera*? – Serge Leclaire, even Charles Melman, to name them in alphabetical order, and others besides ... Well, setting aside the share of absent-mindedness that now and again drives me to say *yes* when someone asks me to do something, I did, even so, have a few reasons to be there. Namely, all of this was happening in the framework of a teaching which is that of my old friend, my old comrade, Henri Ey.

This generation of ours, because it's the same, Henri Ey's and mine, will therefore have played some role. This old comrade in particular will to my mind have been the one to whom I should give pride of place when it comes to a function that is none other than one which I shall call a civilising function.

You can scarcely fathom what the house physicians' office was like at Sainte-Anne when the two of us arrived, along with others, too, who had loosely the same vocation, but who in the end didn't make it to the finish line. The underdevelopment, if I may say so, when it came to logical dispositions, because it's a question of logic here, was truly, in 1925 – hey, it's not yesterday – something extraordinary. Well, since that time, Henri Ey has introduced his big machine, organo-dynamism. It's a false doctrine, but incontestably a civilising one. In this regard, it has fulfilled its role. It can be said that not a single soul in the field of the psychiatric hospital has not been touched by the questions that this doctrine brings to the fore, and these questions are questions of the greatest importance.

That the doctrine should be false is, in view of this effect, almost secondary. First, because it cannot be otherwise. It cannot be otherwise because it's a medical doctrine. It is necessary, it is essential to the status of medicine, that it should be dominated by a doctrine. This has always been so. The day when there will be no more doctrine will be the day when there will be no more medicine either. On the other hand, it is no less necessary, and experience proves as much, that this doctrine should be false. Without it, it couldn't lend its support to the status of medicine.

The day when the sciences – with which medicine now surrounds and sustains itself – come to join up in the middle, well, there will be no more medicine. There might still be psychoanalysis, which will then constitute medicine. But that will be most vexing indeed because it will be a definitive hindrance to psychoanalysis becoming a science. This is why I'm not wishing for it.

So, yesterday evening, I was brought before the audience thus chosen, to speak about the operation of alienation, which I think most of them had never heard mention of before, given how people don't like to go out of their way – from Sainte-Anne to the École normale, *It is a long way* . . . I thought therefore that for them – for they who constitute the sector of a calling upon psychoanalytic responsibilities, in other words, upon those who are going to train psychoanalysts – I ought to pinpoint, because it truly was the place for it, how this inaugural choice is posed, so to speak, which as you know is a false choice because it's a forced choice.

What appellatives are suitable for this choice in this central sector of those who are going to be in charge in the future? It was a matter, just like that, of accustoming their ears to the appropriate appellatives. I really am compelled to allude to this because it is rare for such talks, even when restricted, as this one was, to remain secret, above all when the house physicians' office is involved, and so perhaps you will get wind of these appellatives in the form of some gloating.

Obviously, these are not necessarily obliging appellatives. But to put forward *I am not thinking* and *I am not* as the fundamental constituents of this first alienation is not very obliging either for this vaster zone that I am bringing out as a whole from the human field in the form of the field of the subject – *either he is not thinking or he is not*. Moreover, it changes if you put it in the third person. What is at issue here is indeed *either I am not thinking or I am not*. This tempers a good deal the value of the terms I used yesterday, above all if one considers that, in keeping with the operation of alienation, one of the two terms is always excluded.

I then showed them how the term that remains takes on a wholly different value, which is in some sort positive, by proposing itself, by imposing itself even, as a scale term that offers itself to criticism from those I was then invoking, in considering the position specific to candidates to be one of criticism. This was very urgent because, while the former situation was that of underdeveloped folk so far as logic was concerned, the current situation among this generation, through a sort of paradox and an effect that is precisely that of analysis, is altogether different. The occurrence, *casus*, of the best, *optimus*, can in a good many cases be *pessimus*, the worst. The others were underdeveloped in logic, but they tended to be monkish. I mean that, in the same way that monks withdraw from the world, they would thus withdraw from logic. They used to wait until their analysis was over before pondering any logic.

I roundly urged them to give up this standpoint. Moreover, I'm not the only one. It so happens that there are others. There is one right beside me, for example, who is one of those who, in this realm, has been trying to rouse, while there is still time – I mean, not at all necessarily at the end of didactic analysis but during its course, too, and perhaps this is even more worthwhile – the critical vigilance of those whom he might have on occasion to indoctrinate.

Nevertheless, I must say that it is in the capacity of psychoanalyst, in the capacity of a representative of this field, the problematic field in which for the time being the whole future of psychoanalysis is still being played out, that Monsieur Green finds himself today receiving the floor, in view of the altogether sizeable fact that he himself stepped forward to do so. I mean that it is not at all in the capacity of one of my pupils, or one of my followers, that he is going to be telling you today what the reflections that the latest terms I brought forward in connection with the logic of the fantasy have inspired in him. I will now give him the floor, for exactly as long as he would like, and will allow myself to take advantage, for both your use and mine, of what he will have put forward today.

Green, the floor is yours. *(There follows the presentation by Dr Green.)*

Many thanks to Green for the contribution he has brought us today. I think I don't need to underscore, for the informed ears, what has gratified me so deeply in his exposition. While he has introduced a number of questions on sundry planes concerning my concurrence with or my distance from Freud, or concerning the elucidation, the calling into question, of such and such a point of what here amounts to work in progress, to something that is being constructed and is developing in front of you and with you in mind, I do owe him an extra acknowledgement. Thanks to the step that his talk constitutes, the level of these questions has now been posited which ought to enable us presently not only to reply to him – which I most surely will do, and in designating the spot where I join him – but also to pursue the edification, I shall say, by taking up the pinpointing of this level which has been contributed by a study that is truly so profound, so substantial, which he has produced in front of you today in reference – I can say this and I think he will feel the homage in it – to my disquisition. I can only add my compliments on the forbearance he has shown throughout the test, to which we have all been exposed, of the unpleasant rumble of various noises and for which I must in some way apologise because it was most surely not his person that was being targeted on this occasion.

The next appointment will be on 12 April. Contrary to what some people were expecting, there will be no seminar on 5 April.

15 March 1967

XIII

THERE IS NO SEXUAL ACT

A language emptied of the subject
On the difficulty of being a sexuated subject
Contradictory and contrary
Enjoyment value
The he-man

Non licet omnibus adire . . . Since no one finishes it . . . *Corinthum*. I've used a Latinate pronunciation for the first word to suggest the translation – *This is not the omnibus for Corinth*.

The adage that was transmitted to us in Latin from a Greek wording does not merely signify, I think, that the prostitutes were dear in Corinth. They were dear because they initiated you into something. I would thus say that it's not enough to pay the price. This is rather what the Greek wording meant.

Likewise, it is not open to everyone to – inverted commas – become a psychoanalyst. This is how it has been for centuries when it comes to being a geometrician.

1

Let none enter here . . . you know the rest . . . *who is ignorant of geometry*. This requirement was inscribed on the pediment of the most famous school of philosophy in Antiquity, and it indicates very well what is at issue, namely the introduction of a certain mode of thought.

We can specify this with a further step. It's a matter of categories. The equivalent in Latin to the Greek word κατηγορία is *praedicamentum*, this being what is the most radically predicable for the defining of a field.

It brings with it a specified register of demonstration. This is why, in the wake of the Platonic requirement, the claim to demonstrate *more geometrico* could be heard being expressed in a reiterated fashion, which bears witness to just how much the said mode of demonstration represented an ideal.

It is known, it is wished that you should know – I'm pointing this out to you so far as I am able, that is to say, within the limits of the field that is my reserve – that metamathematics is now coming to radicalise yet further the status of the demonstrable over the full range of categorial remodelling that historically punctuated the conquests of the geometrical.

As you know, geometry is moving further and further away from the intuitions that ground it, spatial intuition for example, and is endeavouring to be no more than a specifiable form of demonstration, and moreover one that is multi-tiered, to the extent that ultimately metamathematics has been dealing only with the order of this terracing, in the hope of getting to the most radical stringencies so far as demonstration is concerned.

Imagine a science that begins only with the terminal point of the remodelling of a certain field thus evoked. It would be needless for it first to stammer through land surveying, in which a first familiarity with the measurable comes to take on order, or even the transmission of the most substantial formulae that were to come, which emerged in the singular guise of the secrets of calculus. It would be needless, and at the very least deceptive and idle, for it to tarry over the Babylonian stage of geometry, because any template of measure that you meet at the start taints this science with a mirage that is impossible to clear away. This is what we pointed out to begin with in our teaching, denouncing the trickery of narcissism – without yet naming it with the term we have now pinned on it, the *imaginary* – when we established the function of the mirror stage.

Running into an obstacle like this was effectively the fate of a good many sciences, and this is even where the special privilege of geometry lies. It is here, of course, that the purity of the notion of magnitude presents. That this is not *what the rabble believe* ought not to hold us back here. For the science that we are entertaining, it's a wholly different tablature. Not only is the template of measure inoperative here, but the very conception of a unit is a shaky one so long as the sort of inequality in which its element is instituted has not been generated, that is to say, the heterogeneity that is concealed within it.

Recall the equation of value in the first steps of *Das Kapital* – by Marx, for those who are unaware. You never know, some people might have got distracted. What is made patent in his writing on this equation is the ratio that results from the price of two pieces of merchandise, *so much of some such = so much of some such*, an inverse relation between price and the quantity of merchandise obtained. Now, what is at issue is not at all that which is patent in the equation, but that which it harbours, that which the equation withholds, which is the discrepancy in nature between the values thus combined and the necessity of this discrepancy. Indeed, what founds the price cannot be the ratio, the degree of urgency for example, of two use values, nor the ratio, and with good reason, of two exchange values. In the equation of values, one comes up as use value and the other as exchange value. We know that a similar catch occurs when labour value is at issue. The important thing is that it is demonstrated in this critical work that *Das Kapital* is, as can be read in its subtitle, that in failing to acknowledge these catches, any demonstration remains moot or leads astray.

Marxism's contribution to science – I am certainly not the one who carried out this work – is to reveal this latent element as being necessary at the start. I mean, at the start of political economy. The same goes for psychoanalysis. This sort of latency is what I, for my part, call *structure*. My reservations are drawn to the side of any effort to drown out this notion – in narrowing down the necessary points of departure within a certain field that cannot be defined otherwise than as a critical field – in something that I identify, poorly, under the vague name of *Structuralism*.

It ought not to be thought, of course, that this latency is missing in geometry. But history is proving that it is at its end, now that they can just perceive as much, because biases about the notion of magnitude, which stem from its handling in the real, have not done a disservice to its logical furtherance by chance alone. Still, it is only now that this can be known, upon noticing that the geometry that has come about has no need of measurement, of metrics, nor even of the space that is said to be real.

As I said, this is not so for the other sciences. Why is it that some of them cannot get going without having worked out these facts, which might be said to be final in that they are structural? Perhaps we may pose this question as of now as a pertinent one, if we know how to make it homologous with these facts.

In truth, we are ready for this because we have taken note of this structure as much as we have practised it, on meeting it in our psychoanalytic experience, and because, while we have introduced our remarks, from a few insights which, moreover, are trivial, into the realm of the sciences – I'm stating the obvious here – these remarks of ours are not without setting their sights on such results as this realm ought really to come to terms with.

For as long as I've been teaching, though not so long as I've been writing, I've been teaching that structure comes down to how the subject is a fact of language per se. The subject thus designated is that to which is generally attributed the function of speech. What distinguishes this subject is the introduction of a mode of Being that is its own specific energy, in the Aristotelian sense of the term ἐνέργεια. This mode is the act in which the subject is taciturn.

Tacere is not *silere*, and yet they do overlap at an obscure frontier. It is nonsense to write, as has been written, that it is fruitless to search for any allusion to silence in my *Écrits*. When I inscribed the formula for the drive at the top right of the graph as barred S, lozenge, capital D for demand, ($ ◊ D), it was so as to indicate that the drive begins where demand becomes taciturn. But if I didn't speak at all about silence it was precisely because *sileo* is not *taceo*. The act of being taciturn does not free the subject from language, even if the essence of the subject culminates in this act, if it agitates the shadow of its liberty. Being taciturn remains laden with an enigma that for so long made the animal world such a heavy presence. We no longer have any trace of it except in phobia, but let's not forget that for a long while the gods could be housed here.

The *eternal silence* of anything whatsoever, of everything that you are aware of, only half spooks us now due to the appearance, which science gives to common consciousness, of positing itself as a knowledge that refuses to be dependent upon language, without this claimed consciousness being struck for all that by the correlation that, by the same token, it refuses to be dependent upon the subject.

What has actually been happening is not that science has been bypassing the subject, but that it has been emptying it of language. I mean that it has been expelling language from the subject. It creates its formulae from a language that has been emptied of the subject. It begins with a prohibition on the subject effect of language, and this has but one result – to demonstrate, in effect, that the subject is but an effect, and one of language, but that it is a void effect. Thenceforth, the void encircles it, that is to say, makes it appear as a pure structure of language. This is the meaning of the discovery of the unconscious.

The unconscious is the moment at which there speaks, in the stead of the subject, pure language, an utterance about which the question remains as to who said it. The unconscious, its status which can indeed be said to be scientific because its origin is the doing of science, is the subject that, rejected from the symbolic, reappears in the real, presentifying there what is now a fait accompli in the history of science, namely its only support, language itself. This is the sense of the appearance of the new linguistics in science.

What does language per se talk about when it is thus unfastened from the subject but is thereby representing it in its radicalised structural emptiness? We know this in broad strokes. It talks about sex.

It talks about sex in a speech whose silence is represented by the sexual act. That is to say, it talks in a speech that is necessarily tenacious and obstinate in forcing it, and with good reason.

This sexual act is what I am going to examine now.

2

Even so, I will take the time to clear away, in a fashion that I don't think unhelpful, the first prejudice to rise up. It's not a new one, of course, but shedding new light on it always has it impact.

We shall situate the first prejudice, which rises up in a psychologising context, in contradistinction to the reference to enunciation which we have just made, the only true enunciation, from the unconscious. It may be formulated through the remnant, in what we have stated, of an index that is essential to structure. As I said, the unconscious talks about sex. Here, the frivolous mind, and goodness knows they are aplenty, swallows the *about* and has it that *the unconscious talks sex*.

It bellows. It rants. It mews. It bills and coos. It doesn't belong to the realm of all the vocal noises of speech. It's a *sexual aspiration*. This is the sense that is presupposed, in the best cases, in the use that is made of the term *life instinct* in psychoanalytic ruminations. Each erroneous use of the discourse on the subject has the effect of bringing this discourse down to the level of what it fantasises in the stead of the subject.

This psychoanalytic discourse of which I speak is itself a rant. It rants in calling upon the figure of an Eros that would supposedly be a unitive power and, what is more, enjoy universal impact. To regard what withholds the cells of an organism as being of the same essence as the force that is purported to impel the individual thus composed to copulate with another belongs strictly to the domain of delusion, in a period when meiosis is sufficiently distinct from mitosis, at least under the microscope. I mean, for everything that is presupposed by the anatomical phases of the metabolism that meiosis and mitosis represent.

The idea of Eros as a soul with aims that are contrary to the aim of Thanatos, and which are active through sex, is the discourse of a starry-eyed girl in springtime, to echo the erstwhile expression of the late lamented Julien Benda, *midinette au printemps*. He is long forgotten nowadays, but he represented for a while that sort of swashbuckler who is the result of an intelligentsia that has lost its usefulness.

To place those who have gone astray back onto the axis of the unconscious structured like a language – isn't quite sufficient evidence provided by those objects which had never been specified in the way that we have managed to specify them, to wit the phallus and the different part objects? We will be coming back to what results from their immixing in our thought, to the twist that has been taken by the fumes given off by one or other of the waves of contemporary philosophy loosely qualified as existentialist. For us, these objects bear witness to how the unconscious does not talk sexuality any more than it sings it, but rather, in producing these objects, it finds itself precisely, as I said, talking *about* it, since it is by being in a relation of metaphor and metonymy with sexuality that these objects are constituted.

As firm and as straightforward as these truths may be, it has to be believed that they generate a very strong aversion because, in preventing them from remaining in the centre, they are unable thereafter to be the fulcrum of any articulation of the subject. And so is begat that sort of bland liberty to which I have already alluded more than once in these last sentences and which is characteristic of the lack of seriousness.

What are we to say of what is said about the sexual act by the unconscious? I could do a little Barbey d'Aurevilly number here. He once made one of those diabolical clergymen, whom he so excelled at portraying, say, *What is the secret of the Church? The secret of the Church* . . ., so well crafted to give fright to old ladies in the provinces, . . . *IS THAT THERE IS NO PURGATORY*. Thus shall I amuse myself by telling you what might, even so, have a certain effect on you – after all, I'm not punctuating what I'm about to say about this stage just for the sake of it – the secret of psychoanalysis, its big secret, is that there is no sexual act.

This is something that can be upheld and illustrated.

To do so, I will remind you about what I have called *act*, namely the doubling of a motor effect as simple as *I'm walking*, which means that simply in being uttered with a certain accentuation, it finds itself being repeated and, through this doubling, takes on the signifying function that makes it capable of being inserted into a certain chain so as there to inscribe the subject. Is there in the sexual act anything comparable whatsoever? In the sexual act, is the subject able to inscribe himself, in the same form, as sexuated, establishing by that same act his conjunction with the subject of the sex that is called opposite? It is quite clear that everything in the psychoanalytic experience speaks against it.

There is nothing in this act that does not vouch for how the only discourse thereof that can be established is one in which all that counts is the same third-party element which I just stated quite amply enough as the presence of the phallus and part objects. We now need to articulate its function in such a way as to demonstrate what role this function plays in the sexual act. It is a function of substitution that is constantly sliding, that is almost equivalent to a sort of juggling, and which in no case whatsoever allows us to posit that, in the sexual act, man and woman stand as opposites in some eternal essence.

And yet, I will scratch what I said about the big secret that there is no sexual act, on account of how it is no big secret, on account of how it is patent that the unconscious keeps shouting it out at the top of its voice. And this is precisely why psychoanalysts say – *Let's shut it up when it says this, because if we repeat as much along with it, no one will come to seek us out anymore. Why would they, if there is no sexual act?*

So, they lay the emphasis on the fact that there is sexuality. Indeed, it is precisely because there is sexuality that there isn't any sexual act. But the unconscious might perhaps mean that it gets messed up. At any rate, it certainly seems that way. Only, for this to assume its full scope, it does need to be accentuated to begin with that the unconscious says it.

You remember the anecdote about the cleric who preached about sin? *What did he say? – He was against it.* Well, the unconscious preaches too, in its own way, about the subject of the sexual act. And it's not in favour of it. This is the most suitable point of departure for conceiving of what is at issue when it's a matter of the unconscious. Even so, the difference between the unconscious and the cleric deserves to be pointed out here. It's that the cleric says that the sin is sin, instead of, perhaps, the unconscious turning sexuality into a sin. There's a small difference.

What arises for us here is the question of how the subject has to measure up to the difficulty of being a sexuated subject. This is why I introduced into my last logistical comments a reference – the aim of which I think I sufficiently underscored as being to establish the status of the object *a* – which goes by the name of the golden section. It is what imparts its status, in a form that is readily handled, to what is in question, namely the incommensurable.

In the little *a*, we indicate what is in some sense the substance of the subject, if you understand this substance in the sense that Aristotle designates it in οὐσία. What specifies οὐσία, and which people forget, is precisely that it cannot in any way whatsoever be attributed to any subject, the subject being understood as ὑποκείμενον. The *a* serves as a module to examine him who is supported by it. He doesn't need to go in search of his complement in the dyad – that which he lacks to become twain, and which would be altogether desirable. The solution to this relation, by virtue of which 2 might be established, hinges entirely on what will bypass the referring of *a*, the golden section, to 1 insomuch as it engenders lack. This lack is inscribed here through the simple carryover effect, which is likewise an effect of discrepancy, in the form $1 - a$. This is an altogether straightforward calculation, which I have already written up on the board to invite you to find it for yourselves, formulated as $1 - a = a^2$.

I am calling this to mind only so as to bring in, here on the cusp of what I want to introduce, what it is essential to articulate for you as the point of departure for our science, namely that which introduces us necessarily, albeit paradoxically, to the sexual nexus wherein the act that at the present time is forming our interrogation steals away and flees from us. What is at issue is the bond with the *a* insomuch as the *a* represents, *darstellt*, supports and presentifies first of all the subject himself. It is the same *a* that will appear in an exchange which has a formulation which we are now going to show, an exchange capable of using this object that we touch upon in the dialectic of the treatment under the heading of the part object. What is at issue, then, is the relation between these two facets of the *a* function and the index of the object that lies behind the principle of castration.

I won't be bringing this cycle to a close today. This is why I want to preface it with two formulations that correspond to a sort of problem that we are posing ourselves a priori. If the object *a* really is there as having to represent discrepancy in the sexual dyad, what value ought to be ascribed to it so that it can yield the two results between which our question hangs? This question can be broached only along the path down which I have been leading you, the path of logic.

The dyad and its points of suspension are what logic has been elaborating since the very beginning, if one knows how to follow its trace. I'm not going to be rehearsing the history of logic for you, but let it suffice me to mention that Aristotle's *Organon*, which stands at its dawn, is something quite different from mere formalism, if you know how to plumb its depths. The first point in his predicate logic is the opposition between contraries and contradictories. We have come a long way since then, but this is no reason not to take an interest in the status of these terms and how they entered history.

Furthermore, as an aside for those who sometimes open up textbooks on logic, when we track closely what Aristotle set out, nothing should forbid us from introducing at the same time what the likes of Łukasiewicz, for instance, has filled it out with since then. I'm saying this because in the Kneale and Kneale, which for that matter is quite excellent, I was struck by a declaration that pops up just like that at the turn of a page, in which Łukasiewicz comes to distinguish, in what Aristotle says, what belongs to the Principle of Contradiction from the Principle of Identity and from the Principle of Bivalence.

The Principle of Identity is that A is A. You know that it's not clear that A is A. Fortunately, Aristotle didn't say that. But, even so, that this should be pointed out holds a certain interest. Second, that a thing should be both A and not A is a different matter entirely. As for the Principle of Bivalence, namely that a thing must be true or false, this is a third matter. I find that pointing this out rather clarifies Aristotle. Pointing out that he surely never pondered all these niceties has nothing to do with the issue.

This is what allows its full interest to be accorded to this coarse business of contraries to which I'm now returning.

We will designate this contrary by *not without*. This is not in Aristotle, but it's already indicated in my past teaching. It will be helpful to us later. Don't fret. Just allow me to steer you a little.

The contraries are what are raised by the whole logical question as to whether, yes or no, the particular proposition implies existence. People have always found it enormously shocking that, in Aristotle, it does incontestably imply as much. His logic even hinges upon this.

It's curious that the universal proposition does not imply as much. I mean that the universal proposition *Every centaur has six limbs* is absolutely true. Only, there are no centaurs. If, however, I say, *There are centaurs who have lost one*, in Aristotle this implies that centaurs exist. I'm trying to reconstruct a logic that would be a little less shaky on the centaur side. But this isn't of interest to us for the time being.

There is no male without female. This belongs to the realm of the real. It has nothing to do with logic, at the very least not in our times. And then there is the contradictory, which means the following and nothing else – *If something is male, then it is not non-male.* It's a matter of finding our path through these two distinct wordings.

The second, that of the contradictory, belongs to the symbolic order. It is a symbolic convention, which precisely has a name – *the excluded third*. This ought to be sufficient to give us a sense of how it is not from this angle that we are going to be able to sort things out for ourselves because, at the start, we sufficiently accentuated the function of a discrepancy as essential to the status of the sexual dyad. If it could be founded, subjectively I mean, then we would need this third.

Let's not pull a useless face now to claim that we are attempting what we have already introduced, namely the logical status of the contrary. Over here, *one and the other* stands in opposition to *one or the other*, over there.

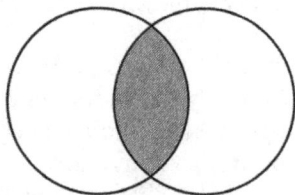

This *one and the other* is an *intersection* in Boolean algebra and can be most fittingly inscribed in the shape of this small overlapping lunular space.

I am much dismayed at having to present this figure yet again, because you can see very well that it's not satisfactory in the slightest. What you would like is for there to be one that is male and the other female, and for them to be treading on each other's toes once in a while. This is not what this is about. It's about logical multiplication.

The game of heads or tails – to which I tried to attune, at least for a term, those who were following me over the early years, just to get across to them what the signifier is – is quite evenly inscribed into a sequence of pluses and minuses. Contrary to this, the relation of *one and the other* is inscribed in the form of a multiplication. I mean, a logical multiplication, a Boolean multiplication.

What value – because this is what it at issue – can we suppose for the element of discrepancy so that the result would be the bare net value of the dyad? This really does lie in the reach of everyone. At least this much should have been dyed fast into you by the maths you were taught, so mindlessly, if you are over thirty. If you are in your twenties, you might be fortunate enough to have heard it being spoken about a little differently. No matter. You are all on the same footing with regard to the formula $(a + b) . (a - b)$. Here is the discrepancy – there is one that has it as a plus, the other has it as a minus. If you multiply them, it gives $a^2 - b^2$. What value needs to be ascribed to the discrepancy so that $a^2 - b^2$ should be equal to 2, to the dyad? It's very easy. On the one hand, b has to be equal to the square root of minus 1, $\sqrt{-1}$, that is to say, a numerical function that is known as an *imaginary number*. These imaginary numbers crop up in all sorts of calculations nowadays, in the most commonplace fashion, to found what are called *complex numbers,* an extension of the real numbers. As for a, if it is a matter of specifying it in two opposite ways, with plus something and with minus something, so that both should give the result of 2, then it suffices to make a equal to 1. Meanwhile, b is equal to i, which is how the imaginary function $\sqrt{-1}$ is usually written, and indeed it is far wieldier.

Don't believe that what I'm explicating for you here will be of no use to us. I'm introducing it here at the outset because it's going to be of use to us for what comes next. But right away this can be clarified by a parallel formula that presents to us as the other possibility, if we ask ourselves in advance what has to be obtained. This, too, holds a certain interest for us. For it is also very interesting to find out why, in the unconscious, with regard to the sexual act, we are indeed compelled to say that what marks out discrepancy – in the first line of which stands the subject himself – still remains at the end, but also that it is required that it should remain at the end for this to be a sexual act. In other words, this time around it is required that (a + b) . (a − b) should be equal to a. Clearly, this is not the same a as in the formula from just now, when it was a matter of obtaining 2. What value should be given to a in the new formula?

Well, for $(1 + a) \cdot (1 - a)$ to be equal to a, this a has to be equal to the golden section. This is an opportunity to say once again that I have been using the golden section to introduce for you the function of the object a. You can confirm that when a is equal to the golden section, the product of $(1 + a) \cdot (1 - a)$ is a.

It is at this juncture that I will suspend for the time being what I wanted to bring forth for you in a logical grid.

3

Let's turn our consideration now to what is at issue with respect to the sexual act.

What is going to be of service to us in dealing with this, and which justifies my having earlier introduced Marx's famous slogan, is the following formulation, which we owe to his mentor, Feuerbach. *The subject's object is nothing else but the objective essence of the subject itself.* Thus, the object to which any subject refers, in essence and necessarily, is none other than the specific essence of this unobjectified subject.

While this formulation has a simplistic and approximate aspect with regard to what the doctrine developed by Marx was to be, as has been shown very well by certain persons, some of whom are my listeners, it would be curious for us to be standing much further ahead of it. What can give the object at issue here, which is the specific essence of the subject qua unobjectified, its veritable substance? Well, who else can do this but us, analysts?

Let's take as our starting point what psychoanalysis has set out concerning the subject of the fundamental law of sex, which we have long taken as our fulcrum, namely the incest prohibition, to the extent that for us it is another reflection, and a very sufficient reflection, of the presence of the third-party element in any sexual act, insomuch as it requires the subject's presence and foundation. Psychoanalysis made its entrance in the world with the announcement that there is no sexual act that does not bear the trace of what is called, improperly, the traumatic scene, in other words a fundamental referential relation with the parental couple.

You know how matters stand at the other end. As Lévi-Strauss showed in *Structures élémentaires de la parenté*, in the order of exchange upon which the order of kinship is instituted, it is woman who bears the costs. Women are exchanged. No matter whether the logic is patriarchal or matriarchal, the logic of inscription prevails on any ethnologist to look into how the women are transported between lineages.

It seems that there is something of a gap between these two ends. Well, today we are going to indicate how, in our field, this gap is articulated and filled in.

Earlier we marked out how the origin of the unmasking or the demystification of the economy can be seen in the combining of two values that are discrepant in nature. This is precisely what we are dealing with here.

What poses a problem in the sexual act is not social. Rather, it is here that the principle of the social is constituted, namely the law of exchange. The exchange of women no longer concerns us, but if we perceive that the problem belongs to the order of value, I would say that everything starts to become quite clear enough in giving it its name. We saw earlier that the founding of the merchandise-object results from falsely identifying exchange value with use value. And it might even be said that it takes capitalism for this thing, which far antecedes capitalism, to be revealed. Likewise, the principle of what structurally splits value in two at the level of the unconscious is that there is something that holds the place of exchange value. For us to perceive what is at issue, it requires the status of the subject such as it is wrought by science, which reduces this subject to its function as an interval. We shall call this – and why not? We shall be justifying it presently – *enjoyment value*. The equating of the two discrepant values, use value and enjoyment value, here hinges on how the latter plays the role of exchange value.

You should have an immediate sense of how this truly does concern what lies at the very heart of analytic teaching, and how this enjoyment value is perhaps what will allow us to formulate in a completely different way what is involved in castration.

However muddled the notion of drive maturation may be in the theory, it does, even so, put the emphasis on how there is no sexual act – I mean, in the sense whereof the necessity I have just spelt out – that does not entail, strangely enough, castration.

What is it that we call castration? It's not that the little tap gets unscrewed, as in the formulations that are so nicely put forward by little Hans, because the tap really does need to stay in its place. What is at issue is that it could never take its enjoyment in itself.

Moreover, they go on about this everywhere in analytic theory.

4

I'm nearing the end of my lesson for today, such that, as you may suspect, I'm abridging.

I will accentuate the following, from which I should like to start again – the equating of the two values known as use and exchange, and what is essential about this in our field.

Imagine if you will man reduced institutionally to the function of a domestic-animal stud. This has never been done, it has to be said.

To designate him, let's use English. As you know, in English they speak of a he-goat or a she-goat. Well, let's call this man, as most befits, a *he-man*. As an instrument, this is altogether conceivable. In fact, if there is something that gives a clear idea of use value then it is what is being done whenever one brings in a bull to perform a certain amount of servicing. It is quite peculiar that no one has ever entertained inscribing the elementary structures of kinship into this circulation of the almighty phallus.

The curious thing, and we are the ones who discovered it, is that this phallic value is represented by woman. If enjoyment, penile enjoyment I mean, bears the mark that is said to be that of castration, it seems that this would be so that, in a way that we might call fictive, in echo of Bentham, woman should become that which procures enjoyment. This is a singular claim, which for us opens up all the ambiguities peculiar to the word *enjoyment*, in so far as, in the terms of the juridical development it now entails, it implies possession.

In other words, what we have here is something that has turned around. It is no longer the sexual organ of our bull – use value – that will serve in this sort of circulation in which sexual order is established, but rather woman, in so far as she herself has become on this occasion the locus of transfer of the value subtracted at the level of use value, in the form of an object of enjoyment.

It's really very curious, because this sweeps us along with it. Having introduced the he-man, you will now hear me calling woman the *she-man*. This is quite in line with the wit of the English language. Goodness knows the fun that has been poked at the *wo* of *woman*, which promises nothing but woe. In French, I shall call her *l'hommelle*. This word will also be poked fun at, and widely misapprehended I suppose. I present you *l'hommelle*, the she-woman. I'm holding her by the little finger. She will be of great service to us.

Everything that the analytic literature has been able to articulate about woman in the sexual act concerns her only insomuch as she plays the she-man function. May the women here present not look askance at this, because in truth I am making this remark precisely to set aside, there where she is, the place of this woman about whom we have been speaking from the start. In everything that is pointed out to us in this literature with respect to women's sexuality, and in keeping with long-standing experience for that matter, masquerade plays an eminent role. It has to do with the way in which she makes use of an equivalent to the phallic object, which has always made of her a wearer of jewellery. Well, we are perhaps at last about to make this jewellery speak, in the manner of Diderot's *bijoux indiscrets*.

It is most peculiar that, from the subtraction, somewhere, of an enjoyment that is chosen only for its character of ready handling, if I may dare thus to designate penile enjoyment, we can see being introduced here – with what Marx, and we, too, call *the fetish*, which is to say a use value that is extracted and frozen – a hole that is the sole necessary nook of insertion for any sexual ideology. This subtraction, somewhere, of enjoyment, is the fulcrum.

Doubtless woman does constitute the alienation of analytic theory, and that of Freud himself, who is the father of this theory and one who was great enough to have noticed this alienation, as is shown by the question he was wont to repeat – *What does woman want?* Don't believe, for all that, that woman is faring any worse. I mean that she still has her own enjoyment at her disposal in a way that utterly eludes this ideological seizure. She has no lack of resources when it comes to playing the she-man, and it is in this respect that even the feminist claim has nothing original about it –

it's still the same masquerade, simply revamped to the tastes of the day – but where she remains inexpugnable, inexpugnable as woman, lies outside the system that the sexual act is said to be.

It is on this basis that we must gauge the difficulty at issue concerning the act with regard to the respective status of the originary sexes, man and woman, in what is instituted by the sexual act to the extent that it is a subject that can found itself therein. Here they are brought to the utmost pitch of their disjunction. I spoke to you about the she-man, but what about the he-man? Where is he? Well, he's vanished. They are no more. Precisely because, as such, the he-man has been withdrawn from use value.

Of course, this doesn't prevent them from really circulating. Man as a penile value circulates very well. But it's clandestine. Regardless of the value it may hold, which is certainly essential, in social climbing. By the left hand, generally speaking.

I will say more. We oughtn't to omit that, while the he-man is not recognised in the status of the sexual act in the sense that it is foundational in society, there nevertheless exists a Society for the Protection of the He-Man. This is even what is known as male homosexuality.

On this somewhat marginal point, mirthfully highlighted, I will come to a halt for today, simply because the time is putting a stop to what I had prepared for you.

12 April 1967

XIV

ON ENJOYMENT VALUE

> Enjoyment value and discourses of truth
> Schema for the sublimation operation
> Were sexual relationship to exist . . .
> *He enjoys* versus *he has enjoyment of*
> Castration complex versus primary narcissism

I set out a certain number of items in front of you last time. I stated, for instance, *there is no sexual act*. I daresay the news has been going all around town.

Well, I didn't impart this as an absolute truth. I said that this was what was strictly speaking articulated in the discourse of the unconscious.

That said, I did frame this formulation, and a few others, into a sort of reminder, which I must say was fairly dense, about what provides its meaning and its premisses as well.

The lesson was a sort of waypoint dotted with assembly areas, which will perhaps be of service as a written introduction to something that I should like therefore to pursue today in a form that is perhaps more accessible. At any rate, it has been envisioned as an easy stroll.

It will be a first way of unravelling the articulations into which I shall be advancing, which are those I have been presentifying for you over the last two or three lessons, namely an articulation between three units. There is the *a*. There is a value 1 which is there only to give its meaning to the value *a*, given that the latter is a number, and strictly speaking the golden number. And then there is a second value 1.

|—— *a* ——|—— 1 ——|—— 1 ——|

I could of course rearticulate these units once again in such a way as to show their necessity, in other words in a way that I might call apodictic. I shall be proceeding differently, beginning instead by exemplifying the use I am going to be making of them, even if it means taking things up again thereafter in the required fashion, the one that for now I'll be steering away from.

I'm going to be proceeding in a fashion that could be called *eristic*, doing so therefore with a thought for those who don't know what this is about.

1

What this is about is psychoanalysis.

It's not necessary to know what is at issue in psychoanalysis to benefit from my discourse. One still needs to have been practised in this discourse for a certain amount of time.

I must suppose that this is not the case for everyone here, especially among those who are not psychoanalysts.

While I am mindful of those who have to be introduced to what I have called *my discourse*, this is not of course without a thought for the psychoanalysts. Yet I also need, to a certain degree, to address those whom I am coming first to define, and whom I did indeed one day find myself labelling, as *the great numbers*. I need to address them so that my discourse should in some way come back from a point of reflection to the ears of the psychoanalysts.

Indeed, it is striking, and inherent in what is at issue, that the psychoanalyst doesn't enter this discourse in full flight, and this is so, precisely, to the very extent that this discourse concerns his practice and that this is demonstrable. The ensuing part of my disquisition today will be laying the accent on why it is conceivable that the psychoanalyst should find in his very status, I mean in what establishes him as a psychoanalyst, something that might put up some resistance, and especially to the point I introduced, inaugurated, in my last disquisition.

To say the word, introducing *enjoyment value* poses a question at the very root of a discourse, of any discourse, that might go by the title *discourse of truth* – at least, understand me on this, in so far as this discourse may come to compete with the discourse of the unconscious, if indeed this discourse of the unconscious is, as I said last time, really articulated by this enjoyment value.

It is peculiar to see how psychoanalysts always do a little touching up to this competing discourse. It is right where their potential utterance stands squarely in truthfulness that they invariably find themselves going back on it. It is enough to have a little experience to know that this wrangling is strictly correlative, when one can take stock of it, to the sort of graspingness that is linked to the psychoanalytic institution and which adds up to the idea of getting oneself recognised on the plane of knowledge.

Enjoyment value, so I said, lies behind the principle of the economy of the unconscious. I also said, underlining the article *du*, not that the unconscious *parle sexe*, but that it *parle du sexe*, it talks *about* sex. What the unconscious designates for us are the pathways of a knowledge. To follow them, one must abstain from wanting to know prior to having wended one's way along them. The unconscious talks about sex, but can it be said that it tells us about sex? In other words, does it tell the truth?

To say that it talks always leaves what it is saying in abeyance. One can talk to say nothing, which is even commonplace. It's not the case for the unconscious. One can say things without talking. This is not the case for the unconscious either. And even, the full depth of what I articulated about the unconscious at that point of departure was that *it speaks*. Of course, this has gone unnoticed, like a good many other features I have spelt out.

If anyone had a good ear, they could deduce from this that, to say something, it has to speak. But I have yet to see anyone pluck this out, even though it's said in my *Discours de Rome* in at least a dozen different ways, one of which was recently presented to me in the course of a few interviews with some young people, who were most congenial and very taken with one part of my *Discours*. It had to do with my famous formulation that the subject in analysis speaks to you, the analyst, then he speaks of himself, and then, when he speaks of himself to you, everything will go just fine. This formulation has had a better fortune, of course, on account of being a formulation. Always be wary whenever anyone wants to pack everything into a formulation. Formulations which have the good fortune to be gathered up, like this one, need to be placed back into their context to avoid giving rise to confusion.

So, does the unconscious tell the truth about sex? I haven't said so. Freud, you will recall, raised the question. He did so, it should be specified, in connection with a dream of one of his patients and her dream was manifestly designed to lead him, Freud, up the garden path, to make him think the moon is made of green cheese. That generation of disciples was fresh enough back then for him to have to explain this to them by making a fuss. In truth, one can easily get out of it by noting that the dream is the royal road to the unconscious but is not in itself the unconscious.

Posing the question of truth at the level of the unconscious is another kettle of fish, which I have already unpacked. I did it as I always do, at great speed and leaving no room for ambiguity, in my text *La Chose freudienne*, written in 1956 for the centenary of Freud's birth. I made this entity loom up that says, *I, Truth, speak*. Truth speaks. Since it *is* truth, it doesn't need to *tell* the truth. We hear truth, and what truth says cannot be heard but for whosoever knows how to articulate it. What truth says where? Well, in the symptom, that is to say, in something that is not quite right. Such is the relation between the unconscious, insomuch as it speaks, and truth.

It no less remains that there is a question that I raised during the year of my last course. It was in the session from November 1965, the one that was published in the *Cahiers pour l'analyse* under the title *La science et la vérité*. The question remains open as to wherefore the theory will win out because it is true, this being the statement from Lenin which introduces this *Cahier*. What I have just been saying about psychoanalysts does not give this statement an immediately convincing endorsement. Marx himself allows something to linger over this that is not unenigmatic, as indeed did many others before him, starting with Descartes. With respect to truth, Marx proceeded in keeping with a peculiar strategy which he sets out somewhere in these pungent words – *the advantage of my dialectic is that I say things little by little – and when they think I have finished, and rush to refute me, they merely make an untimely manifestation of their asininity*. It seems peculiar that someone from whom comes the idea that *the theory will win out because it is true* should express himself thus.

To spell it right out, this politics of truth is complemented by the idea that, in sum, only what earlier I called *the great numbers* could never be in the wrong, that is to say, the same that are reduced to being no more than numbers and which in the Marxist context are called *class consciousness*, in so far as it is the class of these great numbers. It's a peculiar principle, and yet none of those who have the merit of having pursued Marxist truth along its path have ever been at odds with it. But why should class consciousness be so surefire in its orientation when it doesn't know anything, or knows precious little, of the theory, and when, being strictly reduced, according to the theorists themselves, to those who belong to the class that is defined on this occasion as excluded from capitalistic profits, it emerges at the level of the uneducated?

Perhaps the issue concerning the force of truth is to be sought out in the field into which we have inserted ourselves, which is the metaphorical field that we may call – I repeat, by metaphor – *the market of truth*. If the mainspring of this market is, as you were able to perceive from last week's lesson, enjoyment value, something does indeed get exchanged there which is not truth per se. In other words, the bond between whoever is speaking and truth is not the same depending on the point at which he sustains his enjoyment.

It is here that the whole difficulty of the psychoanalyst's position lies. What does he do? What procures him enjoyment at the place he occupies? This is what lies on the horizon of the question I did no more than introduce by marking it out, along its hairline crack, with the term *the psychoanalyst's desire*.

So, in this exchange that is transmitted by speech, the horizon of which is set for us by the analytic experience, the truth is not in itself an object of exchange. This can be seen in practice, and the psychoanalysts who are here vouch for this through their practice. They do not, of course, count for nothing in this. They are there for what might fall from this table by way of truth, and even for what they might make of it by rigging it a little. Such is the necessity to which they are compelled by the fact of a status that is hindered with respect to the enjoyment value attaching to their position of psychoanalyst.

I can say that I have had confirmation of this and I will most certainly have further confirmation of it. I'll take one example.

Someone who is not a psychoanalyst, Monsieur Deleuze to name him, has prefaced *Venus in Furs* with a *Présentation de Sacher-Masoch*. He has written what is incontestably the finest text that has ever been written on masochism. I mean, the finest text compared with everything that has been written on this theme in psychoanalysis.

Of course, he has read the analytic texts. He hasn't invented his subject. He begins with Sacher-Masoch, who all the same has a little word to say about masochism. I know they've cut a bit away from his name and that now [in French] people say *maso*, but still, it's up to us to mark out the difference between *maso* and *masochist*, even *masochian* or simply *masoch*. Whichever the case may be, we shall surely be coming back to this text.

I can say that it's a subject on which I have not kept quiet, because I wrote *Kant avec Sade*, but there is actually just a glimpse of it in there, notably of the following – that sadism and masochism are two strictly distinct pathways, even though, of course, they each have to be plotted out in the structure. No sadist is automatically a masochist, nor is every masochist an oblivious sadist. It's not like a glove that can be pulled inside out. In short, it may well be that Monsieur Deleuze has drawn some benefit from these texts – I would swear to this all the more readily because he quotes me at length – but isn't it striking how his text truly does pre-empt everything that I am going to have to say about this, along the path that we have opened this year, when there is not a single one of those analytic texts that, within this new perspective, does not have to be taken up and gone over in full?

I have made sure to check with the author himself – the one I'm citing – that he has no experience of psychoanalysis.

These are the points I wish to mark out here, with their date, because, after all, with time they may change.

They are points that take on an exemplary value and which deserve to be retained, if only to require of me that I account for them in full. I mean, in detail.

With that, it just remains for me to go into the articulation of this structure. The single line on the board sets out its base and foundation.

2

I did not leave you without some clarification about how this schema is going to be of service to us. None the less, I'm going to repeat it.

The *a*, here, designates the object of the same name, which I have already given you a sense of as what might be called the subject's *monture*, the subject's frame or setting. This metaphor implies that the subject is the gemstone while the object *a* is what it is set into, its support and frame.

I will remind you, however, that we have already defined and illustrated the object *a* as what falls away in the structure at the level of the most fundamental act of the subject's existence, because it is the act from which the subject begets itself as such, namely repetition. The fact of the signifier, signifying what it repeats, is what begets the subject, and something falls away from this. Recall how the cut of the double loop, which is carved out of the mental object known as the projective plane, produces two cutouts that are respectively the Möbius band, which we can think of as the subject's support, and the ring that necessarily remains, which is ineliminable from the topology of the projective plane.

In this schema, the object *a* is supported by a numerical reference, the golden section, as a figuring of what is incommensurable about it. It is incommensurable with what is at issue in the subject's functioning at the level of the unconscious. In other words, it is quite simply incommensurable with sex.

Of course, the golden section is here merely as a support, a symbolic function. We have chosen it because of its special privilege, which I have indicated as best I can, for want of being able to give you the strictest and most modern mathematical theory thereof, which would have taken us too far off course. It has the privilege of being, as it were, the incommensurable that narrows down least rapidly the intervals in which it can be localised. In other words, of all the forms of the incommensurable, which are multiple and, I believe, well-nigh infinite, the golden section is the one that requires the most operations in order to reach a certain limit of approximation.

I'll remind you at this juncture of what is at issue. The a that is here on the left is carried over to the 1. This allows the discrepancy between them, $(1 - a)$, to be marked as a^2. This hinges on the specific property of the a, which is that $(1 + a)$ is equal to $1/a$, from which it is easy to deduce that $(1 - a) = a^2$. Do a little multiplication and you will see this straightaway. This a^2 will then be carried over to the a, which is here in 1, and will generate a^3. This a^3 will be carried over to the a^2, and what will come out of it at the level of the discrepancy is an a^4, which will be carried over in the same way so that a^5 should appear, here.

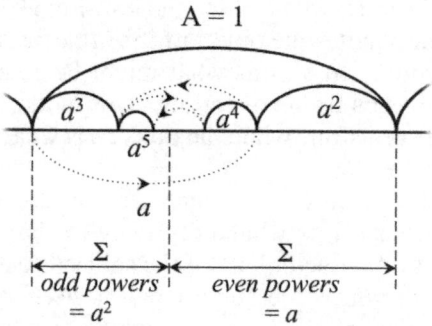

Limits of the odd powers and even powers

You can see how all the even powers of a are staggered out on one side of the line and the odd powers on the other. In continuing these operations to infinity – because they will never meet any halt or end-term – their limit will nonetheless be a for the sum of even powers and, for the sum of odd powers, a^2, namely the initial discrepancy. This is how, at the end of the operation, what was marked out here in the first operation as a discrepancy will come to be inscribed. Here, at a, the a^2 will come in the end to be added, bringing about in the sum, here, the 1 that is constituted by the complementation of a by this a^2. What is here constituted by adding up all these remainders is equal to the first a from which we began.

I think that the suggestive character of this operation will not escape your notice, and all the more so given that for a good while now, for a month or a month and a half, I've been noting for you how it could support and form an image for the operation of what is brought about along the path of the sexual drive under the name *sublimation*. I won't be coming back to this today because I have to move forward. I will simply make do with pointing out to you the aim of what we are going to have to do by making use of this support.

As you can sense already, and as you are going to see, this support won't be able to suffice us due to the very success – such a sublime success, make no mistake – of what it presents to us in allowing us to reach this perfect 1. If this were so in the case of sublimation, if it allowed us to reach a 1 such as this on the horizon of sex, it would be known by now. Everything in experience indicates to us that between the two series, that of the even powers and the odd powers of the magical *a*, something must remain as a gap, an interval.

Nevertheless, it is no bad thing to see, from the support that is most conducive to such traditional articulations, the necessity of a complexity that must be our starting point in every case.

Let's not forget that the first 1, the one that lies in the middle of the three elements on my little pocket measure, the 1 onto which I have just projected the sequence of operations, is here only to figure the problem with which the subject articulated in the unconscious is to be faced, namely, the problem of sex. The 1 is the locus of sexuality.

Let's pause here, because we are standing at the gates of the problem.

3

Sexuality. Now then, that's a genre. It's a pond. A puddle. A *black tide*, as we've been saying for a little while. Dip your finger into it and lift it to the end of your nose. There, you can smell what's at issue.

When one says *sexuality*, it's drawn from sex, but for it to be sex, one would have to be able to articulate something with a little more firmness.

Here, at this fork in the path, I don't know which branch to go down, because this is a point that is contentious in the extreme. Ought I to give you right away some idea of what the subjectifying of sex could be, if it could work out?

Of course, you can dream about it. You even do nothing but that, because this is what forms the text of your dreams. But that's not what this is about. What could this be, if it were – and if one gives meaning to what I'm developing here in front of you – a signifier? You're going to see straightaway in how much of a bind we will be with such a signifier, because if I say *male* or *female*, well, even so, that's animal through and through. So, then, how about *masculine* and *feminine*? That would be splendid, but it is promptly borne out that Freud, the first to have made progress down this path of the unconscious, states in no uncertain terms that there is simply no way. It's not that I would be telling you by what measure you are masculine, by what measure feminine. It's not about that. Nor is it about biology, the Wolffian duct and the Müllerian ducts. Rather it's about how it is impossible to give meaning, analytic meaning, to the terms *masculine* and *feminine*.

And yet, if a signifier is what represents a subject for another subject, then this should be the elect ground. You can see how things would be splendid, how they would be pure, if only we could manage some subjectification, I mean some pure and valid subjectification, under the term *male*. We would get something suitable, namely a subject who manifests as male would be represented as such for another signifier designating the term *female*, and which wouldn't need to determine any subject whatsoever, the inverse being true.

I underline that, while here we have been examining sex with respect to its possible subjectification, we are not evincing any clearly exaggerated manifestation of intersubjectivity. It could well be that it holds together like this, without one having to deal with another subject. Indeed, this might even be desirable. However, if you ask what earlier I called *class consciousness*, which is the class of all those who believe that *man and woman* is something that exists, it couldn't be anything else, and as such, it would be just fine, were it so. I mean the principle of what is called, ridiculously, the sexual relationship.

I must say that the ridiculous is compelling here. If, before the present gathering, a gathering that is becoming familiar to me, a gathering in which I can drive home as befits that there is no sexual act – which means that at a certain level there is no act and this is precisely why we need to seek out how it is constituted – I could get the expression *sexual relationship* to assume in each of your heads the buffoonish connotation it deserves, I would have achieved something.

Were sexual relationship to exist, it would mean the following – that the subject of either sex may touch something in the other at the level of the signifier. I mean that this would entail in the other neither consciousness nor the unconscious, but simply concord. It would be a pure relating of signifier to signifier.

This is most surely what fills us with wonder when we come across it in the animal world, at a certain number of spots in animal tropisms that are quite enthralling. When it comes to mankind, we are a long way from this. And, for that matter, perhaps so too are those animals for whom things come to pass only through the intermediary of certain markers of adnexa, which must certainly lend itself to a few abortive attempts.

Be that as it may, the virtue of what I articulated thus is not entirely disappointing. I mean that these signifiers, designed for the one to present and represent to the other the opposite sex in a pure state, do exist at the cellular level. They are called sex chromosomes. It would be surprising were we to be able one day to establish, with some chance of certainty, that the origin of language, namely that which comes to pass before it engenders the subject, should bear some relation to this play in matter that offers up those aspects we find in the coming together of sex cells. This is not where we are, and we have something else to do.

Quite simply, let's not be astonished by the distance that separates us from the level at which something manifests that is not designed in an unenticing way, and which I shall call *transcendence of matter*. Please believe me, I'm not the one who came up with this. It has already occurred to a few others. I am designating this extreme point – while expressly underscoring that it is utterly unresolved, that the bridge has not been made – simply to mark out for you how, within the realm of what is more or less properly called *thought*, over the course of the centuries, at least those that are known to us, one has never done anything else but speak as though this point had been resolved. For centuries, in a form that is to a greater or lesser extent masked, to a greater or lesser extent figured, to a greater or lesser extent clandestine, cognisance has done nothing but parody what would be involved were the sexual act to exist – were it to exist to the point that would enable us to define what is involved in *Purusha* and *Prakṛti*, as the Hindus say, in *animus* and *anima*, and *Toute la Lyre*.

What is required of us is to carry out more serious work. This work is necessitated simply by the following. Amid the play of primordial significations, such as they would be inscribable in terms that, I will underline, implicate some subject, we are separated therefrom by all the thickness of something that you will name as you wish – *flesh* or *the body* – but on the condition that you should include in this what is specifically brought into it by our condition as mammals, that is to say, a condition that is utterly specific and on no account necessary, as is borne out abundantly by a whole kingdom. I'm referring to the animal kingdom.

Nothing implicates the form that the subjectifying of the sexual function takes for us. Nothing implicates that what comes into play here in a symbolic capacity should be necessarily linked to it. It suffices to reflect on what this can be for an insect. Moreover, let's not refrain from making use of the images that might pertain to them in order to make one or another singular feature of our relations to sex unfold in fantasy.

Well, here we are. A moment ago, I took one of the two paths that were open to me. I'm not sure I took the right one. I shall now have to go back to the other. The other path consists in designating why the 1 comes to the right of the *a*, to the point that I designated as representing locally, with a signifier, the fact of sex.

There is a surprising convergence here between what is truly at stake, that is, what I am in the process of telling you, and, on the other hand, what I will call the major point of psychoanalytic abjection. I must say that it is owing to Jacques-Alain Miller alone, who put together a comprehensive index of the concepts in my *Écrits*, that it doesn't have the alphabetic index which I must say I had rather set my heart on, imagining it would begin with the word *abjection*. It was not to be so. This is no reason for the word not to take up its place.

I'm putting this 1 here through pure mathematical reference. I mean that it simply stands in for how, in order to speak about the incommensurable, I need to have a unit of measure and there is no unit of measure that is better symbolised than by 1. The subject, in the form of his support, the *a*, measures himself by sex. Hear this in the same way as one might say *he measures himself by the bushel* or *by the pint*. The 1 is the sex unit and nothing more.

Well, this 1 is no small matter! It's a question of finding out up to what point it converges, as I said earlier, with the 1 that to this day has been reigning as the very base of the psychoanalysts' mindset in the shape of the unitive property that is professed to be the principle behind everything they unfold in the way of a discourse on sexuality.

The vanity of the slogan *sex unites* does not suffice them. They also require the primordial image given to them in the fusion whose beneficiary would be the enjoyer in this joyance, the little baby in his mother's womb. Nothing has thus far been able to vouch for this baby's being any more comfortably positioned than the mother herself who bears him. In this is purportedly exemplified the lost paradise of fusion between *me* and *not-me*, which it has been said is necessary to the psychoanalyst's thought, as you were able to hear in this room last year in the disquisition of Monsieur Conrad Stein,

On enjoyment value

whom, I regret, we have not seen since. I repeat that, going by the psychoanalysts, this is where the cornerstone is to be found without which nothing of the economy of libido could be thought through. For this is what is at issue.

I think that there is indeed a veritable cornerstone here, which I will allow myself to point out to anyone who means to follow me, and which is that anyone who remains attached in any way whatsoever to this schema of primary narcissism can thread as many Lacanian carnations as they would like through their buttonhole, they will never come anywhere close to what I teach.

I'm not saying that primary narcissism is not something that poses a question in the theoretical economy and that it wouldn't deserve to be accentuated one day. Indeed, as of today, I'm starting to draw attention to how enjoyment value finds its point of origin in the lack that is marked out by the castration complex, in other words, in the prohibition on auto-eroticism, which bears on a specific organ, and which here plays its role and function only by introducing this unit-element into the inauguration of a status of exchange, upon which depends everything that thereafter will amount to economy in the speaking being who is at issue in sex. Clearly, what is important is to perceive the reversion that results from this, which is the following. On the basis of something that is carried over to value by the minus which the castration complex constitutes, the phallus designates this something that amounts precisely to the distance between the *a* and the unit of sex. It is on this basis, as all experience teaches us, that the being who will be carried over to the function of partner – woman, to bring an image into my disquisition – in this test to which the subject is put, that of the sexual act, will take on her value of an object of enjoyment.

Yet, at the same time and by the same stroke, look what's happened. It's no longer *he enjoys* but *he has enjoyment of*. Enjoyment has gone from the subjective to the objective, to the extent of sliding in the direction of *possession* in the typical function, such as we have to consider it as inferable from the impact of the castration complex. It is constituted – and this I brought up last time – by the shift that turns the sexual partner into a phallic object.

I am only shining light on this operation in the direction from *man* to *woman*, both of them in inverted commas, in so far as it is most scandalous, if I may so, in this direction. For it can of course be articulated in the opposite direction, with the proviso that woman doesn't have to make the same sacrifice because it has already been carried over onto her account from the beginning.

In other words, I've been underscoring the position of what I shall call *male fiction*, which might be expressed roughly as – *we be the have gots*. There is no greater picture of contentedness than a fellow who has never seen further than the end of his nose and who gives voice to the provocative slogan, *to have or to have not* . . . They are those who've got what you know, and then, *they've got what is* – both hold up. *What is*, is the object of desire, woman.

It has been noticed for some time that this simplistic fiction is actually a little more complicated and is in the process of being seriously reconsidered. However, even though I thought I ought to spell it out again in a report entitled *La Direction de la cure et les principes de son pouvoir*, people don't seem to have perceived terribly well what is entailed by my setting in opposition to this male fiction, to take up one of my words from last time, the *she-man* value. *One is not what one's got*. Be careful, because this is not quite the same sentence. They be have gots, but they are not what they've got. In other words, it is insomuch as man *has* the phallic organ that he *is not* it. This implies that on the other side they *are* what they *don't have*, that is to say, it is precisely insomuch as she doesn't have the phallus that woman can take on its value.

These are the points that it is exceedingly vital to spell out at the start of any induction into what the unconscious says about sex, because this is strictly what we have learnt to read in its discourse.

Whenever I speak of the castration complex, it is not to misrecognise, of course, everything that is contentious about it. For the least that may be said is that it can lead one somewhat into error, and especially on the male side, as to the person in whose regard we have such a fine description in Genesis, to wit woman conceived from this something of which the man's body has been deprived. This is called, in the chapter that you know so well, a *rib* – for modesty's sake.

Only, whenever I speak of the castration complex as originative in the economic function of enjoyment, psychoanalysts start delighting in the term *object libido*. What is important is to see that if there is something that deserves this name then it's precisely the carryover of this negativised function which is founded in the castration complex, namely the enjoyment value that is forbidden at the precise point of the organ constituted by the phallus. This is what is carried over as object libido, contrary to what they have been saying, to wit that the libido that is called narcissistic would be the reservoir from which what would amount to object libido would have to be extracted.

This might strike you as a mere subtlety. *After all*, you will tell me, *if in narcissism there is libido that is brought to bear on one's own body, well – even though you've specified these matters – what is at issue is a portion of this libido*. In what I have been setting out, it is no such thing. And very precisely because, in order to say that one thing is extracted from another, it has to be supposed that it is purely and simply separated from it by way of what is called a cut. And not only a cut, but something that can thereafter function as an edge.

Now, this is very precisely what is dubious and even what can be settled as of now. The fact is that there is no homomorphism, there is no structure such that the phallic shred, so to speak, could be graspable in the manner of a portion of narcissistic investment. The fact is, it doesn't constitute this edge – this is what we have to maintain – the in-between edge that would allow narcissism to construct a false assimilation of the one to the other, which is the doctrine in traditional theories of love.

Indeed, the traditional theories of love leave the object of good within the limits of narcissism, but the relation that is truly at issue, the economy of enjoyment, is distinct from it.

Object libido, in so far as it introduces something that, if I may say so, leaves us wanting when it comes to the exact note of the act that claims to be sexual, is of another nature, make no mistake. It is properly speaking *entrenched*, discrete.

It is here that the keen point lies, on which it is essential not to yield. For, as you will be seeing in the next sequence, around this point alone can everything that occurs in the field of the analytic act, whether this concerns the relation between the analyst and the one being analysed or the effects of regression, find its proper place.

Excuse me for leaving this hanging. The law of my disquisition doesn't always allow me to perform the slice at the drop-off point that would suit me best. The clock is cutting us off today. I'll resume next time.

19 April 1967

THE ECONOMY OF
THE FANTASY

XV

FROM TRUTH TO ENJOYMENT

Logic, metadiscourse immanent to language
Metaphor and the golden section
On the unary trait
The rotten, distinct from shit
Enjoyment questions truth

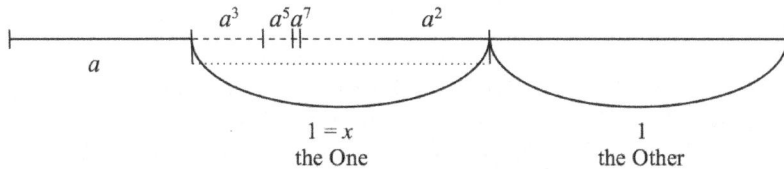

I have made this drawing for you, which is incomplete in the sense that it is unfinished, but let's not waste any time.

I have already indicated quite amply that these two segments may be qualified [respectively] as the One and the Other. *Other* carries the sense that I usually intend – the locus of the *Autre*, A, the locus where the signifying chain is articulated along with what it sustains by way of truth.

These are the terms of the essential dyad in which the drama of the subjectifying of sex has to be forged, that is to say, the very matter we have been speaking about for a month and a half now.

Essential, I say. For those whose ears have been trained to Heideggerian terms, which, as you will see, are not my privileged reference, I will specify, not an *essential dyad* in the sense of that which *is*, but in the sense of that which – it really does have to said in German – *west*, as Heidegger expresses it, moreover in a way that already forces the German tongue. Let's say, in the sense of what operates as *Sprache*, that is, the connotation left to Heidegger of the term *language*.

It's a matter here of nothing else but the economy of the unconscious, indeed what is commonly called *the primary process*.

1

Let's not forget that we have to start from the *effect* of the terms of our dyad, the One and the Other. Their effect has something paltry about it, which is that it lends itself to the rough-and-ready metaphor that this effect might be the child himself.

Yet subjectifying sex gives life to nothing if not mishap.

What it has already produced, however, and which is given to us in a univocal manner in the psychoanalytic experience, is the discard from which we begin as the necessary bearing for constructing the full logic of this dyad. This we do by allowing ourselves to be steered by that of which this object is properly speaking the cause, to wit the fantasy.

2

What is logic, if it is true that I can posit as its initial thesis – and this is what I'm doing – that there is no metalanguage?

Logic is this – that one can extract from language the loci and the points at which, so to speak, language speaks by itself.

This is indeed how it has been panning out in our times. You need only to open a book on logic to see that it has no pretension to be anything else. It has nothing ontic about it, in any case, and scarcely anything of the ontological.

Since I'm going to be affording you a fortnight's breather after today's lesson, go and have a look at Plato's *Sophist*. Read this dialogue to see just how accurate this formulation about logic is and how its point of departure doesn't date from today, nor even from yesterday. You will understand that this is in fact the dialogue from which Martin Heidegger begins for his reinstatement of the question of Being. In any event, it would be a no less wholesome discipline for you to read *Introduction à la Métaphysique*, the excellent [French] translation that Gilbert Kahn has made [of *Einführung in die Metaphysik*].

I say *excellent* because, in truth, Kahn hasn't sought to do the impossible. For all the words for which an equivalent, if not an equivoque, could not possibly be found, he has coolly forged, or re-forged, some French words, as best he could, even if this has meant adding a lexicon at the end to give the precise references in German.

I have only just received the book, from a press office because I hadn't been informed of it, and so only now am I able to recommend it to you. But this is just a parenthesis.

It's a straightforward read, which might perhaps be disputed for other texts by Heidegger, but I assure you that this one is unusually straightforward and even has a sharply cutting note of easiness. The way in which he intends there to be a re-posing of the question of Being at our historical juncture could not be made more transparent. It is certainly not the case that I deem what is at issue here to be anything else but an exercise in reading and, as I said a moment ago, in wholesomeness. It clears things up, but it no less goes astray in issuing the single instruction to return to Parmenides and Heraclitus, however brilliantly he locates them, precisely at the level of this metadiscourse which I've been speaking about as immanent to language. The metadiscourse immanent to language, which I've been calling *logic*, is of course what warrants being refreshed by this reading.

To be sure, as you might notice, I am not on any account making use of the etymologising procedure with which Heidegger admirably breathes life into those phrases that have been termed pre-Socratic. Furthermore, the direction that I mean to indicate differs from his precisely in that I hold the one indicated by the *Sophist* to be irreversible. The *Sophist* is also an extraordinarily straightforward read, and one which doesn't fail to make its reference to Parmenides in order to stress how far Plato was from, and how sharply against, the proscription that Parmenides expresses in these two lines of verse:

No, never shall you bend with force non-beings to be;
Rather turn your thinking away from this search.

It is precisely the route opened with the *Sophist* which impresses itself upon us, strictly speaking upon us analysts, if only we might come to know what we are dealing with.

Had I succeeded in creating a lettered psychoanalyst, I would have won the round, which is to say that, from that moment forth, the person who is not a psychoanalyst would thereby become unlettered. Let the many lettered persons who people this room rest assured, they still have their little leftover.

Psychoanalysts have to manage to conceive of the nature of what they handle, this scoria of Being, this discarded stone which becomes a cornerstone and which is specifically what I have been designating through the object *a*.

It is a product of the operation of language, in the sense that the term *product* is necessitated in our discourse by the raising, since Aristotle, of the dimension of ἔργον, of labour.

It's a matter of rethinking logic on the basis of this *a*, because this *a* – although I named it, I didn't invent it – is properly what has fallen into the hands of analysts on the basis of the experience they have passed through in what is involved in the *res sexualis*.

Everyone knows what I'm trying to say and they know, too, that they speak about nothing but that. Since analysis, this *a* is you yourselves, each of you in your essential core. It gets you back on your feet, as they say. It gets you back into the delusion of the celestial sphere of the subject of cognisance.

That said, this explains why – it is even the sole reckonable explanation – one starts in analysis, as everyone can see, with the child.

It is for reasons that are strictly speaking metaphorical, because the *a* is the metaphorical child of the One and the Other, insomuch as he is born as the discard of the inaugural repetition, the one which in order to be repetition requires this relation of the One with the Other.

The real reason for the reference to the child in psychoanalysis is thus on no account whatsoever the G.I. Joe in the making, the seed destined to flower into the happy blighter who appears to Mr Erik Erikson to be sufficient motive for his cogitations and his troubles, but rather this problematic essence, the object *a*, the exercises of which bemuse us in the child, and not just anywhere – in the child's fantasies, very sufficiently brought to execution. In order to appreciate how it is at their level that the games and pathways are to be seen opening out most fully, one has to be receptive to confidences that are not within the reach of child psychologists.

In short, this is what means that it is in the child's merest sexual frolicking, in his *perversion* as they say, that we find the single, the only, the sole worthy presence that has to be ascribed to what is designated by the word *soul*.

3

What is the 1 doing here?

Well, as I said last time, in this logic the 1 is simply the bringing into play of the operation of measure, of the value to be ascribed to the *a* in this operation of language that will amount, in sum, to an attempt to reintegrate the *a* into the universe of language, which, as I posited at the start of the year, doesn't exist. Why doesn't it exist? Well, precisely because of the existence of the object *a* as the effect thereof.

What is at issue, therefore, is an operation that is contradictory and hopeless, but which, fortunately, the existence of arithmetic,

From truth to enjoyment 233

however elementary it may be, ensures to be a fruitful enterprise for us. For even at the level of arithmetic, they have realised – recently, it has to be said – that the universe of discourse does not exist.

So, how do things present at the start of this attempt? We need this 1, and we will content ourselves with this for the measure of the object *a*.

$$1 + a = \frac{1}{a}$$

You may well suspect that, once my theory starts to be subjected to serious scrutiny from logicians, there will be a great deal to say about the introduction of the three signs that feature as *plus*, *equals*, and the bar between 1 and *a*.

So that my lesson doesn't drag on forever, you really do need to trust provisionally in my having carried out these tests for myself, only allowing the tip of it all to show through here at the level at which it may be useful to you. While this does come about of its own accord, and while it really is most convenient, we still have a long path to travel. I have simply set down here the formula that happens to cover what I have called *the largest incommensurable*, or else *the golden section*, which strictly speaking designates the following. The relation of the greater magnitude to the lesser – the relation of 1 to *a* in this instance – is the same as the relation of their sum to the greater magnitude.

If I am proceeding in this way it is certainly not in order to drive home – and, moreover, too hastily – hypotheses that it would be untoward for you to take as decisive. I mean, it would be untoward were you to give too much credit to this paradigm, which is simply intended to make the object *a* function for you, for a while, as incommensurable with the reference to sex. It is in this capacity that the 1 is tasked with covering sex and its riddle.

Besides, there is nothing to indicate that we cannot right away bring the mathematical notion of proportion into this formula. Such as it has been written up here, it implies for anyone who reads it at the level of its common mathematical use, that –

$$\frac{(1 + a)}{1} = 1 + a$$

However, so long as this has not been expressly written, the formula can be regarded as far less compressed. It indicates nothing else but how we understand ourselves to see something arising from the coming together of 1 and *a*. What? Why not, on occasion, that 1 should represent *a*?

I am hardly employing symbolisations randomly. Indeed, there are some here who might remember my symbolisation of metaphor.

$$\frac{S \ldots S'}{S} \longrightarrow S'\left(\frac{1}{s''}\right)$$

The metaphor

They will recall the following. I write out the sequence of signifiers with the indication that this chain comprises on its lower level a signifier that has been substituted, capital S. From this substitution, a new signifier obtains. Let's call it S' in that it harbours the signifier for which it has been substituted. This new signifier takes on the value of the origin of a new signified dimension that belongs to neither one nor the other of the two signifiers at issue, and which is connoted here by the notation on the right-hand side of the formula.

Is it not apparent that something analogous – which here would be strictly the surfacing of the dimension of measure or proportion, as an originary signification – is implied in this interval moment between the initial formula, $1 + a = 1/a$ and its completion with the 1 that was absent from it, albeit immanent to it?

By dint of being singled out in a second phase, this 1, the one that lies below the bar, assumes the figure of the function of the signifier *sex* qua repressed. This is so to the extent that the relation with the enigmatic 1, taken in its pure conjunction of $1 + a$, can in our symbolism imply a function of 1 as representing the riddle of sex qua repressed. This riddle of sex will present to us as capable of making a reality of this substitution, this metaphor, by covering the *a* itself with its proportion.

What does this mean?

You will object that the 1 is not at all repressed as it is here, where, sticking to an approximate formula, I have made a chain of signifiers of which none is suitable to reproduce the repressed signifier. This is precisely why I need to distinguish the repressed.

Does the 1 on the first line go against the articulation I'm trying to give you for this? It most surely does not, as you know, and as you have taken the trouble to practise a little with what I showed you in the way of the use that may suitably be made of the *a* in relation to 1. That is to say, having marked out its discrepancy and brought about its subtraction from 1, it came to be noticed, as I told you, that $(1 - a)$ is equal to nothing else but an a^2. So long as you fold this a^2 back over the *a*, brought in here in the first operation, this is succeeded by an a^3, which reproduces itself here over the a^2, by the same mode

From truth to enjoyment

of operation, in order to obtain an a^4 here. All the even powers are threaded out on one side, reaching towards the odd powers on the other side which trail off here. All together, they bring about this sum that is enciphered with the little 1. Thus, what we have up here in this proportion is nothing other than $a + a^2 + a^3 + a^4$, and so on, starting with a^2 and on up to infinity, this being strictly equal to the big 1.

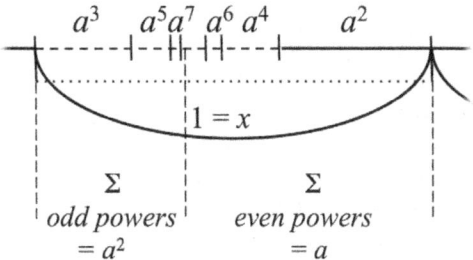

What results from this is that you have a fairly good figuring of what I called *the metonymic effect in the signifying chain*, and which I have already been illustrating for some time now with the sliding of the figure of the a within this chain.

This is not all. If the measure that is thus given in this play of writing – for it is nothing but that – is exact, it immediately ensues that this suffices to make the total block of $(1 + a)$ pass over to the function of 1, upon which it impresses itself as a substitution, to obtain –

$$\frac{1 + (1 + a)}{1 + a} = \frac{(1 + a)}{1} = \frac{1}{a} = \frac{a}{1 - a} = a$$

Substitution of $(1 + a)$ by a

By way of amusement, I can go so far as to refrain from writing the last 1, instead reproducing at its level the earlier manoeuvre. This allows me to write thereafter $1/a$.

If you keep proceeding in the same way, the formula $a/(1 - a)$ ensues. $(1 - a)$ being equal to a^2, this is none other than a/a^2, that is to say a.

This final identification in some way sanctions how all this circuitry – which is no small matter because it is here that we can learn to make the relations between the a and sex play out – brings us back purely and simply to the identity of a.

For those for whom this still remains a little difficult, do not leave out of account how this a is something that is altogether existent.

I have not done so thus far, but I can write out its value, with which everyone is acquainted. Is that not so?

$$\frac{\sqrt{5}-1}{2}$$

The value in figures is something along the lines of 2.236068 ... Don't hold me to it. In my time, we used to learn mathematics by memorising a certain number of figures by rote. When I was fifteen, I knew the first six pages of my tables of logarithms by heart. On another occasion, I'll tell you about its purpose.

It's quite certain, however, that this wouldn't be one of the least sound methods for selecting candidates for the job of psychoanalyst. We're not there yet. I have so much trouble getting into people's heads the slightest item on this subject that I haven't so much as suggested using this criterion. It would be just as good as any of those currently in use.

So, we shall be taking up these phases that follow on one from the next in order to designate within these formulations the stage of $(1 + a)$ as what best designates what we might call *the sexual subject*.

In its first phase of enigma, 1 designates the signifying function of sex. When $(1 - a)$ emerges as the denominator of the equivalence, such as we can see it developing here, always the same, the 2 of the dyad looms up here on the upper level. You can see this, even though I did, heedlessly, neglect to write it up. Actually, it can't be written in the form of a 2 without advising you of a few further remarks concerning what is called in this instance the *associativity* of addition. In other words, I will tease apart the second 1, here in this parenthesis, to group it into this same parenthesis with the other 1 that precedes it, but which has a different function.

$$\frac{1+(1+a)}{1+a} = \frac{(1+a)}{1}$$

Associativity of addition

Now, it's not hard to notice within these three terms – the two 1s and the a – the three intervals at issue, namely those that problematise the a with regard to the two 1s. What can all this mean?

In order to confront the a with the unit, which is simply to institute the function of measure, needs must begin by setting this unit down in writing. This is the function that I introduced long ago under the name of the *unary trait*, which it is essential to bring about when it comes to measuring up the object a with regard to sex.

From truth to enjoyment

So, where is it to be written? Well, surely not on the back of the object *a*, because no object *a* has a back. I think you have known from the start that what serves this writing is what I have termed *the locus of the Other*, precisely insomuch as it is represented here, as called upon by this whole logical process. This is to say that the locus of the Other introduces as such the doubling of the field of the One.

Here we have nothing else but the figuration, properly speaking, of what I have articulated as originary repetition, as that which means that the first 1 – so dear to philosophers even though it poses a few difficulties for them in the handling – emerges, in truth, only as retroactive, once a repetition has announced itself as signifying.

With respect to the unary trait, I recall the despairing cries from a listener of mine when I simply gathered up the *einziger Zug* from one of Freud's texts. It had passed unnoticed by this suave interlocutor, who should have liked very much to be making the discovery himself. Don't believe, however, that it exists there alone. Freud wasn't the one who uncovered it. Naturally, I'll be speaking in a short while about the Greeks, but, to keep up with current events, leaf through the latest issue of the excellent journal by the name of *Arts asiatiques* and you will see the translation of a very nice treatise on painting by Shitao, one of whose little kakemonos I have the good fortune to possess. Well, he makes a rather great deal of this unary trait. Over few but splendid pages, he speaks of nothing but this. In Chinese it is called – and not only for the painters, because the philosophers, too, speak much of it – *yī*, which means *one*, *huà*, which means *stroke*.

yī   *huà*

It's the unary trait. I can assure you that it functioned for a long while prior to my harping on about it. You will recognise here the essential function, which is a long-standing feature in my graph, of the S(Ⱥ). It calls for the field of the Other across from it, as though in a mirror, facing up to the field of the enigmatic One. In an article entitled *Remarque* [*sur le rapport de Daniel Lagache*], which provides the formulation for what in psychoanalysis and in Freud's texts is called *identification with the Ego Ideal*, I set down the decisive trait for this form of identification in the Other. That is, I indicated this mirrored reference, from which begins the lode of everything that amounts to identification in the subject, at the level of the Other.

Identification is to be distinguished in particular from the two other functions of the register of the dyad we are speaking about today, namely repetition and relationship. We will place identification in the middle. I told you last time what ought to be thought about anything that might be entitled by the sexual dyad. I qualified this relationship as buffoonish. It is spoken of as though it might be something that should have some whiff of consistency when sex is at issue.

At this juncture I should like to make a simple remark. I have already urged you to take up the little treatise from the time when Aristotle enters the fray, just after the time of the *Sophist*. Whatever dissolution we have managed to bring about since then in the operations of logic, it is fair to say that his *Categories* still maintain an unshakeable character. The treatise may be admired purely for all that concerns the exercise that can allow a meaning to be given to the term *subject*. I don't need to go over the list of categories – place, time, quantity, the why and the wherefore, and so on. Now, is it not striking that Aristotle didn't introduce, after such an exhaustive list, this sort of relationship that could be written – well, have a little go and tell me how you get on – as the sexual relationship?

Any logician is used to exemplifying the different types of relationship which he distinguishes as transitive, intransitive, reflexive, and so forth, by illustrating them with terms of kinship – *if So-and-so A is the father of B, then B is the son of A*, etc. It's rather curious, at least as curious as the absence of sexual relationship in the Aristotelian categories, that no one ever ventures to say, *if A is the man of B, then B is the woman of A*.

Even so, this relationship forms part of our question concerning what is at issue, namely that of the status which could provide a foundation for the terms I have just brought forward – *man* and *woman*.

It is altogether unavailing to go about this by projecting – to employ a'term that psychoanalysts use wildly and indiscriminately – the 1 that comes to mark the field of the Other into what I am now going to call x, so as to mark out how thus far this One has been nothing but a denomination [thus, $1 = x$]. What lies here between the a and the big Other needs to be named *unary trait* because to regard this field x as unifying is misleading. Making it unitive is even more so.

Of course, such slipping and sliding is nothing new and is not the special privilege of psychoanalysts. The conflation of a Being – what Being? The Supreme Being – with the One as such is what is incarnated eminently in the writings of Plotinus. This is no secret to anyone.

I referred to this prevalence of the median function of the Ego Ideal as fundamental, insomuch as a whole cascade of secondary identifications is dependent upon it, notably that of the ideal ego which is the ego's core. All of this was laid out and remains set down in its time and place. In and of itself it brings out quite well enough the question of what grounds necessitate the multiplicity of these identifications. It suffices to consult the little optical diagram which I provided for this. It's merely a metaphor, though this has nothing metaphorical about it because these are metaphors that are operative in the structure.

In short, that the bond of the One to the Other by identification should take on the reversible form that turns the One into the Supreme Being is, properly speaking, typical of the philosophical error. If I told you to read Plato's *Sophist*, it's because back then people were a long way from falling into this One, and the said Plotinus is the best reference here when it comes to testing that out.

I should just like to draw a contrast here with the mystics. We may define the mystics as those who went ahead, to their cost, from the *a* towards this Being which did nothing but announce itself as unutterable, as having an unutterable name, and through nothing else but these enigmatic letters that reproduce – do we know this? – the general form of *I AM* – not *the one who follows* or *the one who is*, but – *THAT I AM*. In other words – *Keep looking*.

You can see nothing there that really specifies – although it warrants being specified at another level for the reference that is therein made to the father – the God of the Jews. Since in our times Zen is cropping up here, there and everywhere, you must have garnered from somewhere or other that the Tao that can be named is not the true Tao. Well, we're not here to delight in this age-old banter.

When I speak about the mystics, I'm simply talking about the holes they encounter. I'm speaking for instance of the *Noche oscura*, which proves that when it comes to whatever there might be that is unitive in the relations between the creature and anything whatsoever, it can always, even with the subtlest and most rigorous methods, hit a snag. To spell it right out, I must say that this is the sole point of interest to the mystics so far as I am concerned. I'm not trying to furnish you with a *mystic theory*, in inverted commas. I think you can perceive this amply enough.

We are speaking about them to steer to our attention how a mystic is less of a fool than a philosopher, just as a patient is less of a fool than a psychoanalyst.

This is due solely to how this amounts to a renewed instance of the alternatives I have often set out as formulations of alienation, *Your money or your life, Freedom or death*. There's no choice. Here, it's *Foolery or knavery*.

When this question is posed at the level of philosophers or psychoanalysts, well, foolery wins out every time, never knavery.

4

Anyhow, let's get back to the drawing on the board.

You can see that the field that lies between *a* and the big A consists of a line that comprises two segments, a dashed line and then a solid line. The dashed segment is to show that *a* is equal in its first portion to the outer *a*. The unbroken segment marks how there is this leftover, a^2.

But I have made a second line, which could well be the only one, to indicate that we analysts have to consider this field in its entirety as at least liable to participate in the function of the *hole*.

If only out of recognition for the contribution that Monsieur Green kindly brought to my work, I cannot help but introduce here – why not? – the reference that he was good enough to add. It's the one he introduced, I must say – don't get carried away – very remarkably, in the form of the cauldron of the *Es* which he extracted from Freud's lecture 31.

The cauldron, according to a certain image one may form of it, expresses something along the lines of – *it's bubbling away in there*. In truth, this is very much what is at issue in Freud's text. One would of course have to study the irony with which Freud allowed such images to pass through. This is not within our immediate reach. One would first have to give oneself over to a solid scrubbing operation, as I have many times noted, to cleanse away what has covered the text – *the black tide*.

Let's not say too much about this except that, after all, one of the most essential differentiations to be drawn is that between rot and shit. When one fails to make an exact distinction here, one cannot perceive, for example, that what Freud is designating is this something that is rotten in enjoyment.

I'm not the one who invented the term. It crops up already in courtly literature. These are poetical terms used in the Round Table romances, and we can see them being taken up – we find what is of benefit to us wherever it happens to be – by the pen of that old reactionary, T.S. Eliot. Read *The Waste Land*. It's another very fine read, and very amusing I must say, albeit not so clear as the

Heidegger read. Eliot knows very well what he's talking about. It concerns nothing else, from end to end, but the sexual relationship.

Clearly, one of the most useful things would be to decant from this field of the rotten the shitty coal tar – strictly speaking, in view of the privileged function the anal object plays in this operation – with which current psychoanalytic theory has been covering it. So, instead of what I had defined as the *Es* of grammar – and you will be seeing which grammar is at stake – Monsieur Green reminded me that I oughtn't to forget the existence of the cauldron that goes *blip, blip, blip, psst*. The question is indeed essential and I will absolutely pay him this homage, that he took a path that is very much one of mine, in right afterwards making function what he modestly called the association of ideas and which was a reference to the book on the *Witz*, to remind us of the other use that Freud makes of the cauldron. To wit, in connection with the celebrated cooking pot that we are reproached for having returned with a hole in it, the exemplary subject replies in the usual way that, first of all, he never borrowed the pot, second, it had a hole in it already, third, he gave it back intact. It's a wording that most surely has all its value of irony and *Witz*, but which is especially exemplary here when it's a matter of the function of analysts and the use they make of this place.

I readily concur that it ought to be represented by something like a cauldron, on the condition precisely that one bears in mind that it has a hole in it, that it is therefore pointless to borrow it to make jam and that, besides, we are not borrowing it. All analytic technique consists precisely in leaving the place of the cauldron empty, and it is wrong not to take note of this. So far as I am aware, one doesn't make love in the analyst's consulting room and precisely because, for this place and what one has to take measure of within it, one operates with the *a* and the A, and this is why we might perhaps be able to say something about it.

So, I will say that these three amusing references to the bind in which the debtor of the cooking pot finds himself merely cover a threefold refusal from analysts to acknowledge what is at stake. *Primo*, while they haven't borrowed this pot, they deny this *not* and imagine to themselves that actually they did. *Secundo*, even though they know full well that the pot has a hole in it, and that to promise to return it intact is adventurous, it seems they prefer to forget this for as long as they can. It is only on this basis that one might account for what is at issue in the phenomena of truth that I have sought to pinpoint with the slogan, *I, Truth, speak*.

This is true, whatever the psychoanalysts think about it, and even if they prefer to think something that doesn't compel them to plug up their ears to the words of truth.

What does the element of analytic theory teach us here? Well, that acceding to the sexual act is to accede to a guilty enjoyment, even and above all if it is innocent.

Full enjoyment, the enjoyment of the king of Thebes, the people's saviour, he who picked up the fallen sceptre we know not how, is without descent. How so? It's been forgotten. What does this enjoyment cover? It covers the rot, the rot that ultimately bursts out in the pestilence. Yes, King Oedipus, for his part, did carry through the sexual act. The king prevailed.

Rest assured, it's a myth. It's a myth, like nearly all the other myths of Greek mythology. There are other ways of carrying through the sexual act. In general they meet their inevitable punishment in Hades. Oedipus' punishment is the most humane, as we say nowadays, with a word that has absolutely no equivalent in Greek, where even so the linen closet of humanism is to be found.

What ocean of womanly enjoyment, I ask you, did it take for Oedipus' ship to float without sinking, until the plague showed him at last what the sea of his happiness was made of?

This last sentence might strike you as enigmatic. Indeed, the riddling character that a certain knowledge has to maintain is to be respected here. It's a knowledge that concerns the span of what is marked out here on the blackboard by the hole.

Likewise, there is no possible entry to this field without breaking the riddle. As you know, this is what is designated by the Oedipus myth. It also requires the notion that this knowledge, which is figured by the riddle alone, whether it has been reasoned out or not, is intolerable for truth. Indeed, the Sphinx rears her head whenever truth is at issue, and Truth casts herself into the abyss when Oedipus slices through the riddle. This means that what he evidences here is that sort of superiority, of ὕβρις, as is said [in the text], that truth cannot abide.

What does this mean? It means enjoyment, insomuch as it lies at the source of truth. It means that which is articulated in the locus of the Other so that enjoyment, which it is a matter of locating, should poise itself as asking questions in the name of truth. And it has to be in this locus of the Other in order to ask questions, because one doesn't ask questions from anywhere else but there.

This indicates for you that the locus of the Other, which I introduced as the locus in which the discourse of truth is inscribed, is certainly not, whatever one fellow or another might have understood, that sort of locus which the Stoics called *incorporeal*. I will have something to say about what is involved in this locus of the Other, namely that it is the body. But I won't be getting into that yet today.

In any case, Oedipus knew a thing or two about what was being put to him as a question, but the form of the question ought really to arouse our perspicacity, too. Hasn't the simple-minded face of the reply been deceiving us down through the centuries, with its four legs, its two legs, and the dodderer's cane added on at the end? Isn't there something else in these figures, the formula for which we would better find in following what is going to be indicated to us by the function of the object *a*?

Knowledge is thus necessary to the instituting of the sexual act, and this is what the Oedipus myth says.

Deliberate for a while the power of dissimulation that Jocasta marshals, along the pathways of encounter, of τύχη, which is the one that comes along just once in a lifetime, the only one that can lead to happiness, because Oedipus was able not to know the truth any sooner. For, in the end, over all those years that his happiness was to last, whether he was making love in his bed of an evening or during the day, did Oedipus not once have cause ever to bring up that strange scuffle which occurred at the crossroads with the elderly man who succumbed? And what's more, the servant who survived, and who sees Oedipus ascending to the throne, got the hell out of there. Come on now. Isn't this whole story, this fleeing of all the memories, the impossibility of meeting a single one, evocative of something for us? Besides, why does Sophocles put in the whole story of the servant if not to keep us from thinking about the fact that Jocasta at least could not have not known?

Even so, Sophocles couldn't avoid putting into her mouth the cry that bursts forth when she tells Oedipus to hold off – *I mean you well*, she says, *I give you sound advice*. – *This snaps my patience*, replies Oedipus. – *Oh, unhappy man. May you never learn who you are.* She knows. Of course she already knows. And this is why she kills herself, for having caused the loss of her son.

But what is Jocasta? Well, why not the lie incarnate, when it comes to what is involved in the sexual act? Even if no one has thus far been able to see or to say as much, it's a locus to which one accedes only upon having set aside the truth of enjoyment. Truth cannot make itself heard here, for if it does, everything gives way and turns to desert.

And yet, as you know, the desert is usually a place that is populated. Namely, this field *x* on the blackboard, into which measurements alone can penetrate. There is as a rule a whole crazy crowd in the desert – masochists, hermits, demons, phantoms, *larvae* and *lemures*. One just has to start preaching, psychoanalytical preachifying in particular, for everyone to scarper. That's what this is about. Whence is one to speak about it? Well, my word, from right where everyone brings enjoyment into it, because, as I told you, enjoyment is not there. What is there is enjoyment value.

And this is put very well by Freud, precisely when he reveals the ultimate meaning of the Oedipus myth, namely that enjoyment is guilty, enjoyment is rotten. Doubtless so, but this still says nothing so long as one hasn't introduced the function of enjoyment value, that is to say, that which transforms enjoyment into something of another order.

What is the master's enjoyment in the myth that Freud forges? He enjoys, so they say, all the women. What does that mean? Isn't there something of a riddle here, to do with those two senses of the word *enjoy* which I stated last time, the subjective aspect and the objective aspect? Is the master the one who enjoys in and of his essence? But then, all these objects are in some sort fleeing the field. Or else, is what holds importance in that which procures him enjoyment the enjoyment of the object, to wit woman? This is not said, and it shrinks away, for the simple reason that this is myth.

What it is a matter of designating in this field is the originative function of enjoyment, an absolute enjoyment, which, as the myth says quite amply, functions only when it is an enjoyment that has been killed off, or, if you wish, an aseptic enjoyment, or even a canned enjoyment.

I'm turning to my own purpose the word *canné* which I've learnt – from reading Monsieur Dauzat or Monsieur Le Bidois – that Canadians use. They take the [English] word *can*, which as you know is in *jerrycan* for example, and they employ the word *canné*. That's some fine Franglais right there, once again.

A canned enjoyment. Now that is indeed what Freud, forging the myth of the originary father and his murder, designates for us as being the originative function of enjoyment. Without this, we cannot even begin to conceive of the problem that now is ours, to wit, what is it that is being played out in these operations, by dint of which the functions of enjoyment, such as we have to face up to them in the psychoanalytic experience, become exchanged, economised and overturned?

After what I have put forward today, I think I'll be able to wrap up, though it shall still be preparatory, what we shall be moving into on 10 May.

26 April 1967

[NB: the present lesson includes two mathematical mistakes, corrected at the start of the following chapter.]

XVI

THE OTHER IS THE BODY

>   Bergler, neurosis and being refused
>   The askesis of Diogenes
>   The third element in the sexual act
>   Perception, the model of ideology
>   Triplicity of the holed One, the Other and the *a*

First, I should like to announce that to my great regret I won't be holding this seminar next Wednesday for the reason that there is going to be a strike and, after all, I do intend to respect it, aside from the inconvenience it would cause me were I to do otherwise. The next seminar will therefore be in a fortnight's time, on 24 May.

Does anyone have any observation to put to me in connection with what I conveyed in the last session? Has anyone reflected at all on what I wrote on the board? It doesn't seem so. I don't know whether I should be breathing more easily or not. Is this due to the profound absent-mindedness with which what I inscribe is received?

When I got back home I started fretting over what I'd written on the board as the formula for the a, $(\sqrt{5} - 1)/2$, and, right after it, the value of $\sqrt{5}$ in numbers. Instead of indulging in some banter about the table of logarithms, I'd have done better to specify that what I was writing there was not the figured value of a, but of $\sqrt{5}$. The value of a is not 2 point something, because it's less than the unit. It's a figure that's just slightly above six tenths, which is useful to know when you want to draw out the lines I've been using by putting the length of the a in exact proportion alongside the length defined to equate to the unit. The second mistake I made was to write $= a$ at the end of a long series of equivalences beginning with $(1 + a)/1$, when in fact what ought to have been written was $1/a$. Well, for those who copied down these formulas, you'll have to correct them.

We shall keep on advancing into this year's object.

THE ECONOMY OF THE FANTASY

1

The logic which I've been elaborating under the heading of the logic of the fantasy has an end that I have many times defined and which will have to come to be applied to what can only be a work of sifting, or even properly speaking of critique, aimed at what has been put forward at a certain level of experience and in a theoretical form that at times leads to error.

With this design in mind, I have opened, or rather reopened, a book which didn't fail to strike me as important when it first popped up and which is accessible to you all because it was translated into French not so long ago under the title *La Névrose de base*. It's by someone who most surely is not lacking in talent or penetration, and who goes by the name of Dr Bergler. Since you have another fortnight ahead of you, I commend it to you, by way of example and by way of an occasional support to the purpose our work here might serve.

To commend it to you by way of example is not to commend it to you as a model, and yet it's a work of considerable merit. While we won't see any clarification whatsoever of the nature of neurosis along the paths he takes, this isn't to say that some essential mainspring is not perceived in it.

Certain notions of structure are brought to the fore in this work. Moreover, in the sense that I have been employing this word for the moment, they are not the special privilege of this author. It's a matter of what is usually stated in the notion of *layers*, layers which for the same reason are arranged in tiers from shallow to deep, or the other way around. The author bases himself on cases defined in his own manner as what he calls *oral regression* and which he regards as the most numerous in neurosis. How exactly does he define these cases? Well, there's no reason not to take the definition directly from his text because it's summed up in a few lines.

I quoté. *Oral neurotics are people who constantly provoke the situation of the following triad of the 'mechanism of orality': (1) 'I shall repeat the masochistic wish of being deprived by my mother, by creating or misusing situations in which some substitute of my pre-oedipal mother-image shall refuse my wishes.'* This is the deepest layer, the one to which access is most difficult, the revelation of which the subject will defend himself against most firmly and at the greatest length. I'm saying this for the more inexperienced listeners in this room. *(2) 'I shall not be conscious of my wish to be refused and initial provocation of refusal, and shall see only that I am justified in self-defense, righteous indignation and pseudo-aggression because of the refusal.' (3) 'Afterwards I shall pity myself because such an injustice "can happen only to me," and enjoy more psychic masochistic pleasure.'*

I will pass over what Bergler adds to this under the name of what he calls *the clinical picture*, namely the peculiar differentiation he makes between, on the one hand, the genetic picture, which he regards as encapsulating the genesis of the disturbance, and, on the other, this clinical aspect which for him defines the intervention of a superego whose watchfulness consists precisely in maintaining the presence of the element designated as masochistic, and which will be forever active in maintaining the defence. This second standpoint is in itself debateable, but I won't be going into that today.

What I should like to move into on this topic is the following.

To say that in the oral drive the subject wants to be refused is accurate. But nowhere is it spelt out why it is not true to say that the oral drive consists in wanting to obtain, specifically, the breast. While the hard-line position is well founded, it no less remains that nowhere in this work by Bergler has what this means with regard to a drive defined as oral been taken into account. Why does the tendency that seems, let's say, *natural*, come to be overturned in some sort at the very start of the oral drive? This is an important point insomuch as it is precisely its natural position that the subject will use as an excuse in order to sustain the aggression that Bergler terms, quite rightly, *pseudo*, because it is not aggression per se. Of course, this leaves open the matter of what is involved at the level of any aggression that would not be *pseudo*.

On this subject, I introduced a register that is properly speaking the register of narcissism and is equivalent to what the widely accepted theory calls *secondary narcissism*. Having counted aggressiveness as its constitutive dimension, and as distinct in this respect from pure and simple aggression, we find ourselves amid a range of notions. There is raw aggression, which doesn't really match any case when it's a matter of neurotic phenomena, there is narcissistic aggressiveness, and lastly there is this pseudo-aggression that Bergler specifies as emerging at a certain level of oral neurosis. I'm simply pointing out these distinctions without for the moment giving them their full development.

Be that as it may, the question arises as to whether it is suitable to maintain the status of a certain phase of the oral drive thus far defined as *aggressive*. Furthermore, why in oral neurosis is the accent of *being refused* posited by Bergler as the most radical?

It is not within the scope of my remark to make a decisive slice through the facts, apart of course from how making such a slice would entail seeking out exactly what he is speaking about, that is, which neurosis at which moment of his approach. The import of my remark bears rather on something that is lacking in a text that is theoretical, namely whether there might be cause to look, at the very spot where things come to a standstill, into what is meant by the term *being refused* and why it is pertinent. *Being refused* suggests something of a question left unanswered. Being refused in what capacity? Being refused as what?

All the same, *being refused* is nothing new for us, if we suppose ourselves to be standing on the threshold of analytic theory, when, for example, we present ourselves in a relationship that would be qualified as intersubjective. You know in this regard what was promulgated within a certain mode of thinking, the Hegelian thought off of which Sartre himself pulled a branch in order to highlight the accent it can assume at a certain level, one which has been qualified as the radical and mutual exclusion of consciousnesses, as the incompatible character of their coexistence. An *it's either him or me* is reckoned to surge up as soon as the dimension of the subject strictly speaking appears. This is also to say just how far this relief map falls within the scope of criticisms that may be voiced against the genesis that initially takes hold in the life-and-death struggle, which itself derives its status from this radical conception of the subject as utterly autonomous, as *Selbstbewusstsein*.

Is it something of this order that is at issue in aggressiveness? It certainly doesn't seem so, because everything that the analytic experience contributes concerning the stage that is termed *oral* involves a good many further dimensions, most notably the bodily dimension of oral aggressiveness – the need to bite and the fear of being devoured.

So, is *being refused* to be taken on this occasion to concern the object? In truth, the justification could easily be seen emerging in how, within this register, *being refused* would amount to saving oneself from being swallowed up by the maternal partner. But to give this reply to the question of the status of *being refused* might perhaps be somewhat overly simplistic, as is indicated well enough by the fact that in the few lines from Bergler which I have just quoted, oral neurosis is twice associated with the dimension of masochism as though it were essential to it.

The *being refused* in question here is, as the author writes, a *pleasure of refusal, humiliation, and defeat*, and it is in this respect that he allows himself to introduce the masochism label, which he here qualifies as *psychic masochism*, thereby consecrating in some way a vulgar use of the term *masochism*. I'm not saying that there isn't in some text or other by Freud a pretext for introducing such a term, but, stretched out and taken up within this usage, which is now becoming increasingly prevalent, it is strictly speaking ruinous.

The only thing that might justify introducing the dimension of masochism at the level of *being refused* is the reference to the object, to which allusion is made. It is inaccurate to say that what characterises masochism is the painful side of a situation that is assumed as such. Broaching things from this angle can, for example, culminate in the excess which some have produced of turning sadomasochism into the register that is essential to the entire analytic relationship. This is a veritable perversion of Freud's thought, and of his theory and practice with it. It is strictly untenable, so much is the dimension of masochism defined precisely by the fact that the subject assumes an object position, in the most accentuated sense we can give to the word *object*, thus to define it as the remnant, discard, or residuum effect of the subjective advent.

The fact that the masochist establishes a situation that is set out in advance, and settled in every detail, which can go so far as to lead him to stay under a table in the position of a dog, forms part of a staging, a script, which has its meaning and its benefit and the principle of which is incontestably to the profit of enjoyment, whatever note we might add or not concerning the maintaining, the respect and the integrity of the pleasure principle. This enjoyment is tightly bound to a manoeuvre of the Other which is most commonly expressed in contractual form. In the form of a written contract, I mean. It dictates his entire conduct as much to the Other as to the masochist – actually, a good deal more to the Other than to the masochist himself.

This is what ought to instruct us concerning the relation to the Other that gives its specificity and its originality to masochistic perversion. It is very well cut out to clarify for us, down to its base, the part played by the Other in the sense that I understand this term, this being the Other as the locus in which a word is deployed, which in this instance is a contractual word. After this, how can one fail to see that reducing the term *masochism* to something that presents merely as an exception or an aberration, to the simplest access to pleasure, is liable to give rise to every sort of misuse?

The first such misuse is what I shall call exasperation with respect to the patient. I don't believe I'm employing a term that is too strong or inappropriate. Over the full length of Bergler's book, which even so is remarkable and full of meticulous observations, all of which are highly instructive, one picks up on a certain exasperation that is not far from evincing a malicious attitude to all those people whom he calls, as though it were a great wrong on their part, *injustice collectors*, as though when all is said and done we lived in a world where justice was such an ordinary state that one would have to go well out of one's way to have something to complain about.

The most covert operation that Bergler detects in all these so-called *injustice collectors* is the fact of being rejected, but in the end we cannot avoid countering him with the idea that, in certain cases, being rejected is something else. Fantasy is one thing, but here I'm talking about reality. In reality, perhaps it's better once in a while to be rejected than to be accepted too quickly. When you meet someone or other who asks only to adopt you, the best solution is not always not to escape. Why, then, this partiality that implies an orderliness, that it is in the nature of things, that everything is on the right track, whenever everything is being done to gain acceptance?

It is assumed here that to gain acceptance is invariably to be allowed to sit at a beneficent table, and such an assumption is not a little unsettling. It seems to me that this is something that needs to be picked up on occasionally in order to notice something or other that might be happening in the world, for instance, right now in a certain district of South-West Asia, where efforts are being made to persuade certain folk that they are quite wrong not to want to be accepted into the benefits of capitalism. They prefer to be rejected.

It is on the basis of such a moment that, so it seems to me, questions about certain significations ought to be asked. Take the following. Just as Freud wrote somewhere that *anatomy is destiny*, so too the day may come, when we have reached a sound perception of what Freud uncovered for us, that one might be able to say, not *politics is the unconscious*, but quite simply, *the unconscious is politics*. But today is not the day for taking the first steps in this direction. I shall limit myself to saying that what binds men together, and what pits them against one another, is to be explained by that for which we are trying for the time being to spell out the logic.

For want of this logical articulation, a slippage can occur. Prior to noticing that being rejected is essential as a dimension for the neurotic, it should in each case be noted that he supplies himself. As I have written somewhere, what the neurotic does, just as what we do ourselves, and with reason because we follow these paths of neurosis, is to try to create demand out of supply. Of course, neither in neurosis nor in analytic treatment does such an operation invariably succeed, especially if it is conducted clumsily.

This enables us to realise that while the key to the neurotic position does hinge on this tight relation to the Other's demand, insomuch as the neurotic tries to make it emerge, it is through his supplying himself. Likewise, we can see here the fantasised and thus outmoded character of the myth introduced by analytic preachifying, and which is called *oblativity*. It's a neurotic's myth. Well, we can note at this juncture that examining the analytic discourse never fails to give us occasion to perceive what it involves by way of a certain innocent discourse. Indeed, this analytic discourse never knows just how far it will go in what it articulates.

How can one possibly account for these needs that the subject evinces, which are expressed in these paradoxical ways and which are always so poorly defined, if one refers solely to the benefits that the subject may or may not reap thereafter in reality and if one omits this essential first stage, in the light of which all that results in the real can be judged? Should the subject marry this man or that woman? What do you know about it? He messed up his marriage at some juncture of other, but what if that was a stroke of good luck? What do you know about it? What are you getting mixed up in? The only thing you ought to be dealing with is the logical structure of the subjective position at issue, whether it is neurotic, as in the present case, or otherwise.

Now, the logical structure at issue in the present case could be qualified as the *desire to be rejected*. You need to know first of all what the subject at this level is pursuing. What necessity and benefit might there be for the neurotic in being rejected? Pinning the term *masochist* onto this as an extra is to introduce a pejorative hint, which is immediately followed, as I noted just now, by a directive attitude from the analyst which can, on occasion, go so far as to become persecutory.

This is why it is utterly necessary to take things up as I mean to this year.

2

Since we are here, I remind you that I started with the sexual act in its structure as an act.

I did so in connection with the fact that the subject comes to light only through one signifier's relation to another, and that this requires material of these signifiers. To act is to introduce this relation of signifiers through which conjuncture is consecrated as significative, that is to say, as an occasion to think.

People lay the accent on mastering the situation because they imagine that this is the will that governs, for example, in the famous *Fort/Da*, in the child's game. It is not the active aspect of the motor function that is the essential dimension here, because it is deployed only in the dimension of play. It is its logical structure that singles out this appearance of *Fort/Da*, which was taken as exemplary and has since become pat. This is because the *Fort/Da* game is the first signifying topicalisation, in the form of a phonemic contrast, of a certain situation that may be qualified as active, but only in the sense that henceforth we shall not be calling it *active* unless it has the structure of the act in the way I have defined it.

In what capacity is this structure of the act implicated and called into question in a relationship that is so distorted, so concealed, so shut out, so pushed into the shadows, as the relationship between two beings belonging to one of two classes, which are definitive both for the register of births, marriages and deaths, and for the medical board, but which our experience has taught us to see as being no longer obvious at all, for instance in family life, and as being fairly blurry so far as private lives are concerned? In other words, what defines man and woman? Well, this is where analytic theory and experience contribute, as essential to this act, the notion of satisfaction.

Satisfaction, *Befriedigung* in Freud's text, introduces the notion of a supervening peace. What is this satisfaction? Is it the satisfaction of discharge, of detumescence? It is a satisfaction that is simple in appearance and altogether fit to be received. Nevertheless, all the differentiations which we introduce and describe, in terms that are more or less suitable or unsuitable, when we distinguish, for instance, the satisfaction that would belong to the pregenital realm from the one that is genital, imply another dimension, a dimension implicated by this very difference.

That a term like *object relation* should have become so insistent goes without saying, yet this alleviates nothing of the farcical character that arises whenever one tries to diversify the term and to stagger it out in accordance with the greater or lesser ease with which the relationship comes about. It is a matter of nothing else but this when people single out the genital relationship using the traits of tenderness and break-up. On the one hand, one could easily maintain, and this is what I pride myself on doing, that what is claimed to be tenderness is never anything else but the reversing of contempt. On the other hand, what people accentuate in the claimed essence of a break-up, even of grieving, shows that the progression of the relationship said to be *sexual*, insomuch as it would become genital, would be that one would find it that much easier to think with respect to one's partner, *I wish you dead*.

Let's take things up on another plane of certitude. What would the sexual act satisfy? It is quite clear that one could reply simply and legitimately that it satisfies pleasure.

Yet I know of only one register in which this reply would be fully tenable and that is the ascetic plane. This plane is occupied in history by Diogenes, who made the public gesture of masturbation, exhibiting the sign of the theoretical affirmation of a hedonism that is termed, on account of this mode of manifestation, *Cynical*. It might be regarded as a medical treatment, or *Handlung*, of desire. It doesn't fail to exact its price, namely that, curiously enough, this philosophical fellow excluded himself from the political dimension I introduced a moment ago. Cynicism lands you with exclusion from the dimension of the city-state. This is palpable not only from the anecdotes reported about this personage but also from his placement in his barrel, even if he really was visited by the likes of Alexander. I repeat, there is something here that it would be wrong to smirk at, a mode of life that is properly speaking ascetic. It is probably not so widespread as it seems. I can't say. I've never tried it out.

This locus of pleasure, of the lowest degree of tension, should not therefore be overlooked. Only, it is quite clear that this locus is not sufficient. A good many further modes of gratification, a very wide variety of them, become apparent at the level of the search for satisfaction implied by the sexual act.

Our thesis, the one that is fleshing out our course this year, is the following. It is impossible to grasp the full set of these modes of gratification in their breadth and variety without logical scrutiny. The set at issue here is the one that establishes what we shall call, tentatively and with reservations, *a masculine being and a feminine being*, in this founding act which we brought up at the start of our disquisition this year by calling it *the sexual act*. If I said that *there is no sexual act*, this is in the sense that this act is assumed to conjoin, in a straightforward form of apportionment, a male piece and a female piece, to use a terminology that evokes an everyday technical use like that of the locksmith. This simple sharing out is presumed to constitute the inaugural pact whereby subjectivity would be generated as such, male or female.

In its time and place, I mentioned the notorious *Thou art my woman*. Well, it's quite clear that it's not enough for me to say as much to remain her man. But then, would the fact that it resolves nothing be sufficient? That I should ground myself as her something or other is a wish of belonging that is laden with a pact, at the very least a pre-emption pact, but it locates absolutely nothing of either man or woman.

The very most that can be said is that these are two contrasting terms. It is indispensable that there should be two of them, but as to what either one or both of them is, this is utterly excluded from any foundation in speech. When it comes to union, matrimonial union, if you wish, or any other, that a certain dimension should raise it to the dimension of sacrament changes absolutely nothing about what is at issue, namely the being of man and the being of woman.

In particular, it leaves completely to one side the category of womanliness. Since I took the example of *Thou art my woman*, it is never a bad thing to refer to this example, which is the example of the mentor of psychoanalysis himself, in whose life this pact was extraordinarily prevalent. It was something that struck all those who got close to him. *Uxorious* is how Jones qualifies it, after so many others. But, after all, it's no mystery that his thought should have stumbled to the very end over the theme, *What does a woman want?* – which amounts to asking, *What is a woman?* It has to be added that sixty-seven years of psychoanalytic procedures have not led us to find out anything more about feminine enjoyment, even though we speak endlessly of women and mothers. This is, even so, something that deserves to be pointed up.

The heuristic diagram that I have given you in the shape of the line with three segments – the *a*, then the 1 that follows, which is the 1 with a hole in it, and then the 1 of the Other – simply reminds us of this, which is the everyday fare of what we articulate, namely that the sexual act implies across all the levels a third-party element.

This element is, for instance, the Mother, the Mother in the Oedipus complex to whom all the debasements of love life are attached. In any case, ipso facto, a prohibition remains forever present in desire.

The third-party element is also the phallus, insomuch as it must be wanting for the one who has it, that is to say, for the man. If the castration complex means something, it is something that has not as yet been brought to light at all, because it entails our inventing in its regard the scope of a special negation. To wit, that there should be a register in which man doesn't have it – to the extent that the sexual act may exist – does not mean, for all that, that he should lose it. I hope that the subject of this negation can be broached before the end of the year.

On the other hand, that this phallus should become the being of the partner who doesn't have it doubtless accounts for Aristotle's peculiar omission. As I reminded you last time, however subject to grammar he was, so we are told, he developed the list, the catalogue, of the *Categories* and curiously enough, after having said it all – quality, quantity, πότε, ποῦ, πρός τι, and the whole kit and caboodle that follows – he never thought to maintain in connection with any entity whatsoever what was insistent in his time as much as in ours, namely that there might be a category of sex.

And yet the Greek language, like our own, is subject to what Pichon calls *sexuisemblance*, to wit there is *le fauteuil* and there is *la photo*. Furthermore, in passing, amuse yourselves by switching the spelling – it will instruct you a great deal about an altogether concealed dimension of the analytic relationship – *le photeuil* and *la fauto*. So, it is one of two things. Either Aristotle was not guided by grammar to the extent they say he was, or else there is some reason behind this omission.

It is probably linked to this. When I spoke earlier of being masculine or being feminine, there was an inaccurate use of the word *being*. It may well be that being is, as Pichon expresses it, *unsexuable*, that the τὸ τί, the quiddity of sex, is perhaps lacking, and that there is perhaps the phallus alone.

That would explain a good many things, in particular the wild struggle that sets in around the phallus. It is surely what furnishes us with the visible reason, and thus also the ultimate reason, for what is called *the battle of the sexes*. However, I do believe that, once again, history shows for that matter that the battle of the sexes is something which has been tarried over by the more superficial psychoanalysts.

It none the less remains that a certain ἀλήθεια, to be taken in this sense, with the accent of *Verborgenheit* which Heidegger lends it, perhaps ought to be instated for what is at issue with respect to the sexual act.

And it is what justifies the use I'm making of this diagram.

3

I will underline in passing that this is not to be confused with other things that I said in other circumstances, and notably with regard to the structure and function of the cut.

I have sometimes told you that when I symbolise the cut by making it play across the projective plane, I claim not to be turning it into a metaphor. Rather, I speak about it as the *real support* of what is at issue.

Of course the same does not hold for this very simple little diagram, which articulates this One, which last time I drew with a dotted line and with a hole, to this Other and this little *a*.

A certain number of points can and must be developed around this very simple triplicity, and we have to give these points their contour in connection with what is involved in the symptom insomuch as it refers back to sex. My intention now is to repeat what is going to serve as a base. I cannot repeat things often enough when it's a matter of new categories.

To begin in the middle, the One is the most contentious. It concerns what is claimed to be sexual union, that is to say the field in which is called into question whether the act of partition might occur which would necessitate the dividing up of functions defined as male and female. We designate this field, and we number it, as One. But we do not assume it to be unifying, at least until we have had some evidence of it. A whole analytic theory clings to this fictive One, and you have heard me speak out many times against its fallacy.

We have already said, with the metaphor of the cauldron that I brought up again last time, that there is something here that we cannot help but designate provisionally as the presence of a gap or, if you wish, a hole. There is something that doesn't tally, something that isn't self-evident, and which is precisely what I was calling up earlier in terms of the chasm that separates any promotion, any proclamation, of the male–female bipolarity from everything that is afforded us by experience with respect to the act that founds it.

It is important to state that it is from this field that any truth speaks up, insomuch as for us analysts, and for many others before we even came along – though not long before, for a thinking that dates from what we may call by its name, the Marxist turn – truth takes no other form but that of the symptom.

The symptom may also be said to be the *signifiance* of discordances between the real and the wherefore of its playing out. Ideology, if you like. But on the condition that you go so far as to include perception itself within the term *ideology*. Perception is the model of ideology. It is a sieve in relation to reality. Why be surprised at this? Everything that has existed by way of ideology for as long as the world has been teeming with philosophers has never been constructed on anything else but a primary reflection that bears on perception.

I shall come back again to what Freud calls a *tide of mud* in connection with the widest field of cognisance, this whole share of utterly inundating knowledge from which we are barely emerging, to pinpoint it with the term *mystical knowledge*. At the root of everything of this realm that has been made manifest in the word, *there is but the sexual act*, which is the nether side of my slogan, *there is no sexual act*. It is quite needless to purport to refer to the Freudian position in any aspect whatsoever, if not to take altogether literally the fact that, at the base, the principle, of everything that has been contributed until now, my goodness, by way of satisfaction by knowledge – which I have here labelled with the adjective *mystical* so as to distinguish it from what has been given birth to in our times in the form of science – there is but the sexual act.

When you read in Freud that there are desexualised functions in the psyche, it means that sex has to be sought out at their origin. It doesn't mean that there is what is called, on certain shores and for political requirements, the famous *conflict-free sphere* – for instance, a more or less strong ego, which is more or less autonomous, which may have a more or less aseptic prehension of reality. To say that there are relations with truth that the sexual act doesn't concern is strictly untrue. There are no such relations.

I apologise for these formulations, the trenchancy of which may I suppose be a little too keenly felt. All of this is implicit in everything I have set out, to the extent that I know what I'm saying. But I've also observed that the fact that I know what I'm saying is not enough for you to recognise it therein because, in the end, the only sanctioning of my knowing what I'm saying is what I don't say. This is not my own lot. It's the lot of all those who know what they are saying.

This is what makes communication so very difficult. One knows what one is saying, and one says it, but in a fair number of cases it has to be regarded as unprofitable because no one notices that the sinew of what you have to get across is precisely what you never say. It's what the others say that carries on making a noise and, further still, having effect. This is what compels us once in a while, and even more often than is our turn, to apply ourselves to making a clean sweep. Once one has started down this path, there is no reason to end. There once was a certain Heracles who, it seems, completed his work in the stables of a certain Augeas. This is the only case of stables being fully cleaned out that I know of, at least when one particular domain is involved.

There is only one domain, it would seem, and even then I'm not so sure, which bears no relation to the sexual act insomuch as it concerns truth, and this is mathematics at its point of confluence with logic. But I think this is what allowed Russell to say that in mathematics *we never know whether what we are saying is true* – not *truly true*, but quite simply *true*. In fact, it is true from a definitional position of truth. If such and such an axiom is true, then a system develops which has to be judged as to whether or not it is consistent. What relation might there be between truth thus defined and truth insomuch as it would necessitate the presence, the bringing into question, of the sexual act as such?

Well, even after saying this, I'm not sure that this modern deployment of logical mathematics, which is both marvellous and magnificent, is altogether without relation to the question in the balance as to whether or not there is a sexual act. It is enough to hear the groaning from the likes of Cantor. For it is in the form of a groan that at one point in his life he stated that people don't realise that the great difficulty, the great risk, of mathematics is that it is the locus of freedom. We know that Cantor paid a high price for this freedom.

At the point we've reached, the formulation that strikes me as the most accurate is *truth concerns the real insomuch as we are therein engaged by the sexual act*, by this sexual act which, I have claimed, we cannot be sure exists, even though there is this alone that is of interest to truth.

Therefore, it is in this locus of the One with a hole in it that the symptom, any symptom, builds up. And it is in this respect that it always entails, however astonishing this might seem, its facet of satisfaction. Sexual truth is exacting, and it is better to satisfy it a little more than not enough. From the standpoint of satisfaction, we can appreciate that a symptom may be more satisfying than reading a whodunit. There is more of a relation between a symptom and the sexual act than between truth and this fundamental *I am not thinking* wherewith, as I reminded you at the start of these reflections, man alienates his so barely tolerable *I am not*. In relation to which, our excuse of *being rejected*, from earlier, even though not so very agreeable, might strike us as more tolerable.

We are done for the time being with the One. Let's move on to the Other, as the locus in which the signifier takes up its place.

I haven't told you yet that this is where the signifier sits. It is here because it exists only as repetition, because it is the signifier that ushers in the thing at issue as true. At the point of origin, one doesn't know where it comes from. It is nothing else but that trait which is also a cut, from which truth can be born.

The Other is the reservoir of material for the act. Material accumulates, very probably due to the fact that the act is impossible. When I say this, I'm not saying that it doesn't exist. Saying so is not enough, because impossibility is, quite simply, the real, the pure real. Since the possible is defined as always requiring a first symbolisation, if you exclude this symbolisation you will see how much more natural seems the slogan, *the impossible is the real*.

It's a fact that no one has ever proved, in any formal system, the possibility of the sexual act. You can see that I'm being emphatic. I'm coming back to it again. What does the fact that it can't be proved prove? Well, we now know very well, now that its status has been perfectly circumscribed and whole volumes have been written about this sector, that incomputability, even undecidability, on no account implies irrationality. It can perfectly well be defined logically. So, what is this Other? What is its substance?

For a while I allowed myself to say – in truth, it has to be believed that I'm allowing myself to say so less and less because no one hears it anymore, or at least I don't, it doesn't reach my ears anymore – that I was camouflaging under this locus of the Other what is agreeably termed, and why not, *spirit*. The trouble is, this is wrong. At the end of the day, the Other is, if you haven't guessed yet, the body.

Why should one call something like a volume or an object, something subject to the laws of motion in general, a *body*? Why should one speak in terms of a free-falling body? What a curious extension of the word *body*. What relation is there between a little ball falling from the Tower of Pisa and the body that is ours? Well, there is the one basis that the body, our presence as an animal body, is the first locus in which to place inscriptions.

Everything in our experience is there to suggest to us what the first signifier is, except that we are always enthralled by things. When people speak of a wound, they add *narcissistic* and think right away that it must really be a nuisance for the subject who, naturally, is an idiot. It doesn't occur to them that what is interesting about a wound is the scar.

Reading the Bible, with the rods placed in the troughs where Jacob's flocks would graze, ought to remind us that the different tricks for imposing a mark on the body are nothing new and are altogether radical. The hysteric symptom in its simplest form, that of the *rhagade*, is not to be regarded as a mystery but as the very principle behind any signifying possibility. There's nothing to rack your brains over. The body is made for inscribing something that is called a *mark*. The body is made to be marked. People have always done it and the first beginnings of a gesture of love are always to adumbrate this gesture just a little or more.

That said, what is the first effect, the most radical effect, of this bursting in of the One insomuch as it represents the sexual act at the level of the body? Well, this is, even so, what makes for our advantage over a certain number of dialogued speculations on the relations between the One and the Multiple. We know that it's not at all as dialectical as all that. When this One bursts into the field of the Other, that is to say at the level of the body, the body falls to pieces. The body in pieces, this is what our experience demonstrates to us as existing at the subjective origins.

The child dreams of dismemberment. He breaks up the nice unity of the empire of the maternal body. And what he feels as a threat is to be torn apart by his mother. It is not enough merely to uncover these things and explain them away with a little mechanics of aggression, a little ball game, *aggression is reflected, reflects, returns, re-embarks, who was it who started?* Before this, it could be useful indeed to suspend the function of this body in pieces. In fact, the only angle from which the body in pieces has interested us is its relationship with what might be involved in truth, in so far as it is itself suspended from ἀλήθεια and from *Verborgenheit*, and from the concealed character of the sexual act.

On this basis, what is the notion of Eros? I recently jeered at it in the form it can take as the force that is presumed to unite through its irresistible attraction all the cells and organs that our bag of skin gathers together. This is a conception that is at the very least mystical, because they don't put up the least resistance to their being extracted and the rest don't fare any the worse. Well, this Eros is plainly a compensatory whimsy for all the terrors bound to the Orphic fantasy I have just described.

Besides, it is not explanatory at all. It is not enough for terror to exist for it to explain anything whatsoever. It is rather terror itself that should be explained, which is why it's better to head down the path of what I have called a *logically consistent system*.

Hence the question to which we have now to turn – why is there this Other?

Let's begin by asking what the strange double position of the 1 is, because the Other itself is not twain. It's the position that the single unit takes on when it's a matter of explaining the curious One that mounts up in the beast with two backs, in other words in the clasping of two bodies. It's not about the strange 1 that the Other is. Stranger still, between them, between the field of the One and the field of the Other, there is nothing. There is no link. Quite to the contrary. It is even for this reason that the Other is also the unconscious, that is to say the symptom without its meaning, deprived of its truth, yet laden still more with what it contains by way of knowledge. What cuts the One from the Other is very precisely what constitutes the subject.

There is no subject of truth, unless it is a subject of the act in general, of the act that, perhaps, cannot exist qua sexual act. This is very specifically Cartesian – the subject knows nothing of himself except that he doubts. *I doubt*, as the jealous man says, having just seen through the keyhole some hindquarters in the thick of it with legs he knows so well. . . . if it's not God and his soul, the foundation of Descartes' subject. The subject's incompatibility with *res extensa* is not sufficient reason to identify the body with *res extensa*, and yet its exclusion as a subject is thereby founded. In taking this from the angle I am presenting, the question of its intimate union with the body – I'm speaking of the body, not the soul – is no longer a union. It suffices to reflect on how, when it comes to the signifier, that is to say structure, a surface, for instance, has no further support than the hole that it constitutes by its edge. It is this alone that defines it. Raising matters by a degree, let's take things at the level of volume.

There is no other support for the body but the cutting edge that governs its carving up.

These are topological truths for which I won't be making the decisive slice here as to whether they bear any relation to the sexual act. But any possible elaboration of what is called Boolean algebra requires the subject to be always at a structural degree below what makes for his body. This also explains why his passivity, to wit the fact whereby he depends on a mark of the body, can on no account be compensated by any activity, even were it affirmed in an act.

So, of what is the Other the Other?

I am quite disconsolate. The time, a certain immoderation, perhaps, too, a certain paradoxical use of the cut – but then, in that case, take it as intentional – means that today I am taking leave of you now, at the end of the hour.

The Other is not Other save in this, which is the first phase of my three linear segments, namely the a. I started from this in our last talks to tell you that its nature is that of the incommensurable, or rather that it is from its incommensurability that any question of measure emerges.

It is with this a, object or not, that we shall be picking up our talk next time.

10 May 1967

XVII

FROM CASTRATION TO THE OBJECT

The norm of the act
The object in orgasm
There is enjoyment only of one's own body
Laying bare the phallic object
The law of the sexual act

Today I'm going to try to lead you into an arcanum which, though trivial in psychoanalysis, is no less of an arcanum.

At every turn in the recent psychoanalytic literature you can read that it is desirable for the analysed subject, the analysable subject, to adopt what is called a *regressive* position, or even *pre-oedipal, pre-genital* – in short, *pre*-something. You might well be surprised that this is not instead designated *post*-, because the subject is presumed to be taking refuge here to evade the impact of castration.

For my part, I have been trying to put together here this year a structure that promises to be logical. It's a logic that is risky and, perhaps, highly precarious.

On such a path I cannot claim at all to be giving you the definitive steps, nor even to have trodden them myself, but rather to be making tangible for you just how preferable is a path that derives its surety from some truth concerning the subject's dependence. And so I am meting out to you, not offering them up too quickly, the forms in which I trusted in my own scribbling. I'm trying to show you what is accessible in one particular articulation which consists, in this easy form which I chose among others, in quite simply seizing hold of what there is that is most incommensurable with 1, namely the golden section.

This is far preferable to giving oneself over to the gruelling exercises of the common analytic prose that is distinguished by that sort of jiggling, by those ludicrous detours, which always seem to be required in order to account for this interplay of libidinal positions. A whole population of subjective entities which you are well acquainted with, which are lying about all over the place, are brought into play – the ego, the ego ideal, the superego, the id, not to mention what can be added by way of the novel and refined by distinguishing from the ego ideal the ideal ego, or even, as has been done for some time now in the Anglo-American literature, further enlisting the *self* which, while clearly called upon as a backup to remedy the ridiculous proliferation of this throng, no less fails in that it merely represents, given how it is handled, an additional entity. This entity, a rational being, is always inadequate once we start bringing into play in a correct fashion the function of the subject as nothing else but that which is represented by one signifier for another signifier.

A subject is on no account an autonomous entity. Only its proper name can give the illusion of this. It is too much to say that the *I* is suspect. For as long as I've been speaking to you about it, it ought no longer to be so. It is very precisely this subject alone that *I*, as signifier, represents for the signifier *walk*, for example, in *I walk*, or for the pair of signifiers *button it*, as in *I'm buttoning it*.

You can sense that if I have taken this wording it is so as to avoid the form that is claimed to be reflexive, *I'm silencing myself*. It would surely lead us very far were we to ask ourselves what this *myself* might mean, in this form as in a good many others. You would see just how far its so-claimed acceptation as reflexive spreads across a range that doesn't allow it to be lent any degree of consistence whatsoever. This is just a reminder. I won't be expanding any further in this direction.

I will now tackle what I had announced.

1

There is, then, a subjective function that is known as *castration*.

It is presented – and this had never been said before psychoanalysis – as essential for access to what is called *genitality*.

Were the expression fitting to the highest carat – I mean that it is not – someone who might approach this from the outside, and after all we are all still there, wouldn't fail to marvel at how the organ's passing over to fantasy is, within the genital function such as it is being privileged, necessary for this function to be brought about.

I don't see any way out of such a deadlock unless to assert, as did one psychoanalyst of note in the political topography, in a turn of phrase and without even properly noticing the scope of what he was saying, that, after all, castration is a dream. The word was being used to mean that it's just a story told by patients. Now, it is no such thing. Castration is a subjective structure that is utterly essential for something of the subject, however slight, to move into this affair that psychoanalysis labels *genital*.

I must say that I believe I've made a little opening in this deadlock. I think I've made a change, as they say, in that not so long ago, four or five lessons back, I introduced the remark that it could not be merely a matter of introducing the subject into the genital function, if indeed we are able to know what we mean when we call it thus. It's about passing from function to act. It's about knowing whether or not there is an act that might warrant the title *sexual act*. There is? There isn't? *Chi lo sa?* There might be. We shall perhaps find out some day whether there is a sexual act, whether sex, as I have commented, mine, thine, yours, does hinge upon the function of a signifier capable of operating in this act.

Whatever the case may be, on no account can one escape what is not merely asserted by the doctrine but which we meet at every turn in our experience, to wit, only the subject who is, let's say, castrated, that is to say – to repeat in the manner of a dictionary – who has straightened things out at the level of what is called *the castration complex*, is capable of performing in the sense of the sexual act in a way that would not be at fault. I'm speaking about something that resembles the sexual act and which is not that to which I am going to try to refer today to introduce the register of perversion.

To have straightened things out at the level of what is called the castration complex does not mean, of course, that one has a complex about it. On the contrary, it means that one is in the norm with regard to the sexual act. This is what is set out in any psychoanalytic literature worthy of the name. I mean, any sound psychoanalytic literature, not the chatter of people who don't know what they are saying, which is something that can happen even among the higher authorities. To be in the norm with regard to the sexual act does not mean that one reaches it. It means that at the very least one is on the right path.

The *norm* has a very precise meaning in the passage from affine geometry to metric geometry. In short, one enters a certain order of measure, the same that I have been trying to touch on with my golden section which, I repeat, is merely metaphorical. You need only reduce it to the term of the most widely spaced incommensurable there is with regard to the 1.

At any rate, I hope I shall only have to say for the ears of novices that no one should be content with supporting the castration complex with a little story of the kind, *Dad said so, it's gonna be cut off if you keep on about taking your father's place*. First of all, most of the time, as everyone has been able to see for a long while now, the one who came out with this slight remark was mum herself, just when little Johnny was in effect taking his father's place, but to the modest extent that, as Dad had already done at his age, he was fiddling with himself in a corner in all tranquillity.

This has nothing to do with the castration complex. It's a little yarn that is not made any the more plausible by the fact that guilt over masturbation is to be met at every bend in the genesis of the disturbances we deal with. It's not enough to say that masturbation has nothing psychologically harmful about it and that it takes on its importance due to its place in a certain subjective economy.

As I reminded you on one of the recent occasions, masturbation can even take on an altogether clear-cut hedonistic value because it can be pushed as far as askesis, and because such a philosophy can turn it into the foundation of the subject's well-being, on the condition, of course, that he should have a conduct that is comprehensively coherent with its practice. It was familiar to the likes of Diogenes, who went so far as to promote it as an example of how one ought to treat what lingers on, within this perspective, of the minor excess of an organic tickling, *titillatio* in Latin. It has to be said that this perspective is more or less immanent to any philosophical position and even encroaches onto a certain number of positions that may be qualified as religious, if we consider the hermit's withdrawal to be something that in and of itself entails it.

This starts to take on its interest and, therefore, on occasion, its value of guilt, only where one endeavours to reach the sexual act. It then becomes apparent that enjoyment, which is sought for its own sake, is the enjoyment of a part of the body, a part of the body which plays a role.

I'm saying *which plays a role* because one should never say that an organ is made for a function. If you generalise a little, if you turn yourself once in a while into a mussel or some other little creature, and if you try to reflect how it might be to be in what can scarcely be called their skin, you would understand fairly quickly that it is not the function that makes the organ but the organ that makes the function. But still, this is a stance that swims too much against the tide of the transformist obscurantism in which we bathe for me to insist. If you don't want to believe me, go back to the main current.

It is therefore quite out of touch to profess, in keeping with the moralising tradition – well, in keeping with how this is explained in the *Divine Comedy* – that masturbation is shameful, and indeed a grave sin, on the grounds that it would divert a means from its end, this end being the production of little Christians or even, to come back to this even though it was felt to be scandalous the last time

I said it, little proletarians. That masturbation should consist in raising a means to the rank of an end has absolutely nothing to do with the question such as it ought to be posed. What is actually at stake is the norm of an act, in the full sense of the word, and not at all the reproductive scions that it might churn out to ends of perpetuating the animal. We have to situate what is at issue here in relation to the subject's passage to the signifier function at this problematic point that the sexual act is and which lies quite outside the ordinary field in which we are at ease with the word *act*.

That the passage from enjoyment, where it might be grasped at through such a prohibition – to stick to a word that has been used – to a certain negativation – to be more prudent and to maintain the possibility that it might be given a more precise formulation – should bear the most manifest relation to introducing this enjoyment to a function of value is something that can, after all, be said without imprudence.

The profound adulteration of enjoyment due to the fact of its passing over to the function of a value is what is called *castration*.

2

I am now going to broach what is involved in the correlation of this castration with the object. You will be seeing which object.

On this point, one may turn to experience, and even to an experience to which a certain empathy of the listener is no stranger. I have no reason to refuse what is afforded us here by the literature because, as I have just said, the only means of access here is empathic. It will have to be purified afterwards, but when we are on difficult ground this is not to be sneezed at.

What emerges from it is that there is a tighter relation between castration and the appearance of what is called *the object* in the structure of orgasm.

I repeat, we are still being empathic. Orgasm is singled out here as distinct from an enjoyment that is . . . Ah, what are we to call it? *Autoerotic*? That would be a concession. Let's call it *masturbatory*, and leave it at that, given that what is at stake is an organ and a very precise one.

Goodness knows what will be made of it, just like everything that has already been made of autoerotism, even though the latter can have a very precise meaning, that of an enjoyment that is local, and manageable, like everything that is a local. Soon enough they'll be turning it into the oceanic bath in which we shall have to pinpoint all of this. As I told you, anyone who grounds anything whatsoever on the idea of a primary narcissism and starts from there in order to generate what would amount to object investment is quite free to carry on, because it's with this that psychoanalysis functions throughout the world as an industry of guilt. You can be sure that everything I have to spell out here is made to repudiate it absolutely.

I have admitted, then, by having mentioned it, the presence of the object in orgasm. Nothing is easier than to dash from here to the mummery of the dimension of the person. *When we couple, those of us who have reached genital maturity, we treat the person with reverence.* This was how they used to express it some twenty-five or thirty years ago, especially in the circle of French psychoanalysts, who did, after all, hold some interest in the history of psychoanalysis.

Well, nothing is less sure than this reverence for the person, because to speak of the object concerned in the sexual act is to introduce the question of whether this object is man per se or *a* man, woman per se or *a* woman.

In short, the whole point of introducing the word *act* is to open the question that really does deserve to be opened, and which circulates among you without my having anything to do with it. It's a matter of knowing whether the sexual act, to the extent that any of you should ever have happened upon it, bears any relation to the advent of a signifier representing the subject as sex for another signifier, or whether it has merely the value of what I have called, in another register, *encounter*, in the sense of the single encounter, the one that, once it comes along, is definitive.

Naturally, people do talk about all this. And that's what is so serious, because they talk about it light-mindedly. In any case, mark well that there are two distinct registers. The question as to whether in the sexual act man reaches Man in his manly status, and likewise for woman, is an altogether different question from the one as to whether one has, yea or nay, encountered one's definitive partner, because this is what is at issue when one brings up encounter. More curious still, the more poets bring it up, the less efficacious it is in the consciousness of each as a question.

At any rate, the notion that it should be the person that is implied here can bring a faint smile to the lips of anyone who has a little glimpse of womanly enjoyment. This is quite surely a first point that it is most interesting to bring to the fore as an introduction to any question that might be posed about what is involved in women's sexuality, when what is at issue is very precisely her enjoyment.

One thing is quite certain, and worthwhile pointing out, and this is that psychoanalysis seems to make all those subjects who have settled into its experience, namely the psychoanalysts, incapable of facing up in the slightest to the question I have just voiced.

For the males, it has been evinced and abundantly so. When coming from a subject defined to all appearances as male on account of his anatomical constitution, this question of women's sexuality has never taken a single step that could be regarded as serious.

The most curious thing, however, is that when the women psychoanalysts approach this theme, they manifest all the signs of a misstep which can only point to one fact – that they are utterly terrified of what they might have to formulate on this matter. Consequently, the question of women's enjoyment doesn't seem close to being properly studied any time soon, because here, my goodness, is the only place where something serious might be said about it.

At the very least, by bringing it up in this way, by suggesting to each of you, and especially to what there might be by way of the feminine in this gathering of listeners, the fact that one might express oneself in this way with regard to womanly enjoyment suffices us to place it in such a way as to inaugurate a dimension that, even if we won't be entering it, since we can't, is absolutely essential when it comes to situating everything that we have to say in other respects.

3

Let's come back to the object.

The object is not, therefore, given in and of itself by the reality of the partner, by which I mean the object concerned in the normalised dimension, said to be genital, of the sexual act. It stands a good deal closer to the function of detumescence. At any rate, this is the first inroad that is afforded us.

To say that there is a castration complex is to say that detumescence on no account suffices to constitute it. This is what we took care to assert at the start, somewhat long-windedly, upholding the experiential fact that copulating and wanking are not the same thing. It no less remains that the dimension of detumescence ought not to be overlooked, because the question of enjoyment value finds its handhold, its point of reference, its pivot point, where detumescence is possible.

Regardless of what we might have to say about it on the physiological plane, the function of detumescence has been utterly neglected by psychoanalysts, who haven't shed the faintest clinical light upon it apart from what was already in all the textbooks concerning the said physiology of sex before psychoanalysis came into the world. Yet this merely bolsters what is at issue, to wit that detumescence is there only for its subjective use, in other words, to call to mind the limit that is known as the pleasure principle.

On account of being what characterises the functioning, in the genital act, of the penile organ, to mention it by name, and precisely to the extent that what it supports by way of enjoyment is left in abeyance, detumescence is there to introduce, legitimately or otherwise, that is, as something real or as a supposed dimension, the indication that there is an enjoyment that lies beyond. The principle of pleasure functions here as a limit on the edge of a dimension of enjoyment insomuch as it is suggested by the conjunction that is called *sexual act*.

Everything that experience shows us concerning what is called *premature ejaculation*, and which in our register would be better termed *premature detumescence*, gives rise to the idea that the function of detumescence can in itself represent the negative of a certain enjoyment. Clinical practice shows us only too well that what is at issue here is an enjoyment in face of which the subject refuses, even shies away, precisely in so far as this enjoyment is as such too coherent with the dimension of castration, which in the sexual act is perceived as a threat. All these precipitations of the subject with regard to this beyond-zone allow us to conceive of how it is not without foundation that in this stumbling, in these lapses of the sexual act, what is at issue in the castration complex is demonstrated, namely that detumescence is cancelled out as a good in itself, that it is reduced to the function of protection against a dreaded evil, whether you call it *enjoyment* or *castration*, castration being conceived of here as a lesser evil. On this basis, the lesser the evil is, the further down it is scaled and the more perfect the evasion is. Such is the mainspring we can put a finger on clinically, every day in treatments, from everything that can arise across the various modes of impotence, and especially in so far as they are centred on premature ejaculation.

So, the only enjoyment that can be pinpointed is the enjoyment of one's own body. What lies beyond the limits that are imposed upon it by the pleasure principle is not chance but necessity, which, by making it apparent only in the conjuncture of the sexual act, associates it as such with the evocation of the sexual correlate, without our being able to say any more about it.

In other words, for all those who already have their ears open to the usual terms in psychoanalysis, it is upon this plane and this plane alone that Thanatos is to be found in any way whatsoever brought into connection with Eros. The possibility of conjunction between Eros and Thanatos is posited only to the extent that the enjoyment of the body – of one's own body, I'm saying, beyond the pleasure principle – is evoked, and is evoked nowhere else, in the act that puts a hole, a void, a gap, in its centre, around what is localised with hedonistic detumescence. It is on this basis that it becomes conceivable that what psychoanalysis introduced into the economy of instincts, and which it designated not by chance with these two proper names, is not some crude flight of mythical fancy.

Well, as you can see, all this still amounts to beating about the bush, and yet goodness knows the effort I'm making for things not to be this way. It has to be reckoned that if we are still here, beating about this bush, it's because it's not so easy to enter. We can at the very least glean the following truths. First, that the sexual encounter of bodies does not pass in its essence by way of the pleasure principle. Second, that nevertheless, to orient oneself in the enjoyment that this encounter entails – that it entails as *supposed*, because to orient oneself within it does not yet mean that one has entered it, but rather that it is very necessary to orient oneself within it – it has no other marker but the sort of negativation brought to bear upon the enjoyment of the organ of copulation, insomuch as this is the one that defines the presumed male, namely the penis. Third, that it is from here that emerges the idea – these words are carefully chosen – of an enjoyment of the feminine object.

The *idea*, I said, and not enjoyment itself, of course. It's an idea. It's subjective. Only, what is curious, and which psychoanalysis affirms, though for want of accurate logical expression no one has been able to glimpse what this means and entails, feminine enjoyment itself can pass only via the same marker. This is what is called in women the castration complex.

It is for this reason that the woman subject is not easy to articulate, which is why at a certain level I proposed the *she-man*. This doesn't mean that all women are limited to this. There is something of woman somewhere, *odor di femina*, but she is not easy to find. I mean, she is not easy to place, because, to arrange a place for her requires a reference, the organic accidents of which mean that she finds her place only over with what is called, anatomically, the male. It is only on the basis of the suspension brought to bear on the male organ that an orientation for the two of them, man and woman, can be found. In other words, only on this basis can the function take on its value of being in a reversed position in relation to the hole, the gap, of the castration complex.

A reversal is a direction. Prior to the reversal, it may well be that there is no subjectifiable direction. After all, it is perhaps to this that should be referred the striking fact I mentioned a moment ago, namely that the women psychoanalysts have taught us nothing about their enjoyment besides what the men psychoanalysts have been able to concoct, that is to say, hardly anything. But once there

From castration to the object

is a reversal, there is an orientation. However little this may be, if this is all that can orient the enjoyment concerned here, on the woman's side, in the sexual act, we can understand how, unless otherwise notified, we have to make do with this.

It leaves us at a precise point which has its characteristic. We shall say that what can at present be formulated when it comes to the sexual act is the dimension that is called, in other registers, *good intentions*, a straight-up intention with respect to the sexual act. This is what, going by what psychoanalysts say, we can and must reasonably content ourselves with concerning the sexual act.

All of this is expressed very well in the fundamental myth. When the originary Father is said to enjoy all the women, does this mean that the women enjoy, however little this may be? The subject is left intact. And I bring this up here not merely with a humoristic intention. As you are going to see, it's a key question.

In our next meeting I shall have to take up and spell out everything I left open last time.

I showed you that we have to leave the central field of the three segments, the field of the One, of sexual union, as a deserted wasteland insomuch as the idea of a process of partition, whatever it might be, such as would allow for a grounding of what are called the *roles*, and which we call the *signifiers*, of man and woman, turns out to be somewhat slippery.

I left you on the threshold of another conjunction, the relation between, on the one hand, the Other, on the registry, on the tablets, with which this whole adventure is inscribed and which, as I told you, is none other than the body itself, and, on the other, the partner that remains to it, the *a*. This *a* is your substance, your substance as a subject to the extent that, as a subject, you have none save for this object which has fallen from the signifying inscription, save for what makes this *a* a sort of fragment of belonging of the rambling capital A, that is to say yourselves who are here as a subjective presence, but who, no sooner than I have finished, will be showing your nature as an object *a* in the unfolding of the great clearance that will promptly take place in this room.

I will leave hanging the question as to what is involved in the phallic object, because I need – and this is a necessity that is not imposed upon me alone – to lay it bare in the way that it is supported as an object. And all of this is done precisely for me to realise that in itself it is not supported. This is what the castration complex means – that there is no phallic object. And this is what leaves us our only chance – that there might be a sexual act. It is not castration, it is the phallic object that is the effect of the dream around which the sexual act runs aground.

To give you a sense of what I'm spelling out for you, there is no finer illustration than the one offered us by the Holy Book, by the One and Only Book, the Bible itself. If you have made yourselves deaf to its reading, go to Saint Mark's in Venice. It's none other than the chapel of the Doge, but its narthex is well worth the trip. What is there in the text of Genesis is nowhere else more deeply expressed in images. Among others, you will see there, cunningly magnified, what I shall call God's infernal idea, when He says of Adam Kadmon – he who was One – needs must that he be twain. He was Man under its two facets, male and female. *It is good*, says God, *that he should have an helpe meet for him*. This would still be nothing were we not to see that, in order to proceed to this adjunction – which is all the stranger in that it seems that hitherto the Adam in question, a figure formed from red clay, had been doing very well without – God takes advantage of his slumber to remove one of his ribs, from which he fashions, so we are told, the first Eve. Can there be a more gripping illustration of what is introduced into the dialectic of the sexual act by the fact that man, at the precise moment when divine intervention comes, supplementarily, to be marked upon him, finds himself having thenceforth to deal with a part of his own body as an object?

Everything I have just said is entailed by Mosaic Law itself, along with the accentuation that is lent by circumcision when we underline how the fragment in question is not the penis, because the latter is in some way incised to be marked by this negative sign. Isn't this designed to make loom up before us what there is that is, I shall say, perverse in the instauration of the Commandment that stands on the threshold of the sexual act, *And they twain shall be one flesh*? This means that within a field that is interposed between us and what might be involved in something that would go by the name of the sexual act – to the extent that man and woman could assert themselves within it, one for the other – there is, beforehand, the body's autonomous relation to something that is separate from it, after having been part of it. It's a matter of knowing whether the full scale of this interposed field can be crossed.

Such is the acute threshold wherein we can behold the law of the sexual act in its crucial datum, which is also enigmatic. Castrated man can be conceived of as never clasping anything else but this complement, by which he can be deceived and goodness knows he is sure to be, in taking it for a phallic complement.

I will posit today, as I bring my disquisition to an end, this question – we don't yet know how to designate this complement. Let's call it *logical*.

The fiction that this object should be other surely necessitates the castration complex. It is hardly astonishing, then, that we should be told, in the Bible's mythical side issues which are to be found, oddly enough, in rabbinic marginalia, that it is the primordial woman, the one who was there before Eve and whom they name Lilith – this is what the rabbis say and I'm not about to get mixed up in these stories – who took on the form of the serpent and, by Eve's hand, made sure that Adam was presented with, what? The apple. The oral object.

Why does this object crop up here? Perhaps it is there for no other purpose but to awaken Adam to the true meaning of what occurred to him while he was asleep. This is indeed how matters are taken in the Bible, because we are told that thenceforth he entered the dimension of knowledge for the very first time.

It is precisely owing to the effect of psychoanalysis that we have been able to pinpoint, within this dimension of knowing, the nature and the function of the object, here fully concentrated into this apple, in at least two of its major forms, oral and anal, and one might say its two others also, scopic and vocal, though the link has not yet been made.

This is the only pathway along which we might manage better to specify, and precisely by a series of effects of contrast, what is involved in the phallic object, which as I said, in order to articulate at last, I must first lay bare.

24 May 1967

XVIII

ENJOYMENT OBTAINS BY THE BODY ALONE

Enjoyment, beyond pleasure
Master, slave and enjoyment
Enjoyment and subjectification of the body
Does that of which one has enjoyment itself enjoy?
Perversion, *cosa mentale*

For those who find themselves here again today having followed my teaching for a while, I do need to point out what I have of late been able to insert into it by way of fresh articulations.

One important articulation, dating from our antepenultimate meeting, was to have designated – purposely, I will say, especially since the matter was not inaccessible for those who have been listening to me – the locus of the Other in the body. Quite so, the body itself has been, from the start of my teaching to the present day, what I have articulated as the locus of the Other insomuch as it is there, from the beginning, that the mark qua signifier is inscribed.

It was necessary for me to issue a reminder of this today, just as we are about to take the next step in this logic of the fantasy.

1

It so happens that the logic of the fantasy can put up with a certain logical looseness. You will see this being confirmed as we move forward.

This logic, qua logic of the fantasy, presupposes a dimension that is said to be of fantasy insomuch as exactitude is not required of it there at the point of departure.

Likewise, what we can find that is most rigorous in the exercise of an articulation that warrants this title of logic includes within itself a mode of approximation that entails not only growth but a growth that, as far as is possible, is the most rapid there is towards the calculation of an exact value. It is in this respect that we have chosen to refer to an algorithm of very wide comprehensiveness, the most apt to secure the relation of an ideal incommensurable, the simplest there could be, the most widely spaced out also, for narrowing in on what it constitutes in the way of the irrational through its very progression, namely the golden section.

I mean that it is only for the legibility of my text that I am figuring this incommensurability of the a using the golden section, since those who are in the know, know that this sort of number constituted by the very progression of its approximation is actually a whole family of numbers, so to speak, such that one can start from anywhere, from any exercise of relation, on the sole condition, which the incommensurable requires, that the approximation should have no end-term while still being perfectly recognisable at each instant as rigorous.

It is on this basis, therefore, that what we are confronted with in the shape of the fantasy has to be grasped as reflecting a necessity.

In other words, the problem that the likes of Hegel faced could be contained within the simple limit constituted by the certainty that is included in the consciousness of the self. Given certain conditions which I will mention in a moment, which are conditions of history, Hegel was able to allow himself to call into question the relation between self-certainty and truth. With this is concluded a whole process through which philosophy is an exploration of knowledge. If Hegel is able to allow himself to introduce into this the τέλος, the finality and end, of an absolute Knowing, it is to the extent that, at the level of certitude, he finds himself being able to indicate that it does not contain in itself its own truth.

It is in this respect that we find we can, not merely take up the Hegelian formulation, but complicate it. The truth we are coming to grips with hinges on this act whereby the foundation of self-consciousness, self-certainty, is confronted with something that by its very nature is radically foreign to it. What we therefore need to bring in today is that the psychoanalytic experience introduces how the truth of the sexual act forms a question in this experience.

Of course, the importance of this discovery only takes on depth on the basis of a positioning of the term *sexual act* as such. I mean that, for ears that have already been sufficiently trained to the notion of the prevalence of the signifier in any subjective constitution, it's a matter of perceiving the distance that lies between a positing of the term *sexual act* as such and a vague reference to sexuality that can scarcely be called a function, as a dimension specific to a certain form of life, notably the one that is most profoundly knotted, tangled up and intertwined with death.

This is not the whole story because, once we know that the unconscious is the discourse of the Other, it is quite clear that everything that brings into the balance the realm of sexuality in the unconscious can penetrate it only on the basis of a calling into question of the sexual act. Is the sexual act possible? Is there such a thing as this nexus, definable as an act, wherein the subject could be grounded as sexuated? That is to say, if the subject is not male or female per se, can the subject proceed through such an act to something that might culminate, even if only at its end-term, in the sheer essence of male or female? I mean, could a culmination in the sifting apart, in the sharing out in a polar form, of that which is male and that which is female, be reached precisely in the conjunction that unites them in what I have named *enjoyment*? This is a term that I am not bringing in here, at this hour, for the first time. I introduced it long ago, notably in my seminar on ethics.

It is indeed required that the term *enjoyment* be used, and in specific contradistinction to pleasure, as constitutive of a beyond-zone. This is indicated in psychoanalytic theory by a series of convergent terms, chief among which is the term *libido*, which represents a certain articulation of it. At the end of this year's talks we will have to show how the use of this term can be rather slippery, such that the essential articulations which we are trying to introduce today can be led to buckle rather than find support in it.

Enjoyment is this something that bears a certain relation to the subject insomuch as, in this confrontation with the hole left in a certain register of the act – the eminently questionable register of the sexual act – the subject is suspended by a series of modes or states of dissatisfaction. Here you have what in itself alone justifies introducing the term *enjoyment*, which is also what comes to the fore, and notably in symptoms, as indiscernible from this register of satisfaction. Indeed, the problem for us from one moment to the next is to know how a nexus which is sustained by unease and suffering alone is precisely the very thing through which the instance of suspended satisfaction manifests itself, that is to say, the locus in which the subject holds himself insomuch as he tends towards this satisfaction.

The law of the pleasure principle, the law of the lowest degree of tension, does no more here than indicate the necessity of the detours on the trail along which the subject sustains himself on the path of his search, a search for enjoyment. It does not yield its end. This end is, however, entirely masked for us in its final form, to the extent that it might equally be said that its full term is so questionable that one may start as much from the fundament that *there is no sexual act* as from the fundament that *there is but the sexual act* which actuates this entire articulation.

This is why I have been keen to bring in here the reference to Hegel, which everyone knows I have been using for a long time.

The process of dialectic across the different levels of self-certainty in the *Phänomenologie des Geistes*, as he put it, is suspended from a movement he calls *dialectical* and which can most surely from his perspective be taken to be dialectical only for a relation he articulates from the presence of this consciousness, in so far as its truth escapes it. Its truth escapes it in what constitutes the interplay of the relation between one self-consciousness and another, in the relation of intersubjectivity. Now, it is quite clear, and has long been demonstrated if only through the disclosure of this social gap, that we are not permitted to encapsulate what presents as a struggle, namely the struggle between master and slave, in the face-off between one consciousness and another. It doesn't even fall to us to critique what is left open by the Hegelian genesis because it has been done by others, and most notably by one other by the name of Marx, leaving the question of its outcome and its modes in suspense.

Freud comes along and takes things up at a spot that is only analogical to the Hegelian position, but is already sufficiently inscribed into the term *enjoyment* insomuch as Hegel had introduced it. Hegel tells us that the point of departure lies in a life-and-death struggle between master and slave, after which it is established that the one who declined to risk the stake of death falls into a state of dependency upon the other, which is not for all that shorn of the whole future of the dialectic in question. This is where the term *enjoyment* comes in. After the close of the life-and-death struggle for pure prestige, enjoyment will be the special privilege of the master while the path traced out for the slave will be that of labour.

Let's look at things more closely in the text, though time will not allow me to do so at any great length. Of what does the master have enjoyment? In Hegel's text, the thing is very amply perceived. The relation established by the articulation of the slave's labour means that, while the master does perhaps enjoy, he on no account enjoys absolutely. At a pinch and forcing things a little – which we would do to our cost as you are about to see – we might almost say that he derives his enjoyment only from his leisure, which means, from having his body at his disposal. In fact this is far from being so, but we can admit that he is separated from everything he might enjoy in the way of things by the very one tasked with putting them at his mercy, to wit the slave. Meanwhile, for the slave there is a certain enjoyment of the thing insomuch as he doesn't merely fetch it for the master but he has to transform it for the master to receive it. This is a vital point which I don't need to argue out because it is amply indicated by Hegel.

After this reminder, it is time to ponder with you, to get you to ponder, what the word *enjoyment* implies in such a register.

Surely nothing is more instructive than to refer to what is known as the lexicon, in so far as it sets to such precarious goals as the articulation of signifiers. As we can read somewhere in a note from the preface to the magnificent work that is called *Le Grand Robert*, *the terms included in each entry constitute a chain of cross references that should culminate in the means of thought expression. The asterisk* – you will be able to observe that in each of these entries which fulfil their programme very well – *the asterisk refers to entries that develop at length an idea suggested by one headword.* Thus, the lemma *jouissance* opens with the word *plaisir* marked by an asterisk.

This is merely one example, but it is surely not by chance that this word presents these paradoxes here. Of course, *jouissance* was not tackled for the first time by *Le Robert*. You can also study it in the *Littré*, where you will see that its most legitimate use varies from the aspect indicated by its etymology, which has its roots in *la joie*, to that of possession and ultimately to that which one has at one's disposal, the exclusive enjoyment of a title, be it a legal title or some piece of paper representing listed stock. To have the enjoyment of something, of dividends for example, is to be able to hand it over. The sign of possession is to be able to resign it.

Having enjoyment of is different from *enjoying*. Nothing more than these slippages of meaning, in so far as they are discerned in the lexical comprehension exercised in a dictionary, shows us the degree to which reference to thought is indeed what is most unsuitable when it comes to designating the radical function of one signifier or another. It is not thought that provides a signifier's effective and ultimate reference. It is the instauration that results from the effects of introducing a signifier into the real.

It is insomuch as I am spelling out in a fresh manner this relation between the word *enjoyment* and what is, for us, in practice in analysis that the word meets and is able to conserve its ultimate worth.

I mean today to give you a sense of the scope of this at its most radical point.

2

The master derives enjoyment from something, be it from himself – *he is his own master*, as they say – or, equally, from the slave.

But of what does he have enjoyment in the slave? Precisely, of his body. As we can read in the scriptures, *the master says go and he goeth.*

I once allowed myself to write, more or less – if the master says *Jouis!, Enjoy!*, the other can only reply, *J'ouis, I hear.* I amused myself with that, and in general I don't amuse myself willy-nilly. It means something, which could have been picked up by one of those who hearken to me. I am too often to regret that I don't receive any more than what I am compelled to do for myself.

The question is this. If there is this enjoyment that is established in the *I* of the subject in so far as he possesses, does that of which he has enjoyment itself enjoy? It does seem that this is the veritable question, because it is quite clear that enjoyment is on no account what characterises the master. In so far as he is one who, in the city-state, can on no account be just anybody but who is marked by his function of master, he has a good deal else to do besides giving himself over to enjoyment. The mastery of his body – for it is not a mere matter of leisure – is achieved and maintained only by tough discipline. In any era in civilisation, he who is master does not have time to allow himself to slacken off, even in his leisure pursuits.

Different types could be singled out here, but the type of the master in Antiquity does not belong to a realm that is so purely ideal that we don't have any reference points for it. I would say that it is sufficiently inscribed in the margins of the first philosophical discourse for us to be able to say that Hegel gives adequate testimony of it. The question is precisely as follows. Why shouldn't the one who has clung on to enjoyment, such that he submits and alienates his body, not remain with enjoyment in hand? After all, this would only be fair and in conformity with the opening stakes of the first round, because at the start he was not able, if Hegel is to be believed, to sustain the possible risk of losing his life, which is indeed the surest path to losing enjoyment.

A short-sightedness, goodness knows what fantasy, would like everything to be always on the same side, for the full bouquet to be held in just the one hand. But this is simply not the case. We have a thousand testimonies of how what characterises the position of him whose body is put at the mercy of another is that on this basis there opens up for him what can be called *pure enjoyment.*

Furthermore, following the clues which afford us at the very least a way of cross-checking this, it may well be that certain questions that have been asked about certain paradoxical positions, in particular masochism, would fade away. But then, after all, it is sometimes better not to go through those doors that are most promptly opened. Just because they are easily walked through, it doesn't make them true.

So, I'm not saying that the condition of the slave is the mainspring of masochism, far from it, even if it is thinkable that this condition might be the only one that would afford access to enjoyment. To the very extent that we are able to formulate the question, as subjects we shall never know anything about it. Now, the masochist is not a slave. He is, on the contrary, as I will be telling you presently, a smart Alec, someone very firm. The masochist knows that he is in enjoyment. It is precisely for your use, for you to understand what is at issue in his regard, that the present disquisition is proceeding.

And to make it proceed, what first had to be shown was how there is more than one flaw in Hegel's construction. The first of these was the one that gave me occasion, in front of those who were listening to me back then, even before promulgating it and speaking about it in connection with the mirror stage, to mark out how on no account whatsoever is that sort of aggressiveness which is active and present in the life-and-death struggle for pure prestige anything else but a red herring. On this basis, any reference to this struggle as a primary articulation is rendered null and void.

I am merely pointing out again in passing the problems that arise and are left wide open by the Hegelian deduction with respect to the society of masters. How do they get on with one another? And then, gracious me, there is the elementary reference to the slave. For him to be transformed into a slave, he can't be dead, and so the life-and-death struggle didn't result in anyone being put to death. The master has only the right to kill him, and this is precisely why he is called *servus*. The master *servat*. He safeguards him. It is on this basis that the veritable question arises – what is it that the master safeguards in the slave? Here we are brought back to the question of the primordial law, of what the rule of the game establishes, to wit, he who will be vanquished *could* be killed and if he is *not* killed, at what price does this come?

It is indeed here that we move back into the register of *signifiance*. What is at issue in the master's position is still the consequence of introducing the subject into the real.

To take measure of what is involved in its effects on enjoyment, a certain number of principles need to be set out at the level of this term. We have already introduced the term *enjoyment* in the logical mode of what Aristotle calls an οὐσία, a substance. That is to say, something that, as he expresses it in his book of *Categories*, very precisely can be *neither predicated of a subject nor exists in any subject*, something that *seems not to admit of more or less*, that cannot be introduced into any comparative, into any indication of greater or lesser sign, or indeed lesser or equal. Enjoyment is this something in which the pleasure principle marks out its traits and its limits, yet it is something substantial and which it is important to state in the form that I am going to spell out in the name of a new principle – *enjoyment obtains by the body alone*.

Allow me to say that I consider the upholding and the affirming of this principle as essential, and it strikes me as having a greater ethical scope than that of materialism. I mean that this formulation has exactly the scope and the depth that the affirmation that *there is only matter* introduces into the field of cognisance. You need only take a look at how, with the evolution of science, this matter ultimately blends so well with the interplay of elements into which it is resolved for it to become, at a push, all but impossible to discern what is playing out in front of you, whether it is those elements, στοιχεία, those ultimate signifiers, or those of the atom, so much do they possess in themselves something that is well-nigh indiscernible from how your mind is proceeding, from how your search is playing out. But, in the end, what is involved is a structure that you no longer know in any way whatsoever how to bring back to what is yours by way of a common experience of matter.

But to say that *enjoyment obtains by the body alone*, and in particular that this forbids you everlasting enjoyment, is very much what is in play in what I have called *the ethical value of materialism*. It consists in taking seriously what happens in your everyday life and, whenever the question of enjoyment should arise, in facing up to it and not putting it off until better tomorrows.

This principle, *enjoyment obtains by the body alone*, responds very precisely to the truth requirement which is there in Freudianism.

3

Here we are, then, having left wholly unto its own errancy the question as to whether what is at issue is to be or not to be, whether what is at issue is to be man or to be woman, in an act that would be the sexual act.

If this is what dominates this entire suspension of enjoyment, then this is what we also have ethically to take seriously. It is to this that we ought to bring to bear what we might call our right of inspection.

Oedipus is not a philosopher. He is the model for what is at issue when it comes to the relation of what is involved in a certain knowledge.

The knowledge he evinces – this at least is what is indicated in the form of the riddle – is a knowledge concerning what is involved in the body. It is with this that he breaks the power of a fierce enjoyment, that of the Sphinx, who is most strangely presented to us in the shape of a vaguely feminine creature – half-bestial, half-feminine, let's say. After which, he gains access to what is assuredly an enjoyment. This doesn't for all that secure his triumph. No sooner has he entered it, he is already in the snare. I mean that this enjoyment is the one that marks him already, ahead of time, with the sign of guilt.

Oedipus didn't know from what he was deriving his enjoyment. I have posed the question as to whether Jocasta knew and even, why not, whether she derived enjoyment from allowing Oedipus to remain in ignorance of it. Let's put it like this – what share of Jocasta's enjoyment corresponds to her allowing Oedipus to be in ignorance? This is the level at which, thanks to Freud, serious questions concerning what is involved in truth can now be posed.

Now, what can we say with respect to what interests us, and which was set out at the start, namely that enjoyment obtains by the body alone? The effect of the introduction of the subject, itself an effect of *signifiance*, is properly to bring the body and enjoyment into the relation that I have defined through the function of alienation, insomuch as this function is coherent with the genesis of the subject as determined by the vehicle of *signifiance*.

As I have just been spelling out to you for the last half an hour, the subject is founded with a mark of the body, which privileges it, and this is what means that this subjective mark will thenceforth dominate everything that will be at issue for this body. That it should go hither and thither and not elsewhere, that it should be free or not to do so, this is doubtless what distinguishes the master, because the master is a subject.

Enjoyment, in this first grounding of the subjectification of the body, is what falls into dependence upon this subjectification. To spell it right out, it is what gets effaced because the master's position is, at the point of origin, a relinquishing of enjoyment. This is what Hegel glimpsed. There is the possibility of engaging everything on having the body freely at one's disposal or not. Not only one's own body, but also that of the other party. And this other party is not just one 'body. It is, once the interplay of social struggle has been introduced, the full set of bodies. Indeed, by this fact alone, relations between bodies thenceforward fall under the dominion of this something that is called law. One might say that this law is bound to the advent of the master, but only if one understands this to mean the advent of the absolute Master, that is to say, death become legal sanction.

This then allows us to glimpse that, if the introduction of the subject as a signifier-effect lies in this separation between body and enjoyment, in the division placed between these terms which subsist only one from the other, then it is here that for us the question must be asked as to how enjoyment can be handled on the basis of the subject. Well, the response is given to us by what analysis discovers as an approximation of this relation to enjoyment, in the field of the sexual act. What it discovers is the introduction of what I have termed *enjoyment value*, that is to say, the annulling of the enjoyment that is, as such, most immediately concerned in sexual conjunction. It is what analysis calls *castration*.

This resolves nothing. It does, of course, explain for us how it is that the simplest and clearest legal form of the sexual act, insomuch as it is instituted in a regular concretion that is called *marriage*, is originally the special privilege of the master alone – not, of course, the master in contrast with the slave, but, as you know if you have absorbed a little history and Roman history in particular, the master in contrast with the plebs. Access to the institution of marriage is not for just anyone who wants it. It is for the master alone.

Yet everyone also knows – from, goodness gracious, life experience, in view of what this marriage, which has since then been put within reach of us all, still drags along with it in the way of heartache – it doesn't go off without a hitch. If you open up Livy, you will see that there was a period, not so late on in the Republic, when the Roman gentlewomen, those who were marked for sure by the true *conubium*, throughout a whole generation poisoned their husbands with a perseverance and on a scale that didn't fail to leave its trace in memory. It was not without good reason. It has to be believed that the institution of marriage, when it functions at the level of veritable masters, must entail a few drawbacks. And they are not tied solely to enjoyment, because these little incidents result rather from the accentuated character of the hole that lies at this level, namely the fact that enjoyment is a far cry from conjugal choice.

The sexual act interests us, us analysts, only at the level where, precisely, enjoyment is involved. As I reminded you last time, God has not deigned to keep watch over this. It suffices that woman should enter the game of being this phallic object, which is so well designated for us by the Biblical myth, for man to be content – which means, exactly, to be perfectly bamboozled, to wit, encountering only his bodily complement.

The discovery of psychoanalysis is precisely to notice that it is solely to the extent that man might not have been bamboozled to the point of finding nothing more than his own flesh – and there's nothing astonishing about there now being only *one flesh* here, because it's his own – that there should be some chance of there being a sexual act.

For there to be some chance of this, yea or nay, this operation of bamboozling must not occur, namely right where castration occurs.

But then, what about enjoyment, since the characteristic of a sexual act that would be grounded would lie precisely in the fact of this lack of enjoyment, somewhere? What about this enjoyment in its third-party function?

4

The response to this questioning is afforded us by another approach, which goes exactly contrariwise to the step forward, to the breaching, in the direction of the sexual act. It is called, precisely and solely on account of its reverse direction with respect to a certain logical progression, *regression*.

It is here that our algorithm can be of service to us in so far as it confronts the a with 1.

As I have already drawn out here, the a can fold back towards the inside, onto the 1 of the middle segment, that is, the field of the One, leaving as a remainder the discrepancy $(1 - a)$, which is at the same time a^2. Another way of treating the question is suggested to us by the function of the Other. The 1 of the field of the Other comes to inscribe itself in the a that is at issue, but without folding back, that is to say, leaving between itself and the A the large interval of the One. You cannot help but notice the fact that is thereby privileged, which is that $1/a$ is precisely equal to $1 + a$, and that this is what establishes the worth of this algorithm. We have thereby set down the locus, the topology, of what is involved in connection with enjoyment.

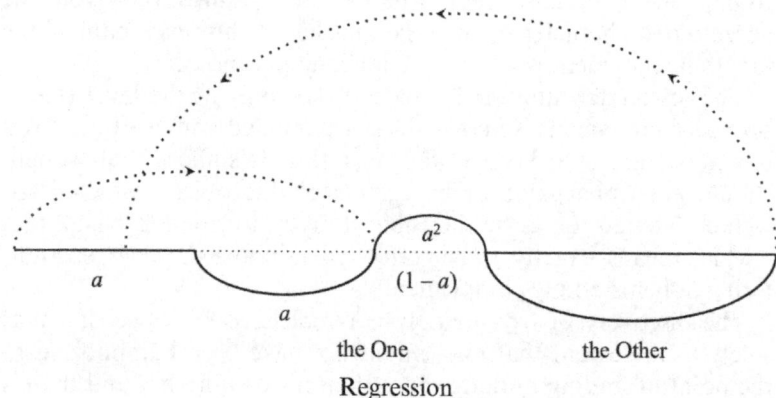

Regression

In the case of the slave, how are we to know what is involved in his enjoyment, given that he has been divested of his body? How are we to know, unless, precisely, it lies in that which of his body slips outside subjective mastery? Everything that is involved for the slave, insomuch as his body goes hither and thither at the master's whim, nevertheless leaves preserved those objects that are given to us as having emerged from the signifying dialectic, those objects that are its stake, but also its forging, those objects prehended at the edges, those objects that function at the level of the body's rims. We know them well in the dialectic of neurosis and we shall have to come back to them again and severally, to define in full what makes for their price and their worth, their exceptional quality.

I don't need to remind you of these objects when it comes to the oral and also what is called the *anal* object, but there are the higher objects too, which are less known, which belong to a more intimate register that, in contrast to demand, is constituted as desire. They are called the *regard* and the *voice*.

Insomuch as they can on no account be captured by any kind of dominion of the signifier, even when such dominance is amassed in full at the level of social oppression, these objects by their very nature elude it.

What does this mean? Where is the enjoyment? The decisive question is the one I posed earlier – *does that of which one has enjoyment itself enjoy?* Hegel was mistaken in that it is *for the slave* that the master's enjoyment obtains. It is an enjoyment taken for granted. Yet perhaps there is something of the real of enjoyment that may subsist only at the level of the slave. And should this be so, then it is to be found in that place that is left at the margins of the field of his body, constituted by those objects I have just listed. It is in this place that the question of enjoyment must be posed. Nothing can take away from the slave the function of his regard, nor that of his voice, nor that of what is involved in the function of a wet nurse which Antiquity so frequently shows us to have been carried out by bondwomen, nor in the slave's function of a deformed object, an object of scorn. It is at this level that the question of enjoyment is posed, which is even, as you can see, a scientific question.

Now, this is what the pervert is. Perversion is the search for this perspectival point in so far as it can make the accent of enjoyment loom up. But the pervert hunts it out in an experimental way. Indeed, while it does bear the most intimate relation to enjoyment, perversion is, like the thought of science, *cosa mentale*, as Leonardo said of painting. It is an operation of the subject who, having perfectly pinpointed the moment of disjunction wherein the subject wrenches the body away from enjoyment, knows even so that there is more to this process of the alienation of enjoyment. He knows that somewhere there remains some chance of something having escaped it, that not the whole body has been caught in the process of alienation. It is from this point, from the locus of the *a*, that the pervert interrogates what is involved in the function of enjoyment.

Psychoanalysts have only ever grasped this in a partial fashion. I won't say that they take up the standpoint of the pervert, because really it has to be said that they comprehend nothing of it. Wasn't there even one who recently set out a sort of equation whereby the pervert could never be subject and enjoyment at once, whereby, to the extent that he was enjoyment, he was no longer a subject? No, the pervert remains a subject for as long as it lasts, throughout the exercise of what he poses as a question to enjoyment. The enjoyment that he targets in this question is that of the Other, insomuch as he himself, the pervert, is perhaps indeed the only remainder of this enjoyment, but he posits it through an activity of the subject.

What this allows us to reassemble can be done only on the condition that we realise that, for example, the terms that are yoked together in so-called *sado-masochism* carry meaning only when considered as lines of research along the path to what the sexual act is, or else that, speaking of *sadistic relations* between some or other vague cell of the social body only carries any interest when they stand in for something that concerns the relations of man and woman. You will see next time that, by overlooking what is fundamental in these relations, one allows any means of grasping what is involved in sadism and in masochism to slip away. This doesn't mean on any account whatsoever that these two terms stand in for relations comparable to those of male and female.

A person of, I must say, incredible naivety, somewhere wrote this truth that *masochism has nothing specifically feminine about it*, but the reasons he gives for it lie at the level of – *if masochism were feminine, this would mean that it isn't a perversion, because it would be natural for woman to be masochistic*. On this basis one might thus surmise that, naturally enough, women cannot be qualified as masochistic because, being a perversion, masochism cannot be something natural. This is the kind of reasoning people can become mired in.

And yet his first line of thought is certainly not without a certain intuiting of how a woman is not naturally masochistic. Quite so. She is not naturally masochistic, and for good reason, because were she naturally masochistic, it would mean that she is capable of fulfilling the role that the masochist ascribes to a woman, which, of course, gives an altogether different meaning in this case to what feminine masochism would be. It so happens that woman has no vocation for fulfilling the role assigned to her by the masochistic enterprise, and this is precisely what constitutes its worth.

You will allow me to finish today with this point, while promising you that we shall be bringing, at least so I trust, some order and at the very least a little more clarity to the forefront of what is called into question by thus introducing perversion.

31 May 1967

XIX

THE QUESTION OF ENJOYMENT

> The subject's relation to the body
> The disjunct between body and enjoyment
> Woman's body, metaphor of my enjoyment
> On comedy in Antiquity
> Perverse act and neurotic act

What do what have very recently been called *structuralisms* have in common? Well, their common point is to make the function of the subject dependent upon signifying articulation.

This is to say that this distinctive sign can remain more or less elided and that in a sense it always is.

I am of course aware that some of you can in this respect find that the analyses by Lévi-Strauss, which have for some years now been focused on myth, leave this central point in abeyance, thus leaving us faced with the question, to spell it right out – in the end, should it be thought that honey had been awaiting in tobacco the truth of its relation with ash?

In a certain sense it's true. And this is why the suspending of the subject follows on from any approach of this kind. It is also what suffices to lead us to contribute to something which, even so, is not a doctrine, which is merely the acknowledgement of an efficacy, which does indeed seem to be of the same nature as the one that grounds science. It no less remains that a notion of class, a minimum sequence of characteristics, such as the structuralisms would imply, could in no way whatsoever coalesce a certain number of lines of research into one set.

To take my research as an example, it is after all merely as a facilitator, as an adjuvant apparatus, that it was pressed to encounter at the start the necessity of the subjective articulation in the signifier. It was in some way a preface to this research, without which nothing could have been thought through correctly.

And yet it was not without good reason that something that was articulated too quickly in that same field did ultimately have to be produced by us, namely the fundamental relation between the subject thus constituted and the body.

1

I am turning at last to the subjective relation to the body, which is something that for years I had to put to one side, precisely due to the fact that symbolism had always traditionally been articulated as bodily symbolism, that is to say, in a fashion that missed what was essential, as does tend to happen when things are overly hurried.

The members and the stomach. A good while back, I brought up on the horizon the fable by Menenius Agrippa. It wasn't a bad one. Comparing the nobility to the stomach is better than comparing it to the head, and then, it puts the head back in its place among the members. Even so, this rushes matters somewhat. And if we know as much, it's on account of what lies at the centre of our research.

Our research, that of us analysts, doubtless passes only along the pathways of structure, in other words, the signifier's repercussions in the real in so far as it introduces the subject into it. But what lies at its centre? It is a sign that I am only able to call it to mind with such force at a moment when, strictly speaking, I am establishing my disquisition in what I have been able justifiably to call *a logic*. It is a moment when I am able to call to mind how everything revolves for us, in our research, around what is involved in what has to be called *the difficulty*... – not *of being*, as a certain someone said in his twilight years – *the difficulty inherent in the sexual act*.

Introducing the function of difficulty is no small matter. There are other difficulties that have heralded this one. On the day the difficulty of social harmony took on the legitimate name of *class struggle*, a step forward was taken. The difficulty of the sexual act can carry a certain weight if one pauses over it, I mean, if everything that we have to articulate in our field comes effectively to be centred upon this difficulty.

I suspect that one of the reasons psychoanalysts prefer to limit themselves to positing that placing the Thing at the centre, with a capital T if you wish, sheds light across a whole surrounding zone is that, apart from something which I shall have to point out presently, it presents first and foremost a logical difficulty. One could in this connection take as a pointer how the institution of marriage is proving to be ever more – I won't say solid, it's far more than that – resistant, the more rights are provided in our society to align oneself with all sorts of aspiration, as the psychologists say, to the sexual act. While it does seem that a corner has been turned in clarifying the difficulty of social harmony, it is quite striking indeed that it is not especially here that the greatest openness is to be found with respect to the right to align oneself with aspirations to the sexual act. Marriage has shown itself to be – I won't say *more resistant*, there's no call for resistance – more instituted here than elsewhere. Across all the fields where aspirations are aligned in hundreds of forceful forms, in all the fields of art, cinema, the spoken word, not to mention the field of the great neurotic discontent of civilisation, marriage still remains centre-stage, having budged not an inch in its fundamental status.

In other words, to sum up this institution, see how it is founded upon this one enunciation, once uttered, *Thou art my woman*. I used this, in a different way, to exemplify the structuration of the message in and of itself. This utterance doesn't even need to be met by another, such that asking her whether she agrees is all but a purely formal matter. In every shape and form in which this institution persists, at least for the time being, the inauguration of what we will call *a couple*, defined as productive, hinges upon this utterance.

This is not to say that what is at issue is the couple alone, in the sense of the sexual pair. Of course this is required, but it has to be noted that we can say that its product is something else besides the child reduced to biological offspring, to the effect of the function of reproduction. And this is what we mean by designating as *a* what we need to examine at the start of its entry into the sexual act. It is already its product, and not merely as biological offspring.

I told you that – if you absolutely must slot this into one of your philosophical pigeonholes – we could identify this *a* in broad terms with the residuum at which the philosophical tradition ultimately arrived. After having brought to perfection the isolation of the function of the subject, and having had to keep shtum beyond that, it was to bid us farewell and wave us off – *Bye bye, sail away now on the waves of whatever will follow me, drift away in this world into which you have taken a brief dip, this world all astir and about to come out with the latest of its contradictions.* This is beginning, in fact. But then, at that very moment, this same tradition told you in the very same breath that, even so, a little residuum did remain, in the shape of this advantageous dialectics to which total order, absolute Knowing, was promised, and which is called *Dasein*.

This residuum of presence, insomuch as it is bound to subjective constitution, is in fact the sole point at which we remain in continuity with the philosophical tradition. We gather it up from its hand. We meet it again precisely as the by-product of what was masked in the dialectic of the subject, to wit, how it has to do with the sexual act.

This subjective residuum is already there when the question is posed as to the mode in which it will play out in the sexual act. While the whole of human discourse is structured such that it leaves wide open the very possibility of the subjective instauration implied in the sexual act, this same human discourse has as a whole already produced – not in each subject, but at the level of its subjective effect in itself – the raining down, the trickle down of residua that accompanies each of the subjects concerned in the process. At the end of the day, this residuum, as wholly partial as it may be in its essence, is the surest junction there is between the subject and the body. I think you will recall that it is by this inroad that we have already approached the *a*.

The *a* certainly presents as a body, but not as a *total body*, as some say. It presents as an offcut, as misplaced with regard to the body on which it depends. It depends upon it in keeping with a structure that must be maintained very firmly if it is to be understood, and it can only be understood by referring to what forms its centre. What is this centre? Certain indications allow us to have a glimmering of it, like the following, and I'm the first to have stated it. There is the repercussion of these objects which I have been calling the *a*, each of which are tied, I won't say to the sexual act, but, even so, to something that tends towards it because it revolves fully around it, to wit what is termed prematuration.

It's not only a matter of biological prematuration, which calls forth the appeal to the body towards the locus of the act. It is not only a matter of prematuration or its attempt at the level of what is called prepubescence, the first shoot that reaches out to indicate the future and the horizon of this locus. Already, by itself, but not without calling forth a whole conjunction, a whole social circumstance of suppressing, of appraising, at the very least of discursively referencing, demand and desire, it preforms the subject as *a*. It brings the subject, as a by-product of this central point of difficulty, to this difficulty itself.

The shortcoming of psychoanalysts with respect to their role, a shortcoming that however relative it may be remains no less radical, is perhaps due – I'm saying perhaps – to how they don't posit themselves as being engaged in experiencing to the utmost the extreme difficulty of the sexual act.

Indeed, while didactic analysis is of course more than a requisite on the side of these analysts in order, let's say, to cicatrise the chance effects of this difficulty, as is the case for each and everyone, this doesn't mean that analysis constitutes in and of itself the fact of experiencing this difficulty. Once through the cleansing phase – call it whatever you will – the phase of prerequisite purification, it is rather convenient to get back into one's slippers, which are not, whatever some might say, the place of choice for the sexual act.

Certainly this is already an inroad towards being poised to think through desire. Are you going to believe that I'm giving you the watchword that what is at issue is to think through the sexual act?

2

If you care to recall how I introduced the notion of act, you will note that an act doesn't need to be thought through to be an act.

The question even arises as to whether it is an act by dint of not having been thought through. I won't be going any further in this direction, which is overly favourable to the semblances of an act.

This business is not especially amenable, but what is quite certain is that, whether or not it ought to be thought through, it can only be thought through after the event. It is in the very nature of an act that it first has to be performed, which perhaps doesn't exclude its being thought through. This tells you that, if we are starting from the difficulty of the sexual act, this is not to bring within arm's reach the time to think it through.

Let's pick up at the base level the matter of how the thing is posited. If it's an act, the constitution of a signifier in an act, on the basis of some motion, we will say, here merely invoking the register of movement, of something measurable in a body's weight, there must be, if the signifier is reduced to the most straightforward chain, the opposition that in one of my articles I have already inscribed on two little unforeseen panels, and which we shall here translate anew, lopping off the *I*, with *am a man* and the relation it bears to *am a woman*.

While the earlier wording, *Thou art my woman*, presented with the structure of the message in an inverted form, we absolutely cannot in any case whatsoever account for a link between these two terms that would justify one being taken to be the inverse of the other. Isn't this utterly fabulous? And so, on this basis, we need to examine them as they are, that is to say, in our complete incapacity – as you are well aware and as is spelt out on every line in Freud's work – to give them any certain correlate whatsoever. For example, activity and passivity are in this respect mere substitutes which, whenever we use them, as Freud underlines, show their, I won't say inadequate, but suspect character.

So, let's pose the questions afresh with the apparatus we have been furnished with by our fine little tradition of subject handling. It ought to be able to be put to the test here, and even if it cannot serve any purpose, the way in which it will be rejected by the object will perhaps instruct us about a property of the object itself, like its elasticity for example. We will take *being male* first, but note that at this level of discourse both being male and being female are in exactly the same position.

If we are to find something analogous to whither our handling of the subject is leading us, it, too, must have two facets. Indeed, this leaps out straightaway. There exists an *in itself* and there exists a *for something*, but what can be seen right away here is that this is not at all a *for itself*, due to the fundamental requirement of the sexual act. It cannot remain *for itself*, yet let's not say that it is *for* the one who forms the pair. This is where the introduction of the function of the big Other should be of service to us. What corresponds here to our examination – as contrasted with this *in itself* of the τό that tends rather to drift off course and which corresponds to being male and far more still to being woman – is a *for the Other*, that is to say, what we had to bring up first, the locus whence the message comes back to it in an inverted form.

I'm going to slip in a brief reminder here. I'll be elaborating on it next time as I can only touch on it in passing today. I broadened the scope of the alternative, *either I am not thinking or I am not*, by showing that it exceeds the simple reach of alienation because it has already enabled us, back in the first term, to establish the logical operation of alienation in its relationship with two others. You may have forgotten, but these two others can form with the operation of alienation something that can be examined in the manner of a Klein group. I situated the subject's fundamental alienation at the starting point of this little rectangle, precisely in its relation with a possibility that was nothing else but the place marked out for the sexual act in the logical form of sublimation.

This alternative, a seductive choice as you can see, is the starting point for what is offered to the subject once the perspective of an unconscious is introduced, insomuch as this unconscious is formed from the difficulty of the sexual act. How are the terms of the alternative shared out? *I am not thinking* is assuredly the *in itself*, the *for itself* – should ever it manifest itself – of being male or being woman. *I am not* stands on the other side, namely the side of *for the Other*. What the sexual act is called upon to secure, because it grounds itself there, is something that we may call a *sign* coming from *I am not thinking*, whence I am as not thinking, to arrive at *I am not*, right where I am thinking as not being.

This is the opportunity to recall what I once put in a written piece, that *I am where I am not thinking*, and that *I am thinking where I am not*. Indeed, the locus where the act arrives might well bear the title *I am not*, but even so it is here – in this locus where *me, male, I am not, at the level of woman* – that my destiny plays out and this locus is that of *I am thinking*. Whatever philosophers' pretensions might be to detach τὸ φρονεῖν, *I am cogitating*, from τὸ χαίρειν, *I am enjoying*, my destiny plays out at the level of the former. The fact of having dialogued with Socrates has never stopped anyone from having niggling obsessions that greatly disturb one's τὸ φρονεῖν.

So, the next step is afforded us by the function of the message, which is why I called it to mind. It is a fact that, being rash and absolutely not knowing what I'm saying, I proclaim myself as being man right where I am not thinking. Furthermore, the form of *Thou art my woman where I am not* carries all the same the interest of affording woman the possibility of proclaiming herself, too. Moreover, this is what requires that she should be there as a subject, because she becomes one, like me, as soon as she proclaims herself. This encounter which occurs under the pure form of message – and which is all the purer, I insist, on account of one absolutely not knowing what one is saying – brings right to the fore the function of the subject in the sexual act. It is even as a pure subject that we perceive ourselves at the level of the fundament of this act. This pure subject is situated at the juncture, or, to put it better, the *disjunct*, between body and enjoyment. It is a subject commensurate with this disjunct.

How is this best to be seen? We know it from the tradition, since earlier I was evoking the *Philebus*, in particular where the τὸ φρονεῖν and the τὸ χαίρειν are subjected to the operation of separation with a rigour that led me, on the eve of the last break, to recommend that you read it.

At this turn you might want to tell me that, after all, we can very well do without the requirements of this act, that perhaps we have no need of the sexual act to fuck in a perfectly seemly fashion. Actually, it's a matter of finding out what, in the contours of the act, is required there by the subject. Perhaps to say that everything hinges on the opposition between the signifiers *man, woman*, is to say very little, if as yet we don't even know what they mean. And indeed it is not so very much in the word *woman* that the repercussion of the subject is to be seen as in the word *male*.

I observed that the term *enjoyment* is an ambiguous one. It slides from having us say that enjoyment obtains by the body alone, which opens the field of substance where those severe limits come to be inscribed within which the subject contains himself with repercussions of pleasure, to the meaning where to enjoy, as I stated, is to possess, where it's *my* ... – I have enjoyment of something. The latter leaves in suspense the question as to whether this something, by my having enjoyment of it, itself enjoys. It is here, around this *my* ..., that the separation between enjoyment and the body is located. It was not merely for the sake of it that I led you into this last time by way of the articulation from the *Phänomenologie des Geistes*, that of the master and slave, which is so fragile on account of being limited to the traditional field of the subject's genesis.

My ... Henceforth *I have enjoyment of your body*, that is to say, *your body becomes the metaphor of my enjoyment*. Even so, Hegel doesn't forget that this is just a metaphor. If master I am, my enjoyment is already displaced. It depends upon the metaphor of the serf. It still remains that for him, and for what I am questioning in the sexual act, there is some other enjoyment, which is adrift.

Need I write it out again on the board, with my little bars?

$$\frac{(my) \text{ body}}{?} \quad \bigg| \quad \frac{\text{body}}{my \text{ enjoyment}}$$

The body of the woman who is *my* ... – *my woman* – is henceforth the metaphor of my enjoyment. It's a matter of knowing what is there in the shape of my body. Of course, I don't even think, innocent as I am, to call it *my* ... It, too, will have its relation of metaphor, which would most surely ground everything in the easiest and most elegant fashion with the enjoyment that is in question and which makes for the difficulty of the sexual act.

You will ask me – *why is it at the level of woman that enjoyment forms a question?* We shall reply right away and very straightforwardly. Every psychoanalyst knows the answer. They don't necessarily know how to say it, but they do know it. They know it from how, men or women, they have not yet been able to articulate the slightest thing that would hold up on the subject of women's enjoyment.

I'm not telling you that women's enjoyment cannot take up this place, but rather bringing you to a halt just when it's a matter of not going too fast, to tell you that it is here that the difficulty of the sexual act lies.

3

With regard to what I have called *enjoyment adrift*, last time I took the reference of the master–slave relations, a reference that is less intolerable solely because it's a myth.

You can fairly imagine that when the slave is at issue there is no reason for the enjoyment not still to be there, and all the more so because unlike the master he hasn't been possessed by the idiocy of putting it at risk. So, why shouldn't he have kept it? Just because his body has become the metaphor of the master's enjoyment, this doesn't mean that his own enjoyment shouldn't go on with its own little life, as everything proves to be so.

If you read the comedy of Antiquity, if you re-read the cherished Terence, for example, you will see that he is very precisely not primitive at all and is even quite the contrary. It may be said that things are pushed so far in his plays, matters are so thoroughly exhausted, that they outstrip in simplicity anything we might ponder. It's far more simplistic than a film by Monsieur Robbe-Grillet, even when it's slipshod. Nothing in Terence's plays is slipshod. Yet we can no longer make out what is at issue.

There is a certain story about *Andria*, for instance. You will read it and tell me, *Good gracious, what a carry on! All that just because a boy who has a father and who must or mustn't marry a girl of high birth or low birth, and in the end, the one of low birth turns out to be of high birth after all on account of this eternal business of recognitions, having been abducted when she was little, and so on and so forth. What blithering idiocy!* Only, what is vexing is that if you reason thus, you won't see the matter at hand, which is that there is but one interesting person in the whole comedy, and he goes by the name of Davus.

He is well and truly a slave, for he can be taken altogether seriously, him who runs everything, who is the most intelligent of all these folk, and no one dreams of suggesting that any of them could even come close to being as much. The father plays the paternal role to just the right degree of stupor. The son is a poor minion who is utterly disoriented. The girls are nowhere to be seen and of interest to no one. But there is a bondman who fights for his master, so much so that from one minute to the next he runs the risk of being crucified. It's there in the text. And he conducts this business masterfully, it has to be said.

This is what is at issue in the comedy of Antiquity, with the slight difference that for us there is just one point of interest, which is that of showing us that there can be a questioning of what becomes of enjoyment when this little shift occurs, this *Verschiebung*, which is properly speaking constituted when the function of the subject is introduced between the body and enjoyment.

This is not done with the enjoyment proper to one body, insomuch as this enjoyment defines it. A body is something that can enjoy, yet, there you have it, it is made to become the metaphor of the enjoyment of another. And so, what becomes of one's own? Is it exchanged? The whole question lies here. It has not been solved. And why not? Even so, we analysts know why, which doesn't mean that we are always able to say why. This is a general observation. I'm not going to keep repeating it.

Let's write it up here. We'll make this the body. This way it will be more amusing. It looks like my little panels from one of my articles [to which I alluded earlier], on which I wrote *Gentlemen* and *Ladies*, as can be seen at the entrance to public urinals.

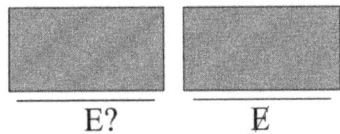

A little panel will be able to serve us as a body, with a certain number of things inscribed upon it. Indeed, this is the function of the body, since we have been reminding ourselves that this is the locus of the Other. So, we shall draw the same little bar, so that you won't be disturbed, and underneath we shall write E for *enjoyment*.

There is a question mark here because we do not know ultimately whether enjoyment does come to this place, whether the woman's body is really what the male asserts, because he does no more than assert as much. This is what we began with in *Thou art my woman*, namely that the woman's body is the metaphor of his own enjoyment.

Indeed, in the sexual act, there is not merely the couple in play. As other structuralisms functioning in other fields have reminded you, man's relation to woman is subject to functions of exchange which, by the same token, imply an exchange value. To constitute this exchange value as such, the locus where something is of use has to be struck through by the necessary negativation. Here, for reasons arising from the natural constitution of the function of copulation, this negativation is derived from masculine enjoyment insomuch as, for its part, they know where it is. Well, they believe they do. There is a little organ which they can catch hold of. This is what the male baby does, promptly and with the greatest of ease.

As a parenthesis, I really must show you this. I have been given a fanciful little book on masturbation, with illustrations, and it's such a delightful thing that I can't imagine it would find its way back to me were I to circulate it here. I'm not sure what to do. There must be devices for projecting such things. The book is called *Le Livre sans titre*. There are a score of images showing the ravages brought upon the unhappy wretch, upon any young man of course – you know what a bad reputation masturbation had in the early nineteenth century – the ghastliness, at any rate, that it produces. And all this is rendered in pen and ink . . . well, to behold the unfortunate young man vomiting blood . . . it's most sublime.

Please forgive me. This has nothing to do with my disquisition. Nothing at all. It's going to cost me horribly dear, which is one of the reasons I'd prefer not to part with it. Indeed, it is of a beauty to surpass anything else. I've never seen something of the like.

3

Anyhow, this embargo on masculine enjoyment, in so far as it can be apprehended somewhere, is something structural, albeit concealed, with respect to the founding of value.

As for woman, she is after all a subject in the sexual act. I would even say, and I have just spelt out, that there couldn't be any sexual act were she not grounded as a subject at the start. Now, for her to take on her function of exchange value, she has to cover over what is already established as value, which is what psychoanalysis reveals under the name *castration complex*.

I am not trying to tell you that the exchange of women is comfortably retranslated by the exchange of phalli. Were that the case, I don't see why ethnologists wouldn't draw up their tables of structures by calling things by their name. It is about the exchange of phalli, but in so far as the phallus is the symbol of an enjoyment that is subtracted as such, which is to say, not the penis, but that which, since the woman becomes the metaphor of enjoyment, makes it such that one can in its stead take a new metaphor, namely this negativised body part which we call *the phallus* to distinguish it from the penis.

This leaves the problem that we have just spelt out no less wide open. In other words, something is established, another process, that of social exchange, in the founding of the material, so to speak, that is destined for the sexual act. And this leaves no less in abeyance the question as to whether we are able, on account of this external element, to situate something concerning woman in her function of metaphor in relation to an enjoyment that has passed over to the function of value.

This is expressed in many a myth. I don't need to recall for you Isis and her eternal mourning for the last portion of the body she gathered up. I will simply point out to you in passing that in this extreme myth the goddess is defined – and this is what distinguishes her from a mortal – precisely as being pure enjoyment, an enjoyment that is also separated from the body. But whyever so? Well, because nothing of what constitutes a body in its status as a mortal body could hold worth for a goddess.

This does not mean that the gods have no bodies. They simply change bodies, as you well know. Even the God of Israel has a body. One has to be a fool not to notice that. This body is a pillar of fire by night and of cloud by day. So we are told in The Book, and what is at issue there is properly speaking His body. These are matters that I would have developed better had I been able to deliver the seminar on *The Name-of-the-Father*.

The goddess is enjoyment, and it is very important to call this to mind. Her status of goddess is to be enjoyment, and to fail to recognise this is to condemn oneself to understanding nothing of everything that has to do with enjoyment. It is in this respect that the *Philebus* is exemplary. One line from the dialogue announces that on no account do the gods have anything to do with enjoyment, that it would be unworthy of them. It is here, so to speak, that the weak spot in the starting point of philosophical discourse lies – to have radically failed to recognise the status of enjoyment in the realm of entities.

I am only making this remark in an incidental fashion and to remind you of the scope of this reading of the *Philebus*. It permits of pinpointing with exemplary accuracy the limited field in which is developed everything that will be involved in the status of the subject and in what is signified by the reclaiming of those questions that have thereby been isolated.

4

Here we are, then, turning around this question of what is involved in enjoyment in the sexual act.

To introduce the close of our disquisition today, I need to begin by articulating what now needs to be set out and to give it the most emphatic punctuation. We shall say that it's a matter of pinpointing how those acts that get placed within the register of perversion, and legitimately so, concern the sexual act.

If they concern the sexual act, it's because the point at which enjoyment is in question lies at the level of the man's body – it can be no less in question at the level of woman's body, as you will see, but from another angle – given that the model that allows the perverse attempts at solution to become apparent is afforded us in the instauration of enjoyment value, that is to say, in the negativation of the function of a certain organ, which is the very organ wherewith Nature, through the supply of pleasure, ensures the copulatory function. Yet the way in which it does so is perfectly contingent and incidental, because in other animal species it does it quite differently, by hooks for example, such that nothing can reassure us that there should be in this organ anything whatsoever that concerns enjoyment properly speaking.

To read this on our schematic – here, on the left above the bar, we have the male term through which enjoyment value is introduced, which means that at the level of enjoyment, this enjoyment comes into play very precisely in the form of a question.

Posing the question of women's enjoyment . . . well, this already opens the gate to all the perverse acts. This is why men, in appearance at least, have the special privilege of the major perverse positions and why the question is asked – it is already something that one is able to ask this – as to whether woman has even a hint of it. Of course, through the reflection of what is introduced into her by the man's want of enjoyment, she does enter this field, along the path of desire, which is, as I have been teaching, the desire of the Other, that is to say, in this instance, the man's desire. But the question of enjoyment arises for the man at a more originary stage insomuch as this enjoyment is concerned from the very start, at the very foundation of the possibility of the sexual act.

The man will test out this enjoyment by means of objects, those same objects which I have been calling *a*, in so far as they lie on the margins, eluding a certain structure of the body. Specifically, they elude the structure that I have been calling *specular*, which is the mirage wherewith it is said that the soul is the form of the body, that everything of the body passes into the soul. This is what can be retained, the body image, and it is through this that so many analysts believe they are able to grasp what is involved in our reference to the body. Hence the number of absurdities they proffer. For, precisely, it is not here that the question of enjoyment lies, but in those parts of the body on this strange limit which, as I would say by way of commentary upon these images, form a ball or a symphysis. It is here, in these parts of the body which we shall call the *anaesthetic parts*, in contrast to the specular reflection, that the question of enjoyment takes refuge. And it is these objects that the male subject addresses in order to pose the question that concerns him as his highest priority, that of enjoyment.

Of course, in delivering you this just as I am about to take leave of you, it might strike you as a closed formulation, and so it is. At the very least, for each of the major objects I have just brought up, how they serve as questioning elements would have to be demonstrated in an exemplary fashion. This is something that can be done only on the basis of what I have been spelling out, last time and again today, as the constitutive separation between body and enjoyment.

I just need to make a brief inroad into this by pointing something out, so that your thoughts may head straight down the path of the drive that is called, wrongly, *sadomasochistic*, but which is even so, along with scoptophilia, the only term which Freud enlists as a fulcrum when he sets to defining the drive.

What is in question in the game that is played out in full by the sadomasochistic drive is here, in this disjunct, amply marked out by my siglum or, if you wish, my algorithm, of $S(\bcancel{A})$, namely the disjunct between enjoyment and the body. I will be showing you this next time in all its detail, starting from the masochist.

The masochist interrogates the completeness and the rigour of the separation between body and enjoyment, and supports it as such. It is through this that he comes to prise out, so to speak, from the field of the Other, what remains available for him in the way of a certain interplay of enjoyment. He yields a solution that is not the path of the sexual act but which comes to pass along this path.

There you have it for what is going to allow us to situate in an accurate way the fundamental position of the masochist as a perverse structure, when what is usually said about it is always so approximate. As I have the sense that I haven't said all that much about it today, and because it might serve some of you already as a theme for reflection, I can as of now indicate, having already spelt it out in its time, that the level of the masochistic position is an essential reference when it comes to distinguishing, because they have to be distinguished and radically so, the perverse act from the neurotic act. The perverse act is located at the level of the question about enjoyment. The neurotic act, even if it refers to the model of the perverse act, has no other end but that of sustaining what has nothing to do with the question of the sexual act, namely the effect of desire.

It is only by posing these questions in this radical fashion – and this cannot be radical but in being articulated in logic – that we can perceive how the perverse act is distinct from everything that resembles it on account of having borrowed from its fantasy.

7 June 1967

XX

THE SADIST AND THE MASOCHIST

The fantasy sets the measure of comprehension
Symptom and fantasy
The pervert finds his enjoyment in the object a
Re-conjoining body and enjoyment
Subject to enjoyment

An analysis can be interminable, but not a course. A course has to have an end. And so the last of this year will take place next Wednesday. Today is therefore the last but one.

My choice this year was that there wouldn't be a closed seminar. I nevertheless made a place for at least two people – forgive me if I am forgetting others – who brought their contributions to me and maybe, here at the start of this penultimate lesson, there could be someone among you, or a few, who might perhaps care to tell me what they would like – who knows? – to accentuate further, or to reply to, or to open up for a future resumption, either in this last lesson but one or in the final one. I will see whether I can give a response today. I shall at least endeavour to indicate the direction in which I am able to respond, or not. In short, if some of you might like to give me, right here right now, some sign of their wish and of what I might have left to be desired regarding the field I have articulated this year upon the logic of the fantasy, I would be most grateful to them.

Well, who will take the floor? Then again, there's no time for dawdling. Who wants the floor? [*silence*]. It's a tall order. OK. Let's not speak of it any further, at least for now. Those who might be visited by the *esprit de l'escalier* can send me a brief note. My address is in the directory, rue de Lille. I don't think you will have any doubts. So far as I know I'm the only one, at least on that site, to be identified as *Docteur Lacan*.

I'm going to be pursuing from the point at which we left matters. As we no longer have much time to wrap up what can be taken as having shaped a certain field which has been circumscribed by what I have set out over the year, I'm going to endeavour to indicate the last remaining points of reference in the most straightforward way I can.

1

I'm going to try to keep things simple and this entails forewarning you of what this simplicity might mean.

The term *logic of the fantasy* is amply justified by the fact, which I am today about to re-accentuate yet again, that the fantasy is, in a far narrower manner than all the rest of the unconscious, structured like a language. At the end of the day, the fantasy is a sentence with a grammatical structure. To articulate the logic of the fantasy does therefore seem to be appropriate.

This means first of all posing a certain number of logical questions. Some of these questions, for instance that of the relation between the subject of the statement and the subject of enunciation, however straightforward they may be, have not been voiced so often. I'm not saying that this was done for the first time by me, but perhaps it was done for the first time by me in the analytic field. This does not exclude that at the end of this first disentangling, an indication could be given as to the direction in which the thrust of the matter might develop in a fuller, more articulated and more systematic fashion. I can only claim to have opened up this year the furrow of this logic of the fantasy.

This first disentangling has of course indicated that the *logic* of the fantasy somewhere hooks onto, inserts into, hangs upon, the *economy* of the fantasy. This is indeed why at the end of this disquisition I have brought in the term *enjoyment*. I brought this term in while underlining, while accentuating, that this is a new term, at least within the function I am giving it.

Enjoyment is not a term that Freud brought to the forefront of his theoretical articulation. If my teaching is, in sum, able to find its axis in the slogan *making the case for Freud's doctrine*, then this implies that I should announce and broach any such function, any such marker, that is in any way discerned, outlined, required or implicated by this doctrine. To make the case for Freud is to do what I have always been doing. This entails first of all rendering unto Freud that which is Freud's, as they say, which doesn't rule out any other allegiance, for example making a case for him with regard to what he indicates and entails in the way of the relationship to truth. I would even say that, if something like this is possible, then it is precisely to the extent that I never fail to render unto Freud that which is Freud's, that I don't arrogate to myself what is his.

This is a point that carries its importance and I shall perhaps have time to come back to it at the end. It is rather curious to see that, for some, it is by appropriating as their own – I mean, by not rendering unto me – that for which they are most manifestly indebted to me in their formulations, as is plain for anyone to see, that they promptly find themselves prevented from taking the next step, which even so it would be very easy indeed to do in many a field. Alas, they leave it to me do so, then to despond, feeling that I've beaten them to it.

So, let's start our approach to the function of the fantasy and, first of all, to take stock of the very point of departure of our question, let's simply state something that leaps out here, which is that it is something closed. In our experience, for those subjects who usually, most commonly and most customarily sustain it, namely neurotics, it presents as a closed signification.

Notice that this closed aspect is thus to be doubly situated, in the two terms I have been accentuating since I first introduced this year's schemas, and which I recommend you refer back to once you have gathered together whatever you might have been able to take down in the way of notes, whether extensively or less so, in order to form a grasp of the ground that will have been covered.

The first of these terms is correlative to the choice constituted by *I am not thinking*, in which *I* is constituted precisely by the fact that it comes in reserve, so to speak, as having been lopped off, as a negative. In the exemplary examination that he makes of the fantasy, not *Someone is Beating a Child*, but rather, to be strict, *A Child is Being Beaten*, as is written in German, *Ein Kind wird geschlagen*, Freud notices firmly that the fantasy unfolds as a grammatically structured sentence. It is this structure that is inscribed at the level of *I am not thinking*.

This structure stands at the level of the only possible term from the forced choice of the alienating alternative, *Either I am not or I am not thinking*. If it stands as the only structure that is offered to us then this is to the extent that it can be called upon to unveil the other, the rejected one, that of *I am not*. It is the unconscious *Bedeutung* that comes correlatively to bite into the field of the *I* that is there qua not being there.

The *Bedeutung* at issue here is precisely the closed signification of which we were speaking. It slips away, and yet it is so important to underscore that it is this signification that sets the measure of comprehension, the accepted measure, the intuition, the experience that is called upon whenever someone holds a discourse of false pretence that appeals to understanding as opposed to explication. Jaspers stands in the front line of such purveyors of philosophical vanity and haughtiness. It's that spot in your guts which he aims at to lead you every so often to believe that you are understanding things. It's that little isolated, secret thing that you have within you, in the form of the fantasy. You believe you understand whenever it awakens within you the dimension of desire.

It is quite simply this that is at issue in what is called *understanding*. Calling this to mind here has all its importance, and I'm not saying this because, in the main, such as you all are – I'm saying this for the majority – you're a little neurotic around the edges. The fantasy sets for you the measure of comprehension, precisely at this level where the fantasy awakens desire within you, which is hardly piffling because it's what centres your world.

For all that, this is no reason for you to imagine that you understand what only the logic of the fantasy can deliver, namely perversion. Don't imagine that the fantasy plays the same role for the pervert. As I've been trying to explain, what the pervert does is rooted in what cannot be defined but in relation to the term that I have introduced, which is likewise novel on account of having been accentuated – *the sexual act*.

Between the enjoyment concerned in perversion and the difficulty or the deadlock of the sexual act, there are terms to be distinguished and connections to be articulated. I reminded you just now of the example of *A Child is Being Beaten*, where the fantasy is given to us in a closed state. The function of this fantasy cannot as such present as anything else but the strict formulation *Ein Kind wird geschlagen*. Just because it might have a configuration which you can point out and refer back to the economy of perverse enjoyment by making some such terms of one correspond to terms of the other, this doesn't mean that they are in any way whatsoever of the same nature.

In support of this I will right away underline the vital point that can easily be gathered up in passing in this text of Freud's which is so clear, namely that, in the cases of neurosis in which he met it, the fantasy in question *subsists apart from the rest of the content of the neurosis*. In the structure of a neurosis, this fantasy – to take this one because we do indeed need to take something to know where to focus our attention – *finds no proper place*. Here we have something that might indeed call for a moment's attention.

Well, with respect to what is involved in the structure of symptoms, I mean, what the symptoms signify in the economy, it cannot be said that this makes the same thing fall into place in one neurosis as in another. I can never repeat this too often, even if I might seem to give rise to astonishment when, across from one of those who put sufficient trust in me to come to be supervised by me, I take a firm stand against their using such terms as, for example, hystero-phobic structure. Why so? Well, a hysteric structure is not the same thing as a phobic structure. They stand no closer to one another than they do to the obsessional structure.

The symptom represents a structure. This is the striking point. As Freud indicates, this fantasy can, unlike the symptom, wander around in very different structures.

Another point – for the moment, I'm reading Freud and repeating what he says – the fantasy has the special privilege of being confessed to *only with hesitation*. We could tarry over what is unmentionable here, which could include a good many things. In any case, to stay at the level of the rough-and-ready approach of 1919, the year he wrote the text, *a sense of guilt* attaches to the fantasy, like a cherry on a stem, and Freud at any rate pauses here to relate it to what he calls a *scar*. The scarring of the Oedipus complex.

This is well cut out to make us say that, on account of how it has surfaced in our experience, the fantasy partakes of the experimental aspect of a foreign body.

By dint of the veritable theoretical bridge that Freud constructs, we start to have an inkling of how this closed signification was related to something else that is far more open to development and far richer in its potential, and which is called, properly speaking, perversion.

Just because Freud takes this leap very early on, this is no reason for us not to have to reinstate the full and proper distance.

It falls to us now to restore the proper ratios and to question ourselves, now that we have after all acquired a great deal of experience on the matter, about what is involved in perversion.

2

So, I said that perversion is something that is articulated and presents as an inroad to the difficulty that is generated by, let's say, the *project* – put this word in inverted commas because it is merely analogical and I'm bringing it in here as a reference to another discourse than my own – of a calling into question that, to be more exact, lies at the corner where two terms meet, *there is no . . . , there is but . . .* , the sexual act.

There is no sexual act, so I said, to the extent that we are unable to articulate its resultant postulations. This does not mean, of course, that there are not some subjects who have gained access to it and who can legitimately say, *I am a man, I am a woman*. But we analysts, we are the ones who are incapable of saying as much, and this is what is striking.

And yet, *there is but this act*, held in suspense at this level, to account for what is called perversion.

The matter has, however, remained, and remains still, ambiguous. After all, perversion could be separated off from the sexual act. This is the case when what is at issue is perversion in the absolute sense, in the sense that Aristotle takes it, for instance, when he prescinds from the field of his ethics, as τέρας, as monstrosities, a certain number of practices which were perhaps – why not? – more manifest, more visible, more persistent even, in his world than in ours, where, moreover, it oughtn't to be believed that they are not still present. To cite one example that he gives us, there is bestial love, and even, if I remember rightly, the allusion he makes to the tyrant Phalaris who liked to enclose his victims, whether friends or otherwise, in goodness knows what contraption in which they were steam cooked for a certain while.

For us this is not, of course, a univocal model because in his ethics, as in any ethics from the Greek philosophical tradition, the sexual act has no central value. I mean it has no patent, declared value. It is up to us to read into it. The same is not so for us, due to the inclusion of the Judaic commandments in our morality.

With Freud, however, the matter is clear-cut. We are dealing with sexual perversions. Even if we find it more convenient to slacken off its chains in the shape of a reference to goodness knows what endogenous development, goodness knows what stage which we claim, no one knows why, to be biological, it still remains that perversion assumes its value only in being articulated to the sexual act.

I will say – to the sexual act *as such*. And this is why I have chosen this little model of incommensurable division par excellence, this little model of the a, the largest there is to develop its incommensurability, which is defined as $1/a = 1 + a$. This fact allows us to inscribe it into a schema, in the form of a double development. Am I going to have to draw it up again today?

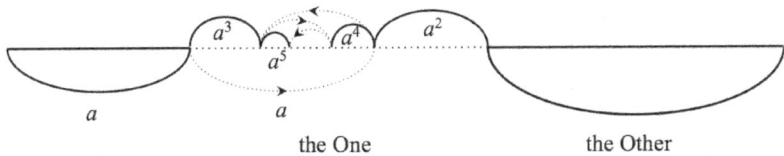

the One   the Other

I will simply indicate that, the middle segment being 1, there is a way to fold back into it the a that is here. Then, this leftover which as though by chance turns out to be a squared, that is, a^2, is itself equal to $(1 - a)$. This can be easily checked straightaway. When folded back into this a^2, an a^3 produces here an a^4, which in turn ... and so on and so forth, culminating here in a sum of odd powers that happen to be equal to a^2, while the sum of even powers happen at the end to be equal to a. Through this, what you initially saw being projected into 1, namely a to the left, the a^2 to the right, turn out to be separated in a definitive fashion, inversely.

It would be easy for us to show that this schema can represent fairly well, albeit in a purely transumptive way, that which of the sexual act could present for us in a way that tallies with Freud's hunch, namely that the sexual act is achievable, but only in the form of sublimation. It is precisely to the extent that this path and what it implies remain problematic that I have excluded it this year.

Indeed, to say that the sexual act can be achieved in the form of sublimation is to move away from what we are dealing with, namely this whole chain of difficulties that arise structurally and uncoil across this field, and which includes a major gap. The wide open gap that remains here is that of castration.

Correlatively, it is along a path that runs away from the bedrock of castration that perversion is articulated. This is the least that can be said, and on this point the common vote, so to speak, of those authors who have experience of this is quite clear.

The interest of this schema is to show that the measure a, which here is first projected onto 1, can also develop in an outward fashion. Namely, the relation $1/(1 + a)$ is also equal to the fundamental relation designated by the a, which means, here, as I called to mind back at the time, $a/1$.

What is at issue at the level of perversion? Well, to the extent that the One is left intact – not the One of the act but the presumed One of sexual union, of the sexual pact, if you wish – to the extent that the partition is not established here, the subject said to be perverse comes to find his enjoyment at the level of this irreducible thing that he is, this originary a.

What renders this conceivable is that there could be no sexual act here, nor any other act, unless in the signifying reference which alone can constitute it as an act. By this fact alone, the signifying reference does not concern the two natural entities, the male and the female. By the mere fact that this signifying reference is dominant, because this is a lower field of the sexual act, it introduces these beings – which we can on no account maintain in the state of natural beings – in the form of a subject function. As I have spelt out over the previous sessions, this subject function has the effect of a disjunct between body and enjoyment.

It is here, at the level of this partition, that perversion most typically steps in. Perversion strives to re-conjoin enjoyment and body, which have been separated by the fact of the signifying intervention. It is in this respect that perversion is situated along the path of a resolution of the question of the sexual act. As I showed you in my little schema last time, there is in the sexual act, for whichever of the two partners, one enjoyment that remains in suspense, that of the other party. An inter-crossing is required if either body is to be turned rightfully into metaphor, into the signifier of the other's enjoyment, but this inter-crossing is held in suspense, which is why, from whichever side we might approach it, we cannot help but behold a displacement which shifts an enjoyment into dependence upon the body of the other party. In view of which, the enjoyment of this other party remains, as I termed it, *adrift*.

In the case of man, for the structural reason that a levy is taken from the enjoyment that is his, then to be raised to the function of enjoyment value, he finds himself, more readily than woman, caught up in the consequences of this structural subtraction of a share of his enjoyment. The man is effectively the first to bear the reality of this hole introduced into enjoyment. It is not, of course, that the question of enjoyment carries greater weight for him – it carries just as much for his partner – but as such he can provide articulate solutions to it.

He is able to do so on account of it being in the nature of this thing that is called a body to have something that duplicates the alienation that constitutes the subject's structure – the alienation of enjoyment. Next to subjective alienation, I mean, the introduction of the function of the subject which bears on enjoyment, there is another alienation that is embodied in the function of the object *a*. Eurydice twice lost, as it were.

Where is the pervert going to find again the enjoyment which he does indeed re-find? He won't find it in the totality of his body, where an enjoyment is perfectly conceivable and perhaps even requisite, but where it is clear that this is where it poses a problem when it's a matter of the sexual act. The enjoyment of the sexual act can in no way whatsoever be compared to the enjoyment that may be felt by a runner as he paces along freely in his higher realm.

Nowhere more than in the field of sexual enjoyment does the pleasure principle become apparent as that which sets this limit upon the law of enjoyment, since the pleasure principle is properly the limit, the obstacle and the end point that is brought to any form of excess in enjoyment. It is here, and especially for the man insomuch as the castration complex already articulates the problem for him, that the field will be found in which certain objects in the body are defined as being, with regard to the pleasure principle, in some sort *outside the body*. These are the *a* objects.

The *a* is something ambiguous. However little it may belong to the body, even to the individual object itself, it is in the field of the Other that the subject has to make his appeal for it and take up its trace, and with good reason because this is where the subject himself takes shape.

First, the breast. It really does have to be defined as something that is stuck onto the mother's body, hooked onto the surface like a parasite, in the manner of a placenta, and thus remains something which the child's body can legitimately claim to belong to it. This belonging is enigmatic, of course, as can be seen very well whenever some mishap in the evolution of living beings makes it apparent that, for some of them, something of them has remained appended to the body of the being that engendered them.

We have already mentioned excrement. It hardly needs to be stressed that it has something marginal about it with respect to the body, but not without being tightly linked to the body's functioning. It is fairly plain to see in all its weight what living beings add to the natural domain in the way of these products of their functions.

Next come those objects which I have designated with the terms *regard* and *voice*.

I have already spelt out plentifully what is entailed by the fact that, in the relation of vision, the question is always left hanging as to what is involved at the root of the visible. This question, which is such a straightforward one to articulate, cannot, in spite of everything, be resolved by phenomenology, as Merleau-Ponty's last work proves. It's that this root has to be found in the question of what a regard is most radically.

The regard is no more graspable as a reflection of the body than any of the other objects in question are liable to be seized in the soul, I mean, in the regulating aesthesia of the pleasure principle, in this representative aesthesia, wherein the individual finds himself identified with his own self in the narcissistic relation wherein he asserts himself as an individual.

The object *a* is a leftover, a remainder that rises up only at the moment when the limit that founds the subject becomes appreciable. This is where enjoyment that doesn't fall under the sway of the pleasure principle takes refuge, and here, too, stands the *being-there*, in that the *Dasein*, not only of the pervert but of any subject, is to be located outside the body. There is something like a foreshadowing of this in the passage from the *Philebus* which I asked you to look up, where Socrates speaks of what he calls ἀναισθησίαν in the soul's relationship with the body. It is precisely in this anaesthetic, insensible part that enjoyment lies.

3

To show you this, and to whip you into shape, as it were, with the said inroad, I shall turn now to the structure of the subject in the two exemplary terms defined as those of the sadist and the masochist.

Need I evoke for you what we may imagine at the most elementary level in the way of a puppet which is toyed with by the sadistic act? This is of course on the condition that you be good enough to grasp that it is not a matter of understanding what might be moving about such a practice, imagined or otherwise. I began by taking out my guarantees, reminding you that you are all more or less teetering on the edges of neurosis, to ask you to pause on something else besides the empathy that might be stirred up in you by the merest little fantasy of this type, to avoid, for example, questions about the economy of pain in the sadist's act, which I do hope people have stopped racking their brains over.

We shall say that what the sadist toys with is the subject.

I'm not about to come out with a prosopopoeia on this, because I've already written something about it which is called *Kant avec Sade*, to show that the two of them, Kant and Sade, are in the same vein. The subject is toyed with. Which subject? Well, since I said somewhere that one is *subject to thought*, or *subject to vertigo*, I shall say in response, *subject to enjoyment*. This introduces an inflection that makes us pass from the subject to what I have marked out as the subject's leftover, the object *a*.

It is at the level of the Other that the sadist brings about this subversion, by adjusting the dose of tickling, of *titillatio* as Spinoza puts it, thereby giving its true name to what the philosophers have always deemed worthy of being disdainfully qualified as the body's relations with the soul. So, the sadist toys with the body of the other party, apparently. But you can see very well that the question needs to be displaced to the level of the question I formulated in a field where things are less captivating, when I gave an image to this relation between master and slave by asking, *does that of which he has enjoyment itself enjoy?* You can see, then, the immediate relation with the field of the sexual act.

Yet the question at the level of the sadist is this. He doesn't know that it is to this question as such that he is attached, that he becomes its pure and simple instrument. He doesn't know what he himself is doing as a subject. He is essentially in *Verleugnung*, and he can interpret it in umpteen different ways, which he doesn't fail to do. Of course, he does need to possess some power of articulation, which was the case with the Marquis de Sade, in view of which his name remains attached to the thing and rightly so.

Sade remains essential on account of having marked out the relations between the sadistic act and what is involved in enjoyment, and for having made a derisory attempt to give voice to the law in the shape of a universal rule worthy of one of Kant's maxims, in the famous line, *Yet another effort, Frenchmen, if you would become Republicans*. My commentary in the article I have just mentioned bore on this. It shows that the formulation of this law could never concern the enjoyment of the total body, but rather – mark this well in the text – a part of the body. In the fantasmatic State that Sade imagines, founded upon the right to enjoyment, each citizen would be duty-bound to offer, to anyone who betrays the intent, the enjoyment of any part of his or her body. So writes the author, and not to no avail.

This part is a refuge of enjoyment, and the sadist subject doesn't know that this is very exactly his own *Dasein*, that this is what makes a reality of its essence. Here we have what is already given to us by Sade's text as a key.

I won't have time to spell out all over again what results from this redeployment, one in relation to the other, of enjoyment and the subject, and how close this is to the fantasy, which is promptly articulated by Sade, of enjoyment raised to its absolute in the Other. This lies very precisely in this part of the 1 that is here on the far right of our schema, just where we saw, at the start of the problem, enjoyment sliding away, bereft of support. And this is why Sade, being an atheist, has to construct the figure of God, the most manifest and the most manifestly plausible God, that of the enjoyment of an absolute malice.

Then and only then – carried along, as it were, by the logic of the fantasy – does Sade confess that the sadist is merely a servant of this essential and sovereign evil. He avows that the sadist has to clear the way, with maximum destruction, for the radical evil that Nature constitutes. But, let's not forget, it is merely a question of the logic of the thing. The actual endeavours of the sadist have a plainly futile and buffoonish character, and are always miserably aborted. I developed this in *Kant avec Sade* and suggested that you should refer to its sources, because the truth of it can better be seen on the basis of this unfolding.

The truth of the matter is afforded properly by the masochist's practice.

Here it is clear that, in order to prise out, as it were, to tease out the object *a* at the only spot where it is manifestly graspable, the masochist gives himself over – with deliberation in his case – to an identification with this object as a rejected object. Less than nothing. Not even animal. An ill-treated animal. Yet also a subject, albeit one who has contractually abandoned, through his subject function, all his privileges. His dogged search for an impossible identification with that which dwindles to the most extreme aspect of discard is a construction which for him is bound to the requisition of enjoyment. It is here that the economy of the masochist's practice becomes apparent, laid bare as an exemplum.

Let's take a look, here, without lingering, at the sublime lines of Baudelaire's verse which humanise, as it were, this manoeuvre –

Tandis que des mortels la multitude vile,
Sous le fouet du Plaisir, ce bourreau sans merci,
Va cueillir des remords dans la fête servile . . .

All this is mere trickery. It is the reflection of pain brought upon the law of pleasure. Pleasure is not a *bourreau sans merci*. Far from being a merciless tormentor, pleasure keeps you within a limit that is sufficiently buffered to be, precisely, pleasure. When the poet expresses himself thus, it is very precisely to mark out his distance from what is at issue, namely –

Ma Douleur, donne-moi la main; viens par ici,

Loin d'eux.

It's a fluting chant, to show us the charms of a certain path that is obtained by this pain, thus reversed.

We can observe now the necessity of our schema when we are dealing with the sexual masochist. What Reik stresses, with a tactlessness that may truly be said to make your head spin, in masochism's imaginary or fanciful character, more exactly *phantasiert*, shows that he really didn't grasp, even though everything that he brings by way of examples designates it quite well enough, that what is at issue is precisely what we have projected here, at the level of the 1 on the right-hand side, namely the absolute 1 of sexual union.

On the one hand it is that pure yet detached enjoyment of the woman's body, as evidenced by Sacher-Masoch, who is just as exemplary as Sade, for having delivered us the structures of the masochistic relation.

Sacher-Masoch essentially embodies in the figure of a woman this Other whose jouissance he has to tease out. It is an enjoyment of absolute Otherness, but it is entirely enigmatic. There is no question of this enjoyment giving so much as a moment's pleasure to the woman, as it were. But this is the least of the masochist's worries. And this is why, when Sacher-Masoch's wife set to writing her memoirs – she upon whom the moniker Wanda is bestowed in *Venus in Furs* – she shows us just how much she was in a bind with his requests, truly a fish with a bicycle.

On the other hand, given that this enjoyment is purely imaginary, what point is there in racking one's brain over its being embodied on occasion by a couple? It is manifest that the couple is necessitated here by the structure of this Other, insomuch as it is merely the folding back of the as yet un-partitioned 1 into sexual division. To spell it right out, there's really no need to tire oneself out going into Oedipal evocations to see that it is necessary for the being who represents this mythical enjoyment – I'm referring to feminine enjoyment – to be, on occasion, represented by two would-be sexual partners, who are there for the theatrics, for the puppetry, and who alternate.

Therefore, the masochist manifestly situates himself, and can only situate himself, in relation to a representation of the sexual act and he defines, through his place, the locus in which enjoyment takes refuge from it. This is even what is derisory about it. And it is not simply derisory for us. It is derisory for him, too. This is where the explanation lies for the double aspect of derision.

One face is turned outwards, in so far as he never fails to include in the staging – as was noted by someone who is conversant with it, Monsieur Jean Genet – this little thing that marks out, not for an eternal audience, but so that anyone who might roll up can make no mistake, how this whole business is mere trickery, even clowning around. It's part and parcel of the enjoyment.

The other face, which may properly be termed *mockery*, is turned inwardly. It's enough to have read *Venus in Furs*, since you now have it in easy reach following the admirable *Présentation* by Gilles Deleuze. Although somewhat lordly as Sacher-Masoch was, he envisages the protagonist in his novel, whom he casts as a nobleman, playing the role of manservant and scurrying back and forth after his lady. Look up the moment when this personage has a hell of a job keeping a straight face, even though he is sporting the saddest look he can muster. It is only with some trouble that he manages to stifle his laughter.

There should further be underlined here the essential aspect – which also struck Reik, though he couldn't fully account for it

– of what I shall call the *demonstration* side of the thing. It forms part of the masochist's position. He demonstrates – like me at the blackboard, it has the same value – that there alone lies the locus of enjoyment. Demonstrating it is part and parcel of his enjoyment. And the demonstration is no less valid for that. Perversion as a whole, in its every variety, always has this demonstrative dimension. I don't mean that it demonstrates for us, but that the pervert is himself a demonstrator. He is the one who has this intent, not the perversion, of course.

It is on this basis that questions may soundly be posed as to what is involved in what we shall call, more or less prudently, moral masochism. Indeed, before introducing the term *masochism* at every turn in our remarks, we do need first to have clearly understood what masochism is at the level of the pervert. Earlier, I pointed out fully enough that neurosis is tied to perversion by nothing else but the fantasy, but that within its own field of neurosis, this fantasy fulfils an altogether special function which no one really seems to have pondered. It is solely on this basis that we will be able to ascribe its correct value to that upon which, at some turning point in neurosis, we might pin the label *masochism*, more or less reasonably.

I've been caught unprepared. Not being able to delve any further into neurosis, what I have to say finds itself being literally cut in two. This is of course bound to how I always gauge poorly what I can manage to say in one sitting.

Even so, I have spelt out fairly clearly today the mainspring of perversion per se. By the same stroke I have shown you that sadism is not at all to be seen as a mere switching of sides from masochism.

Indeed, each of them, sadism and masochism, operate in the same fashion, with the slight difference that the sadist operates in a way that is more naïve. Intervening in the field of the subject, insomuch as he is subject to enjoyment, the masochist does after all know that what happens in the field of the Other matters little to him. Of course, the other party does have to play along, but the masochist is the one who knows the enjoyment that he has to prise out.

As for the sadist, in truth he finds himself being a serf to this passion, to this necessity, of bringing what he targets as the subject under the yoke of enjoyment. But he doesn't realise that in this game he is himself the dupe, turning himself into the serf of a power that lies fully outside him. In view of which, he spends most of his time getting only halfway to what he targets. On the other hand, unbeknownst to him, without striving for it, without positioning himself there, what he doesn't fail in fact to achieve is the function of the object *a*. That is to say, he is objectively, really, in a masochistic position, as the biography of our divine Marquis demonstrates well enough. I stressed this in my article.

What indeed could be more masochistic than to have put himself wholly in the hands of his mother-in-law, the Présidente de Montreuil?

14 June 1967

XXI

THE AXIOM OF THE FANTASY

The unconscious in the field of logic
Truth represented by interpretation
Erections are autoerotic
Cowardice and the *désirpas*
The fantasy plays the role of signifying truth

I have to come sharply to an end today.

I announced last time that this would be my last lesson for the academic year. I therefore have to bring this subject to a close having done no more than open it. It is my wish that some of you might take it further, should I have been able to spark this desire in you.

To bring this sharply to an end, my intention is to close with what might be called *a clinical reminder*. This is certainly not to say that when I speak about logic, and the logic of the fantasy in particular, I'm leaving the clinical field behind for so much as an instant. Everyone knows, and all those who are practitioners can vouch for it, how my principal terms can be found very commonly, in the day-to-day utterances of their patients. Nor did I go off hunting for them anywhere else.

1

With these terms of reference from my teaching, I am bringing some order to the place of the psychoanalytic discourse itself.

No later than the start of this week, I received a report that ran in some way contrariwise to those that are most often brought to me. The most usual scenario is that a patient has seemingly given to his analyst, the day after my seminar, something that sounded like a repetition of it, to the point that the analyst is given to wonder whether he might be hearing an echo. They marvel at this all the more in those instances where it would clearly be impossible.

So, contrariwise, as it were, I can say that no later than the start of the week, in remarks reported to me in three different sessions – it matters little whether these sessions were didactic or therapeutic – I met the very terms that, because it was a Monday, I had just excogitated the day before, in the country retreat where I prepare my seminar for you.

Therefore, with respect to this analytic discourse, I am doing nothing more than setting out the coordinates with which its whereabouts can be located.

What does this mean?

Just because I can draw parallels between this discourse and the discourse of a neurotic, as everyone so frequently does, this does not specify it. This discourse is the discourse of a neurotic in the conditions, in the conditioning, that is set by the fact of being held in an analyst's consulting room. And so I shall point out right away that it is not just for the sake of it that I am bringing to the fore this condition of the locality.

Should these echoes, indeed these calques, really signify something so very strange? Everyone knows, everyone can see and anyone can experience for himself, how my discourse is not, of course, a discourse of free association. Does this mean, therefore, that whenever this discourse, the method and way of which we single out for our patients, fails to follow our recommendation – whenever it speculates, whenever it introspects, whenever it elucubrates, whenever it intellectualises, as we so amiably put it – it intersects with this discourse of mine? Without a doubt it does not, and for the following reason.

There must still be something that allows it to be said that the patient who is obeying the recommendation to associate freely is able, even so, to say such things in some way legitimately. Indeed, everyone knows that if he is asked to go down the path of free association, this is not to say that it prescribes a discourse that is loose or broken up. Yet even so, for something to reach, sometimes even in its finer points, such delicate distinction regarding the repercussions of his relation to his own demand, to the question of his desire, ought to be of a nature to give rise to a moment's reflection on what is conditioning this discourse beyond the instructions we issue. It is here that we need to bring in the element that is known – today I'm really sticking to the level of what is most widely evident – as *interpretation*.

Asking what interpretation is and how and when it ought to be done tends increasingly to put analysts in something of a bind, perhaps for want of posing beforehand the question as to how free discourse, the free discourse that is recommended to the subject, is conditioned by how it is in some sort on its way to being interpreted.

This is what is leading us simply to mention a few markers that logicians have been giving us for a long while now, and this is what has pressed me this year to speak about logic. I have certainly not been led to give a course on logic. That would not have been compatible with what I had to cover. I have tried to set out the framework of a certain logic that is of interest to us at the level of two registers, that of alienation on the one hand and that of repetition on the other. These two schemas were each laid out in a quadrangle and are basically superposable, one upon the other.

I do hope, though, that I have also managed to encourage some of you to dip into, to cast an eye over, a few books on logic, if only to remind yourselves of the value distinctions that logicians introduce into discourse when they distinguish, for instance, between sentences that are called *assertive* from those that are called *imperative* or *implorative*. According to the logicians, only the former, the assertive sentences, are non-exempt from critique, provided we define this as a critique that requires reference to those conditions that are necessary for one statement to be deduced from another statement. Oddly enough, these same logicians only broach the others – the sentences I have called imperative or implorative, which of course are words that are no less brimming with repercussions – by skirting around them. They take them in some way obliquely, which means that to this day the field has been left fairly intact. These sentences solicit something that, if we refer to what I have defined as an act, cannot help but be of interest to logic. If they solicit active interventions, this can sometimes be in the capacity of acts.

Someone who might have parachuted in today for the first time, who had never heard tell of such things, might find this to be all rather dull. But come on, I must suppose, even so, that in your ears the distinction between statement and enunciation is resonating. Furthermore, having heard what I have just said, you know that the statement is constituted by a signifying chain. That is to say, that which in discourse constitutes an object of logic is limited to begin with to formal conditions. This is indeed what leads this logic to be designated by the name *formal logic*.

Here, at the start, we find the function of Negation being brought to the fore. Not that it wasn't set out from the very beginning by him who was the great initiator, to wit Aristotle, but he only stated it in an ambiguous and partial manner. It was more surely educed in later progress. In what Aristotle sets out, Negation is brought to the fore, at the level of what I have just called *necessary conditions*, in so far as it excludes any third possibility. This means that something cannot be both affirmed and denied at the same time from the same standpoint. Here, we could after all bring in straightaway, in the margin, what Freud asserts, namely that, even so, we do not find the restrictive principle of what is called *non-contradiction* arresting what gets stated in the unconscious.

You know that right back in *The Interpretation of Dreams* Freud stresses how contradiction – that is to say, that a thing should be affirmed and denied at the same time from the same angle – is the special privilege, the property, of the unconscious. If something were required to confirm for those who have still not been able to get it into their noggins that the unconscious is structured like a language, I would ask them, how can you yourselves explain why Freud should take such care to stress this absence of the principle of non-contradiction in the unconscious? For the principle of non-contradiction has absolutely nothing to do with the real. It's not that there are no contradictions in the real. It's that there is no question of contradiction in the real.

There are those who, tasked with speaking about the unconscious in places where, in principle, teaching is provided, start by saying, *Anyone in this room who believes that the unconscious is structured like a language can leave now*. Certainly they would be quite right to leave, because it proves that they already know as much as there is to know. In any case, if it's to learn that it's something else, there's no reason to stay.

Whether this something else is pure tendency or tension, there is still no question of it being anything else but what it is. It might on occasion be composed in accordance with the parallelogram of forces, it might reverse, to the extent that we suppose it to have a direction, but it is in a field that is still non-exempt, as it were, from composition. In the principle of contradiction, on the other hand, something else is at issue. It's a matter of Negation. Negation isn't just lying about in a stream somewhere. If you go looking under a horse's hoof, you won't find any Negation.

Freud must have known a thing or two about this. If he takes care to stress that the unconscious is exempt from the principle of contradiction, then it is indeed because there could be some question of its being non-exempt. And if it is a question of its being non-exempt, then it's quite obviously on account of what is there to be seen, namely that it is structured like a language. It is only in a language, in the use of a language, that the interdiction issued by the principle of contradiction can have a sense. After all, this interdiction can partake of a certain convention. The principle either functions or it doesn't. If it is to be noted that the principle is not functioning somewhere, then it's that what is at issue is a discourse. To invoke this principle [as Freud does] amounts to saying that the unconscious contravenes this law yet proves, by the same stroke, that it is well within the logical field and that it articulates propositions.

So, to call this to mind is not, of course, to come back to basic principles, unless incidentally, but rather to issue the reminder that, in this regard, what logicians teach us is that the law of non-contradiction is to be distinguished from the law of bivalence. They are not the same thing, even though people did manage to get this wrong for a rather long time. It is one thing to disallow contradiction in logical use, to the extent that it has limited its field to assertive sentences which have the restricted goal of educing from a statement the necessary conditions for a correct chain to be deduced, that is to say, one which allows the same assertion, affirmative or negative, to be made about another statement. It is quite another to ground another law, the law of bivalence, by saying that any proposition is either true or else false.

I'm not going to expand upon this here because in my first lessons of the year I already dropped a few hints to give you a sense of what is eminently problematic about this bivalence when it is sharply sliced. All the nuances that there are and which get inscribed into *it's true that it's false that* . . . or *it's false that it's true that* . . . show that this is not at all something that is linear, univocal and sharply sliced.

Now, this is precisely what ascribes all its worth to the presence of this dimension, which is our dimension, within which is located the discourse that we ask not to look any further, as it were, than the end of its nose. *You just have to be asking yourself,* I say to those who come into analysis with me, *whether you ought to say this or not, for the question to be settled – indeed, you ought.* This is the clearest way to lay out the analytic rule.

Yet, even so, there is something that I don't tell them, even though it is the foot they set off on, and this is that ultimately it is nothing else but truth that is here being posited as what has to be sought out in the fault lines of their utterances. In sum, I put them at their leisure to multiply these fault lines and almost recommend that they do, but all this thenceforward assumes, as the principle of the very rule I have set out, a coherence that implicates an eventual rehabilitation of the said fault lines. And by what norms is this rehabilitation to be carried out if not by those that are evoked and suggested by the presence of the dimension of truth? This dimension is inevitable in the instauration of the analytic discourse.

The analytic discourse is a discourse subject to this law, that of soliciting a truth that speaks. I have already spoken of this, in the terms that are most appropriate. In sum, it's a matter of soliciting the utterance of a *ver-dict*, a veritable *dict*. Of course, the rule thereby assumes an altogether different value. This truth that speaks, and whose verdict is awaited, is caressed and treated gently. We steer it from behind with a guiding hand. We seek to take it under our wing. And to do so, we affect a semblance – this is, all in all, the true sense of free association – of not being preoccupied with it, of not caring less, of being mindful of other matters. And that is how this truth will perhaps come to spit it out.

There you have it for the principle. I almost blush to be making so much of it. But don't forget, I'm dealing with psychoanalysts, that is to say with those who – even if what I'm saying is tangible and well-nigh in anyone's reach – are most inclined to forget this principle. Furthermore, they have the strongest reasons for doing so and I'm going to say what these are right away.

The question, then, is this, as I shall point up in passing. What is being examined is the truth of a discourse which can say *yes* and *no* of the same thing at the same time. It is a discourse that, going by Freud, is exempt from the principle of contradiction and which, in being spoken, in being put together as a strange old discourse, introduces a truth.

This, too, is fundamental, although it is not always brought out in the type of teaching I mentioned earlier. It is so fundamental that this is where the jitter which Freud had to face arises from. It is known and it was felt and we have testimony of it. It is what surely arose when Freud explained to his gang, the Viennese Wednesday chums, that a patient had been having dreams that were expressly designed to reel him in.

It set them ajitter, and very likely gave rise to clamour from the gathering. We can see that Freud went to a fair amount of trouble to resolve the question. He accounts for it, of course, as best he can. He explains that dreams are not the unconscious and that they can lie. It no less remains that the least that can be said is that this unconscious is not to be pressed. I mean that if this dimension must be preserved, then what Freud does is done in the name of the following – that the unconscious preserves a truth that it does not avow, and so if one presses it, it can start lying abundantly with whatever means it has. But what does all this mean?

The unconscious has no meaning – except for those imbeciles who think that it's evil incarnate – unless one can see that it is not a fully fledged subject, or more exactly, that it stands prior to the fully fledged subject. There is a language from prior to the subject's knowing anything whatsoever. There is therefore a logical anteriority of the status of the truth of anything whatsoever, qualifiable as a subject, which might lodge itself there.

I know full well that when I say these things about truth, when I wrote them for the first time in *La Chose freudienne*, it had a little romantic resonance. What do you expect? I can't do anything about it. Truth is a personage that people have long been kitting out with skin and hair, and even a well in which to dwell and bob around like a bottle imp. It's a matter of finding out the reason for this.

What I simply want to tell you is that if, as I said earlier, it is impossible to exclude truth, then this is for the following reason. If interpretation doesn't bear this relation to what there is no other way of naming but as *truth*, if it is merely that behind which it is sheltered, then what does it become? You can fairly suppose that, in our day-to-day hands-on work we are not going to bother the little minions whom we supervise by saddling them with the load of truth. So, we tell them that an interpretation has, or hasn't, *succeeded*, as they say, because it has had – this is the criterion – its discourse effect. This discourse effect can be nothing else but . . . a discourse. That is to say, there was some material. It started over. The fellow went on speechifying. OK. But if that's it, if it is just a sheer discourse effect, what does interpretation become? Well, this has a name which psychoanalysis is perfectly familiar with and which, moreover, is a problem for it. It's a funny old thing. It's very precisely what is known as *suggestion*.

Were interpretation merely that which begets more material, were one radically to eliminate the dimension of truth, then any interpretation would be mere suggestion. This is what puts in their proper place some most interesting speculations that have been made only to avoid the word *truth*. When Dr Glover speaks of exact or inexact interpretation, he does so only by avoiding the dimension of truth. The dear chap knows very well what he is saying. But you will see that ultimately he can't avoid it. There you have it. The fact is that one can speak about the dimension of truth, but it is hard indeed to speak about false interpretation. Bivalence is polar, but it leaves us in a pickle when it comes to the excluded third, and this is how Glover can admit the potential fruitfulness of inexact interpretation.

Consult his text. *Inexact* does not mean that it is false. It means that it is a far cry from what is at issue at that moment as truth, but that sometimes it doesn't for all that fall necessarily wide of the mark. Truth rebels, and however inexact the interpretation might be, it has still given truth a tickle in some locality.

So, within this analytic discourse designed to capture truth, the latter is represented by the interpretative response. In being possible there, even if it doesn't occur, interpretation orients the discourse as a whole. Now, the discourse that we have commended as a free discourse has the function of making room for interpretation. It inclines towards nothing else but establishing a place of reserve so that this interpretation can be inscribed within it as the locus reserved for truth.

This locus is the one occupied by the analyst. I will point out that he does occupy it, but that this is not where the patient puts him. This is the interest of the definition I have been offering of transference. After all, why not remind ourselves that it is specific? The analyst is placed in the position of the subject supposed to know. He knows very well that this doesn't function unless he holds this position, because this is where the very effects of transference are produced, those upon which he has to intervene so as to adjust them in the direction of truth. Put otherwise, he has a foot in each camp. He is between the false position of being the subject supposed to know, which he knows full well he is not, and the position of having to adjust the effects of this supposition by the subject in the name of truth.

It is in this respect that transference is a source of what is called *resistance*. If it is true, as I say it is, that truth in the analytic discourse is placed elsewhere, in the place of the one who hears, then the one who hears can in fact function only as a relay post in relation to this place, which is to say that the only thing he knows is that he is himself, as a subject, in the same relation to truth as the one who is speaking to him.

This is commonly expressed by saying that the analyst is, by necessity, beleaguered by his unconscious just like everyone else is and that this is what lends the analytic relationship its characteristic unsteadiness. Now, it is precisely this difficulty, the analyst's own, which alone can respond in a worthy manner right where one awaits – where one awaits and where sometimes one waits for a long time – the interpretation. Yet, as you can see, a difficulty, whether it's a difficulty of being or a difficulty of relating to the truth – it probably amounts to the same thing – does not constitute a status. It is for this reason that they do everything they can to camouflage the analyst's condition. The analyst can respond only with his own difficulty of being . . . an analyst. But they try to camouflage this by telling stories, saying for example that, for their unconscious, the business is settled, they've done an analysis, and a didactic one at that, and so of course this has enabled them to be a little more at ease on that score. But we are not in the realm of more or less. We are dealing with the very fundament of what constitutes the analytic discourse.

This is not going at a very great pace, is it? Well, this is how it has to go.

2

To posit that this truth refers back to desire will perhaps account for the difficulties we meet in handling this truth, just as logicians can have.

Let it be enough to mention that the truth of desire is indeed not something that can be so simply defined, just like that.

Now, the truth of desire is tangible. We are always dealing with it because this is why people come to seek us out. They come to seek us out on the subject of what occurs for them when desire arrives at what is called the hour of truth. This means, *I much desired this thing, but standing there before it, it's there for my having, but then and there some mishap arises.*

Quite so. As I have already tried to explain, desire is lack. It's been known for a long time. I didn't come up with it. Other deductions have been made, but this is the starting point because one can only start from there. For Socrates, desire is lack in its very essence. The meaning of this is that there is no object with which desire could be satisfied, even though there are objects that are the cause of desire.

What becomes of desire at the hour of truth? Taking advantage of the well-known mishaps that arise, wisdom prides itself on deeming desire to be folly, and then it puts in place all sorts of measures, said to be ethical, to preserve oneself from it. From desire, I mean. The problem is, however, that there is a moment when desire is desirable.

Whenever it's a matter of what happens, and not without good reason, for the execution of the sexual act, the sizeable error is to believe that desire has a function that has been integrated into physiology and that the unconscious does no more than bring trouble. This is a great mistake. I'm emphasising this today because I'm saying my goodbyes for a few months. It can very clearly be seen that this is, in spite of everything, an error that remains deeply inscribed in those minds that ought to be most aware of it. I mean those of psychoanalysts.

It is most peculiar indeed that people do not understand that what appears to be the measure, the test, of desire, in other words an erection, has nothing to do with desire. Desire can function perfectly, can play out with all its repercussions, without being accompanied by it in any way whatsoever. An erection is a phenomenon that has to be located on the pathway to enjoyment. I mean that in itself this erection is enjoyment, autoerotic enjoyment, and precisely what is asked, for the sexual act to take place, is that one shouldn't stop here at this autoerotic enjoyment. Were it otherwise, one can't really see why this enjoyment should be marked with this sort of veil. Normally, I mean when the sexual act carries its full worth – at least this is to be supposed – priapic emblems have been set up at every crossroads. It is not an object to be withdrawn from common contemplation except to the precise extent that this erection is questionable, questionable with regard to the sexual act qua act.

The desire at issue – unconscious desire, the desire that is spoken of in psychoanalysis and in so far as it bears a relation to the sexual act – needs first of all to be properly defined. Whence does this term arise prior to its functioning? It is very important to call this to mind, which, even so, has been my teaching from the start.

If the operation that is indispensable for the sexual act is not posited in these terms, if the operation of copulation and the possibility of its realisation are not placed in the register of enjoyment – and not the register of desire – then one is condemned outright to understand nothing of all that we have been saying about women's desire. We are told that feminine desire, like masculine desire, has a certain relationship with a lack, a symbolised lack, which is phallic lack. How are we accurately to situate the meaning and place of what we are saying here with regard to feminine desire if we do not take as our point of departure what fundamentally differentiates the two partners on the plane of enjoyment?

There is, on this plane, a gulf between them. I will designate this gulf by taking two markers – for man, erections, and for woman, I won't find any better than what I fortunately didn't have to wait until I became a psychoanalyst to have confided in me and which any one of you each can receive, namely the term that young girls use among themselves to designate what seems to them to be closest to what I am designating at this level – what they call *the bonk in the lift*. It's something that happens when the lift goes down a bit suddenly. They know, and they know very well, that it is something of this register that is involved in the sexual act.

This ought to be the point of departure for finding out the distance at which desire – that is to say, what is at issue in the unconscious – stands in relation to the sexual act. It is not a relation of topside and underside. It's not a relation of epiphenomena. It's not a relation of things that hang together. And this is why it's quite necessary to practise for a number of years to know that desire has nothing to do with anything else but demand, that it is what is produced as a subject in the act of demand.

Desire is concerned in the sexual act only insomuch as demand can be concerned in the sexual act, which, after all, is not inevitable, though in the end is common. It's common to the extent that the sexual act – which is what I have defined for you as what never culminates in making a man or a woman – is inserted into something – let's say this to provoke you – which is called *the sexual marketplace*. There, in this place of commerce, one has to deal with demand. And it is from demand, necessarily from demand, that desire emerges.

This is why desire in the unconscious is structured like a language – because it comes out of that. It's unfortunate that I have to bellow out these things which are in anyone's reach but which, even so, are regularly pretermitted and overlooked in everything that is concocted by way of the most simplistic theories about psychoanalysis.

By like token, this means that desire is merely a by-product of demand. I don't need to make a theory out of this for you. One can grasp here why it is in its very nature not to be satisfied. Desire emerges from the dimension of demand, and even if demand comes to be satisfied on the plane of the need that gave rise to it, it is in the nature of demand, because it has arisen from language, to generate the fault line of desire. This fault line stems from how demand is articulated demand, and so something has been displaced, rendering the object of demand unfit for satisfying desire. Such is the breast. Everything that goes in through the mouth for digestive needs is displaced by the breast, which substitutes something for it which is strictly what has been lost and can no longer be given.

There is no chance of satisfying desire. Only demand can be satisfied. And this is why it is accurate to say that desire is the desire of the Other. Its fault line is produced in the locus of the Other, insomuch as it is to the locus of the Other that demand is addressed. It finds itself having to cohabit with that of which the Other is also the locus, in the capacity of truth, in the sense that nowhere is there a shelter for truth but where language has a place. And language finds its place in the locus of the Other.

So? Well, it is here that needs must comprehend a little what is at issue regarding desire in its relation to the desire of the Other. To this end, I tried to put together a short apologue for you. I borrowed it, certainly not by chance but rather for reasons that are quite essential, from what is called the art of salesmanship, that is to say the art of supply. In his design of creating demand, the salesman has to get people to desire an object of which they have no need, to coax them into asking for it.

So, I don't need to describe for you all the tricks that are employed for that. They are told that they will miss out on it, for example, because someone else will get it, which would thereby bar them from having it. I'm using words that echo my usual symbols, but this is quite literally how this works in the mind of what is known as a good seller. Or else they might be made to see that this really is the outward sign that will bring the finishing touch to the vibe they intend to give to their life. In sum, it's through the desire

328   THE ECONOMY OF THE FANTASY

of the Other that any object is present when it's a matter of *l'acheter*, of buying it. *L'acheter, l'acheter . . . lâcheté*. Cowardice. Well, well, that's rather curious. That's quite a word, that is. *Lâcheté, Feigheit. You, sir, are a coward. Tua res agitur*. It's very much a matter of cowardice, but it concerns thee. This can be seen in how the main result – thou knowest it well – that arises from this series of misappropriations which life rounds up under the sign of desire, is that of pressing thee ever further in the direction of redeeming thyself. *De te racheter de la lâcheté*. Redeeming thyself for thy cowardice.

This dimension is of course always masked in analytic interventions, but those others, those who are in on it, I mean those who hold the analytic discourse, do not mask it. It's all very well that the dimension of cowardice should have been of interest, but I do wonder . . .

417   I went to the trouble of opening up, just like that, one of Freud's major clinical observations. In the case of the Rat Man, I soon came across the fact that the patient brings in right away this dimension of cowardice. Yet it's not clear where this cowardice lies. It's like the dimension of truth earlier. Where does the subject's courage lie? The subject's courage is perhaps precisely to play the game of desire, and that of the desire of the Other. Handing over the bounty to something that is perhaps equally the cowardice of the Other who is bribing him, then in the end to find that he can get on with it, this, in the end, is very much the problem when neurosis is at issue.

However, for this it is important to grasp, or more exactly to remember, to bring back to the fore, what I said about desire. Back in its time, what I said about desire was that desire is its interpretation. Now, since after all no one wants to know what is meant by an unconscious desire, the objection might be raised – *What, in principle, can be more conscious than desire?* If one speaks of unconscious desire, it's because it is indeed the desire of the Other that it is possible. If there is precisely what I have just mentioned, through a reminder of the metaphor of buying, about which one doesn't know over whom it has a hold, this art of captivation in the desire of the Other, it's that there's a step, a *pas*, to be taken.

We are told that if desire is unconscious, then it's because a link in the chain of discourse that sustains it has been skipped, such that the desire of the Other has become unrecognisable. This is the best trick that can be found to bring the machine to a standstill. There's a *pas*? Well, we shall create, upstream of this *pas*, not *non-désir*, but the *désir-pas*.

The definition of unconscious desire is this, which the subtleties of negation in French enable us to express, to wit this ending in aught designated for us by the *pas*, the same of which I have already made use on the subject of the *pas de sens*. If you will give me something of a free rein, I will go so far as to turn this into *désirpas*, a written name that holds up in its own, then to give the *dès* that is in charge of it the same accent as in *désespoir* or *désêtre*. This will allow me to say that the unconscious desire of the *désirpas* is something that *déchoit*, that diminishes with respect to goodness knows what *irpas*, an *irpas* that here designates very precisely the desire of the Other.

Interpreting this could be verbalised fairly well with an *irpassé*. It is around this that the inversion could be made. It's that interpretation is effectively that which takes up the place of desire, in the sense that earlier you were raising the objection that, fully unconscious as it was, it was there at the start. But it is there, too, as one passes back over it, because it has already been articulated. Fortunately, when interpretation has come in its stead, this doesn't settle anything because it is not at all sure that the desire which we have interpreted should have its outcome. Indeed, we even count on its not having an outcome. We count on its still remaining a *désirpas*, and so much the better for it. This even affords us quite a bit of elbowroom for interpreting desire.

But then, we ought, even so, to find out what game we are playing by interpreting these unconscious desires, those of the neurotic in particular. It is here that we need to pose the question of what is meant by what supports all this under the name *fantasy*. We have been posing this question unceasingly, but let's pose it again, here at the end, one last time.

3

When the logicians, with whom today's disquisition got under way, limit themselves to the formal functions of truth they find, as I told you, a gap. They light upon a singular space between the principle of non-contradiction and that of bivalence.

You can find this as far back as Aristotle, precisely in the book that is called *De Interpretatione*, in paragraph 19a in the designated notation for the classical Aristotelian manuscripts. It falls on page 100 of the very poor translation by Tricot, which nevertheless is the common one and which I'm commending to you. Aristotle casts doubt upon the consequences entailed by the bivalence of the true and the false when the contingent is at issue, when it's a matter of what is to happen. If we straightaway posit of what is to happen that it is true or false then this means that it is already decided. Naturally this cannot work.

Aristotle's solution is to put bivalence in doubt. But this is not what is at issue for us and I won't be pressing the discussion any further on this point.

What I will note, however, is the commonplace logical solution that is given, for example, in the Kneale and Kneale. They tell us, here in *The Development of Logic*, that *It is not the sentence or form of words* – the signifying articulation – *which is true or false, but what is expressed by it*. This solution is wrong, as the whole development of logic shows. I mean that what is deduced from any formal instauration can in no case whatsoever be grounded upon signification, for the simple reason that there is no possibility of fixing down any signification that could be univocal.

Whichever signifier you put forward to pin down a signification as true or false, it is always possible to implicate it in a circumstance where a truth that is stated as clearly as can be, in the capacity of signified content, will be false. It can even be more than false. It can be a characteristic deception. It is not possible to establish any logical order unless by attributing the truth function to a signifying grouping. This logical use of truth is met only in mathematics, where, as Bertrand Russell wrote, *we never know what we are talking about*. Whenever we think we know, we are quickly disabused of this. A prompt clear-out is called for to sweep intuition away.

I am issuing this reminder in order to examine what is involved in the function of the model fantasy, *A Child is Being Beaten*. The fantasy is merely a signifying arrangement, the formula for which I gave long ago by coupling the *a* to the barred S. This means that the fantasy has two characteristics – the presence of an object *a* and, on the other hand, nothing else but what begets the subject as $, to wit a sentence. This is why *A Child is Being Beaten* is typical. *A Child is Being Beaten* is nothing else but the signifying articulation *A Child is Being Beaten*, except that – read the text and look this up – what hovers over it is nothing less than this thing, which it is impossible to eliminate, which is called the regard.

Before running through the three phases in the genesis of this product that is known as the fantasy, it is important to designate what it is. Just because Freud was dealing with illiterates, it remains no less interesting to set out the crisp edges of the status of the fantasy and to tell you – in keeping with what I brought to you at the start of the year concerning the coupling of a part of *I am not thinking* to grammatical structure – that it is at the very place of this grammatical structure that the object *a* emerges. This place is to be found at the fourth vertex of the quadrangle, at the bottom left. At the vertex on the bottom right, the *I am not* cedes its place, which it lops off at the level of the unconscious, to the complement of the purely grammatical signifying structure of the fantasy, namely my point of departure today which is called a *truth signification*.

What needs to be retained in everything that Freud sets out with respect to the fantasy is simply this little clinical feature, which he most certainly puts forward in order to demonstrate for us so many things relating to its use and handling, but what needs to be emphasised is that the very same fantasy is to be met across very different clinical structures. What also needs to be emphasised is that, as you know, this fantasy remains at a singular distance from everything that is disputed and debated in our analyses insomuch as it is a matter there of translating the truth of symptoms. It seems that the fantasy is there as a sort of prop or foreign body, something to be used. And after all, you know that it has a well-determined function – that of making up for what we can fairly call by its name, to wit a certain *shortcoming* of desire. Desire bears the stamp of this shortcoming to the extent that it is brought into play at the entry to the sexual act. It really does have to be concerned here if only to take the opening steps and to bring some order into the state of play.

The distance of the fantasy from the zone in which is played out what I earlier highlighted as primordial about the function of desire and its bond with demand is especially evident and it is what allows us to take stock of the difference that lies between perverse structure and neurotic structure. Even so, we can see that this same distance has given rise to a change of course in analysis, around registers that are said to have to do with frustration and other analogous terms.

What do I mean when I say that the fantasy plays the role of signifying truth? Well, I will tell you. I'm saying the same thing as the logicians.

You miss out on your order by wanting at any cost to insert this fantasy into the discourse of the unconscious, when either way it is resistant to this reduction. Phase two, the middle phase, in the genesis of *A Child is Being Beaten*, the one when the subject is in the place of the child, is something that you can get to only in exceptional cases. In truth, in your interpretation, and more especially still in the comprehensive interpretation that you will give to the structure of one neurosis or another, the fantasy will always, in the last instance, have to be inscribed into the registers that I have set out, namely – for phobia, forestalled desire – for hysteria, unsatisfied desire – for obsession, impossible desire.

What is the role of the fantasy in this order of neurotic desire? Well, I said *truth signification*. This means the same thing as when you ascribe the connotation of truth – which you mark out with a capital T as is purely conventional in theories such as set theory, for example – to a sequence of signifiers that you will call an *axiom*.

In your interpretation, the fantasy has no other role but this. You have to take it as literally as possible and to define for each structure the laws of transformation that will secure for this fantasy the place of an axiom in the deduction of statements from unconscious discourse.

This is the only possible function that can be given to the role of the fantasy in the neurotic economy. I have demonstrated, and you have seen, that the arrangement of this fantasy is borrowed from the determining field of perverse enjoyment. I believe I set the formulation for this quite well enough in our first talks when I posited that the disjunct in the field of the Other between body and enjoyment leaves a remainder, this leftover part of the body that is a reserve in which enjoyment can take refuge. That the neurotic should thereafter find in this arrangement a support that is made in such a way as to provide against the shortcoming of his desire in the field of the sexual act is not really something we should be surprised at.

If you would like me to give you some reading material in this regard, I will recommend a text, though I can't say that it should be an especially agreeable read for you. Actually, it's about as much fun as choking through pother. It will also serve you as an example of a real nasty piece of work in scientific matters. No text could better illustrate the extent to which a certain style of approach that entails priding oneself on having forced one's way into a field for the sake of goodness knows what objectivity leaves one in the position of having been turned into a serf, through and through, and in a truly most singular fashion, for there is not a single line in this celebrated observation that does not bear the mark of the professor's cowardice. I'm talking about the case of Florrie, by Havelock Ellis.

The History of Florrie is a sensational text. It will certainly become apparent to you, after the markers I have given you, as having every characteristic of being a neurosis. Affected by flagellation fantasies, Florrie does on one occasion come to breach the prohibition that they represent for her. Such a breach can indeed occur for neurotics, but without anything equivalent to perverse enjoyment being produced for them. *Breach* has an ambiguous meaning here, which makes it both a *passage à l'acte* and, for we who read, acting out. This breach deserves to be brought face to face with the absolutely manifest shortcomings of the observation. These shortcomings reach so far that, when Florrie confesses that only once or twice has she made use of a real person in her fantasies, someone whom she must *like and respect and secretly adore*, it truly beggars belief to see how the pen of Havelock Ellis has written, *What real person was introduced into the part on these rare occasions Florrie never mentioned and was never asked*, when it is clear, as clear as in the case of Père Ubu – you can still see the pig's tail, clear as day, poking through his teeth – that it is Havelock Ellis himself.

From beginning to end of the observation, Havelock Ellis is taken for a ride by his patient. After which, you have to hear how he puts on the airs of a grand personage, and the tone he uses to correct the members of the analytic community who have allowed themselves to opine on this same case, with, moreover, a wholly unjustified respect for the gathering of the observation. But it is all the same of such a nature as to show you all at once the full set of difficulties on which I wanted to shine a light today regarding what is involved when it comes to appreciating the fantasy.

From the fantasy such as we, poor neurotics that we are, imagine it at the level said to be *perverse* to its function in the neurotic register, there lies exactly the distance – I will end with this, so as to be *clinical* – from the *chambre à coucher*.

Are there such things as *chambres à coucher*? There is no sexual act. Apart from the *chambre à coucher* of Ulysses, where the bed is carved from a tree trunk rooted into the ground, it leaves serious doubts on the subject of *chambres à coucher*, especially in our times when everything is hitting the wall. But then, it is a place that, at least theoretically, exists. There is, even so, some distance between the *chambre à coucher* and the *cabinet de toilette*.

Pay close attention to how everything neurotic that comes to pass should come to pass essentially in the *cabinet de toilette*, or the *antichambre*, which is the same thing. These questions of house arrangement are very important. For the eighteenth-century man of pleasure, everything happened in the *boudoir*. Each to his own place.

If you want more details, phobia can happen in the wardrobe, or out on the landing, or down in the kitchen. Hysteria happens in the parlour. In the parlours of nunneries, of course. Obsession, in the loo. Pay close attention to these things. It's most important.

All of this leads us to the door which I will be inviting you to pass through next year, to wit, that of a *chambre à coucher* where nothing comes to pass, if not that the sexual act presents there as foreclosure, as *Verwerfung* strictly speaking. This *chambre à coucher* is what is commonly called the analyst's consulting room.

This is the title I shall be giving to my lessons of the coming year – *The Psychoanalytic Act*.

21 June 1967

Index

a see object *a*
Abelard, Peter 72
abjection, abject 222
Abraham *see* God, 'God of Abraham, of Isaac and of Jacob'
absolute Knowing *see* knowledge
act *see* sex, sexual act; *passage à l'acte*; psychoanalytic act
acting out 144, 147, 153–4, 163, 177, 184–7, 332
active voice 66
Adam (Kadmon) 272–3
affective maturity 183
Agrippa, Menenius 289
Aleph (א) 31
aletheia (ἀλήθεια) 260
Alexander the Great 253
algebra 61, 206, 261
alienation 11, 12, 50, 70, 81, 89–90, 91, 93, 94, 95, 96, 102–3, 108–9, 112, 113, 117–18, 122, 126, 137, 140, 142, 143–4, 147, 151, 153, 154, 190, 194–5, 210, 240, 258, 279, 282, 285–6, 293, 304, 309, 319
ambivalence 182
anaesthetic (ἀναισθησίαν) parts of body 300, 311
anal object 14, 241, 273, 285
    scybalum 7
    shit 14, 47, 240
Angelus Silesius
    Cherubinischer Wandersmann 107
anima 221
animals, animal kingdom, animalcules 8, 200, 209, 220, 221, 222, 265, 299–300, 313

animus 221
Anselm of Canterbury
    Proslogium (*Fides quærens intellectum*) 73, 101–2
Antiquity 44, 91, 165, 197, 279, 285, 296
Aphrodite (*Cypris*) 85
apodosis 45–6, 62
Archimedean point 63
Aristophanes
    'Οὐ παντὸς ἀνδρὸς ἐς Κόρινθόν ἐσθ᾽ὁ πλοῦς' 197
Aristotle 48, 60, 68, 147, 200, 203, 204–5, 231, 238, 307, 319–20
    Categoriae 254–5, 280
    De Interpretatione 329–30
    Metaphysics 84–6, 187
    Physics 187
arithmetic 232–3
art 162, 192, 290
    see also techne
Arts asiatiques 237
askesis 130, 252–3, 265
assertive sentences 319
Augeas (Αὐγείας) 257
Aulagnier, Piera 194
autoerotism 223, 266, 325
automatic translation 36
Axiom of Specification 16

Barbey d'Aurevilly, Jules 202
    see de Villiers de l'Isle-Adam, Auguste
Barbut, Marc
    'Sur le sens du mot structure en mathématiques' 56

Index

Baudelaire, Charles
　'Recueillement' 313
　see Vierne, Louis
Bedeutung 14, 92, 93, 95, 106, 107–9, 120–1, 129, 304
Being 42–3, 51, 71, 91, 94, 98, 175, 176, 200, 230–1, 255
　Being of *I* 86–7, 89–90, 92, 133
　Being-laid-waste (*désêtre*) 93
　and existence 6
　'intuition of Being' 43, 50, 64
　non-being 51, 71
　and the One 238–9
　and thinking 84–8, 99, 119
　want-of-Being (*manque-à-être*) 190
　see also Dasein; living being; speaking being; Supreme Being
Benda, Julien 201–2
Bentham, Jeremy 209
Benveniste, Émile 91
　'Actif et moyen dans le verbe' 65
Bergler, Edmund
　The Basic Neurosis – Oral Regression and Psychic Masochism 246–51
Bernard, Claude 41
Bet (ב) 30
Bible 89
　Book of Daniel 29–30
　Exodus 239, 299
　Genesis 259, 272–3, 283
　Gospel according to Matthew 279
Bichat, Marie-François Xavier
　Recherches physiologiques sur la vie et la mort 136
biology 155–6, 159, 160, 220, 290, 307
bipolarity (male/female) 115, 256
birth control 172
'black tide of mud' *see* occultism
body 6–7, 152, 221, 248, 272, 289, 291
　and enjoyment 152, 176, 224, 265, 269–70, 277, 279, 281, 284–6, 294–301, 309–12, 314, 332
　as Other 242, 259–61, 271, 274, 297, 332
Boileau Despréaux, Nicolas
　Épître première ('J'imite de Conrart le silence prudent') 172
Bonneval Colloquium 16, 69, 74
Boole, George 37–8, 67
　Boolean algebra 206, 261
　Boolean group 36

Bosch, Hieronymus (workshop of)
　The Conjurer 199, 232
Bossuet, Jacques-Bénigne
　Traitez du libre arbitre, et de la concupiscence 156
Brahma (ब्रह्मा) 66
breast 7, 121–2, 247, 310, 327
Brentano, Franz 41

Caesar, Julius 146
Cahiers pour l'analyse 215
Cantor, Georg 73, 74, 257
castration 95, 108, 110, 112–16, 119, 153, 162, 167, 176–7, 180, 190, 204, 209, 263–4, 266, 283–4, 308
　castration complex 14, 223–4, 254, 264–5, 268–9, 270–3, 298, 310
　and woman 190, 209, 223–4, 270–1, 298
　see also function, phallic
Centre national de la recherche scientifique (CNRS) 70
Charbonnier, Georges 34
Chomsky, Noam
　Syntactic Structures ('colourless green ideas sleep furiously') 13, 21, 102, 121–2
Christianity 117, 172, 183, 265
chromosome 159, 162, 221
cinema 128, 290
class consciousness 215, 220
class struggle 289
classes (logic) 23–4, 45, 48
Claudel, Paul
　L'Otage 182–3
Cocteau, Jean
　La difficulté d'être 289
cogito (ergo sum) 59, 62–4, 66, 67–8, 71–3, 74, 81, 84, 86–8, 89, 98–9, 109, 116, 145
　cogito ergo 'Es' 125, 126, 127
cognisance 44, 165, 176, 221, 232, 256, 281
'colourless green ideas sleep furiously' *see* Chomsky, Noam
Comédie-Italienne 43
commensurability and incommensurability (maths) 169–70, 203, 217–18, 222, 233, 261, 262, 264, 275, 307

condensation (*Verdichtung*) 105
Conjunction (logic) 44, 70, 106
  see also sex, sexual conjunction
Conrart, Valentin 172
  see also Boileau, Nicolas
contingent, contingency 329
contract
  in masochism 249, 313
contradiction 23, 24–6, 97
  principle of (non-contradiction) 48, 205, 320–2, 329
  vs contrary 187, 204–6
copula 136
copulation 158, 161, 162, 165, 201, 268, 270, 297, 300–1, 326
cosmology 206–7
cowardice 328, 332
creation (artistic) 162, 171
  women's creativity 175–6
Creation (Biblical) 30–1
Cynicism 252–3
Cypris see Aphrodite

da Vinci, Leonardo
  Notebooks ('*cosa mentale*') 285
Damourette, Jacques
  Des mots à la pensée, Essai de la grammaire de la langue française (with Pichon) 254–5
Daniel *see* Bible, Book of Daniel
Dante Alighieri
  Divina Commedia 265
Dasein ('Being-there') 12–13, 70, 290, 310, 312
Dauzat, Albert 244
Davus (*Andria*) 296
de Coûfontaine, Sygne *see* Claudel, *L'Otage*
de Coûfontaine, Toussaint Turelure *see* Claudel, *L'Otage*
de Montreuil, Madame (Marie Madeleine Masson de Plissay) 316
De Morgan, Augustus
  De Morgan's theorem 67, 81–3, 86
de Villiers de l'Isle-Adam, Auguste
  'L'enjeu' 202
death 89, 110, 135, 155, 276, 277, 280, 282
  life-and-death struggle 248, 277, 280
  see also drive, death drive; 'freedom or death'

defence 113, 157, 247
  vs resistance 71
Deleuze, Gilles
  Présentation de Sacher-Masoch ('Le froid et le cruel)' 216, 315
demand 141, 200, 250, 285, 291, 318, 326–7, 331
  Other's demand 141, 250
Descartes, René 62–4, 66, 71, 84, 86–9, 98–9, 107, 114, 215, 260
  Discours de la méthode 62–3, 72, 87, 101
  Meditationes de Prima Philosophia 62–3, 87
  Principia Philosophiae 87
  Recherche de la Vérité par la lumière naturelle 63
  Regulae ad Directionem Ingenii 99
  see also 'cogito ergo sum'
désêtre see Being, *désêtre*
desire 12, 43, 64, 84, 100, 104, 113, 122, 124, 158, 160, 175, 176, 253, 292, 301, 325–9, 331
  and demand 285, 291, 318, 326–8
  desire to be rejected 251
  desire to sleep 122–3
  and fantasy 10–11, 124, 305, 329, 331–2
  and lack 325–6
  and libido 178
  neurotic desire 141, 331–2
  object of desire 224
  of the Other 122, 300, 327–9
  and prohibition 254
  psychoanalyst's desire 216
  and reality 8–9, 10–11
detumescence 174–5, 191, 252, 268–70
Diagonal argument (diagonalisation proof) 73
diagram of the two mirrors ('optical model') 237–8, 239
dialectic 27, 118, 179, 200
  of desire 100
  Hegel's dialectic 277
  Marx's dialectic 215
  of neurosis 285
  of the subject/subjective dialectic 47, 84, 291
  of the treatment 204
Diderot, Denis
  Les bijoux indiscrets 210

Index

Diogenes Laërtius of Sinope 252–3, 265
discharge 144, 166, 175, 252
discourse 14, 19, 20, 86, 92
   of false pretence 304
   human 291
   Lacan's discourse 74–6, 213
   of love 107
   of the Other 9, 276
   philosophical 84, 299
   psychoanalytic 124, 201, 250–1, 317–18, 321, 324, 328
   scientific 133
   on sexuality 222
   subject's 13, 104, 318–19
   of truth 213, 242
   of the unconscious 212, 213, 224, 276, 322, 331–2
   (no) universe of 4, 17, 21–3, 25–30, 39, 48, 49, 50, 58, 59, 60, 62, 151, 233
   see also metadiscourse
discourse effect 323
discrepancy (*différence*) 199, 204, 205, 206–7, 208–9, 218, 234, 284
   see also small difference
disjunct *see* enjoyment, disjunct between body and enjoyment
Disjunction (logic) 44, 70
displacement (*Verschiebung*) 105
DNA (deoxyribonucleic acid) 159
dream 39, 42, 72, 105–6, 107–8, 121, 122–4, 144, 146, 214, 220, 259, 322
   dream content (*Trauminhalt*) 105, 108
   dream thoughts (*Traumgedanken*) 97, 105–6
drive (*Trieb, pulsion*) 92, 103–4, 109, 110, 121, 138, 157, 175, 182, 200, 209, 219, 247, 301
   death drive (*Todestrieb*) 108
Dunajew, Wanda von
   see Pistor, Fanny; *and* Sacher-Masoch, Leopold Ritter von, *Venus im Pelz*
Dürer, Albrecht 170
dyad 206, 236
   sexual dyad (of One and Other) 174, 204, 205, 229–30, 238

École freudienne de Paris 76
École normale supérieure 195
Ego Ideal (*Idéal du moi*) 237, 239, 263
Eliot, T(homas) S(tearns)
   The Waste Land 240–1

ELIZA *see* Weizenbaum, Joseph
Ellis, Havelock
   The History of Florrie 332–3
enjoyment (*jouissance*) 175–6, 180, 209–11, 216, 223, 224, 240, 242, 244, 249, 266, 269–70, 276, 277–84, 285–6, 294–301, 303, 310–12, 313, 314, 325–6
   adrift 295, 309
   bodily 152, 265, 281
   disjunct between body and enjoyment 285, 294, 301, 332
   economy of 224, 225
   enjoyment value 209, 213–14, 216, 223, 224, 244, 268, 283, 299, 309
   and object *a* 121, 286, 309, 310, 311, 313, 316
   Other's 141–2, 175, 176, 190, 242, 286, 312, 332
   perverse 286, 305, 309–10, 312–16, 332
   point of enjoyment 121, 141
   truth of 243
   want/subtraction of 190–1, 300, 309, 310
   womanly/feminine 175–6, 210, 242, 254, 267–8, 270–1, 295, 297, 300, 314
enthousiasmos (ἐνθουσιασμός) 94
enunciation 201, 290
   subject of statement vs subject of enunciation 46, 49, 66, 83–4, 100, 303, 319
erection 325–6
érgon (ἔργον) 231
   see also labour
Eros 201, 260, 269
   'philosophical Eros' 43, 77
Euclid
   Elements 72–3
Euler, Leonhard
   Euler diagram 11
Euripides (Εὐριπίδης)
   Hippolytus (Ἱππόλυτος) 221
Eurydice (Εὐρυδίκη) 309
Eve 272, 273
L'Évolution psychiatrique 139
excluded third *see* principle (law) of excluded third
existence 6, 24–7, 63, 87, 93–4, 124, 130, 147, 161, 205, 217, 232–3
   and Being 6

338 Index

existence (*cont.*)
    and essence 101
    of God 73, 101–2, 107
    of the Other 100–3, 113–14, 118, 122, 129
existentialism 135, 202
Exodus *see* Bible
extension
    and comprehension 51
Ey, Henri 194
    L'inconscient (VIe Colloque de Bonneval) (co-edited with Green) 69–70, 74–5

fantasy
    as axiom 331–2
    and breast 121
    and comprehension 305
    and desire 10–11, 124, 305, 329, 331–2
    and drive 92, 121
    economy of 303
    as foreign body 306, 331
    formula for 4–6, 193, 330
    and genital organ 263
    and guilt 306
    Ich excluded from 92
    and logic 4, 27, 274
    and neurosis 304–5, 315, 329, 331–3
    of a norm 40
    and object 4–7, 230, 330
    and perversion 301, 305, 311–13, 315, 331–3
    and the real 11
    and reality 8–9, 250
    and sex 222
    signifying structure, 'structured like a language' 4, 303, 304, 330–1
    and symptom 306, 331
    and trauma 42
    and truth signification 331
    vs *phantasia* 4
father
    and analyst 189
    and God 239
    in kinship 238
    and Oedipus complex 264–5
    primal father 244, 271
femininity
    feminine masochism 286
    masculine and feminine 115, 220, 253, 255, 326

    see also enjoyment, womanly/feminine enjoyment; woman
feminism 210–11
Fenichel, Otto 157
    'Neurotic Acting Out' 154
fetish 210
Feuerbach, Ludwig
    Das Wefen des Chriftenthums 207
fideism 89, 156
Figaro littéraire 33
Florrie *see* Ellis, Havelock, *The History of Florrie*
fool, foolishness 102, 165, 239–40, 299
foreclosure (*Verwerfung*) 88, 107, 118, 133, 134, 146, 333
Fort/Da 12, 251–2
Foucault, Michel
    Les Mots et les choses, 'La mort de l'homme' 88
Franglais 32, 186, 244
free association 40, 97, 128, 318–19, 322, 323–4
'freedom or death' 89, 240
freethinking 128, 181
Frege, Gottlob
    'Über Sinn und Bedeutung' 14
Freud, Sigmund 3, 4, 30, 33, 34, 40, 42, 47, 48, 50, 58, 60, 71, 74, 75, 84, 86, 93, 95, 96, 97–8, 99–100, 120, 125, 128, 129, 134, 152–3, 157, 158, 164–5, 166–7, 173, 177, 179, 196, 210, 215, 220, 248–9, 252, 256, 277, 282, 292, 301, 303–4, 307, 308, 330, 331
    Aus der Geschichte einer Infantilen Neurose (The Wolf Man) 42
    Bemerkungen über einen Fall von Zwangsneurose (The Rat Man) 328
    Das Ich und das Es 91, 136
    Das Unbehagen in der Kultur 118
    Der Witz und seine Beziehung zum Unbewußten 76, 93, 241
    Die Traumdeutung 40–1, 105, 122–3, 139, 145, 183, 320–1
    'Die Verneinung' 12
    Drei Abhandlungen zur Sexualtheorie 138
    Ein Kind ist geschlagen 92, 304–6
    Entwurf einer Psychologie 40
    'Erinnern, Wiederholen und Durcharbeiten' 35, 137–8

'Formulierungen über die zwei
  Prinzipien des psychischen
  Geschehens' 49–50, 88, 90
Jenseits des Lustprinzips 135, 136, 155
  and Jung 110–11, 156, 165
  see also occultism, 'black tide of mud'
Massenpsychologie une Ich-Analyse
  237, 244
*Neue Folge der Vorlesungen zur
  Einführung in die Psychoanalyse*
  ('Wo Es war ...') 71–2, 94, 240
'Trieb und Triebschicksale' 103–8
'Über die Allgemeinste Erniedrigung
  des Liebeslebens' 250
*Über die Psychogenese eines Falles von
  Weiblicher Homosexualität* 122, 214,
  322
Freudism 134
frustration 141, 173, 331

gender (grammar) 114–15
Genet, Jean 314
genital maturation 162, 267
genitality, genital stage/function 104,
  157, 171, 173, 175, 182–3, 252,
  263–4, 268
geometry 124, 197–8, 199, 264
Glover, Edward
  'The Therapeutic Effect of Inexact
  Interpretation: A Contribution to
  the Theory of Suggestion' 323
God 64, 89, 94, 114, 115, 128, 239, 260,
  272, 283, 299
  and existence 102, 107
  God and enjoyment 312
  'God of Abraham, of Isaac and of
  Jacob' 115
golden section, number 170, 180, 191,
  192, 203–4, 207, 212, 217–18, 233,
  262, 264, 275
grammar, grammatical structure 84,
  92–3, 102–6, 131, 241, 254–5, 303,
  304, 330–1
graph of desire 20, 59, 200, 237
Green, André 193, 196, 240, 241
  *L'inconscient (VIe Colloque de
  Bonneval)* (co-edited with Ey)
  69–70, 74–5
Grimm, Jacob and Wilhelm
  'Pied Piper of Hamelin' 165
guilt 181, 242, 244, 265, 267, 282, 306

Hartmann, Heinz
  'Notes on the theory of sublimation'
  155, 157
Hegel, Georg F. W. 248
  Phänomenologie des Geistes 275,
  277–80, 282, 285, 295
he-man 209–11
  see also woman, she-man
Heidegger, Martin 279, 255
  Einführung in die Metaphysik 230–1,
  240–1
  Was heißt Denken? 98
Heine, Heinrich
  'Die Bäder von Lucca' (Hirsch–
  Hyacinth) 93
Heracles 257
Heraclitus 231
Hesnard, Angelo
  L'univers morbide de la faute 181
Hirsch–Hyacinth *see* Heine, Heinrich,
  'Die Bäder von Lucca'
homosexuality 211
Horapollo
  Hieroglyphica 41
Houssaye, Arsène
  'Dieu' ('nuage éblouissant') 121
human rights 152
hupokeímenon ($\dot{\upsilon}\pi o \varkappa\varepsilon \iota\mu\varepsilon\nu o\nu$) 203
Hyppolite, Jean
  'Commentaire parlée sur la
  Verneinung de Freud' 12, 184
hysteria *see* neurosis

Ich 71–2, 90, 92, 94–5, 104, 105, 110,
  145
Ich/Aussenwelt 49
Lust-Ich 118
id (*Es, ça*) 72, 84, 86, 91–2, 93–4, 95, 103,
  125, 153, 263
ideal ego (*moi idéal*) 239, 263
idealism 119–20
identification 28, 49, 54, 61, 136, 145,
  176, 236, 237–8, 239, 313
identity 22, 53, 61, 123, 137, 235
  see also principle of identity
ideology 71, 95, 134, 145, 210, 256
imaginary 4, 7, 9, 12, 30, 50, 175, 198,
  313–14
imaginary number 206–7
Implication (logic) 5–6, 44, 45–6, 47, 49,
  50, 52, 63, 68, 70

impossible, impossibility 26, 117, 313
  impossible desire 331
  and real 258
impotence 269
infinite (numerical) 73, 170, 192, 218, 235
International Business Machines
  Corporation (IBM) 34
interpretation 5, 30, 39, 40, 61–2, 65,
  92, 93, 120, 184–5, 318–19, 323–4,
  328–9, 331–2
Irigaray, Luce 131
Isaac *see* God, 'God of Abraham, of
  Isaac and of Jacob'
Isis 298

Jacob 259
  see also God, 'God of Abraham, of
    Isaac and of Jacob'
Jakobson, Roman 126, 130–2
Jaspers, Karl 304–5
Jocasta 243, 282
John of the Cross
  Noche oscura 239
Jones, Ernest
  The Life and Work of Sigmund Freud
    254
Journal de psychologie 65
Judaism 307
  Mosaic Law 272
Jung, Carl Gustav 109, 156, 165

Kahn, Gilbert
  Introduction à la métaphysique 230–1
kakemono 237
Kant, Immanuel 60, 75, 95, 100, 311, 312
Kempen, Thomas von (Thomas à
  Kempis)
  De Imitatione Christi 146
Kjökkenmöddings (shell-mounds) 89
Klein, Felix
  Klein bottle 9, 142
  Klein four-group 54–9, 293
knavery 240
Kneale, Martha and William
  The Development of Logic 205, 330
knowledge 64, 188, 200, 214, 242–3, 256,
  260, 273, 275, 281–2
  absolute Knowing 275, 290
  analytic 133, 134
  and Being 71, 87–8
  and truth 188, 242, 260

Kollontai, Alexandra
  Wege der Liebe 181
Koyré, Alexandre
  *Saint Anselme sur l'existence de Dieu
    (Proslogion)* 73
Kris, Ernst
  'Ego Psychology and Interpretation'
    185–6, 189

labour 231
Lacan, Jacques
  'La Chose freudienne' 215, 323
  Écrits 3, 12, 52, 74–5, 85, 131, 160,
    184, 200, 222
  'Fonction et champ de la parole et du
    langage' 127, 185, 214
  'Kant avec Sade' 95, 152, 216, 311, 313
  'La métaphore du sujet' 15
  'Position de l'inconscient' 48
  'Remarque sur le rapport de Daniel
    Lagache' 237
  'La science et la vérité' 215
  'Séminaire sur *La lettre volée*' 35–6
  *Seminar I, Freud's Papers on
    Technique* 12
  Seminar III, The Psychoses 65
  Seminar IV, The Object Relation 7
  *Seminar VII, The Ethics of
    Psychoanalysis* 276
  Seminar VIII, Transference 182
  'La signification du phallus' 160
  'Subversion du sujet et dialectique du
    désir' 53, 59
language (*langage*/*Sprache*) 12, 15–17,
  18, 20, 21, 45, 60–1, 64–5, 93, 102,
  103–4, 105–6, 108, 110–11, 130, 132,
  151–2, 200–1, 221, 229–30, 232, 322
  and metalanguage 230–1
  object language 18
  and the real 97, 200
  'reduced-state language' ('*langage
    réduit*') 16
  and thinking/thought 4, 93, 104, 105
  and unconscious 4, 21, 60, 105–6, 200,
    202, 303, 320, 327
Laplanche, Jean
  with Leclaire, Serge, 'L'inconscient.
    Une étude psychanalytique' 15–17
  see also language, 'reduced-state
    language'
lattice (*treillis*) 40–1

Le Bidois, Robert 244
Leclaire, Serge 194
　with Laplanche, Jean, 'L'inconscient. Une étude psychanalytique' 15–17
　see also language, 'reduced-state language'
Leibniz, Gottfried Wilhelm von 89
　'*salva veritate*' 140
Lenin, Vladimir 181, 215
letter 21, 31
Les Lettres françaises 33
Lévi-Strauss, Claude 132, 288
　Du miel aux cendres 120, 288
　Structures élémentaires de la parenté 208
libido 109, 223, 224–5, 276
life, living being 6, 89, 135–6, 155–6, 176, 201, 275–6, 310
Lilith 273
Lille 52
linguistics 131–2, 151, 200
Littré dictionary 278
Le Livre Sans Titre 287–98
Livy (Titus Livius Patavinus)
　Ab Urbe Condita, Book VIII 283
logarithm 180, 236, 245
logic 4, 5–7, 11, 12, 14, 33, 37–51, 58, 60–4, 67–8, 69–70, 72, 73, 81–3, 86, 92, 95, 96–7, 99, 102, 103, 106, 107, 112, 113, 122, 125–6, 130, 138, 141, 144–5, 156, 163, 194, 195, 204–6, 207, 208, 230, 231, 232, 238, 250, 251, 262, 289, 301, 303, 312–13, 317, 319, 321, 330
　Boolean 37–8, 67, 206, 261
　and fantasy 4, 27, 274
　and mathematics 24, 36, 40, 58, 140, 169, 257, 330
　predicate logic 48, 51, 197, 204, 280
　propositional logic 16, 21, 44–5, 49, 50, 55, 70, 83, 205, 321
　of sets 24–5, 67
　and writing 20–2, 29, 44, 61, 67
Logical Positivism 103
love 7, 50, 106–7, 118, 165, 173, 175–6, 181, 182, 259
　debasements of love life 254
　traditional theories of 225
Łukasiewicz, Jan
　'Aristotle's Syllogistic' 205
Lust-Ich see Ich

Mallarmé, Stéphane 27
Maritain, Jacques
　Le Paysan de la Garonne 43
Markov, Andrey 21–2
marriage 251, 283, 289–90
'La Marseillaise' 145
Marx, Karl 152, 207–8, 210, 215, 277
　Das Kapital 198
Marxism 118, 199, 215, 256
Massachusetts Institute of Technology (MIT) 35
masturbation 252, 265–7, 268, 297
mathematics 21–2, 24, 29, 54, 73, 83, 100–1, 102, 132, 170, 179, 218, 222, 233, 236
　and logic 24, 36, 40, 58, 140, 169, 257, 330
　metamathematics 198
meaning (*Sinn, sens*) 13, 28, 93, 105, 106, 114, 121, 166, 179, 212, 220, 260, 286
medical field, medicine 41, 151–2, 194, 253
meiosis 201
Mélèze, Lucien 131
Melman, Charles 194
Merleau-Ponty, Maurice 310
message 159, 290, 292, 293, 294
metadiscourse 231
metalanguage 18, 92, 230
metaphor 13, 15, 21, 47, 57–8, 61–2, 130, 202, 215, 217, 232, 234, 239, 255, 264, 328
　body as metaphor of enjoyment 295–8, 309
metonymy 202, 235
Middle Ages 41
middle diathesis (middle voice) 65–6, 152
Miller, Jacques-Alain 31, 32, 34, 36, 37, 38
　Index to the *Écrits* 32, 222
minus phi (–j) 109, 161–2, 173
Möbius band 8–9, 129–30, 142–3, 144, 146, 217
mother, maternal being/body/locus 7, 113, 114, 161, 173, 222, 246, 248, 254, 259
Mozart, Wolfgang Amadeus
　Don Giovanni 6
Müllerian duct 220

Musil, Robert
  Die Verwirrungen des Zöglings Törleß 128
mysticism 71, 256
mystics 114, 239
myth, mythology 120–1, 187, 242, 250, 270, 271, 273, 283, 288, 295, 298, 314
  Oedipal myth 173, 242–4

narcissism 49–50, 117, 118, 198, 224–5, 247, 259, 310
  primary narcissism 49, 173, 223, 267
natural numbers *see* number, integers
Nature 43, 120, 187, 299, 312
negation 12, 48–50, 51, 54, 55–6, 67, 68, 82, 83–4, 91, 92, 106, 254, 319, 320
negative therapeutic reaction 136
nervous apparatus 135, 166
neurosis 8, 141, 246–51, 285, 290, 301, 304, 306, 311, 315, 318, 328, 329, 331–2, 333
  hysteria 259, 306, 331, 333
  obsessional neurosis 63, 306, 331, 333
New Criticism 120
Nodet, C. H.
  'À propos de la régression' 139
noein (νοεῖν) 86, 90
nomination 32
norm, normality 39–40, 183, 264, 266, 268, 321
nought 55, 119
number 13, 40–1, 90
  complex 206–7
  and concept 44–7, 236n
  imaginary 206–7
  integers (whole numbers) 19–20, 102–3, 139
  irrational 275
  real 207

object *a* 4–7, 9–12, 14, 71, 95, 111, 112–13, 119, 121–2, 124, 169–70, 174, 186, 188–9, 191–2, 203–4, 207, 212, 217–18, 222, 223, 231–7, 238, 239, 241, 243, 245, 254, 261, 271, 276, 284–6, 291, 307–11, 313, 316, 330
object relation 7, 252
oblativity 250
obsessional neurosis *see* neurosis

occultism
  'black tide of mud' 109–10, 156, 165, 219, 240, 256, 265
Oedipus 242–3, 281–2
Oedipus complex 160, 254, 306
Office de radiodiffusion-télévision française (ORTF) 34
Olbrechts-Tyteca, Lucie
  Traité de l'argumentation: La nouvelle rhétorique (with Perelman) 15
One
  countable One 17, 136, 161
  in the dyad, locus of sexual union 219, 229–30, 232, 237, 255–6, 258, 260, 271, 284, 308
  One of totality, unifying One 17, 28, 136, 161
  and supreme Being 239
  surplus one, one extra, one-to-spare 28–30, 59–60, 61, 139
ontological argument 73, 101, 114
ontology 230
organ 174, 210, 223, 224, 260, 263, 265, 266, 269–70, 297, 299–300
organism 121, 124, 133, 135, 166, 201
organo-dynamism 194
orgasm 266–7
Other (A) 9, 66, 87, 89, 97, 99, 100–3, 105, 106, 113, 114–15, 116, 117, 118, 140, 141, 147, 151, 154, 173, 174, 187, 188, 229, 230, 232, 237, 238, 239, 242, 249, 254, 258, 261, 284, 293, 301, 311, 315, 327
  and the *a* 7, 10, 11, 20, 162, 261, 271, 284, 310
  and analyst 189
  barred Other (Ⱥ) 100, 108, 114, 140, 168, 188
  body as 242, 259–61, 271, 274, 297, 332
  demand of 141, 250
  desire of 122, 300, 327–9
  discourse of 276
  enjoyment of 141–2, 175, 176, 190, 242, 286, 312, 332
  and God 99, 115, 312
  inexistence of 100, 102, 103, 113, 114, 122, 129
Otherness 115, 314
  and truth 115, 152, 188, 242, 327
Oury, Jean 131

ousia (οὐσία) 203, 280
Oxford English Dictionary 186

Parmenides 231
part object 47, 124, 204
Pascal, Blaise 73, 114, 128
passage à l'acte 142, 144, 153–4, 163, 179, 332
Penia (Πενία) 76
penis, penile organ 174, 176, 191, 269, 270, 272, 298
   penile enjoyment 209, 210
   penile value 211
   see also detumescence; erection
Penisneid 190
Perelman, Chaïm
   Traité de l'argumentation: La nouvelle rhétorique (with Olbrechts-Tyteca) 15
Phalaris of Akragas 307
phallus (F) 7, 113, 167, 168, 175, 176, 202, 203, 209, 223, 224, 254, 255, 298
   as *Bedeutung* 95, 109
   phallic complement 272
   phallic connotation, value 209
   phallic function 162
   phallic object 210, 223, 271, 273, 283
   phallic organ 224–5
   signification of 109, 160
phenomenology 93, 310
Philo of Alexandria 46
philosophy, philosophical tradition 39, 41, 43, 84, 86, 91, 97, 98, 102, 113, 114, 115, 116, 117, 119, 128, 134, 140, 147, 157, 197, 237, 239, 265, 275, 279, 290, 294, 299, 307, 311
physis (φύσις) 92, 187
Pichon, Édouard
   Des mots à la pensée, Essai de la grammaire de la langue française (with Damourette) 254–5
Pindar (Πίνδαρος) 94
Pistor, Fanny (wife of Sacher-Masoch) 314
Plato 94, 198
   Philebus 294, 299, 310
   Sophist 230, 231, 239
   Symposium 76
pleasure principle (*Lustprinzips*) 49, 135, 137, 138, 155

Plotinus 115, 238–9
Poe, Edgar Allan
   'The Purloined Letter' 35
poetry 27, 94, 96
Poincaré, Henri 83
Pontalis, Jean-Bertrand
   Lacan's *La relation d'objet et les structures freudiennes* 7
   'truth about the truth' 47
Poros (Πόρος) 76
powerlessness 176, 182
Prakṛti (पुरुकृति) 221
Précieuses 188
preconscious 34, 122
premature ejaculation 269
principle (law) of bivalence 205, 321, 329–30
principle (law) of excluded third/middle (*principium tertii exclusi*) 54, 205, 323
principle (law) of (non-)contradiction *see* contradiction
principle (law) of identity 22, 205
protasis 45–6, 62
La Psychanalyse (journal) 41
psychoanalysis 11, 32, 72, 96, 100, 108, 116, 119, 121, 134, 139, 140, 141, 144, 147, 151, 152, 154, 155, 158, 159, 164, 171, 172, 184, 185, 189, 190, 194, 195, 199, 202, 208, 213, 214, 216, 217, 232, 237, 254, 262, 263, 264, 267, 268, 269, 270, 273, 278, 283, 298, 323, 326, 327, 331
   didactic/training 73, 195–6, 291, 324
   French 267
   and science 59, 133, 194
psychoanalytic act 134, 180, 184, 187, 333
purusha (पुरुष) 221

Racine, Jean 186–7
Radio-Bruxelles 52
real 8, 10, 88, 90, 97, 100, 107, 177, 199, 200, 205, 251, 256, 278, 280, 289, 320
   of enjoyment 285
   as impossible 258
   and knowledge 133–4
   and logic 39, 97
   'real couple' 161–2
   vs reality 10–11
   and truth 258

rebus 105–6, 152
regard 7, 14, 116, 124, 285, 310, 330
　scopic object 273
regression 139, 225, 246, 262, 284
Reik, Theodor
　Aus Leiden Freuden. Masochismus und Gesellschaft 313–14, 315
repetition 3, 21, 28, 30, 33, 124, 129, 135–8, 139, 140, 142–5, 153, 154, 155–6, 159–60, 161, 162, 163, 165–6, 167, 174, 179, 185, 190, 192–3, 217, 232, 237, 238, 258, 319
　repetition-thought 136
　Wiederholungszwang 135, 137, 155
Repräsentanz 146–7, 158
repression (*Verdrängung, refoulement*) 57–8, 100, 184, 234
　primary repression (*Urverdrängung*) 13, 138
　return of the repressed 13, 58, 110
resistance 33, 71, 99, 178–9, 219, 290, 324
reversal (*Verkehrung*) 92
rhagade 259
Rimbaud, Arthur
　Lettre du Voyant ('Je est un autre') 96
RNA (ribonucleic acid) 159
Robbe-Grillet, Alain 63, 296
Robert dictionary 278
Rosolato, Guy
　'The voice and the literary myth' 14
Rothschild, Salomon Mayer von 93
Russell, Bertrand 43
　The Principles of Mathematics (Russell's paradox) 17, 24–6, 58
　'Recent Work on the Principles of Mathematics'/'Mathematics and the Metaphysicians' 101, 103, 257, 330
Ryckmans, Pierre
　'Les *Propos sur la peinture* de Shitao' 237

Sacher-Masoch, Leopold Ritter von
　Venus im Pelz 216, 314
Sade, Marquis de 95, 152, 311, 312–13, 314, 316
Saint Mark's Basilica
　narthex mosaics 272
Sainte-Anne Hospital 12, 31, 193–5
Sartre, Jean-Paul 38, 39, 248
　Huis clos 117

satisfaction (*Befriedigung*) 90, 155, 156, 157, 162, 167, 165, 171, 172, 174–6, 177, 179, 180, 182, 190, 191, 193, 252, 256, 258, 276, 331, 333
Saussure, Ferdinand de 132
Schlöndorff, Volker
　Der junge Törless 128
Schmideberg, Melitta
　'Intellektuelle Hemmung und Essstörung' 185
science 41, 43–4, 50, 59, 86, 88, 90, 133, 156, 176, 194, 198, 199–200, 204, 208, 256, 281, 285, 288, 332
scopic *see* regard
scybalum *see* anal object
Selbstbewusstsein 98, 116, 117, 122, 142, 248
set theory 16, 17, 22, 24, 25, 30, 54, 83, 331
sex 52, 109–10, 171, 201, 214, 217, 219, 220, 221–2, 223, 224, 233, 234, 235, 236, 238, 255, 256, 267, 275–6
　male–female bipolarity 115, 256
　sex cells, sex chromosomes 221
　sexual act 158–9, 160–2, 166–7, 179–80, 181–2, 183, 187–8, 190, 191, 192, 201, 202–3, 207–9, 210, 211, 212, 221, 223, 225, 242, 243, 251, 252, 253, 254, 255, 256–8, 259–60, 261, 264, 265, 266, 267, 268, 269, 271, 272, 275–7, 281, 283–4, 286, 289–95, 297, 298, 299, 300, 301, 305, 306–7, 308–10, 311, 314, 325–6, 331, 332, 333
　sexual conjunction, encounter 162, 167, 168, 173, 175–6, 182, 202, 234, 267, 269, 270, 276, 283
　sexual difference 95, 202
　sexual drive 157, 219
　sexual dyad, couple, pair 161, 162, 167–8, 173, 174, 190, 204, 205, 236, 238, 290, 293, 314
　sexual frolicking 232
　sexual ideology 210
　sexual Other 188, 189
　sexual reality 110, 111
　sexual relationship 162, 168, 171, 174, 175, 180, 220, 238, 241, 252
　sexual reproduction 160, 290
　sexual satisfaction 172, 175, 177, 193

Index

sexuality 108, 109, 113, 156, 158, 165, 179, 192, 203, 219, 222, 267–8
  subjectifying of 219, 222, 229, 230
sexuated subject 202, 203, 276
sexuisemblance 254
Shaw, George Bernard
  Pygmalion 35
shell-mounds *see Kjökkenmöddings*
shit *see* anal object
Shitao (石濤) 237
signifiance 256, 280, 282
signification 15–16, 21, 23, 27, 36, 40, 108, 109, 160, 221, 234, 250, 304, 306, 330
  effect of signification 57–8, 62
signifier 6, 7, 10, 12–16, 20, 21–4, 26–8, 29, 36, 38, 42–3, 45, 47, 57, 58, 59, 62, 105, 108, 134, 140, 144, 158–9, 160, 161, 162, 206, 217, 220–1, 222, 234, 251, 258, 259, 260, 263, 264, 266, 267, 274, 275, 278, 281, 282, 285, 288, 289, 292, 309, 330, 331
  cannot signify itself 16, 21–4, 26, 38, 47, 54, 61, 144, 146
  and the letter 21, 61
  'man' and 'woman' 271, 294
  and signification 15–16, 21, 23, 57, 58, 330
  and signified 15, 27, 47, 57, 62, 234, 330
  and truth 42–3, 47, 62, 330, 331
signifier of the barred Other, S (A̸) 59, 61, 100–1, 113–14, 140, 168, 237, 301
silence 172, 200–1
Sipriot, Pierre 34
small difference 173
Socialist societies 172, 181
Socrates 294, 310, 325
Sophocles
  Oedipus Tyrannus 243
soul 91, 201, 232, 260, 300, 310–12
speaking being 65, 223
speech (*parole*) 20, 44, 66, 97, 100, 101, 102, 114, 127, 131, 200, 201, 215, 253
Spenglerism 133
Sphinx 242, 282
Spinoza, Baruch 11, 113, 140, 311
square root
  square root of 5 (Ö5) 236
  square root of minus 1 (Ö–1) 206–7

Stein, Conrad 222
Stoïanoff-Nenoff, Stoïan 131
Stoics 45, 50, 89, 242
strike action 125–6, 245
structuralism 33, 34, 120, 134, 151, 199, 288, 297
subject supposed to know 324
  see also *hupokeímenon*
sublimation (*Sublimierung*) 154–5, 156–8, 162, 163, 176, 190, 191–3, 219, 293, 308
substance *see ousia*
superego 193, 247, 263
Supreme Being 238–9
surplus enjoyment *see* enjoyment
surprise 93, 116, 152
symbolic 10, 88, 105, 133, 134, 136, 167, 200, 205, 222
symbolic chain 35
symbolic logic 81, 82
symptom 42, 58, 152, 154, 158, 159, 184, 189, 215, 255, 256, 258, 259, 260, 276, 305–6, 331
  and truth 152, 154, 189, 215, 256, 258, 260, 331

Tat Tvam Asi (तत् त्वम् असि) 119
techne (τέχνη) 187
tenderness 162, 182, 183, 252
Terence (Publius Terentius Afer)
  Andria 296
Thanatos 201, 269
theology
  atheology, negative theology 11, 114
Thomas Aquinas 43, 147
topology 34, 130, 144, 145, 146, 148–9, 164, 193, 196, 223, 267, 290
Tower of Pisa 259
transference 35, 185, 324
Tricot, Jules
  Organon (Aristotle) 84, 329
truth 40, 42, 47, 50, 54, 63, 71, 95, 100, 101, 103, 104, 107, 110, 112, 113, 116, 118, 122, 137, 140, 141, 147, 152, 154, 155, 165, 213, 214, 215–16, 241–2, 243, 257, 258, 259–60, 262, 275, 277, 281, 282, 288, 303, 313, 321–5, 327, 328, 329, 330
  and knowledge 188, 242, 260
  and the Other 114, 115, 152, 188, 189, 229

truth (*cont.*)
  and the real 258
  and the signifier 42–3, 47, 62, 330, 331
  and the symptom 152, 154, 189, 215, 256, 258, 260, 331
  truth effect 62
  truth signification 331
  truth value 44, 83
  and the unconscious 110, 112, 213, 215, 322
  see also aletheia
truth tables 44–6, 63, 70
tufting tie (*point de capiton*) 21
tyche (τύχη) 243

Ubu, Père 333
Ulysses 333
unary trait (*einziger Zug*) 25, 29, 33, 136, 236, 237–8
unconscious 4, 16, 20, 38, 39, 48, 51, 54, 57–8, 59–60, 67, 69, 70, 71, 72, 73, 74, 93–5, 96, 97, 104–5, 109, 110, 112, 117, 118, 120, 122, 127, 144, 145, 147, 153, 158, 184, 200, 201, 202, 203, 207, 208, 212, 213, 214–15, 220, 221, 224, 293, 304, 320–1, 322, 324, 325, 326, 328–9, 330, 331, 332
  formations of 93
  and id 84, 86, 93–5, 153
  and knowledge 214
  is politics 250
  'structured like a language' 16, 21, 60, 93, 105, 202, 303, 320, 327
  subject of 20, 58, 67, 68, 135, 160, 217, 219
  and truth 110, 112, 213, 215, 322
Universitas Litterarum 39
Unterdrückt 16, 58

Venice 272
Verborgenheit 260
Verleugnung 146, 158, 159, 312
Verwerfung see foreclosure

Vierne, Louis
  Cinq Poèmes de Baudelaire, Op. 45 313
Vietnam 39, 43, 250
voice 7, 14, 285, 310
vocal object 273

Wahl, François 34
Webster's New International Dictionary, Second Edition, unabridged, Vol. I 186
Weizenbaum, Joseph
  'ELIZA – a computer program for the study of natural language communication between man and machine' 34–5
Wiederholungszwang see repetition
Wittgenstein, Ludwig 22
  Tractatus Logico-Philosophicus 103
'*Wo Es war, soll Ich werden*' *see* Freud, *Neue Folge der Vorlesungen*
Wolffian duct 220
woman 175, 209–11, 253–4, 270–1, 299, 300, 309, 314
  and enjoyment 175, 223, 242, 244, 268, 295, 297, 298, 300, 314, 326
  identification with 176
  in kinship structures 208
  and love 173, 175, 176
  and masochism 286, 314
  as object of desire 224
  and the phallus, phallic value 175–6, 209–10, 223, 224, 254, 283, 298
  she-man 210–11, 224, 270
  'thou art my woman' 290, 292, 294, 297
writing, the written (*écriture, l'écrit*) 3, 4, 13, 19–20, 22, 25, 28–9, 36, 42, 44, 46, 47–9, 51, 60–1, 64, 67, 72, 75, 100–1, 237, 238, 329

yī huà (一畫) 237

Zen 239
zero *see* nought
Zhuangzi (莊子)
  Zhuangzi (*Chuang Tzŭ*) 123–4